THE UNITED NATIONS IN INTERNATIONAL HISTORY

New Approaches to International History

New Approaches to International History covers international history during the modern period and across the globe. The series incorporates new developments in the field, such as the cultural turn and transnationalism, as well as the classical high politics of state-centric policymaking and diplomatic relations. Written with upper level undergraduate and postgraduate students in mind, texts in the series provide an accessible overview of international diplomatic and transnational issues, events and actors.

Published:

DECOLONIZATION AND THE COLD WAR
edited by Leslie James and Elisabeth Leake (2015)

COLD WAR SUMMITS
by Chris Tudda (2015)

Forthcoming:

LATIN AMERICAN NATIONALISM
by James F. Siekmeier

THE HISTORY OF UNITED STATES CULTURAL DIPLOMACY
by Michael L. Krenn

INTERNATIONAL COOPERATION IN THE EARLY 20TH CENTURY
by Daniel Gorman

THE INTERNATIONAL LGBT RIGHTS MOVEMENT
by Laura Belmonte

RECONSTRUCTING THE POSTWAR WORLD
by Francine McKenzie

THE UNITED NATIONS IN INTERNATIONAL HISTORY

Amy L. Sayward

Bloomsbury Academic
An imprint of Bloomsbury Publishing Plc

B L O O M S B U R Y
LONDON • OXFORD • NEW YORK • NEW DELHI • SYDNEY

Bloomsbury Academic
An imprint of Bloomsbury Publishing Plc

50 Bedford Square
London
WC1B 3DP
UK

1385 Broadway
New York
NY 10018
USA

www.bloomsbury.com

BLOOMSBURY and the Diana logo are trademarks of Bloomsbury Publishing Plc

First published 2017

British Library Cataloguing-in-Publication Data
A catalogue record for this book is available from the British Library.

ISBN: HB: 978-1-4725-0883-6
PB: 978-1-4725-1003-7
ePDF: 978-1-4725-1060-0
ePub: 978-1-4725-1322-9

Library of Congress Cataloging-in-Publication Data
A catalog record for this book is available from the Library of Congress.

Series: New Approaches to International History

Cover design: Catherine Wood
Cover image: USA, New York, NYC, the Interior of the United Nations Building, the Marc Chagall stained glass window "Peace and Man" © AGF Srl/Alamy Stock Photo

Typeset by Deanta Global Publishing Services, Chennai, India
Printed and bound in India

To my graduate students, who have taught me so much.

Thank you for choosing me to join you in your intellectual journey.

Leah Vallely
Darrin Haas
Heather Scheurer
James Derrick
Hasan Karayam
Jennie Epp
Jeanna Kinnebrew
Abby Gautreau
Angie Sirna
Evan Buchanan
Kevin Smith
Jessi Klinedinst
Amy Rohmiller
Carolyn Powell
Ashleigh Oatts
Chris Barker
Howard Flemings
Chris Thrasher
Chris Adams
Tara Mielnik
Jerry Colley
Tom Carter
Alex Johnson
Walt Litaker
Marc Hill

CONTENTS

LIST OF FIGURES

COVER ART

This "Peace Window" was a memorial gift to the United Nations from French artist Marc Chagall and the staff of the United Nations in memory of Secretary-General Dag Hammarskjöld. It was dedicated on the third anniversary of his death, September 17, 1964. As such, it represents the history of the organization under consideration in this volume. But it also is indicative of the ways in which various people have sought to create and symbolize the meaning of the physical space of the United Nations, which this book argues created a borderland between nations for the exchange and development of ideas, meanings, and actions throughout the organization's history.

ONLINE RESOURCES

Online resources to accompany this book are available at: www.bloomsbury.com/the-united-nations-in-international-history-9781472510037. Please type the URL into your web browser and follow the instructions to access the Companion Website. If you experience any problems, please contact Bloomsbury at: contact@bloomsbury.com

SERIES EDITOR'S PREFACE

New Approaches to International History takes the entire world as its stage for exploring the history of diplomacy, broadly conceived theoretically and thematically, and writ large across the span of the globe, during the modern period. This series goes beyond the single goal of explaining encounters in the world. Our aspiration is that these books provide both an introduction for researchers new to a topic, and supplemental and essential reading in classrooms. Thus, *New Approaches* serves a dual purpose that is unique from other large-scale treatments of international history; it applies to scholarly agendas and pedagogy. In addition, it does so against the backdrop of a century of enormous change, conflict, and progress that informed global history but also continues to reflect on our own times.

The series offers the old and new diplomatic history to address a range of topics that shaped the twentieth century. Engaging in international history (including but not especially focusing on global or world history), these books will appeal to a range of scholars and teachers situated in the humanities and social sciences, including those in history, international relations, cultural studies, politics, and economics. We have in mind scholars, both novice and veteran, who require an entrée into a topic, trend, or technique that can benefit their own research or education into a new field of study by crossing boundaries in a variety of ways.

By its broad and inclusive coverage, *New Approaches to International History* is also unique because it makes accessible to students current research, methodology, and themes. Incorporating cutting-edge scholarship that reflects trends in international history, as well as addressing the classical high politics of state-centric policymaking and diplomatic relations, these books are designed to bring alive the myriad of approaches for digestion by advanced undergraduates and graduate students. In preparation for the *New Approaches* series, Bloomsbury surveyed courses and faculty around the world to gauge interest and reveal core themes of relevance for their classroom use. The polling yielded a host of topics, from war and peace to the environment; from empire to economic integration; and from migration to nuclear arms. The effort proved that there is a much-needed place for studies that connect scholars and students alike to international history, and books that are especially relevant to the teaching missions of faculty around the world.

We hope readers find this series to be appealing, challenging, and thought provoking. Whether the history is viewed through older or newer lenses, *New Approaches to International History* allows students to peer into the modern period's complex relations among nations, people, and events to draw their own conclusions about the tumultuous, interconnected past.

Thomas Zeiler,
University of Colorado Boulder, USA

PREFACE AND ACKNOWLEDGMENTS

I would like to thank Tom Zeiler for inviting me to contribute to the *New Approaches to International History* series. The more I have talked to my colleagues about this project over the past three years, the more I have heard about the need for just such a set of academic introductions to the key institutions and movements in international history that can be used in upper-division undergraduate and starting graduate courses. It is my sincere hope that in reading this volume more students and colleagues will be empowered to integrate the United Nations (U.N.) into their scholarship as an active arena of, and even actor in, international history in the twentieth and twenty-first centuries. I am so passionate about this topic because the United Nations brings together all the key elements from the new international history—powerful and less powerful state actors (both high-level diplomats and functional technocrats), nonstate actors that aspire to state status (such as the Palestine Liberation Organization and the African National Congress), international civil servants working within the various U.N. organizations, nongovernmental organizations (NGOs) of all sorts who have tried to influence global policies and practices, and a wide array of individuals and groups who have sought redress from the global body, ranging, for example, from the individual victims of war crimes testifying before a U.N. international criminal tribunal to the members of indigenous groups seeking international recognition and protection of their rights within a world of nation-states.

In writing this book, I have accumulated several personal and professional debts that I wish to acknowledge here. Middle Tennessee State University (MTSU) provided me with a sabbatical during the spring 2015 semester, which allowed me to complete this manuscript in a timely manner. Susan Myers-Shirk, my colleague and friend in the History Department at MTSU, faithfully served as my "writing-accountability buddy" over the phone at 5:00 a.m. every weekday morning as well as bringing her wisdom and humor to my writing process at key junctures. Monica Butler (a former undergraduate student and now faculty member at Seminole State College) and Ryan McMahon (a fellow Buckeye diplomatic historian) also served as my writing buddies throughout the final stages of preparing this manuscript. Collectively, their steadfastness and friendly encouragement were key to finishing this project. I also had encouragement during the writing process (even when I didn't particularly want it) from my parents, Leonard and Sally Sayward, and from my dear friends Farris Morris, Janet Kelly, Tara Hayes, Peter Cunningham, Geri Kristof, Solita Morris, and Amy Arlinghaus. On the professional side, Alexandrea Collins and Melissa Hope, as graduate students, assisted me in some of the research and drudgery required to write this book. Two of my former master's students, Jennie Epp and Jeanna Kinnebrew, also provided significant assistance; Jennie read through the entire manuscript in draft to help me avoid errors and to ensure that I had addressed the book's audience, and Jeanna coauthored Chapter 6 with me. Dean Bonnie Allen and her staff at the James E. Walker Library at MTSU, especially Pam Middleton of the interlibrary loan office, were also extremely helpful in processing my numerous interlibrary loan requests and giving me an exception so that I could exceed the maximum number of books that could be checked out at a single time. Additionally, I want to thank Tom Zeiler, Emma Goode, Claire Lipscomb, and the anonymous reviewers of the proposal and book manuscript for their comments, which helped me to fine-tune this book and make sure that it fits the needs of the students who are its primary audience. Thanks too to Grishma Fredric's team and to Steven Jensen, whose last-minute assistance saved me from any number of errors in the text.

Part of my desire to write this book is because of the joy I have experienced partnering with both undergraduate and especially graduate students in developing their own research ideas over my eighteen years in the History Department at MTSU. That is why this book is dedicated to them. I would be remiss, however, if I did not also thank the mentors who served as my role models in how to teach, mentor, and research. Mr. Olick, my inimitable high school history teacher at Starpoint Central School, passed away in 2015; he instilled in me a deep love of history, and he modeled what it meant to be a teacher who was caring, creative, and intellectually rigorous. At St. Bonaventure University, Tom Schaeper first engaged me in historical research and encouraged me to think about pursuing a PhD. Then Ed Eckert and Joel Horowitz helped me to think and work through the challenges of my first long-term research project with my honors thesis. As a diplomatic-historian-in-training at Ohio State University, I benefited from the incomparable duo of Michael Hogan and Peter Hahn, whose patience, care, and attention allowed me to become the professional I am today. I am thankful to all those who have mentored and encouraged me and hope that they are pleased to see this book as one result of their work.

LIST OF ABBREVIATIONS

In this book, I have tried to avoid the overreliance on abbreviations that characterizes the United Nations and much of the scholarly literature on it, with the goal of making the narrative as easy to read and use as possible for students and scholars new to this area of study. Nonetheless, I provide the following as a helpful guide to decoding this and other works on the United Nations. In this book, the abbreviations appear more often in the citations when the organization appears as the author or publisher of a work.

AFSC *American Friends Service Committee* (Quakers)
ANC *African National Congress* (of South Africa)
ASEAN *Association of Southeast Asian Nations*
CAA *Council on African Affairs* (NGO)
CEDAW *Convention on the Elimination of All Forms of Discrimination Against Women*
CEO *chief executive officer*
CEPAL *Comisión Económica para América Latina y el Caribe* (Economic Commission for Latin America and the Caribbean, ECLAC)
CHR *Commission on Human Rights* (within the U.N. Economic and Social Council)
CIDA *Canadian International Development Agency*
CODESA *Convention for a Democratic South Africa*
CSW *Commission on the Status of Women* (within the U.N. Economic and Social Council)
DAWN *Development Alternatives with Women for a New Era*
DD2 *Second Development Decade*
DEDAW *Declaration on the Elimination of Discrimination Against Women*
DPRK *Democratic People's Republic of Korea* (North Korea)
DPs *displaced persons*
ECA *Economic Commission for Africa*
ECAFE *Economic Commission for Asia and the Far East* (later ESCAP)
ECCC *Extraordinary Chambers in the Courts of Cambodia*
ECE *Economic Commission for Europe*

ECLA	*Economic Commission for Latin America*
ECLAC	*Economic Commission for Latin America and the Caribbean* (CEPAL in Spanish)
ECOSOC	*U.N. Economic and Social Council*
EMRO	*Eastern Mediterranean Regional Office of the World Health Organization*
EPTA	*U.N. Expanded Program for Technical Assistance*
ESCAP	*U.N. Economic and Social Commission for Asia and the Pacific*
E.U.	*European Union*
FAO	*Food and Agriculture Organization of the United Nations*
FGM	*female genital mutilation*
FLN	*Algerian Front de Libération Nationale*
G-77	*Group of 77* (of the U.N.'s developing countries; the name stuck even after the number of such countries changed)
G-8	*Group of 8* (of the world's largest economies)
GAID	*Global Alliance for ICT* [Information and Communication Technology] *and Development*
GARP	*Global Atmospheric Research Programme*
GATE	*GARP* [Global Atmospheric Research Programme] *Atlantic Tropical Experiment*
GATS	*General Agreement on Trade in Services*
GATT	*General Agreement on Tariffs and Trade*
GDP	*gross domestic product*
GRPA	*Gouvernement Provisoire de la République Algérienne* (Provisional Government of the Algerian Republic)
HEUNI	*European Institute for Crime Prevention and Control* (affiliated with the United Nations)
IACW	*Inter-American Commission of Women*
IAEA	*International Atomic Energy Agency*
IBRD	*International Bank for Reconstruction and Development* (but more commonly the World Bank)
ICAN	*International Commission for Air Navigation*
ICAO	*International Civil Aviation Organization*
ICC	*International Criminal Court*
ICCPR	*International Covenant on Civil and Political Rights*
ICEM	*International Committee on European Migration*

ICERD *International Convention on the Elimination of All Forms of Racial Discrimination*

ICESCR *International Covenant on Economic, Social and Cultural Rights*

ICJ *International Court of Justice*

ICRC *International Committee of the Red Cross*

ICSID *International Centre for Settlement of Investment Disputes*

ICSU *International Council of Scientific Unions* (after 1998, the International Council for Science, but retaining the historic abbreviation)

ICT *information and communication technology*

ICTR *International Criminal Tribunal for Rwanda*

ICTY *International Criminal Tribunal for the former Yugoslavia*

IDA *International Development Association*

IDF *Israeli Defense Forces*

IDPs *internally displaced persons*

IFAD *International Fund for Agricultural Development*

IFC *International Finance Corporation*

IFRC *International Federation of Red Cross and Red Crescent Societies*

IGOs *international governmental organizations*

IGY *International Geophysical Year*

IIA *International Institute of Agriculture*

ILANUD *U.N. Latin American Institute for the Prevention of Crime and the Treatment of Offenders*

ILO *International Labour Organization*

IMCO *Inter-Governmental Maritime Consultative Organization*

IMF *International Monetary Fund*

IMO *International Maritime Organization*

IMO *International Meteorological Organization*

INGOs *international nongovernmental organizations*

INSTRAW *International Research and Training Institute for the Advancement of Women*

INTERPOL *International Criminal Police Organization—INTERPOL* (after 1954, simply INTERPOL, which was its telegraphic address and a contraction for international police)

IPCC *Intergovernmental Panel on Climate Change*

IPY *International Polar Year*

ITO *International Trade Organization*

ITT	*International Telephone and Telegraph*
ITU	*International Telegraph Union, later the International Telecommunication Union*
IUDs	*intrauterine devices*
IUOTO	*International Union of Official Travel Organisations*
LDCs	*least developed countries*
MDGs	*Millennium Development Goals*
MIGA	*Multilateral Investment Guarantee Agency*
NAACP	*National Association for the Advancement of Colored People*
NAFTA	*North American Free Trade Agreement*
NATO	*North Atlantic Treaty Organization*
NGO	*nongovernmental organization*
NIEO	*New International Economic Order*
OAU	*Organisation of African Unity*
ODA	*official development assistance*
ODA	*Overseas Development Administration* (U.K.)
OECD	*Organisation for Economic Co-operation and Development*
ONUC	*Operation des Nations Unies au Congo* (peacekeeping operation)
OPEC	*Organization of Petroleum Exporting Countries*
PANS	*Procedures for Air Navigation Services* (of ICAO)
PAPP	*Programme of Assistance to the Palestinian People* (of the U.N. Development Program)
PICAO	*Provisional International Civil Aviation Organization*
PIP	*Peace Implementation Plan* (of UNRWA)
PLA	*People's Liberation Army* (of China)
PLO	*Palestine Liberation Organization*
PNC	*Palestine National Council*
POWs	*prisoners of war*
PRC	*People's Republic of China*
ReCAAP	*Regional Cooperation Agreement on Combating Piracy and Armed Robbery against Ships in Asia*
ROC	*Republic of China*
ROK	*Republic of Korea* (South Korea)
RSCSL	*Residual Special Court for Sierra Leone*
SARPs	*Standards and Recommended Practices* (of ICAO)

SCSL	*Special Court for Sierra Leone*
SUNFED	*Special United Nations Fund for Economic Development*
SWAPO	*South West Africa People's Organization* (Namibia)
TOKTEN	*Transfer of Knowledge through Expatriate Nationals* (of the UNDP)
U-18s	*people under eighteen years of age*
UAR	*United Arab Republic* (the political union of Egypt and Syria, 1958–1961)
UDHR	*Universal Declaration of Human Rights*
U.N.	*United Nations*
UNCTAD	*U.N. Conference on Trade and Development* (of the General Assembly)
UNCTC	*U.N. Centre on Transnational Corporations*
UNDOF	*U.N. Disengagement Observer Force* (between Israel and Syria)
UNDP	*U.N. Development Programme*
UNEF	*U.N. Emergency Force*
UNEP	*U.N. Environment Programme*
UNESCO	*U.N. Educational, Scientific and Cultural Organization*
UNHCR	*U.N. High Commissioner on Refugees*
UNICEF	*U.N. International Children's Emergency Fund* (now U.N. Children's Fund but maintaining the well-known historical acronym)
UNIDO	*U.N. Industrial Development Organization*
UNIFEM	*U.N. Development Fund for Women*
UNIFIL	*U.N. Interim Force in Lebanon*
UNIHP	*United Nations Intellectual History Project*
UNIIMOG	*U.N. Iran–Iraq Military Observer Group*
UNIKOM	*U.N. Iraq–Kuwait Observation Mission*
UNIN	*U.N. Institute for Namibia*
UNKRA	*U.N. Korean Reconstruction Agency*
UNOGIL	*U.N. Observation Group in Lebanon*
UNOMSA	*U.N. Observer Mission in South Africa*
UNRPR	*U.N. Relief for Palestine Refugees*
UNRRA	*U.N. Relief and Rehabilitation Administration*
UNRWA	*U.N. Relief and Works Agency for Palestine Refugees in the Near East*
UNSCOM	*U.N. Special Commission* (monitoring weapons in Iraq)
UNTAC	*U.N. Transitional Authority in Cambodia*
UNTAG	*U.N. Transition Assistance Group* (Namibia)
UNTSO	*U.N. Truce Supervision Organization*

UNWTO	*U.N. World Tourism Organization*
UNYOM	*U.N. Yemen Observation Mission*
UPU	*Universal Postal Union*
WHO	*World Health Organization*
WIDF	*Women's International Democratic Federation*
WIPO	*World Intellectual Property Organization*
WMO	*World Meteorological Organization*
WSIS	*World Summit on the Information Society*
WTO	*World Trade Organization*
YMCA	*Young Men's Christian Association*

CHAPTER 1
INTRODUCTION: AN INVITATION

The United Nations (U.N.) has been the victim of idealistic proclamations about its goals and purposes that emerged from the Second World War period. The scale of the horror and misery of that conflict seems to have inspired an effort to build an optimism of equal scale and to embody it in the United Nations. It seems as if almost every subsequent historian, scholar, and commentator on the United Nations since then has felt compelled to judge whether or not the organization has matched up to these ideals and ultimately to judge whether the organization has been a success or a failure. To provide just one example, historian Paul Kennedy's synthesis marking the United Nations' sixtieth anniversary, *The Parliament of Man: The Past, Present, and Future of the United Nations*, introduces the study as an assessment of "what it has done well and where it has failed"; as a study of the United Nations' "evolution, metamorphosis, and experiment, of failure and success"; and finally as "a tale of multiple setbacks and disappointments." Even reviews of the book could not escape the trap of framing the organization in moralistic and emotional language, with *The New Yorker*'s dust-jacket review reading, "Amid the morass of commissions and conferences, and failures like Rwanda, he managed to find something convincingly heroic."[1] Another curiosity about this U.N. historiography (the history of what has been written on this particular topic) is that many scholars and commentators seemingly feel compelled to prognosticate about its future (which seems particularly odd coming from historians) and to call for reform of the international organization. In addition to Kennedy's title, a search of books on the United Nations turned up three with the title *The United Nations: Past, Present, and Future*,[2] and the closing "Part" of even the encyclopedic *Oxford Handbook on the United Nations* is entitled "Prospects for Reform."[3]

By way of contrast, few histories of the United States Congress, for example, judge the institution as a success or a failure based primarily on the ideals established in the Declaration of Independence—on whether or not the body has consistently managed to uphold all of the people's unalienable rights to life, liberty, and the pursuit of happiness. Instead, historians tend to see and interpret the U.S. Congress as an arena where a variety of representatives come together to dispute and debate issues of local, regional, national, and international interest, which they are more or less interested in, depending on their own perspectives and those of their constituents. And historians of American political history are rarely surprised and rarely pass moral judgments when the U.S. House of Representatives and the U.S. Senate disagree on a bill, when the president of the United States decides to veto or to sign a piece of legislation, when the U.S. Supreme Court declares a law unconstitutional, or even when the people or states that constitute the country decide to abide by a new law or not (with the exception, perhaps, of the Civil War and the Civil Rights Movement). Yet scholars examining the United Nations consistently seem surprised and disappointed to find dissension and disagreement within the General Assembly; between the General Assembly, the secretary-general, the Security Council, and the U.N. specialized agencies; and between the international civil servants staffing these intergovernmental organizations and the representatives of national governments. And these same scholars seem amazingly apt to judge such disagreements and disputes as "failures" of the U.N. system.

So what would happen if we viewed the United Nations simply (and significantly) as an arena, an intersection, or a borderland, as a space where the governments and peoples of the world come together to discuss, debate, and dispute the issues of the day? That is what this book will attempt to do. Rather than drawing conclusions about whether the United Nations has succeeded or failed to attain the lofty goals set for it, this volume will examine the organization as a crucial intersection or forum in international history, where nations and peoples came (and come) together to influence and put pressure on other countries and people with their words, their ideas, their actions, and occasionally their combined force of arms. Sometimes this pressure has resulted in the intended change; not surprisingly, at other times it resulted in unexpected changes or intractable opposition to change. I believe that looking at the United Nations through such a lens will allow for a more historical examination of the institution itself and will open the way to examine it as a place where a variety of international actors have made their cases, defined and defended their identities, and pursued another prong of their multivariate strategies to reach their own goals. This is indeed where much of the new scholarship on international history takes us,[4] and it is another of the goals of this book to point to just such areas where additional scholarship could be fruitful.

The current literature on the United Nations consists of several key types of work: intellectual histories, international histories, institutional histories, and histories of the nongovernmental organizations (NGOs) associated with it (often spoken of as civil society today). I will examine very briefly each of these main types. The U.N. Intellectual History Project (UNIHP) is the most prolific in the first category (though it interestingly did not employ any historians),[5] while historian Mark Mazower's book, *Governing the World*, is interested broadly in the history of the idea of global governance, of which the United Nations is the most potent and recent expression. In the introduction, he argues that from the 1815 Congress of Vienna onward, the idea of "organized cooperation among nations" in its multiple variations was attractive as a "vision of a better future for mankind, one that lies within our grasp and power and promises our collective emancipation." It also provided a vehicle for the exercise of British and then American global power.[6] Shifting to international histories, these frame the United Nations as one crucial arena in which national and international actors come together to advance their agendas. Within this category, Soviet historian Ilya Gaiduk's history of U.S.-Soviet relations centers the United Nations within the history of the Cold War while simultaneously filling out the agendas of the two superpowers with research into the archives on both sides of the iron curtain. As a result, he is able to show the ways in which it played a crucial role in de-escalating early Cold War crises between the two.[7] Other works, under the label of "new international history," see the United Nations as a key venue for the discussion and development of international views on specific conflicts or issues. Recent works look at the ways in which the Algerian independence movement, the Palestine Liberation Organization (PLO), and the African National Congress (ANC) actively cultivated its international space and audience to broadcast their revolutionary messages and gain support for their causes as well as how global population control efforts operated through interconnected national and international networks of organizations, including U.N. agencies and fora, individuals, NGOs, foundations, and countries.[8] Institutional histories of the United Nations—which are often technical studies that have escaped the syntheses described earlier in this paragraph—help get us to the actual work (not just the debates or the rhetoric) pursued through its various organs (see the U.N. organizational chart that leads off the online Guide to Further Research at http://www.bloomsbury.com/the-united-nations-in-international-history-9781472510037/). Such studies provide a window onto the important ways in which the United Nations shapes the lives of ordinary people around the globe on a daily basis through its international standardization of medicines and vaccinations, the transportation of emergency food aid, the regulation of transnational air travel, and the global collection of meteorological and epidemiological data—among countless other duties.

Just as diverse and important is the work of the many NGOs recognized from the beginning as a key part of the United Nations. Such groups also act in this global arena to protect and promote the rights of their constituents—whether they be women, farmers, indigenous people, members of an ethnic or religious minority, workers, children, or another subpopulation of the nation-state—by gaining additional recognition of the issues these groups face and additional leverage to work on these challenges both domestically and transnationally. Historian Carol Anderson's books on the global work of the National Association for the Advancement of Colored People (NAACP) to combat racism at home and abroad provide a model for such scholarship.[9] In sum, a study of the United Nations—as a point of intersection—helps us understand the transnational and international aspects of political, economic, social, and cultural change in the last half of the twentieth century and now the twenty-first century.

In many ways the historiography on the United Nations is uniquely suited for renewed study by a new generation of scholars, despite the fact that there is already a large, interdisciplinary body of literature built up over seventy years of scholarly analysis and public commentary. As such this history allows the new scholar multiple and varying entry points based on her/his field and/or interests. To provide a brief illustration, even the scholar interested solely in relations between member states and the United Nations could enter the discussion at several points—looking at an individual country's relations with the United Nations, looking at the U.N. role within the overall foreign policy of a specific government, looking at the various multinational blocs and their operations within the United Nations (such as the Non-Aligned Movement, the Latin American countries, and the British Commonwealth), looking at the impact of U.N. actions within a specific country (e.g., in terms of peacekeeping or development funding), and/or looking at the nongovernmental groups seeking to influence the government's agenda both at home and abroad and how these were articulated and implemented in the United Nations.[10]

Additionally, U.N. history offers the starting scholar very rich primary sources in large numbers that are generally available. Many of the key players in these histories are still alive, have been the focus of oral history projects, and/or have published their memoirs and autobiographies.[11] The United Nations and its specialized agencies have also been prolific authors and publishers; most U.N. entities publish at least one set of periodicals in addition to annual proceedings and official organizational histories.[12] In addition, each of the governments represented in the world body has generated its own records related to these interactions.[13] There are also a number of excellent electronic launching pads for your own research. A good first place to start is Linda Tashbook's "Researching the United Nations: Finding the Organization's Internal Resource Trails." Additionally, the United Nations History Project website at Harvard includes links to a variety of guides and resources. The U.N. Educational, Scientific and Cultural Organization (UNESCO) and the International Council on Archives maintain a "Guide to Archives of International Organizations" that focuses on major intergovernmental organizations (currently eighty) and allows the aspiring researcher to browse by region or category (such as U.N. system or regional or worldwide intergovernmental organization).[14]

Hopefully as this introduction winds up, I have convinced you that the United Nations is an extraordinarily fruitful field not only to read about but also for your own original research and analysis. To that end, the rest of the book is structured to provide a brief introduction to the United Nations as a whole, what scholars have written about it, and some key sources where you can start your own research. Chapter 2 focuses on the forms of international organization that preceded it, including both the forerunners to the U.N. specialized agencies as well as the bodies created by the Treaty of Versailles at the end of the First World War—the League of Nations, International Court of Justice, and International Labour Organization. Chapter 3 provides a brief narrative overview of key events in U.N. history over the past seven decades that integrates the work of the Security Council, the General Assembly, and the Secretariat; this chapter is meant to give you a basic overall history so that the subsequent chapters, which dive deeper into particular aspects of that work, will be easier to understand and contextualize. Chapter 4 provides you an introduction to the Economic and Social Council of the United Nations (ECOSOC), the U.N. organ responsible for overseeing the specialized agencies of the United Nations. This chapter also provides an introduction to some NGOs, which predominantly work through ECOSOC. Chapter 5 provides a chronological history of the economic development efforts of the United Nations, so that students can see the different aspects of ECOSOC working together in this particular area, which is one of the main emphases for the Council. Chapter 6 focuses on the ways in which the work of the United Nations has grown and developed over time in the specific areas of conflict resolution and the care and protection of refugees. While the framers of the U.N. Charter assigned the organization primary responsibility for maintaining international peace, they could not accurately foresee the various ways in which the organization would be called upon to carry out this task over the next seventy years. These efforts have ranged from armed interventions in Korea and the Persian Gulf to blue-helmeted soldiers standing between hostile forces in Cyprus and the Sinai Peninsula among other places. Those original framers also did not foresee the need for a permanent capacity within the United Nations to provide sustenance and care to millions of refugees and internally displaced people around the world. Chapter 7 focuses on the Middle East to give the reader a sense of the complex ways in which all of the United Nations' bodies work in different ways in the same place over time. So we will see, for example, the U.N. Security Council and Secretariat trying to negotiate and maintain peace (especially in the Arab-Israeli crises), the General Assembly comparing Zionism to apartheid, and the United Nations Relief and Works Agency for Palestine Refugees in the Near East (UNRWA for short) providing protection and assistance to generations of Palestinian refugees. Chapter 8 takes us into some of the most innovative work of the United Nations, especially its work in defining and promoting human rights around the globe as well as prosecuting some of those who egregiously violate those rights.

Finally, a note on the notes in this book—one of the joys of research is all of the interesting things that you find above and beyond what you are looking for. Students of history are invariably curious folks who love exploring these rabbit holes, and so in the notes, I have mapped out some of my rabbit-hole ventures that I think you might enjoy. They also reveal some of the innumerable areas of interest that one can explore in researching the United Nations. So be sure to look at the notes and the online guide to further research to learn more about U.N. art, the politics of the Palestine national soccer team, and the early international history of meteorology among others. Also squirreled away in the notes and online guide are historiographical discussions of the literature that can help you get started on the right foot as you begin your own research. I have tried to give you a sampling of both primary and secondary sources from different disciplines, different time periods, and different formats (books, articles, and websites) so that you can see the main lines of the scholarly discussions that have happened up to this point. I have focused largely on the most reliable secondary sources from university presses and academic journals that have met the high standards of the double-blind scholarly review process. However, you will notice that this is less the case for the more contemporary history of the United Nations, since the archival records that historians rely on are less available from the 1970s onward. For the more recent history, you will see more accounts by participants, journalists, and scholars of international law and international relations, who generally make up the first wave of historiography on a topic based on their access to the events and actors constituting that history.

In attempting to do all of this in the notes, the first draft of this manuscript was almost twice the size of the current book! So in order to keep (and even enhance) the richness of these notes and to allow them to remain up to date even after printing, Bloomsbury very helpfully has created an online "Guide to Further Research" for this book at http://www.bloomsbury.com/the-united-nations-in-international-history-9781472510037/, which will take you beyond the shorter notes printed here and provide an overall bibliography for this book. The online guide also allows me to garner your comments and suggestions for additional sources and works that could be included in an updated second edition.

CHAPTER 2
THE NATIONAL AND INTERNATIONAL ORIGINS OF THE UNITED NATIONS

Like all historical phenomena, the U.N. system did not simply burst onto the world stage without lots of preparatory work—both intellectual and organizational. While historians can seemingly find the "origins" of almost anything decades if not centuries prior to its full emergence, the origins of the United Nations are generally quite clearly delineated. The League of Nations and its appendages that emerged after the First World War were its most immediate precedents, but stretching before that was a longer history of international organizations and ideas (generally dated to the 1814–15 Congress of Vienna). Intergovernmental organizations arose in the areas of the modern world in which nation-states could not fully or effectively act without the formal cooperation of their neighbors. In other words, modern internationalism developed in the borderland between states, where an area of work, exchange, and/or interaction exceeded the capacity of a single state to govern and regulate, even through bilateral or regional arrangements. But equally important, other nongovernmental organizations (NGOs) also developed during this period. Scientists and other professionals developed their own borderlands—their spaces where many different people who shared a desire to work together could gather and develop a sense of community. The process usually started with an international congress, often followed by a permanent international professional organization, whose journal and meetings established new spaces where they undertook the transnational work of their respective professions. In these spaces, information from a variety of sources was combined to provide new and more comprehensive understandings, a common professional "language" was developed that transcended national borders (usually in the form of standardized statistics and measurements), and professionals were equipped to take "home" with them new information and best practices to inform national laws and processes. Other nongovernmental groups also organized internationally to promote a certain issue or set of issues and emerged as something of a hybrid between the intergovernmental and the professional organizations. These international activists tended to focus on issues that also escaped the ability of a single state to regulate, such as the rights of workers or trafficking in narcotics, women, and girls; and they sought to influence, if not determine, national policies on these issues. Like the international professional organizations, however, these NGOs also sought to bring together people from many countries to develop a common language and set of strategies for tackling their issues. Collectively, these international interactions—be they professional, governmental, or personal—helped to form an underlying cultural foundation for the further development of internationalism after the

First World War.[1] The scale of the tragedy of the Great War led the trans-Atlantic world to seek new, institutionalized ways of organizing the countries of the world and keeping the peace. The work of the postwar peacemakers at Paris resulted not only in a League of Nations but also in an International Labour Organization (ILO) and a Permanent Court of International Justice. Another innovation was that instead of the victorious powers simply annexing the spoils of war, the territories taken from the Ottoman Empire and the colonies taken from Germany were placed under the supervision of the League's Mandates Commission. Additionally, the League's work through its economic and social divisions became extremely popular, building as it did on decades of prior work by international professional and activist organizations. Ultimately, even as the League's work of promoting peace was falling well short of the mark in the 1930s, its social and economic work grew in prominence and established an important foundation for subsequent work by the United Nations.

So this chapter will introduce you to these three broad categories of international organizations and interactions (intergovernmental, professional/scientific, and activist) within these borderlands, where these actors were laying the intellectual, cultural, and organizational foundations for the subsequent League and U.N. systems. Indeed, within this "preparatory" period, we see a combination of approaches to international organization, action, and thought that collectively constituted the rise of a new "internationalism" in the nineteenth and early twentieth centuries.

A review of the literature and a case study on nutritional science and organization

Governments, businessmen, and technical experts came together during the nineteenth century to remove obstacles to international trade and to facilitate the use of new technologies to speed such trade. Such intergovernmental organizations worked, for example, toward a scientific understanding of how epidemic diseases spread in order to inform and ease national quarantine regulations. The first permanent intergovernmental organizations came from similar motives and standardized telegraph and mail regulations to speed communication through the International Telegraph Union (ITU) and the Universal Postal Union (UPU). The literature on these pre-League intergovernmental organizations is especially sparse and mostly written by insiders as anniversary or "origins" accounts of those organizations that persisted as affiliated organizations of the League of Nations and the United Nations.[2] As such their study is fertile ground for new interpretations. I would especially urge the reader/researcher to tie these organizations more closely to their intellectual and national roots—for example, examining the ways in which government and business worked together within their particular national contexts to establish, maintain, and innovate the work of the ITU would be a fruitful study. Also, understanding which countries chose to join the ITU and when might well tell us about the development and dissemination of information technology and might inform our views of how particular countries aspired to participate in new technologies and trading networks.

Professional/scientific internationalism in the nineteenth century arose largely from the realization by scientists, doctors, and professionals of many sorts that their studies—ranging on a broad spectrum from public health and meteorology to geology, physics, and agriculture—were incomplete if confined to the national borders of the state in which they resided. In other words, these professionals understood that science had a universality that was stunted if studied only within a single national or even regional context. Indeed, many of these early scientists and professionals had studied in one or more countries outside of their homeland in order to develop and refine their craft—a type of "practical internationalism" in which practitioners traveled to and studied in the country where the most advanced scientific education and training were available.[3] Yet at the same time, these scientists worked almost exclusively for national organizations—government bureaux, national or state universities, and more rarely national research institutions. Elisabeth Crawford, a historian of science, has argued that both nationalism and internationalism within these early scientific communities need more study and research, because an assumption about the universality of science has resulted in a lack of rigorous analysis of how this idea actually functioned and informed practice. Such analysis could, she contends, lead us away from the simplistic view that the First World War's retreat to nationalistic science was an aberration.[4]

Supplementing the early scientific and intergovernmental organizations was a diverse set of activists who organized across international borders around a specific issue and took their cues from the eighteenth century's religious and charitable organizations as well as the successful global effort to abolish slavery. A handful of scholars have examined nineteenth-century international organizations as a whole, but these histories tend to read a bit like a catalog of organizations and activities with a handful of case studies, in part due to a relative lack of accessible archives. One of the most recent attempts, Thomas Davies's *NGOs: A New History of Transnational Civil Society*, stretches the origins of these early organizations back to the eighteenth-century transition from much earlier transnational religious and fraternal organizations and points out the Eastern (as well as the Western) origins of such activities. Other efforts at synthesis tend to focus on a particular issue around which a set of organizations developed, such as Leila Rupp's *Worlds of Women: The Making of an International Women's Movement*, which utilized American, British, Dutch, French, and German archives to tell the stories of the International Council of Women (est. 1888), the International Alliance of Women (est. 1904 as the International Woman Suffrage Alliance), and the Women's International League for Peace and Freedom (which developed from the 1915 International Women's Congress that opposed the First World War and then took its name in 1919).[5] These examples point the way to more opportunities for scholars to understand transnational organization in the era before the First World War.

I think it would be most fruitful to examine these early international organizations as "epistemic communities"—a concept developed by political scientist Peter M. Haas. He has argued that these "networks of knowledge-based experts" play an important role in international relations by "articulating the cause-and-effect relationships of complex problems, helping states identify their interests, framing the issues for collective debate, proposing specific policies, and identifying salient points for negotiation." Most efforts to apply this idea of epistemic communities to international organizations and policies have focused on later periods.[6] As a result, the people organizing into groups such as the Society for the Improvement of Prison Discipline (est. 1817) and the International Association for Obtaining a Uniform Decimal System of Measures, Weights & Coins (est. 1855) have rarely been explicitly connected to the development of professional (or even proto-professional) identity, which they expressed through the creation of these international organizations and which in turn fed back into and reinforced their own professional networks.

Let me briefly illustrate what I mean by looking at the development, professionalization, and internationalization of nutrition as a field of study and action. At the end of the nineteenth and beginning of the twentieth centuries, a trans-Atlantic international community of scientists, doctors, and scholars developed at the nexus between agriculture, nutrition, and medicine, especially in the area of public health. In each of these fields, the countries of North America and Western Europe were institutionalizing higher education and professional training. To meet the urgent and dire public health threats raised by urbanization and industrialization, medical training had moved to an increasingly scientific basis with the progressive introduction of statistics, clinical experiments, microscopy, germ theory, and the application of chemistry and other scientific fields to medical practice. In a parallel fashion, agriculture had become increasingly scientific as the same countries invested in higher education facilities (most famously the land-grant college system of the United States), agricultural institutes (such as Great Britain's Rothamsted), experiment stations, and a broad range of agricultural extension activities in order to become more competitive in the increasingly globalized agricultural markets created by steam-powered and refrigerated oceangoing vessels. As the number of scientists employed in these new universities, research institutions, and government agencies reached a critical mass, international scientific communities developed around these professional scientists who frequently had studied abroad to obtain the best training (be it in Scotland, France, Germany, or the United States), who belonged to one or more international scientific organizations, who attended conferences overseas, and who subscribed to journals in their own and allied fields that closely followed global developments in their chosen field of inquiry.[7] They gathered international statistics on agricultural commodities and issued technical studies through the International Institute of Agriculture (IIA, est. 1908). Following the Great War, transnational nutritionists succeeded in putting nutrition on the League of Nations' agenda as well as developing national nutritional programs and standards throughout the 1930s. These nutritionists then worked for their governments throughout the war (designing and implementing rational rationing systems), but they did not forget their international roots. In fact, they were successful in the midst of the war in gaining the support of U.S. President Franklin D. Roosevelt in calling the first of the postwar planning conferences around the issues of nutrition, resulting in the creation of the Food and Agriculture Organization of the United Nations (FAO). Collectively, these scientists helped define national and international nutrition policy agendas in the first half of the twentieth century, and they provided the first three FAO directors-general.[8] As this case study sketches out, there was a clear connection between early international professional networks and intergovernmental organizations (such as the IIA) that laid the foundation for the elevation and institutionalization of their area of interest within the later frameworks of the League of Nations and the United Nations.

The historiography on the League shares many of the characteristics of the broader U.N. historiography, with an even more decided narrative of failure, which is perhaps warranted given that the organization no longer exists and that its collective security mechanisms obviously failed to stop the march toward the second world war of that generation. As leading historian of the League Gary Ostrower has noted, "The men who created the League had one main objective—to prevent war. The League became their monument to the casualties of World War I, and its success would be measured by the degree to which it helped to keep the peace." But he then went on to say, "On another level, however, the League succeeded beyond expectations. It laid a firm foundation for internationalism, a series of ideas that encouraged international cooperation in areas far beyond the narrow focus of the collective-security enthusiasts." This focus on the development of internationalism—as a set of ideas and institutions—has characterized newer works looking at the nondiplomatic work of the League.[9] The field of international relations within the discipline of political science has likewise seen growing attention to the role and importance of international organizations (often called IGOs for international governmental organizations). Previously, international relations scholars who called themselves "realists" had dominated the field, largely dismissing Wilsonian internationalists as idealists and defining IGOs simply as arenas in which nation-states either achieved or failed to achieve their goals based on their exercise of power. However, the end of the Cold War and new research have highlighted a new social constructivist school within the field that studies the ways in which IGOs play an active role in decision-making and in the setting of international norms that can influence governments. This has focused increasing scholarly attention on the idea of global governance, but frequently on the more recent period after the Second World War. Regardless of approach, all of this new work recognizes the League and similar agencies as a fertile borderland in which new ideas grew and developed, escaping or exceeding the ideas of their founders.[10]

The early development of internationalism and international organizations

By the mid-1800s, a new mentality—internationalism—seemed to have burst onto the scene in Europe and North America. It shaped the ideas, imaginations, actions, and views of the world. Most recently historian Mark Mazower has argued that this "radical project" was connected to the rise of the professions and a growing middle class. Historian Frank Ninkovich has specifically and in some depth identified the cultural foundations—especially a stress on international relations as being "grounded in contacts between peoples and societies" rather than states—that made up the late nineteenth century's nebulous liberal internationalism in the United States.[11] Historian Akira Iriye has also identified the creation of a "global consciousness" during this period. Built in part on the relatively peaceful international relations of the Pax Britannica, people began to feel less pessimistic about their ability to reform the ways in which countries interacted, and new institutions—such as the world's fairs—provided the infrastructure to bring together diverse national organizations and activists to form new international organizations.[12] As a result of these diverse trends, many "internationalisms" flourished in the mid-nineteenth century, ranging from communism and pacifism to calls for laws of war and international arbitration of all interstate disputes, and somewhere in between (and striving in some ways to remove itself from these "political" currents) was the development of a scientific internationalism (like the nutritionists just discussed). Their relative strengths waxed and waned throughout a century that saw a great deal of thinking as well as trial and error in trying to implement the various strains of international thought. The general trend throughout the nineteenth century does seem to be, however, a shift toward the more practical and less revolutionary as these ideas became institutionalized.[13]

The first and second Hague conferences (1899 and 1907) initiated by Czar Alexander I of Russia helped expand and institutionalize some of these international trends. Both included a broader range of governments (most notably smaller European powers and a handful of Asian and Latin American countries) and NGOs and considered a large number of international issues, including disarmament and the compulsory arbitration of international disputes. The first conference also gave birth to the Permanent Court of Arbitration, which established a standard set of rules and procedures to govern such international arbitration, laid the groundwork for the subsequent Permanent Court of International Justice after the First World War, and made important contributions in the development of international law.[14] The court was one of several new intergovernmental organizations established during this period to handle issues (especially commercial issues) that exceeded national and regional capacities to regulate. Beyond institutions, an important intellectual shift that undergirded these conferences was the erosion of the racially determined notion of "civilization" and the emergence of a set of supposedly objective criteria that separated more advanced societies from less advanced ones and allowed independent countries (such as Thailand, Japan, and the states of Latin America) to play national roles in international relations. Equally important in the Hague conferences was how NGOs, most notably women peace activists, established a precedent of lobbying such international conferences.[15] These lobbyists were but one visible sign of the growth and vitality of a wide variety of people organizing and working across national boundaries to abolish slavery and human trafficking, to promote women's suffrage and peace (often through arbitration and international law), and to ensure the humane treatment of soldiers in international conflicts—among others.[16]

Among the multitude of international professional organizations that started developing in the mid-nineteenth century, international commercial associations and private foundations have been relatively neglected in the historiography on internationalism. As the economy globalized, businessmen increasingly organized themselves internationally—first within specific professional niches, then in ad hoc ways around particular functional changes in the global economy, and finally developing broader and more permanent international organizations at the beginning of the twentieth century.[17] The explosive growth of modern capitalism also led to the creation of a new form of NGO, the private foundation acting internationally. One of the first—the Nobel Foundation (est. 1900)—was founded by Alfred Nobel, the Swedish dynamite magnate; the Carnegie Endowment for International Peace (est. 1910) and the Rockefeller Foundation (est. 1913) followed in the United States. The work of these organizations in publicizing and promoting a variety of international organizations and actors deserves more scholarly attention.[18]

Despite the seeming abandonment of internationalism brought on by the nationalism that fueled the First World War, internationalist trends resurfaced as the grisly cost of the war mounted. Many of the same people who had advocated for global peace, international arbitration, women's suffrage, and the like came to support grassroots organizations that aimed at the creation of an overarching postwar international organization. Britain's crusading internationalists formed the British League of Nations Society (est. 1915) whose membership swelled to some 200,000; smaller groups also existed in Belgium, Canada, France, Germany, Ireland, and Switzerland, and the publication of U.S. President Woodrow Wilson's "Fourteen Points" plan for peace, which included just such an organization, heartened these activists. After the war, these groups continued lobbying both their governments and those attending the Paris Peace Conference.[19] In doing so, they drew on a century of activism and action and had clear ideas about how to institutionalize their ideas in the new League of Nations.

The Treaty of Versailles creates the League of Nations system

The Great War that raged across Europe from 1914 until 1918 was the breaking point of the international system created at the Congress of Vienna in 1815. This new war clearly indicated that Europe could no longer maintain peace, that the "civilized" nations on the continent would place few (if any) limits on their warfare against one another, and that room would have to be made for the emerging powers of the Atlantic and Pacific who demanded and played a significant role in the creation of a formal, postwar, global organization. Ultimately, at the Paris Peace Conference, the gathered victors created three new international organizations. The Treaty of Versailles included the large and complex League of Nations covenant (whose Article 14 led to the creation of the Permanent Court of International Justice at the Hague) and provisions for the International Labour Organization (ILO). Collectively, these three institutions constituted the "liberal, nation-embracing, and anticommunist version of internationalism" that characterized the interwar period.[20] Wilson believed that these institutions were so crucial to postwar peace that he abandoned many of his other thirteen "points" in order to secure agreement on the League—only to see the entire Treaty of Versailles rejected by the U.S. Senate. Although historians of the United States always point out the ways in which this stubbornness helped to sabotage Senate ratification of the treaty, international historians are more inclined to see his monomaniacal focus on the League as a type of virtue. For example, Ostrower argues that "without Wilson, the fledgling movement to create a league of nations would have died an early death." The conclusion is likely justified since Wilson had to threaten to leave the conference (after the Italian delegate had already stormed out) to ensure that the League's covenant would be an integral part of the reestablishment of peace.[21]

Wilson's League embraced and institutionalized a vision of the equality of all nations. Not surprisingly, this vision attracted the support of a number of smaller states. Belgium's Paul Hymans, Czechoslovakia's Edward Beneš, Greece's Eleutherios Venizelos, South Africa's Jan Christian Smuts, Sweden's Karl Hjalmar Branting, and Switzerland's Giuseppe Motta were outspoken advocates. Wilson's insistence on providing smaller states with a permanent place in international diplomacy helped ensure a League Assembly that consisted of all states meeting regularly and voting democratically on a regular basis. This seems to have been empowering, leading the Japanese and Chinese representatives to sponsor their own failed resolution in support of racial equality. Additionally, Hymans's outspoken advocacy for the League in Paris subsequently earned him the honor of serving as the president of the very first League Assembly in 1920. Indeed, throughout the decade, representatives of small and medium powers used this forum to raise issues of importance to them and to present their own views to an international audience. The Assembly could also be used to put pressure on another of the League's organs—the Council, which originally had four permanent members (France, Great Britain, Italy, and Japan) and met regularly, while the Assembly met only annually.[22] Although the League was more egalitarian than previous international organizations, people in colonized areas, many of whose hopes had been raised by the inclusion of a call for self-determination in Wilson's Fourteen Points, were bitterly disappointed by the League's reinforcement of the status quo of Great Power rule and colonialism, through its mandate system. This disillusionment fed the creation of a "League against Imperialism" in Brussels, Belgium, in February 1927 (supported by the Communist International, the "Comintern"), ideas for a Federation of the Asiatic Peoples among leaders of the Indian National Congress (who increasingly saw themselves as the future leaders of an independent country), and dissatisfaction among Latin American leaders who had hoped for an international counterbalance to the projection of U.S. power into their territories.[23]

Not surprisingly, given the earlier history of the Hague conferences, the Paris Peace Conference attracted the attention and action of a variety of international organizations that sought to incorporate their interests into the peace settlement. They proposed (ultimately unsuccessfully) that representatives of NGOs and national parliaments be incorporated into extraordinary meetings with the League Council and that an intergovernmental commission explore the international concerns of women. More successful was the joint deputation from the International Council of Women and the Conference of Allied Suffragists, which requested appointments of women to the League and the creation of international health and education organizations. The League Covenant ultimately provided an equal opportunity (although this did not result in equal numbers of positions) for male and female employment in the League's Secretariat.[24]

The first meeting of the League's Council in Paris followed just six days after the Treaty of Versailles came into force and created the mechanisms and procedures needed for the League's work.[25] In establishing the Permanent Court of International Justice, it created an elaborate appointment process for the nine judges (after 1931 there were eleven) to ensure their independence from their home states, but from the date of the conditional adherence of the United States to the court's statute in 1929, there was always an American on the international bench. The most important work of the court—undertaken in conjunction with the judicial department of the League's Secretariat (which was responsible for registering international treaties)—was the codification of international law, which had previously consisted primarily of general principles rather than written rules. As part of this process, the court became the declared jurisdictional body for several hundred treaties, conventions, and declarations, testifying to its legitimacy.[26]

While some diplomatic issues eluded League management in its early years, a number of concerns outside of the realm of traditional diplomacy found their way into the League Covenant. Article 23 committed the new organization to a laundry list of general improvements to the state of humankind, including "to secure and maintain fair and humane conditions of labour for men, women and children"; "to secure just treatment of the native inhabitants of territories"; to suppress the trafficking of women and children; to suppress the international opium and drug trades; "to secure and maintain freedom of communications and of transit" and "equitable treatment for the commerce of all" League members; and "to take steps in matters of international concern for the prevention and control of disease." A number of historians have commented positively on the ways in which these articles paved the way for the League to undertake meaningful social, humanitarian, and economic activities that also laid the groundwork for the later work of the U.N. specialized agencies.[27]

Another part of the League's agenda included administering the former colonies of the Central Powers (the focus of Article 22) through its mandate system. Historian Susan Pedersen's impressive international history of this system calls it "one of the Peace Conference's most bitterly contested decisions," made only under American and international pressure. Some of the victorious powers had wanted to annex these areas outright, and others thought the League should directly administer them. Instead, they were placed under the supervision of the League Mandates Commission and the League Council, which the mandatory powers resisted. It was primarily the work of the director of the Mandates Section in the League Secretariat, William Emmanuel Rappard of Switzerland, that helped ensure that the Mandates Section finally met for the first time on October 4, 1921 (after "fierce criticism" in the 1920 and 1921 League assemblies drummed up by Rappard) and that enforced the requirement that each mandatory power provide "an annual report" to the Council on "the territory committed to its charge." Although the mandates system failed to improve the quality of life of those living under such arrangements (compared to colonial powers) and failed to bring even a single state to independence before the Second World War, Pedersen highlights the section's significant, unforeseen impacts on the international system as a whole and on the ultimate form and functions of the United Nations.[28]

In addition to the Permanent Court of International Justice and the Mandates Commission, another innovation arising from the Treaty of Versailles was the International Labour Organization. It is crucial to recall that the goal of the Paris Peace Conference was not just to reestablish peace on the European continent but also to respond to the growing threat of international communism, which had triumphed in Russia and played a role in the unsettled situations in Berlin, Vienna, and Budapest during the Paris Peace Conference. The delegates in Paris designed the ILO to offer the world's workers a concrete expression of the democratic powers' commitment to build a postwar peace that would provide them with a way forward. The ILO built on a history of small experiments in improving the lives of workers and on national legislation with the same goal, it innovated a number of new arrangements in order to offer the world's employees a viable noncommunist alternative, and ultimately it crafted a long-lived institution that formally represents the world's workers as equal partners with its employers and governments. As such, it was a new type of organization that sought to reconcile potentially antagonistic forces and to change domestic social relations so as to address the root causes of war. Though it, like all international organizations, has fallen short of this mark, it created a new and important borderland for these three groups to interact, which at least helped each group to better understand their positions and to organize across borders.[29]

By far the best historical work on the origins of the ILO is international labor historian Elizabeth McKillen's *Making the World Safe for Workers*, which properly situates the history of the ILO in the borderlands between labor, business, and government; between different strands of unionism within the countries attending the Paris Peace Conference; between different visions of unionism within and between different nations; between different constituencies within unions; between ideologies of socialism and corporatism; and between national and international interests. She starts by pointing out that Wilson's concerns about the radical potential of labor (exacerbated by the Russian and Mexican revolutions) led him to court labor support both at home and abroad, believing that it would be crucial as he tried to write his Fourteen Points into the Versailles Treaty. From the beginning Wilson assumed that there would be a price to pay for such support, as he had earlier faced resistance from American labor to his foreign policy toward Mexico, his domestic preparedness efforts in the wake of the outbreak of hostilities on the continent, his declaration of war, and his efforts to fully mobilize the U.S. economy to support the war effort. Therefore, the president came to advocate for some type of international labor organization in order to bring labor support to his League. He chose Samuel Gompers, the founder and head of the American Federation of Labor (AFL), to assist him both with wartime mobilization and with the postwar development of such an organization. Despite the prominence of Gompers and the ILO's decidedly anticommunist purpose, the U.S. Senate rejected it.[30]

Nonetheless, the ILO started its work under the leadership of Albert Thomas, a French Socialist, who served as director of the ILO's permanent staff (the International Labour Office) from its founding until his death in 1932 (when his deputy, Harold Butler of the United Kingdom, succeeded him). At its first International Labour

Conference in November 1919 in the U.S. capital, the ILO established six International Labour Conventions dealing with hours of work in industry, unemployment, maternity protection, night work for women, and minimum age and night work for young people in industry. Such conventions served as models for national legislation as well as global standards.[31] This first ILO Conference seems to have impressed upon the representatives of industry the need to organize themselves more formally; they quickly realized that "they did not know each other; neither had they exchanged any views as regards the serious problems with which production was directly concerned," resulting in their being "absolutely disunited," especially in comparison with the labor representatives who were well acquainted through their earlier international organizations and work. The International Organisation of Employers quickly organized (est. 1920) to work at the ILO for the common interests of its members (who were national organizations) and soon became the secretariat for the employers' section of the ILO.[32]

The operation of the League of Nations system

In much the same way that the Paris Peace Conference had served as a borderland in which the victors, small powers, and NGOs contended and cooperated with one another to influence the postwar settlement, the organization that they established in Geneva also became a vibrant international borderland.[33] Especially when the journalists, lobbyists, and boosters joined the diplomats and their entourages for each fall's Assembly, the Swiss city became "the world capital of rhetoric, diplomacy, and style." Formal and informal diplomacy occurred in the official meetings and at the lavish receptions. Historian Susan Pedersen characterizes the League largely as a social and rhetorical space—"a public arena where [the statesmen of the world, well-oiled by drink] had to perform civility and espouse internationalism, whatever their private or even political inclinations." But because the League required these duties, it functioned as "an agent of geopolitical transformation." The former deputy secretary-general of the League of Nations, F. P. Walters of Great Britain, noted a similar "atmosphere of Geneva" but chose to attribute it to the personal interactions that allowed those gathered at the League "to understand the attitudes of other countries more clearly" and to gain a "sense of the essential unity of mankind."[34]

Even when the high-level diplomats left Geneva following the Assembly meetings, the city was animated by the Secretariat, the League Council, and an increasing number of what we would today call NGOs, who made their home in this international capital so that they could be better informed about and better able to shape global events that they cared about. As the Council largely set the agenda for the Assembly meetings, those states lacking permanent seats constantly vied for the remaining seats, eventually leading to an expansion of the Council. The aspiring researcher might well inquire into how and why these second-tier states (such as Brazil, Poland, and Spain) maneuvered so determinedly for these seats and what they hoped to accomplish on the Council.[35] Behind the scenes of the Council and Assembly's work and tasked with carrying out the work they defined, the Secretariat (led by Eric Drummond of Great Britain until

June 1933 and then by Joseph Avenol of France) formed one of the largest and most competent early international civil services. Drummond had largely drawn that first skeleton staff from those London staffers who had worked in the government's wartime agencies facilitating wartime cooperation. They subsequently gelled as an international staff as they embarked en masse to Geneva, sent their children to the League school, listened to the League radio station, and worked together to establish and maintain an organization that prized loyalty to an international charter and the ability to manage complex, international problems. Indeed, these were the very tasks that national governments on their own could not tackle, making the League indispensable.[36]

Even outside of Geneva and government circles, the League cultivated a host of people who supported its work and lobbied their governments on its behalf. Millions of people belonged to League of Nations societies that ranged from Poland to Argentina. Although initially created to lobby for creation of the organization, they quickly recalibrated their work to keep abreast of the League's work through publications and lectures. Members of these League societies also quickly mobilized to petition their governments when they seemed to be straying from the Geneva orbit. A historian examining the League of Nations Society in Canada has argued, for example, that no other group drew "so many members from the population at large, or . . . sought so consistently to influence the direction of Canadian public thinking and government policy on foreign-policy issues." Additionally, these national societies were organized into the broader Federation of League of Nations Societies, which met annually and helped to set the agenda for the national and local societies.[37] These societies had a wealth of issues to keep up to date on as the League's work ranged around the globe and into a variety of fields.

The history of the League of Nations is littered with spectacular diplomatic failures and underreported but relatively minor diplomatic successes, which are generally familiar and will not be repeated here.[38] Less well known is the League's development of a vibrant arena of technical or functionalist work in health, aviation, economics, law, nutrition, international commerce, and employment, among others. From the beginning, this work, meant to lay the social or functionalist foundations for a lasting peace, was seen as a corollary to its diplomatic work. These early experiments sprang, much like the earliest functionalist international organizations, from the recognition that broad, global cooperation was needed to manage a growing number of areas in the increasingly interconnected world. For example, at the same time that the Entente powers gathered to conclude the peace treaty after the First World War, they also drafted the Convention Relative to the Regulation of Aerial Navigation, as the importance and danger of airplanes moved dramatically from the theoretical to the practical during the war. The resulting International Commission for Air Navigation, coordinating with the League, helped standardize the field of civil aviation and established the principle that each country controls its own airspace.[39]

The useful work of the League's Health Organization and its Social Department seemed to expand in direct proportion to its declining diplomatic stature. In fact, despite the rather desperate economic circumstances of the 1930s, Latin American, Asian, and even African representatives to the League consistently lobbied for the expansion of the health organization and its budget. In response, the League sponsored public health conferences in the Far East (1937) and Latin America (1938).[40] Given the successes that the Social Department was having, League Council member Stanley Bruce of Australia argued that the League should be reconfigured in a way that would free its social and economic work from the diplomatic focus of the Council. Ultimately, the "Bruce Committee" recommended a new, expert "Central Committee for Economic and Social Questions" that would have greater professional authority and a correspondingly higher public profile. Such a committee would also allow nonmembers to actively participate in its work and contribute to its budget. The Bruce Report, which distilled two decades of League experience into a clear vision for the future, was released on August 22, 1939, just days before the outbreak of general war on the European continent. As such, it became the blueprint for the postwar Economic and Social Council of the United Nations rather than a reorganization of the extant League of Nations.[41]

Conclusion: The wartime transition from the League to the United Nations

As German armies stormed across France, the League of Nations found itself threatened by internal disloyalty as well as external pressures. Secretary-General Joseph Avenol, a Frenchman by birth, sought to curry favor with the fascist powers by praising Adolf Hitler and Benito Mussolini before being replaced in July 1940 by his deputy, an Irish politician named Sean Lester, who did his best to maintain a skeleton staff and the League's records and buildings so that the organization (or its successor) could be useful again when the war ended. The League's treasury and its Refugees Department moved to London in the fall of 1940, the section dealing with drug trafficking relocated to the United States in the spring of 1941, the entire ILO moved to Montreal for the duration, and the League Secretariat's Economic, Financial, and Transit Department relocated to Princeton University with assistance from the Rockefeller Foundation and the support of the American government. In Geneva, Lester was left with fewer than one hundred employees, which was for the best since almost none of the organization's members outside of British Commonwealth made monetary contributions any longer.[42]

Although the League was discredited, the Allies relatively quickly came to the conclusion that some sort of postwar international organization would be needed to keep the peace. The 1941 Atlantic Charter envisioned some sort of "permanent system of general security," and as early as October 1943, Franklin Roosevelt, Winston Churchill, and Josef Stalin each committed, for their own reasons, to some sort of "general international organization, based on the principle of the sovereign equality of all peace-loving states." The U.S. State Department began sketching plans for the new organization, and these became the starting point for the Dumbarton Oaks and San Francisco conferences that wrote the U.N. Charter and established the main organization. New specialized agencies of the United Nations had their own organizational conferences during and after the war, while other prewar organizations were simply absorbed or inserted into the U.N. orbit without much fanfare.[43]

The sense of excited possibility that animated the immediate postwar period and heralded the United Nations led more than two hundred large and small cities and towns—mostly American but occasionally Canadian and European—to inquire about becoming the home of its new headquarters. Enthusiasm abounded as citizens imagined this new borderland, this new capital of the world: "It was imagined as something like a perpetual world's fair, or perhaps a cluster of fashionable embassy buildings, or even an entirely new city where the UN's staff could live and work in modern buildings symbolizing a bright, unencumbered future." Even though most of those dreams dimmed in the harsh light of the dawning Cold War, this period of excited imagining gives us insight into the mindset of a particular postwar moment "when so much had been risked, so much lost, and so much achieved, [that] it seemed to be possible, even imperative, to dream."[44]

CHAPTER 3
THE COLD WAR BORDERLAND

The Great Powers, based on their wartime alliance and their collective work in crafting the U.N. Charter, initially expected (or at least hoped) that the United Nations would function as the location from which they could jointly manage international affairs in a cooperative manner. However, conflicts emerged almost immediately between the Big Three (the United States, the Soviet Union, and the United Kingdom) over a variety of issues. America's support of Iran's complaint to the first session of the U.N. Security Council about Soviet interference in Azerbaijan definitely strained U.S.-Soviet relations in the new world body. By March 1948—with the proclamation of the Truman Doctrine committing the United States to a global policy of containing communism—any remnant of Great Power cooperation had disappeared, and it was clear that the Cold War had set in and that the United Nations would become an international arena characterized by confrontation rather than cooperation between the two postwar superpowers. Each attacked the other for its foreign policy and its suppression of citizens' human rights (discussed in greater depth in Chapter 8), seeking to win international propaganda points before the global audience at the United Nations (whose proceedings were televised in ways previously unavailable to the League).

Yet at the same time, since all permanent members of the U.N. Security Council maintained a permanent mission at the New York headquarters, the United Nations remained an area for continuing dialogue and diplomacy—a borderland—between the contending superpowers. Additionally, their international audience and fellow diplomats in New York City provided a curb to escalation of international crises and served as a diplomatic forum where mediation could still deescalate such crises, which happened mostly clearly in the cases of the Berlin blockade, the Korean War, and the Cuban Missile Crisis.

Nor was this U.N. borderland defined solely by the Cold War conflict. Instead, a number of countries (especially new nations) and coalitions of countries sought to exert their own influence over this global organization. If the period after the First World War is appropriately called the "Wilsonian moment" due to the ability of U.S. President Woodrow Wilson to spark colonial peoples' misplaced hope that they could attain self-determination through the new League of Nations, then the period after the Second World War should be named the "Nehruvian moment" due to India's determination to fight nonviolently for full independence for itself and then for the rest of the colonized world. Much of the later fight happened in the halls of the United Nations, where those Indian National Congress leaders who had been jailed throughout the war for their advocacy of independence took up the mantle of international leadership, most prominently India's first prime minister, Jawaharlal Nehru, who assumed office on August 15, 1947. What India had to share with the world was so essential to the worldview of these Indian nationalists that Nehru had begun formulating a foreign policy for an independent India in the 1930s when he served as general secretary of the Indian National Congress.[1]

Nehru—along with other early nationalist leaders like Egypt's Gamal Abdel al-Nasser, Ghana's Kwame Nkrumah, and Indonesia's Sukarno—helped to establish the Non-Aligned Movement, which later developed into the larger G-77 coalition (short for the group of seventy-seven Third World member states in the United Nations at that time). Both movements sought to draw attention to their collective needs. This happened most publicly and decidedly in the U.N. General Assembly, the only one of the six main organs of the United Nations where all members have a single, equal vote and where most decisions require a simple majority. Third World power in the General Assembly was most evident in the heated debates that marked the fifteenth General Assembly session of 1960 promoting decolonization, but it also emerged in its 1967 consideration of the Arab-Israeli conflict (see Chapter 7) and the special sessions dedicated to the development of a New International Economic Order (NIEO, discussed in Chapter 5).

In addition to these national actors, the secretary-general and his staff (the U.N. Secretariat) also played key roles—often behind the scenes—in both the East-West (Cold War) and North-South (economic development) conflicts. The conflict between the Soviet Union and the United States and their shared desire to be the primary decision-maker in the United Nations meant that the highest position in the world organization would always go to someone from one of the smaller countries that was not considered a clear ally of either side. This has weakened the office generally, and activist secretaries-general able to expand the U.N. mandate have been few and far between. The secretariat—given the longevity of service of its members and its global representativeness—has frequently made significant contributions to the United Nations' mission through their diplomacy, their shaping of international conferences and debates, and their functionalist work in carrying out the organization's everyday work. Perhaps because they often could not act independently, they had to develop a keen ability to craft persuasive arguments that could gain traction in international fora.

So if we return to our analogy of the United Nations as a borderland, the permanent members of the Security Council (originally the United States, the Soviet Union, Great Britain, France, and China) were the most powerful property owners (perhaps the ranchers) in this unstable region—each with real material stakes in the area, each trying to gain greater power and influence. Yet they were simultaneously familiar with and willing to reach out to their less powerful neighbors in the area when conflicts escalated and seemed to threaten the safety and security of their shared borderland. These other and newer states can be seen as the smaller family farmers in this borderland who gather once a year for a "town-hall" meeting in which all the white, male property owners have a chance to speak (the equivalent of the General Assembly). Continuing the analogy, the U.N. Secretariat are the shop owners at the center of the town, permanent members of the area as a whole whose livelihoods depend on the survival of the community as a whole but who lack the means to defend it on their own. Finally, the secretary-general is the mayor who tries to get the various groups to work together for the good of the town, but he lacks police power to do so—the sheriff is beholden to the powerful ranchers in the area. Ultimately, the survival of the entire region is dependent on these actors figuring out how to manage the inevitable conflicts and collectively benefit from the borderland's population growth and economic activity. And as the different populations interact over time, they come to know and understand one another a bit better, making them better able to advance their community as a whole. This is the story of the United Nations that I will briefly narrate in this chapter.

The stakeholders

The Security Council

In preparing for the 1944 Dumbarton Oaks Conference, the United States, the Soviet Union, and Great Britain agreed that the main work of safeguarding peace and preventing war would fall to them. They also reached substantive agreement that the security framework should be global, rather than regional. While the Soviets would have been content to have the entire focus of the new United Nations Organization be on the preservation of global security, the Anglo-American delegations insisted on carrying on the League's work in the economic and humanitarian spheres as well. Eventually they agreed on a General Assembly that would be largely deliberative, while the Security Council would bear primary responsibility for maintaining global peace. Despite consensus that the Security Council would be some sort of continuation of the wartime Grand Alliance, there were pitched debates during the conference about the veto power of the permanent members of the Council, with the Soviets holding adamantly to an absolute veto (except on purely procedural matters). Undergirding the Dumbarton Oaks and San Francisco conferences was the absolute commitment by all three Great Powers that they would work together in the new United Nations, making the work of the conferences simply (and complexly) a matter of figuring out how to arrange that, even as relations became strained between the time of the two conferences. At the 1945 San Francisco Conference, the Great Powers notably fought off an effort (led by Australia) to limit their veto power, which included the theatrics of Republican U.S. Senator Tom Connally of Texas literally tearing up a copy of the Charter to illustrate the impact that limiting the veto would have. On June 26, the United States, the Soviet Union, Great Britain, France, and China were the first to sign the documents creating the United Nations; in doing so, they had certainly started out in the way that they intended the new organization to go.[2] But Cold War tensions and the unforeseen power of new countries emerging from colonial rule fractured the Second World War alliance and made the General Assembly more important in the overall work of the United Nations.

Political analyst and journalist David Bosco's history of the Security Council talks about how it creates the "sense of identity and belonging that exclusive clubs usually offer." He goes on to argue that those who focus on the failures of the Council tend to focus on the Charter-based vision of the Council's work as governing and maintaining international peace and security (presumably through collective action), something that no commentator claims that the Security Council or the United Nations has done well. Bosco instead points to a more historical, coexisting, less idealistic, and expansive vision of the Council "as a mechanism for producing consensus among the major powers." This formulation puts it on a functional plane with the Concert of Europe (which is where historian Mark Mazower started his history of the idea of governing the world), and from this perspective, Bosco argues that the council has "allowed the most powerful states to compromise on contentious issues," "offered them face-saving ways out of crises," "expanded and deepened the networks of diplomatic contacts that link the leading powers," and "created a space and process through which the world's great powers struggle to contain conflicts and achieve compromise"—tasks that collectively amount to "no small feat." He goes on: "The habits of consultation and negotiation that the council has cultivated influence, often in subtle ways, the course of crises" and have "helped to train generations of leading diplomats from the major powers in the art of multilateral diplomacy" (including George H. W. Bush). These habits and skills can help prevent miscalculation. A quiet conversation in the Council's hallway helped to ease the dangerous Berlin blockade in the early days of the Cold War, and the dramatic debate in the U.N. Security Council during the Cuban Missile Crisis helped to slow the pace of the conflict and to shape world public opinion in a way that made a peaceful resolution more likely. When the Middle East descended into war in 1967 and 1973, it also served as a ready vehicle for negotiating cease-fires, dispatching peacekeepers, and avoiding superpower entanglement. In the late 1980s, the combined pressure of the Council helped end the long struggle between Iran and Iraq, a conflict that was spilling over into the Persian Gulf and threatening international commerce. Additionally, the end of the Cold War energized the Security Council to play a larger role in resolving a number of regional conflicts (more on peacekeeping and peace-building in Chapter 7).[3]

The General Assembly

The General Assembly is, in my opinion, the most interesting U.N. organ and the richest area for future historical scholarship on the United Nations. Throughout its history, the General Assembly has taken up issues of international peace and security (rather than leaving these solely to the Security Council), supervised the work of the Economic and Social Council (ECOSOC) and the Trusteeship Council (which oversaw colonial territories entrusted to the United Nations), selected judges for the International Court of Justice (ICJ), and defined the work of the Secretariat by approving its budget, drafting staff regulations, and defining its organizational structure. However, because of the sprawling and public nature of the Assembly's work, it has not received sufficient scholarly attention, especially from historians. Nonetheless, as the only truly democratic organ of the United Nations, it is the arena where the "small" states have exercised the greatest power and where the Non-Aligned Movement of Third World countries dominated the discussion after the mid-1960s. Indeed, the General Assembly has consciously designed its work to maximize the participation of even the smallest delegations. For example, it maintains a rule that there cannot be more than three main committees meeting simultaneously, and it privileges those matters that are submitted to the agenda at least sixty days ahead of the convening of the session, providing more time for delegations to prepare for meaningful debate of the many issues before it. The time pressures on the fourteen-week Assembly work cycle created by the first accommodation are partly offset by the second accommodation. The General Assembly's democratic nature has meant that historians can gain ready access to public documents containing the thoughts and operating procedures of leaders from the "periphery" states, who may be actors on the international stage but about whom there are often no large public archives. Later in this chapter, for example, we will see how the General Assembly became one of the primary agents (along with national liberation organizations on the ground) for promoting decolonization by completing the work of delegitimizing colonial rule and aggressively working both on behalf of the colonial peoples and against the colonizers. It also worked early and consistently to isolate the white South African regime and to vilify its apartheid system of strict racial segregation (detailed in Chapter 8). Additionally, these records and deliberations give us insights into the work of a whole host of nonstate actors—leaders of national liberation movements as well as nongovernmental organizations (NGOs) like the National Association for the Advancement of Colored People (NAACP)—that played crucial roles in the postwar period by coordinating and promoting an agenda of human rights and decolonization as diplomatic historian Carol Anderson's books have shown.[4]

Despite the richness of the General Assembly's activities, much of the international relations literature on it is either descriptive (focused on form, function, and needed reforms) or simply uses data from the General Assembly (such as voting patterns) as one way of studying international dynamics. Given the early reliance by both historians and political scientists on a "realist" perspective that privileged the actions of the Great Powers and their exercise of power through military action and high-level diplomacy, this is unsurprising. Instead, the power of the General Assembly is the type of "soft power" that has gained increasing scholarly attention in recent years and that reflects the broader agenda and commitment of professional historians to understanding the ways in which race, class, and gender have undergirded and shaped all historical processes. So while some would dismiss the Assembly merely as "a forum for deliberation," often in desperate need of reform to make it more efficient, others (especially those focusing on issues of global governance) have recognized and begun to appreciate its importance in "providing collective legitimation (or de-legitimation) of norms, rules, and actions." Additionally, new historical scholarship on the Non-Aligned Movement, nonstate actors, and NGOs shows the hard diplomatic work done by such groups to remold international public opinion and practice. This moves us beyond the idea that this work is unimportant and unworthy of serious study or that shaping and moving international opinion about equality and independence in the U.N. General Assembly "has always been easy."[5]

The secretary-general and secretariat

The League of Nations formed the basic ideas about what the new United Nations' permanent staff should be like. The first League secretary-general, Sir Eric Drummond of Great Britain, had successfully argued that he and his permanent secretariat (modeled on the British civil service) should hold themselves to the highest standards of international impartiality and technical expertise; and his staff's performance during his tenure from 1920 until 1933 helped establish this idea as an international norm. Even the fascist bias of Secretary-General Joseph Avenol (who succeeded Drummond and held the League's highest office until 1940) only reinforced the idea that such ideals were essential and should be embodied in the new U.N. Secretariat. There has been a consistent tug-of-war between the secretary-general and the strongest member states throughout U.N. history. Secretary-General Trygve Lie of Norway (who served from 1946 until 1952)—under pressure from the anticommunist, McCarthyite "witch hunt" then happening in the United States—compromised the principles of the secretariat's independence written into the U.N. Charter when he allowed the U.S. Federal Bureau of Investigation to set up an office within the U.N. headquarters building to evaluate the "loyalty" of U.S. members of the organization, but his successor, Dag Hammarskjöld (who served until 1961), remedied this shortcoming, instituted organizational changes meant to enhance his staff's independence, and spoke frequently in public about the importance of such internationalism. But the Swedish secretary-general had to compromise with the Soviet Union on the issue of permanent staff contracts (the Soviet bloc accepted only fixed-term contracts or appointments on the basis of secondment). Taking office after his predecessor's untimely death, Secretary-General U Thant of Burma (now Myanmar) recruited more staff members from the new nations emerging from colonial rule so that the secretariat would better reflect the global population they served. Austrian Kurt Waldheim (who served from 1972 until 1981) sought to highlight the work of economic development by creating a new director-general for Development and International Economic Co-operation. His successor, Peruvian Javier Pérez de Cuéllar (who held office until 1991), continued this initiative, but the post did not survive Egyptian Boutros Boutros-Ghali's (the United Nations' secretary-general from 1992 until 1996) reorganization that divided the secretariat into just two departments (the Department of Political Affairs and the Department of Peace-Keeping Operations). During the tenure of Secretary-General Kofi Annan of Ghana (from 1997 until 2006), the concept of a permanent international civil service eroded under the weight of the membership's criticism and the organizational weaknesses highlighted as a corruption scandal became public in 2004 involving inadequate U.N. oversight of the program that allowed Iraq (which was under strict economic sanctions for its earlier invasion of Kuwait) to trade its oil exports for food imports. As a result, the current secretary-general, Ban Ki-Moon of South Korea (who took office in 2007), inherited a secretariat with little faith in the integrity of senior management. Regardless of member states' criticism and the weaknesses that do exist in the Secretariat, what it has accomplished with its relatively small staff of just over 14,000 is nothing short of phenomenal.[6]

The Trusteeship Council

The U.N. Trusteeship Council was very much the reincarnation of the League's Mandates Commission as well as an effort to live up to the Atlantic Charter's recycled ideal of self-determination. At the February 1945 Yalta Conference, U.S. President Franklin D. Roosevelt had agreed with Soviet leader Josef Stalin about the need for machinery within the proposed United Nations to manage the non–self-governing trusteeships, but British Prime Minister Sir Winston Churchill carried the day in terms of limiting the scope of such trusteeships only to previous mandates, the former colonial areas of Italy and Japan, and any territory voluntarily surrendered to U.N. oversight. Underlying the Soviet-American consent to this narrow scope was both the U.S. military's commitment to maintaining the Japanese territories it was occupying in the Pacific and a secret U.S.-Soviet accord granting the Soviet Union control of parts of Japanese and Chinese territories in exchange for its entry into the Pacific war and its recognition of Nationalist China. Given these covert interests, the agenda of the previous fall's Dumbarton Oaks Conference had not even included the issue of trusteeship.[7]

In the meantime, the British—and especially the French—were working to shore up their postwar empires and were well aware of the dangers such an organization posed. As we saw in Chapter 2, the League's Mandates Commission became a borderland in which other colonial powers, noncolonial powers, NGOs, and the populations of these mandatory areas could publicly criticize colonial administrations. Georges Bidault, the provisional French foreign minister, cabled his ambassador in London as soon as he heard that the Big Three were contemplating a role for the United Nations in the affairs of dependent territories. After Yalta, France's representative in Moscow had also sought (but not received) assurances that its colonial territories would be safe from any such system, and then Bidault had followed up with his counterpart in Great Britain. Anthony Eden assured the Frenchman that he had clearly excluded their colonies from the scheme and framed the trusteeship issue as an American idea that would allow it "to lay hands chastely on the Japanese islands in the Pacific." The French also worked to line up other colonial powers—especially the Netherlands—to support their views and cabled all of their diplomatic envoys to develop support of the French position.[8]

At the 1945 San Francisco Conference, the question of U.N. trusteeship was finally settled. In the lead up to the conference, the American military had argued for another postponement, but the State Department realized that the lack of an agreement would tacitly approve land acquisition by the victorious powers, something that it very much wanted to avoid. So U.S. Secretary of State Edward Stettinius Jr. worked to hammer out a compromise with the War Department that designated the Marshalls, the Marianas, and the Carolines as "strategic" trust territories to be used solely for military bases and to be under the oversight of the Security Council, rather than the General Assembly or the Trusteeship Council. There were other American voices trying to influence the San Francisco Conference on the issue of trusteeship as well, including the National Association for the Advancement of Colored People (NAACP) and the Council on African Affairs (CAA)—both of whom sent delegations to the West Coast to express the strong anticolonial stance that they had already expressed to the State Department. The CAA planned, for example, to distribute tens of thousands of pamphlets and to lobby the delegates from Belgium, Britain, Cuba, Ethiopia, France, India, Liberia, and Panama. On the special preconference train from Washington, DC, to the West Coast, State Department experts (including Leo Pasvolsky and Ralph Bunche) drew up the plans for the Trusteeship Council. In their eleven guidelines, they carved out the exception for the "strategic areas," established the principle that placing territories under the Trusteeship Council would be voluntary rather than compulsory, stated that the goal of trusteeships was "self-government" (because the British and French opposed any mention of "independence"), argued that the Council's composition should be balanced between states having oversight of such areas and those that did not, and empowered the resulting Council with the power to accept reports, collect petitions, institute investigations, visit the territories, and undertake other activities related to its oversight responsibilities. This draft—buffeted by some four hundred pages of proposed amendments (mostly from the French and British)—emerged essentially intact to form Chapters XI and XII of the U.N. Charter. Although this fell far short of what the delegate from the Philippines, the NAACP, and others had hoped for (especially since the Trusteeship Council oversaw only eleven areas), it was a step in the right direction. Perhaps only the government in South Africa recognized the anti-imperialist potential of the U.N. Trusteeship Council. Pretoria refused either to surrender its League mandate over the former German protectorate of South West Africa or to negotiate a U.N. trusteeship for the territory, fearing the higher level of international surveillance and the inclination toward independence that the trusteeship system embodied.[9]

Test-driving the new United Nations

The First Session of the U.N. General Assembly, consisting of representatives of fifty-one member states, convened in London on January 10, 1946, and featured wrangling over who would serve as president of the session (essentially a ceremonial designation for the person serving as chair of the meeting) and, more substantively, who would serve as the organization's secretary-general. Ultimately, Paul-Henri Spaak, the Belgian foreign minister who had represented his country well for many years in the League of Nations, was elected as the session's president by a coalition of European powers and Latin American countries who wanted a prominent role for one of the "smaller" powers. Spaak's pro-Western orientation and anticommunist credentials made the Soviets eager to ensure that the secretary-general would be more neutral or even favorable to their views, as they initially nominated statesmen from Eastern Europe and opposed Canadian Lester Pearson. In the end, the two superpowers—and then the Security Council and General Assembly—agreed on Norwegian Trygve Lie. The Security Council first met on January 17, 1946. With a focus on ceremonial speeches, it went smoothly and quietly. One week later, the very first resolution of the General Assembly (even before the adoption of rules of procedure regarding the official language of the United Nations) called for creation of a commission "to deal with the problems raised by the discovery of atomic energy and other related matters" that would report to the Security Council and seek to harness atomic energy "for peaceful ends" while eliminating "atomic weapons and all other major weapons adaptable to mass destruction" through a system of inspections. This shows the Assembly's early commitment to raising what it identified as the key global issues, bringing them in front of an international audience, and attempting to put pressure on the Security Council to act according to the will of the majority of the world's states. But the Cold War soon overshadowed these early expressions of hope in postwar cooperation and in the possibilities of the new global organization. However, despite the contention, invective, and even yelling that accompanied subsequent Council and Assembly meetings, behind the scenes, the United Nations was still the place where compromises could be worked out, progress made, and crises de-escalated.[10]

Early Cold War wrangling

The beginning of the Cold War largely played out before a global audience at the United Nations, which also had a key role in influencing the unfolding drama. Initial efforts to maintain Great Power unity faded quickly in the face of an escalating set of crises in Iran, Greece, Germany, and Korea. Historian Ilya Gaiduk's *Divided Together: The United States and the Soviet Union in the United Nations, 1945–1965* provides the clearest historical narrative of this ongoing drama based on the most recent archival research and scholarship (in both the United States and the former Soviet Union). By centering the United Nations in his narrative, Gaiduk moves us beyond studies of the Cold War that make it a side arena and gives us instead a broader view than focused studies of specific diplomatic crises.[11]

Despite initial American reservations about bringing a contentious issue before the U.N. Security Council at the very beginning of its work, the continuing presence of Soviet troops in northern Iran (the Azerbaijan region) as well as their support of an independence movement there was one of the first orders of business for the second Council session in February 1946. In fact the Politburo (which guided Soviet foreign policy) had approved a secret resolution on July 6, 1945, calling for just such actions in Azerbaijan and persisted in these plans despite Anglo-American efforts in late 1945 to bring the Soviets into compliance with the 1942 treaty provisions on the removal of troops. The Soviets hoped to secure their postwar oil (and therefore national security) needs, recognized that the Iranian parliament was unlikely to grant them a concession, and were otherwise anxious about having Anglo-American oil interests so close to their border; but these concerns ran head-on into their allies' interests in the area as well as their fears that Azerbaijani autonomy would be followed by similar demands from Kurds that could destabilize the entire area. Therefore, the Americans supported the Iranians in bringing their suit before the Security Council. Stalin might have miscalculated, thinking that his wartime allies would not endanger their cooperative relationship over the issue of Azerbaijan; another miscalculation came when the Soviets were not allowed to veto the inclusion of Iran on the agenda, since this was a procedural matter. Although the first Security Council resolution on January 20, 1946, blandly called on the two sides to settle the issue through bilateral talks, the Soviets responded with bitterness. They subsequently raised the question in February before the Council of similar postwar occupations of Syria and Lebanon by the French and were disappointed over the mild language of the resolution's "confidence" that these troops would be withdrawn "as soon as practicable," leading to the first of its many subsequent vetoes in the chamber. Gaiduk sees the combination of the Iranian issue and the Soviet veto as destroying "the last vestiges of" the Great Powers' unity in the Council, which was a symptom of the hardening attitude of the administration of U.S. President Harry S. Truman toward his erstwhile ally. Subsequently, the Soviets escalated their support of the separatist movement in Iran and failed to meet the March 2 withdrawal deadline, and the United States pressured the Iranians to bring and keep their complaint before the Security Council. American pressure led the Soviet ambassador to the United Nations to storm out of the session on March 27, when he failed to secure even a two-week extension of time before the Council considered the issue again. Ultimately, Moscow and Tehran reached an agreement on April 5, but the United States was reluctant to allow the Iranian issue to fall from the Council agenda. The Americans increasingly saw the United Nations as an arena for mobilizing global opinion against their Cold War foe, and the Soviets responded in kind, leading British Foreign Secretary Ernest Bevin to complain that the Council was "degenerating into a tiltyard."[12]

The British next found the Soviets tilting at them in the United Nations. The continuing leftist rebellion against the U.K.-supported, autocratic monarchy in Greece that was attempting to reassert its power over the peninsula's government in the aftermath of the war's Nazi occupation became the Soviet Union's propaganda counterweight to Iran, despite its actual disinterest in the issue. It introduced the issue to both the Security Council and the General Assembly in 1946. When the Americans suggested an investigation commission, the British were horrified, and the Soviets initially dropped the issue but then picked it up again in December 1946—decisions designed to maximize the issue's propaganda potential but also to show that it was potentially interested in rekindling goodwill between the Great Powers. Truman snuffed that spark with his announcement of aid to Greece and Turkey and his enunciation of the Truman Doctrine on March 12, 1947, which cast both the bilateral aid and the larger American effort to contain the spread of communism in terms of a contest of values, signaled an end to any efforts to compromise, sidelined the United Nations in developing an international plan for Greece, and therefore demoted it to serving primarily as an arena of Cold War propaganda. America's allies criticized the hardening of U.S. policy, but it was the Soviet Union that excoriated the new policy. On September 18, 1947, Andrei Vyshinskii, heading the Soviet delegation to the second session of the Assembly, cast it as an entirely unjustified abandonment of the wartime legacy of great power cooperation that presaged a new world war. As such, his speech urged a U.N. resolution against propaganda, especially the Anglo-American propaganda that aimed to incite a new world war. The fact that U.S. allies rejected outright dismissal of the proposal shows the level of discomfort they had with the turn in American policy. The new substitute resolution (jointly proposed by Canada, Australia, and France) kept the Soviet condemnation of propaganda designed to threaten peace and omitted most of the inflammatory specifics of the original resolution, allowing the U.S. delegation to grudgingly vote for it. The Indian delegation (headed by the new prime minister's sister, Vijaya Lakshmi Pandit) criticized the ideological tone of the entire session "that is plunging the world into gloom and tension [and] seems so sadly irrelevant to [larger] human problems; problems that vitally affect a half, and perhaps even more than a half, of the world's population."[13] India was indeed trying to refocus world attention on these larger problems, starting with the issue of racial discrimination.

South Africa, Indonesia, and the emergence of the "Third World"

The Soviets were not alone in being upset about how the work of the new United Nations was unfolding. South Africa and its apartheid system became the subject of early General Assembly action initiated by the Indians. The Indian delegation objected during the first U.N. General Assembly meeting on June 22, 1946, to South African laws limiting the freedoms of Indian South Africans. Finally, on October 24, the General Committee declined Pretoria's request that this item be removed from the agenda as an issue essentially within its domestic jurisdiction and therefore beyond the U.N.'s competence (under Article 2, Paragraph 7 of the Charter). Both the committee and the General Assembly as a whole maintained that debates and resolutions, although meant to put moral pressure on governments, did not constitute "intervention" and therefore did not violate the Charter. The Indians took a more expansive view of the issue, seeing the discussion as essential to any effort to live up to the Charter's "faith in fundamental human rights, in the dignity and worth of the human person, in the equal rights of . . . nations large and small." During the deliberations of the Indian complaint before the General Assembly, the president-general of the African National Congress (ANC, which was working to abolish the system of apartheid) lobbied other national delegations at U.N. headquarters. Although the subsequent resolution failed to get the two-thirds vote it needed, India raised the issue again later that year, warning that two global standards—one for whites and another for nonwhites—would undermine the entire international endeavor. Chapter 8 covers the long-running U.N. debate about and actions against apartheid in more depth, but this short introduction shows how the General Assembly clearly served as a borderland where both new governments and nonstate actors could raise new issues and change the global discourse in areas that were essential to them, especially racism and imperialism.[14]

The conflicting claims of European empires and the subject peoples bound and determined to exercise their right to self-determination quickly joined the U.N. agenda. In part because the West had raised the Iranian issue before the Security Council, the Ukrainian delegate at the January 1946 meeting turned the Council's attention to the violence that had flared in Indonesia and argued that it had "created a threat to the maintenance of international peace and security." He was referring specifically to violence at Surabaya in late September 1945 between British troops (seeking to disarm the Japanese and liberate Allied POWs—prisoners of war—in the Dutch East Indies) and the people there who had declared their independence on August 17, 1945, as the Republic of Indonesia under the leadership of Mohammed Hatta and Achmed Sukarno. The British were only too eager to leave the sprawling island archipelago in the Pacific, but the government of the Netherlands, which had held the resource-rich area under colonial rule for several centuries, was determined to reassert control. In the Security Council, the Dutch delegate sought to simply dismiss the Ukrainian critique (and Egyptian support of it) by asserting that it was an entirely domestic matter in which the United Nations could not intervene—just like the South Africans had earlier argued in the General Assembly. But the Council did not seriously engage the substantive issues at this point, because the British were in the process of brokering talks between the leadership of the Indonesian Republic and the Dutch preparatory to their own troops' withdrawal. However, when the subsequent Hoge Veluwe Conference "broke down nearly as soon as it began" due to Dutch contempt for the process, the Americans and British intervened to help broker the Linggadjati Agreement (signed March 25, 1947) that affirmed the position of the Netherlands in the islands and envisioned the Republic as part of a "United States of Indonesia" that would remain under Dutch suzerainty. But the Netherlands quickly reneged on its promises, especially when several Arab states extended de facto recognition to the Republic. The Dutch used the Republic's refusal to put its police and army forces under their command as the pretext for launching a "police action" in July 1947 that triggered widespread international condemnation and again brought the issue before the United Nations. This was especially the case as Dutch fighters shot down a plane coming from Singapore with two tons of medical supplies bound for the Indonesian Red Cross and as the Netherlands refused to allow the Australian Red Cross to organize the dispensing of medical supplies to the areas affected by the military action (a violation of the Geneva Convention).[15] By pairing the analyses of diplomatic historians Robert McMahon and Carol Anderson, we can see the ways in which private citizens, NGOs (such as labor unions and the NAACP), and government delegations from traditionally "less powerful" countries effectively assembled an international campaign in this U.N. borderland that moved U.S. foreign policy and ultimately resulted in Indonesian independence.

On July 31, 1947, India and Australia successfully argued that the Dutch actions in Indonesia had created a breach of the peace and called on the Security Council to act. Nehru had already made a forceful statement on the situation to the *New York Times* on July 25, 1947, questioning, "What has become of the U.N. Charter?" He then declared that "the spirit of the new Asia will not tolerate such things. No European country, whatever it may be, has any business to set its army in Asia against the people of Asia." The two petitioning governments argued that the use of more than 100,000 Dutch troops could not be dismissed as a domestic "police action" but instead constituted an international event that would have serious consequences to neighboring states like themselves. The American, British, and Canadian members of the Council were deeply concerned about the implications of the Dutch action for the future of Southeast Asia and their own ability to stave off communist insurrections like those then taking place in China and Indochina/Vietnam, but the Americans refrained from criticizing the Dutch in the

Council. The Canadian representative dismissed the Dutch effort to define the issue in domestic terms by asserting that "the Council had a moral, if not strictly legal, right to be concerned." The Security Council then passed its very first resolution calling for a cease-fire between the two sides on August 1, and when the conflict continued, it reopened debate, received a delegation representing the Republic of Indonesia, and ultimately on August 26 created a three-member Good Offices Committee (with limited powers) to work toward an agreement. The Republic's leadership felt besieged on all sides—in the Renville Agreement, it was forced to accept far less than even the half-measures toward independence offered by Linggadjati, and then in late September 1948, it had to act to crush an effort by the communists to usurp the independence movement.[16]

Then on December 18, 1948, the Dutch launched a second "police action" that solidified the international community's commitment to seeing Indonesian independence under the leadership of Hatta and Sukarno and led the United States to cut off Marshall Plan aid to the recalcitrant and unrepentant Dutch. Although the Netherlands was initially effective in attaining its military goals of seizing the key city of Jogjakarta and half of the Republican cabinet (including both Sukarno and Hatta), it was unable to maintain these gains in the wake of increasingly effective Republican military actions and withering international pressure: both Nehru and the Arab League publicly condemned the Dutch actions; Ceylon, India, and Pakistan announced that their ports and airfields would be closed to any craft waging war against Indonesia; Australian dockworkers refused to service any ships bound for the islands; angry protests against the Dutch erupted in Rangoon, Bombay, and Karachi; and the United States called the Security Council into emergency session on December 22, where it verbally condemned the Netherlands, voted for a resolution calling for a cease-fire and release of the Republican leaders, and then suspended any further Marshall Plan aid to Indonesia. But the acting head of the Indonesian delegation to the United Nations quickly pointed out that only suspension of such aid to the Netherlands could end the war—this call was taken up by other U.N. delegations, by the Congress of Industrial Organizations (CIO, a major American labor union), by the NAACP, by former U.S. Vice President Henry Wallace, by members of the U.S. Senate, and by mainline U.S. newspapers. In early January 1948, Nehru's calling of an All-Asia Conference to discuss the crisis—combined with the investigations and attempted negotiations of the Good Offices Committee—quickly called into question the sincerity of the Netherlands in seeking a peaceful solution that recognized the strong desire for self-determination among the Indonesian people, especially as it maintained a blockade of the islands. In response, the U.S. State Department shifted decidedly to a position of supporting Indonesian independence, which American Ambassador Philip Jessup signaled in his January 11 address to the Security Council condemning both Dutch actions in Indonesia and their flouting of the resolutions and work of the United Nations. The resulting January 28 resolution not only reiterated the calls for a cease-fire and the release of Republican prisoners but also set deadlines for establishing an interim government and convening a constituent assembly so that sovereignty could be transferred to the United States of Indonesia no later than July 1, 1950—all under the supervision of the United Nations Commission for Indonesia (the new name for the

Good Offices Commission). Adding additional teeth to the resolution was the February 7, 1949, introduction of the Brewster Resolution (backed by ten Republican senators) that called for the suspension of all U.S. aid (including crucial Marshall Plan dollars) to the Netherlands. By March the Brewster Amendment linked Indonesian independence to both the Marshall Plan and the North American Treaty Organization (NATO), causing the reopening of negotiations on April 14 that eventually led to real Indonesian independence on December 27, 1949.[17]

Although most of the Latin American countries had gained their independence in the early nineteenth century and sent representatives to the conferences that established the United Nations, it was India, as we have seen, that crusaded from the beginning against South Africa's apartheid system, charted a course of "nonalignment" through Cold War international politics, took up leadership of the cause of decolonization, and undertook an aggressive agenda of economic development as an essential component in its postcolonial nation-building strategy. Prime Minister Jawaharlal Nehru enunciated these key themes in his address at Columbia University on October 17, 1949:

> The main objectives of [India's foreign] policy are: the pursuit of peace, not through alignment with any major power or group of powers, but through an independent approach to each controversial or disputed issue; the liberation of subject peoples; the maintenance of freedom, both national and individual; the elimination of racial discrimination; and the elimination of want, disease and ignorance which afflict the greater part of the world's population.

Given this agenda, a strong United Nations was absolutely vital. So Indian representatives consistently sought an organization that could transcend the rival ideologies of the superpowers and focus on the needs of peace and development. But early on, India found its desire to play a very active role in the United Nations conflicting with its desire to avoid Cold War bipolarity. In the fall 1947 session of the General Assembly, the Americans unexpectedly threw their support behind India, rather than Ukraine, as a candidate for a nonpermanent seat on the Security Council, a position that drew fire from a number of quarters for unnecessarily turning the heat up on the emerging Cold War. After eleven inconclusive ballots, India finally withdrew its candidacy, ceding the two-year appointment to Ukraine.[18]

India sought a democratic United Nations—not very different from its own parliament—in which all spoke and all participated in the negotiations needed to determine what was best for the larger community. Krishna Menon, India's ambassador to the United Nations for much of Nehru's tenure, was an articulate and outspoken advocate on a number of issues with this goal in mind, which often put him on the opposite side of Western delegates on a number of issues. For example, India took a leading role in working toward universal U.N. membership (including the seating of a communist Chinese delegation). Additionally, India's nonviolent struggle for independence made it generally opposed to the U.N. collective security mechanisms (both legally binding and those utilizing military force), which it saw as perpetuating a "climate of war" rather than truly promoting peace. Reinforcing this philosophy was its experience from 1947 until 1949, when the United Nations tried to resolve the issue of Kashmir (claimed by both India and Pakistan during the postindependence partition of the subcontinent). Nonetheless, throughout Nehru's tenure as prime minister (which reached from independence in 1947 until 1962), India maintained a deep and abiding faith in the potential of the international organization, especially if it worked toward the ideals laid out in its Charter and relied on the tools of debate and "the morally pressing resolution." Therefore India took a leadership role in the United Nations that included a large number of its nationals who committed themselves to service in the various U.N. organizations. To the prime minister, the global organization provided a means for India to assume its rightful position as a world leader, given its size, population, and history. A strong United Nations also needed a strong set of countries committed to steering it away from the Cold War and toward the needs of the world's people. Therefore Nehru's work in forging the Non-Aligned Movement was also part and parcel of his commitment to U.N. internationalism. The other members of the United Nations recognized and acknowledged this commitment by electing Nehru's sister, Vijaya Lakshmi Pandit, as the president of the 1953 General Assembly, the first woman to serve in this capacity.[19]

Berlin, China, and Korea: Crisis, compromise, and conflict in the United Nations

The U.N. Charter established the Security Council as an institution that should "be able to function continuously," with each member "represented at all times at the seat of the Organization." Throughout the Cold War, therefore, the United Nations remained the place where Soviet and American diplomats could regularly and personally interact—often cordially, especially when away from the press. But the organization also served as a new arena for conflict, especially when the superpowers clashed over the city of Berlin and when the United States doggedly refused to seat representatives of the communist People's Republic of China (PRC) in place of the representatives from Chiang Kai-shek's defeated National government in either the General Assembly or the Security Council.[20]

The Soviet decision to impose a land blockade of Berlin in the fall of 1948 touched off a potentially explosive crisis that was effectively curbed and de-escalated in the halls of the United Nations—not in the formal organs and deliberations, but in its lounges and hallways. The Soviets contended that the issues that had caused the blockade should be taken up in direct negotiations between the occupying powers, but the United States, the United Kingdom, and France framed the blockade as a breach of the peace that properly fell within the work of the Security Council and marshaled a 9–2 vote to put it on the agenda. The resulting discussion did nothing to change the course of the crisis. But in January 1949, the U.S. State Department sensed a subtle shift in Soviet policy and, as a result, initiated an informal diplomatic initiative through its U.N. Ambassador, Philip C. Jessup. A presumably informal question in the hallway to his Soviet counterpart, Yakov Malik, led to a private meeting at the Soviet mission, six weeks of secret diplomacy among the permanent representatives of the Security Council (minus the Chinese), and finally the opening of the gates on the autobahn leading to Berlin at one minute after midnight on May 12.[21] But more challenges quickly followed on the heels of the Berlin crisis.

On October 1, 1949, the Chinese communists under Mao Zedong proclaimed the People's Republic of China (PRC)—starting what Gaiduk has described "the long year" that was central to the history of the United Nations and one of the most serious crises of the early Cold War. The United States had not developed a policy toward the new government, even as its Nationalist Chinese allies retreated to the off-shore island of Taiwan and as its British allies extended de facto recognition to the new mainland regime in early October. In November, Communist Chinese Foreign Minister Zhou Enlai, in consultation with Moscow, sent a communication to Secretary-General Lie demanding that he immediately deprive the Nationalist delegation of its rights to represent the Chinese people in the United Nations, and Soviet delegate Andrey Vyshinskii spoke on behalf of the PRC's request and declared that his delegation would no longer treat the Nationalist delegation as representing the Chinese people. Malik made the same argument at the Security Council meeting on December 29, while Vyshinskii was meeting with Mao in Moscow, where they decided on a boycott of the Council to bring the issue of Chinese representation to a head. When the Security Council voted against a Soviet proposal to replace the Nationalist representative on January 13, Malik announced that his country would not participate in the work of the Council until the Nationalists were removed and would consider any work undertaken during its absence as illegal—and then he simply left. In the coming days, similar walkouts occurred in twenty-one U.N. councils and committees. On January 19, Zhou again wrote to the secretary-general and informed him that the PRC had appointed its representative to the organization.[22]

In the midst of the Soviet boycott, North Korean troops swept across the 38th parallel on June 25, 1950, with approval from both its Soviet and Chinese allies. Contrary to Soviet expectations, the United States moved quickly and strongly at the emergency meeting of the Security Council the next afternoon to condemn the North Korean action as a blatant violation of the U.N. Charter and to gain U.N. approval for the use of U.S. air and naval forces to assist the retreating South Koreans. Even after this first resolution and a lunchtime meeting with the secretary-general and the deputy U.S. representative at the United Nations, Malik refused to return to the Council, leaving the United States free to pursue full military action against the North Korean forces (under the U.N. flag and American command). The Soviet representative finally returned at the beginning of July to assume his rotation as president of the Council, igniting "a month-long orgy of procedural battles and inflammatory rhetoric" for the listening and viewing pleasure of millions of Americans following the debates live on the radio and television. But beneath the surface, the Soviets were cultivating real concerns about the American position on both the Korean War and the question of Chinese representation.[23]

With the Soviet return, the United States could no longer manage the war through the Security Council, so the Americans shifted (contrary to British counsel) in September to the General Assembly with their "United for Peace" resolution that established procedures giving the Assembly the power to consider threats to the peace when the

Council was deadlocked in doing so. While the maneuver initially worked well for the Truman administration and led to commitments from fifteen member states of combat troops, over time the American-led response generated questioning and criticism from the Assembly delegations, especially the nonaligned Asian countries of India, Burma, and Indonesia. Gaiduk asserts that the involvement of the United Nations in the Korean conflict helped moderate the actions of both superpowers and prevent their direct confrontation: "Not only did the Soviet Union have to take into account the fact that on the Korean question it was dealing not just with the United States, but with the majority of the world community that supported the UN's efforts on South Korea's behalf, the United States was obliged to respect the opinion of other members of the world organization in its actions in Korea as well." Indeed, at the United Nations the British and Indians early on worked to bring the parties together to mediate the conflict, and in November 1950 the delegates from Britain, France, and several of the nonpermanent delegations invited the Chinese communist representatives to address the Council against American wishes. The visit only antagonized the United States rather than promoting any type of diplomatic settlement of the conflict, and after the initial surge of communist Chinese and North Korean forces that pushed the U.N.-U.S. forces back across the 38th parallel starting in December 1950, the battle lines stabilized around the 38th parallel. Again, the Soviet Union used the informal spaces of the United Nations to initiate talks about a cease-fire in early May 1951, and India's Krishna Menon later played an important role in winding down the struggle by facilitating settlement of the prisoner-of-war issue in the 1952 General Assembly. But the role of the United Nations in the Korean War had further antagonized the Soviet Union, which even considered withdrawing from the international organization in the early 1950s. Even some of the closest allies of the United States worried about this possibility and sought to moderate the Americans' strong anti-Soviet attitude and to imagine ways in which the United Nations could foster a rapprochement between the two superpowers. For its part, the U.S. delegation became increasingly concerned about growing resistance to its initiatives at the Sixth General Assembly meeting in 1951, especially among representatives of the Non-Aligned Movement.[24]

A changing of the guard: Eisenhower, Khrushchev, Hammarskjöld, and decolonization

As the battle lines of the Korean War began to stabilize and as a new president took the oath of office in Washington, DC, the United Nations began moving into its permanent headquarters building on the East River in New York City, a property secured by a combination of an impulsive offer of real estate and Rockefeller largesse. The next fall, Swede Dag Hammarskjöld took over the secretary-generalship from Lie, who had been incapacitated by Soviet refusal to work with him after his support of the U.N. effort in Korea. Adding to this sea change in the major U.N. players was the death of Josef Stalin in March 1953, just two months before the Korean armistice. As Nikita Khrushchev emerged as the new leader of the Soviet Union, he sought the input of other Soviet-bloc delegations and turned his attention increasingly to the Third World, which made the United Nations an arena where he could score propaganda points against the United States and other Western countries as he sought the allegiance of the Non-Aligned Movement. For example, the United States had to defend itself at the June 1954 emergency meeting of the Security Council against Guatemalan charges that military forces aligned with the U.S. Central Intelligence Agency sought to overthrow the government there.[25]

The space or borderland of the United Nations also continued to be an area where the leaders of national liberation organizations operated. As historian Matthew Connelly has shown, in the early 1950s, France faced rebellion throughout its North African colonies, which found its way into the United Nations. While the United States and France worked throughout 1951 and 1952 to derail Egypt's efforts to criticize French actions in Morocco and the Tunisian cabinet's efforts to petition the Security Council (since the protectorate's foreign relations were still under French control), U.S. Secretary of State Dean Acheson complained that "the UN has put us in a terrible situation . . . any irresponsible person like Nehru can make us discuss and vote on any question at all. They have us over the barrel." This was indeed the Indian agenda for the United Nations—to bring key issues in front of the international community for debate as a means of dismantling the system of imperialism, which had been withering under such scrutiny. Twelve members of the Non-Aligned Movement finally succeeded in putting these issues on the agenda of the General Assembly, but perhaps more importantly, the Tunisians began to coordinate their actions to better impact the international community; the nationalists of Neo Destour had called for a general strike in Tunisia at the same time that its complaint came before the Security Council, hoping to recreate the 1948 situation that had led to Indonesian independence. They, along with Moroccan nationalists, even established offices in New York City to distribute information on their movements, helping to prompt a series of sympathetic articles in major U.S. newspapers and calls from Eleanor Roosevelt, among others, for a more positive line on these issues at the United Nations. The portents were not lost on the French, with a least one high-ranking official arguing that France should withdraw from the United Nations to avoid such criticism from the Arab and other nonaligned states. When Saudi Arabia petitioned the Security Council in early 1955 on behalf of Algeria, the French credited this action with creating the "Algerian question" in the mind of U.S. public opinion. Clearly issues of national liberation would continue to animate the U.N. agenda, especially as national liberation movements and the Non-Aligned Movement found the United Nations an effective platform for voicing their international agendas.[26]

The Bandung Conference of April 1955 also signaled a new coordination among the countries of the developing world. With the leaders of twenty-nine states (mostly former colonies from Africa and Asia) gathering in Indonesia to discuss common concerns and to jointly develop international policies, India's Nehru, Indonesia's Sukarno, and Egypt's Nasser became the acknowledged leaders of the Non-Aligned Movement, which now committed itself to ongoing meetings, especially to coordinate their actions at the United Nations. Their deliberations focused on accelerating decolonization (especially in the ongoing conflict in Algeria), easing tensions between the United States and communist China, promoting the peaceful settlement of international disputes, loosening economic ties with the First World, and advocating racial equality as well as equality between large and small countries. By the Tenth Session of the General Assembly that started in 1955, they were formally organized as a caucusing group and helped bring about fundamental changes within the United Nations, which paid greater attention to decolonization, economic development (the topic of Chapter 5), and making the Secretariat staff more reflective of the organization's overall diversity.[27]

Canada also sensed the change that was coming in the United Nations. Lester Pearson, Canada's minister of external affairs and the head of its U.N. delegation, had been paying attention to the sensitivities of the former colonies and cultivating closer relationships with them. Tangible proof of this came with his work to break the Cold War logjam over admission of new states to the United Nations that had started in 1946. Pearson helped secure admission of sixteen new members to the General Assembly in 1955 (and another four the next year); this meant that in 1956 the Assembly consisted of eighty members. While the Eisenhower administration had intended to treat the United Nations primarily as a forum for anti-Soviet propaganda, it quickly found that the international scene was shifting in fundamental ways that required it to reevaluate its own strategy and play a more positive role in the global body.[28]

Crises in North Africa and the Declaration on Independence

The 1950s witnessed the growing importance of the emergent Third World and significant power shifts within the United Nations. The Suez Crisis of 1956 that resulted from Anglo-French collaboration with the Israelis in an effort to regain control of Egypt's Suez Canal (described more fully in Chapter 7) showcased the superpowers' desire to dissociate themselves from the colonial powers, and the resulting tensions between the United States and its erstwhile allies diminished the role of the Security Council for much of the decade. While the prestige of the Security Council seemed to be waning, the spotlight increasingly fell on the new secretary-general, Dag Hammarskjöld. He had helped to reenergize the Secretariat and began to emerge as an independent force in global politics. In 1953, he flew to China to negotiate the release of a U.S. flight crew who had been shot down during a mission over Korea. He also sought to play a more proactive role in moving toward world peace, with prominent examples being his work in Lebanon in 1958 (covered in Chapter 7) and the work that ultimately took his life—trying to engineer a peaceful transition in Congo from Belgian colony to independence, which started in 1960 and is covered in Chapter 6. But Hammarskjöld's handling of the Congo crisis led to an alliance of the French and Soviets in opposing the expanding operation in Congo. Khrushchev demanded the secretary-general's resignation, and failing that, he drafted a proposal to replace the unitary office of the secretary-general with a "troika" of three leaders (one each from the First World, Second World, and Third World). Though the proposal did not gain support, it did lead the United Nations to begin a much greater push toward diversity within the Secretariat.[29]

French criticism of the United Nations grew both from its humiliation during the Suez Crisis and its continuing troubles in North Africa, which were regularly paraded before that body. The French foreign minister arriving in New York on September 27, 1955, for the opening of the new General Assembly was impressed by the degree of anti-French sentiment already in the hall—which only increased as Cambodia, Jordan, Laos, Libya, Morocco, Tunisia, and Sudan joined as new U.N. members in 1955 and 1956. On the eve of the 1955 General Assembly vote on whether or not to include Algeria on its agenda, Muslim shopkeepers launched a general strike in Algeria, and the Algerian Liberation Front (the FLN) sponsored screenings of Fox-Movietone footage of a French gendarme gunning down a prisoner in Algiers. When the nationalists won their way onto the agenda by a single vote, the French delegate walked out of the meeting amid the thunderous applause of a Non-Aligned Movement. Later that evening the French representative railed at Soviet Foreign Minister Vyacheslav Molotov for supporting the Algerians, which was just one of the Soviets' moves toward increasing its presence and influence in North Africa at the time. The Algerian nationalists redoubled their efforts in 1956, working through their new permanent office in New York City to pressure the Non-Aligned Movement to bring their cause before the Security Council and a special session of the General Assembly and again supporting these efforts with labor and commercial strikes in Algeria. The Suez Crisis temporarily took the U.N. spotlight off of Algeria, but the dramatic "Battle of Algiers" (which started in January 1957) brought the spotlight back and was accompanied by a complementary "Battle of New York," in which FLN representatives in New York conducted press campaigns and called for U.N.-led negotiations based on recognition of Algeria's right to independence. Despite a general strike meant to foreground the U.N. General Assembly debate on the issue, the resolution failed by one vote.[30]

In September 1958, the FLN sought to shift the terms of its ongoing efforts by unilaterally declaring Algerian independence and reestablishing itself as the Gouvernement Provisoire de la République Algérienne (GPRA, Provisional Government of the Algerian Republic). At the subsequent General Assembly, the French worked diligently to exclude the GPRA delegates from participating (without much assistance from the United States). Although the resolution recognizing the Algerian people's right to independence and calling for negotiations again fell one vote shy of the needed two-thirds majority, the GPRA considered the American abstention on this vote and its winning of a majority to be a significant diplomatic victory, and the result certainly made French President Charles de Gaulle livid. But the simple truth was that the Eisenhower administration was trying not to alienate Third World opinion, and the pomp and circumstance with which the GPRA delegation to Beijing had been received made the Cold War dimensions of this U.N. battle clear to U.S. Secretary of State John Foster Dulles. On July 14 (Bastille Day), 1959, twenty-five members of the Non-Aligned Movement, with intended irony, petitioned for the inclusion of Algeria on the General Assembly's fall agenda. De Gaulle hoped to defuse the issue in the United Nations with the promise of an eventual referendum, but as Connelly points out, the French shift was inconsequential—"the cause of Algerian independence [had taken] on a life of its own at the United Nations and around the world." A key indicator of this was the U.S. abstention (again) on the resolution calling for U.N.-brokered negotiations between the two sides. By the time the General Assembly convened in 1960, Khrushchev had extended de facto recognition to GPRA, and the Americans had started pressuring the French to announce a nationwide referendum on Algerian self-determination by January 1961. Instead de Gaulle went to Algiers and lost the support of even once-friendly countries like Mali and Togo. Although the U.S. resolution calling for an internationally supervised referendum failed narrowly, the January referendum in both Paris and Algeria established the foundation for the first round of negotiations in May 1961; the second round of negotiations (which started in March 1962) resulted in the Evian Agreements, which were affirmed by an Algerian referendum on July 1, 1962. In this drama, those French nationals who adamantly opposed independence thought that the United Nations embodied the forces ripping "their country" from the metropole, in part, because of the powerful forces that resided in that space. In New York, the French found themselves answerable to an entire range of new international norms—especially regarding self-determination and human rights—and buffeted by the Algerians' claims to prerogatives previously reserved to formal states. Indeed, Connelly concludes his history by asserting that "now any movement that called itself anticolonial could expect a sympathetic reception at the United Nations."[31]

As the Algerian example shows, the tide in the General Assembly was clearly shifting as the Non-Aligned Movement felt its power and redirected the organization's agenda toward its priorities—especially decolonization. On December 14, 1960, the General Assembly passed Resolution 1514 (XV), the Declaration on the Granting of Independence to Colonial Countries and Peoples (or the "Declaration on Independence" for short). It built from the principles of human rights and self-determination laid out in the preamble of the U.N. Charter and the earlier work of the United Nations in moving the trust territories toward independence. In this latter work, India played an important role. Starting in 1946, it had successfully called for creation of a committee to gather information pursuant to the U.N. Charter's Article 73 (e) proviso that member states with non–self-governing territories "transmit regularly to the Secretary-General for information purposes . . . statistical and other information of a technical nature relating to economic, social, and educational conditions in the territories for which they are respectively responsible." India and other new nations renewed the committee's mandate in three-year cycles from 1949 until 1958 and used it "as an entering wedge" for expanding the types of information requested and for putting pressure on imperial powers. Now in 1960, the Non-Aligned Movement declared that "the subjection of peoples to alien subjugation, domination and exploitation constitutes a denial of fundamental human rights, is contrary to the Charter of the United Nations and is an impediment to the promotion of world peace and co-operation." It also defined the right by "all peoples . . . to self-determination," which included the right to "freely determine their political status" and to "freely pursue their economic, social and cultural development." The Declaration on Independence particularly condemned the notion that such areas were unprepared for independence and needed further tutelage—"Inadequacy of political, economic, social or educational preparedness should never serve as a pretext for delaying independence." It further declared that "all armed action or repressive measures of all kinds directed against dependent peoples shall cease" and be replaced with "immediate steps" toward independence "without any conditions or reservations." The penultimate proviso that "any attempt aimed at the partial or total disruption of the national unity and the territorial integrity of a country is incompatible with the purposes and principles of the Charter of the United Nations" was its statement on the limits of self-determination; colonial people had a right to govern the territories whose boundaries had been established by the imperial power.[32]

The next year, to institutionalize the work of the Declaration on Independence, the General Assembly created a special committee (initially of seventeen members nominated by the Assembly's president) "to examine the application of the Declaration, to make suggestions and recommendations on the progress and extent of the implementation of the Declaration, and to report to the General Assembly." An associated resolution broadened the reporting requirements from only trust territories to all "territories whose peoples have not yet attained a full measure of self-government"; this expansion of the earlier work of the Committee on Information submitted under Article 73(e) was transferred in 1963 to this new special committee. With these two resolutions, the General Assembly had crafted an ongoing body designed specifically to put pressure on the imperial system; it came to be called the Special Committee or the Committee of 24 when its membership was subsequently expanded. It very quickly developed a reputation for being one of the most active groups connected to the Assembly and for continually pushing the envelope in terms of international law and decolonization.[33]

This work collectively framed decolonization as a moral imperative that grew organically out of Chapter XI of the U.N. Charter and explicitly linked imperialism, racism, and violence. Some of that moral authority came from outrage following the Sharpeville massacre (in which the white South African police forces killed sixty-nine people and injured one hundred and eighty of the unarmed blacks who had gathered to protest the racially discriminatory "pass laws") that preceded the General Assembly session that passed the Declaration on Independence. Increasingly, the link between imperialism and apartheid/racism as a fundamental denial of human rights was also posited as a real threat to international peace and security that required U.N. Security Council action. This argument became increasingly real as guerilla warfare erupted throughout Africa as black majorities fought against white-settler regimes in South Africa, Southern Rhodesia, and the Portuguese colonies of Angola, Mozambique, and Portuguese Guinea. This argument resulted in concrete action when the Security Council imposed an arms embargo on South Africa on August 7, 1963.[34]

Cold War crises and Security Council politics

In the midst of the sea changes occurring in the General Assembly over the issues of decolonization, a Cold War sideshow unfolded in the Security Council in 1960 when U.S. pilot Francis Gary Powers's U-2 spy plane was shot down during a photo surveillance mission over the Soviet Union. While Khrushchev sought a public apology from the United States at the Security Council, U.S. Ambassador Henry Cabot Lodge instead engaged in "show and tell" about Soviet espionage efforts against his country and corralled the votes to soundly defeat the Soviet resolution condemning the American actions. The Soviets were more successful in embarrassing their Cold War nemesis during the 1961 Bay of Pigs incident, in which U.S.-backed insurgents attempted to invade Fidel Castro's Cuba in much the same way they had earlier done in Guatemala. America's new ambassador to the United Nations, Adlai Stevenson, was uninformed about what had actually happened and replied with a faked CIA photo presentation that presumably showed that the planes involved were Cuban Air Force planes that had defected from Castro's government. Despite the public humiliation and his own thoughts of resigning, Stevenson soldiered on and was prepared when the shoe was later on the other foot in Cuba.[35]

After American intelligence discovered that the Soviets were constructing nuclear missile installations in Cuba in October 1962, President Kennedy decided to use the U.N. Security Council to make his case to the world. Although he had already addressed the nation on October 22 and stated that the United States would blockade the island nation, Stevenson presented the U.S. complaint to the Council the next day, and Secretary-General U Thant responded publicly with a call for a cooling-off period during which he was willing to mediate the crisis. Stevenson's presentation to the Security Council, and especially his spontaneous questioning of Soviet ambassador Valerian Zorin, played well with the American people and with global audiences, but the Security Council did not resolve the Cuban Missile Crisis; it did not pass a single resolution on the issue. However, it had helped slow the pace of events, and Thant's mediation helped to bring the crisis to a peaceful end. Reflecting on the events, U.S. Secretary of State Dean Rusk stated, "The UN earned its pay for a long time to come just by being there for the missile crisis."[36]

The United Nations also seemed to earn its pay for its effective interventions in the developing crises in both the Mediterranean island nation of Cyprus and in Kashmir (a disputed territory at the border between India and Pakistan). When violence broke out between the Greek and Turkish populations in Cyprus in late 1963, strong Anglo-American support (and the Soviet preference for a U.N. rather than a NATO force) led to the creation of a peacekeeping force that persists to this day. Then in April 1965, Pakistan sent hundreds of militants into Kashmir, which prompted a full-scale Indian attack a few months later. Because the United States was providing aid to both countries and the Soviet Union supported the Indians and feared communist Chinese intervention, the Security Council was willing to work together to broker a cease-fire, despite dramatic gestures before the body by both countries' foreign ministers. In fact, Nehru's death, a deadly border conflict with China in 1962, and the U.N. intervention in Kashmir had taken a toll on India's confidence in its relationship with the United Nations and the Non-Aligned Movement and led it in subsequent years to focus more on its own national security and less on the global politics of nonalignment.[37]

The year 1965 seemed to many in the Non-Aligned Movement to mark a step backward from the positive trend toward decolonization in the previous several years. Both the American intervention in the Dominican Republic and the Unilateral

Declaration of Independence by the white-minority government of Rhodesia seemed to be serious setbacks. On April 28, 1965, U.S. Marines were dispatched to prevent former Dominican President Juan Bosch and his Constitutionalists from regaining control of the government in an unsettled and violent political atmosphere. Stevenson found himself having to defend an action that much of the Council saw as an act of aggression or armed interference in the domestic relations of a sovereign state. Although the U.S. ambassador was able to marshal the votes needed to avoid using the American veto (which it had never used), the action elicited criticism in the General Assembly, with the growing number of African and Asian states commenting on how this reflected a clear double standard in which permanent members of the Security Council could effectively do whatever they wished without repercussions and that the affected Third World nations simply had to suffer the consequences. Then, on November 11, 1965, the white government of Rhodesia unilaterally declared its independence from the British Empire and published a new constitution, holding its ground against immediate British sanctions and U.N. Security Council condemnation of the "illegal racist minority regime." Although the Council called on all states to refrain from recognizing Rhodesia and called on Great Britain to end the rebellion, Third World leaders were struck by the contrast between the use of armed force to reverse regime change in the Dominican Republic, while the white regime in Rhodesia was allowed to stand (and would until the March 1980 election of Robert Mugabe as democratically elected president of the renamed Zimbabwe).[38]

Given the increasingly unrepresentative nature of the Security Council, its makeup finally changed in August 1965 from eleven to fifteen members. U.N. membership had grown from seventy-six members in 1955 to one hundred and seventeen in 1965 (with about fifty coming from Africa and Asia). But the six nonpermanent seats had been traditionally apportioned with one going to a British Commonwealth member, one to Eastern Europe, one to Western Europe, two to Latin America, and just one to Africa or Asia. In the newly constituted Security Council, nine votes were needed to pass a resolution, meaning that the ten nonpermanent members could, if they acted unanimously, pass resolutions and determine the Council's agenda.[39]

The Third World's agenda for the United Nations, 1963–80

In 1963, the independent nations of Africa organized themselves into the Organisation of African Unity (OAU) to serve as a unifying voice for the concerns of its leaders and peoples in promoting the twin goals of decolonization and self-determination. The OAU's headquarters in Addis Ababa, Ethiopia, worked closely with the Committee of 24, and the later OAU committee headquarters in Dar es Salaam, Tanzania, quickly became a source of training and arms as well as other types of support for guerilla movements fighting for independence against colonial and white-minority governments.[40] As the voices and power of the Non-Aligned Movement grew stronger in the United Nations, the United States felt increasingly estranged from the organization it had helped create.

The dismissal of Chinese Nationalist representation, the New International Economic Order (NIEO), and the strength of OPEC (the Organization of Petroleum Exporting Countries) all reinforced this sense of American enervation.

Decolonization and Southern Africa

An early focus of the OAU and the Committee of 24 was on Portugal's colonies of Angola, Portuguese Guinea/Guinea-Bissau, and Mozambique. Although Lisbon identified them as "provinces" of the metropole, these arguments failed in exactly the same way as the Dutch arguments about Indonesia and the French arguments about Algeria being integral parts of their countries had failed. As Portugal fought on three national fronts between 1961 and 1974 in what it called "the Overseas War," the United Nations worked systematically to undermine that effort. The General Assembly, in taking up the report of the Committee of 24 in 1965, first criticized the NATO powers for their military assistance to Portugal, which allowed it to continue suppressing the national liberation struggles in its African colonies. In 1969, the Assembly recognized the legitimacy of the struggle of the oppressed people of Southern Africa and called for these "freedom fighters"—if captured—to be treated humanely under the auspices of the Geneva Convention. And the next year, the Committee of 24 and the General Assembly as a whole called on U.N. member states to "render all necessary moral and material assistance to the peoples of colonial Territories in their struggle to attain freedom and independence" and invited "representatives of liberation movements" to participate in U.N. proceedings—bestowing on such movements the privileges previously reserved for internationally recognized states. Then, in 1973, the General Assembly recognized the national liberation movements of Angola and Mozambique, rather than Portugal, as the legitimate representatives of their people. The financial cost and increasing diplomatic and economic isolation that Portugal faced as a result of its effort to retain its colonies helped catalyze the 1974 military coup (led by veterans of the war in Guinea and called the Carnation Revolution) that unseated the Estado Novo government and brought the colonial conflicts to a quick end by transferring power to the indigenous independence movements. As a result, Portugal subsequently worked with the Committee of 24, and South Africa and Rhodesia found themselves even more isolated.[41]

South African rule of Namibia also eventually gave way to a similar combination of U.N. and indigenous military efforts. Pretoria had imposed apartheid on South West Africa in 1948, worked to confine the indigenous African population to "homelands" analogous to the South African bantustans, and maintained the status quo in which white settlers—0.2 percent of the total population—owned 74 percent of the country's arable land. The Herero Chief's Council responded by submitting petitions to the United Nations requesting independence throughout the 1950s. Then, in 1960, the South West Africa People's Organization (SWAPO) took up this work of seeking peaceful regime change. But when the International Court of Justice (ICJ) dismissed a complaint against South Africa's continued governance of the territory in 1966, SWAPO created the People's Liberation Army of Namibia and initiated an armed struggle. The General Assembly also acted, formally revoking the South African mandate in October 1966, establishing the U.N. Council for South West Africa in 1967 to administer the territory in absentia until its independence, and renaming the territory Namibia on June 12, 1968. In an August 1969 Security Council resolution, the South African presence in Namibia was termed an "occupation," and in 1971 the Security Council asked the ICJ to revisit its earlier opinion. The ICJ indeed reversed itself, declaring the South African administration illegal. In 1973, SWAPO became the official representative of the Namibian people and was granted observer status at all U.N. meetings; the next year the Security Council approved the use of U.N. funds to defray the expenses of SWAPO representatives engaged in this work. U.N. Security Council Resolution 435 in 1978 envisioned a comprehensive transition to independence for Namibia, the first resolution of the decade to garner no vetoes. But these plans were only taken up in 1988 as part of a multinational settlement between South Africa, Angola, and Cuba. In fact, historian Piero Gleijeses credits bold Cuban action with freeing Namibia and helping to break the back of the apartheid regime in South Africa. The U.N. Transition Assistance Group came to Namibia on April 1, 1989, to help monitor the peace process, organize elections, and supervise the withdrawal of all foreign military forces. Some 46,000 SWAPO exiles returned and participated in the first free elections for the constitutional assembly in November 1989. After adopting a constitution, Namibia officially became independent on March 21, 1990.[42]

The former British colony of Rhodesia was another target of the U.N. decolonization campaign led by the Non-Aligned Movement and the Organisation of African Unity (OAU). When the white-minority government of Rhodesia refused to abide by the earlier U.N. resolutions condemning its 1965 unilateral declaration of independence, it found itself the target of the very first Chapter VII sanctions imposed by the U.N. Security Council. The resolution called on all member states to immediately sever all diplomatic, consular, trade, military, and other relations with the rogue government. But when the African and Asian members of the Security Council pressed in March 1970 for a resolution that would have required Great Britain to use military means to overthrow the Rhodesian government, not only the United Kingdom but also the United States vetoed the resolution; this was the very first U.S. veto in the Council. The Committee of 24 was especially vehement in its criticism of the United States, which after approving the mandatory economic sanctions against Rhodesia, resumed importation of embargoed Rhodesian chromite on January 1, 1972, as a result of a law passed by the U.S. Congress against the advice of the State Department.[43]

American disillusionment and Indian reengagement

Although the Committee of 24 could take pride in the role it had played in seeing thirty formerly non–self-governing territories with a population of almost seventy million gain their freedom during the 1960s, the U.S. veto and importation of chromite both indicated the increasing disillusionment of the American government and people with the Non-Aligned Movement's agenda for the United Nations. A classified U.S. memo from January 1970 stated, "What we really want from both [the United Nations and Africa] is no trouble. Our policy is therefore directed at damage limiting, rather than at accomplishing anything in particular"—a huge change from the early years of the United Nations when U.S. diplomatic action had largely defined the international organization. In 1971, both the United States and the United Kingdom resigned in protest from the Committee of 24 after having established the U.N. Charter provisions that initially gave it life. Of course, part of this American sensitivity to its seeming inability to shape international affairs to its liking was also a result of its failed effort to sustain a noncommunist government in South Vietnam.[44]

The Third World's influence was increasingly felt even on the Security Council. The Council had met in Addis Ababa in early 1972 and in Panama City in 1973 as a result of the Non-Aligned Movement's effort to focus the Council on particular issues of peace and security in their respective regions. More concretely, on December 15, 1973, a Security Council resolution passed without a single affirmative vote from any of the five permanent members, and the Council's agenda (which had been relatively sparse in the 1950s and even the 1960s) was increasingly crowded with the issues and agendas of the Non-Aligned Movement, which ranged from perennial issues related to national liberation to the New International Economic Order (NIEO). The foundation for the growth in the agenda was an expansive interpretation of Article 31 of the Charter, which allows all states to participate in Council meetings in which their interests are "specially affected"; as a procedural issue, such invitations were immune from the veto.[45] All of these developments pointed to the fact that Third World representatives, though barred from the old boys' club of the permanent members, did have the power to reshape debate, not only in the democratic General Assembly where their numbers gave them a clear majority but now also in the Security Council where they coordinated their work and agenda, much as the United States and its allies had done earlier.

A symbol of the changed power relations within the United Nations became the issue of Chinese representation in the world organization. U.S. intransigence on seating a representative of the communist PRC had been aided by that country's military attack on the armed U.N. forces in Korea and then by the internal turmoil of China's cultural revolution in the 1960s. When the PRC detonated an atomic bomb in 1964, international opinion shifted more decidedly to changing the status quo in the United Nations, which forced the United States to resort to ever more elaborate procedural maneuvers to maintain Nationalist representation. But following Soviet-Chinese clashes along their shared border in mid-1969, U.S. National Security Adviser Henry Kissinger secretly sought to open diplomatic relations with the PRC. Although the United States was subsequently ready to have the PRC take the "Chinese" seat on the Security Council, it also sought unsuccessfully to retain a position for the Nationalist Chinese government in the General Assembly. The Americans at the United Nations also found themselves fighting increasingly pitched battles on behalf of another of their allies—Israel—as the General Assembly became increasingly supportive of the Palestine Liberation Organization (PLO), which is discussed in Chapter 7. The appointment of Daniel Patrick Moynihan to serve as the U.S. ambassador to the United Nations in June 1975 indicated that the United States was fed up with serving as the Non-Aligned Movement's punching bag. The abrasive American saw his job in the United Nations as one of fighting rhetoric with rhetoric, which made the completion of constructive work in the international organization more difficult.[46]

The United States did its best to remain neutral as the increasingly acrimonious relations between the Soviet Union and the PRC were revealed by the 1970 conflict between India and Pakistan over the effort of eastern Pakistan to secede and establish its independence, an effort that the Indians supported. China and most of the Non-Aligned Movement backed Pakistan, while the Soviet Union backed India. In December, in response to Pakistani air attacks on Indian military bases, the Indians wiped out the Pakistani airbases in the eastern part of Pakistan. On three separate occasions, the Soviets used their Security Council veto to protect India from resolutions that might have stopped the military clashes between Indian and Pakistani troops and tanks that ultimately laid the foundation for Bangladesh's independence. The Chinese and Soviet delegates then openly sparred in the August 1972 Security Council debate about whether or not to admit it to the United Nations.[47]

Although the Bangladesh crisis had exposed fractures in the Chinese-Soviet relationship, it helped to resuscitate India's role in the life of the United Nations. The Soviet Union's diplomatic support and India's 1974 explosion of a nuclear device in contravention of the Nuclear Nonproliferation Treaty helped it reestablish diplomatic distance from the West and demonstrate its own strength. In light of these developments, a major foreign policy review in 1976 led India to again place a high priority on its participation in international affairs through the United Nations and other venues. Part of this renewed focus led it to exchange ambassadors with China and to resume diplomatic relations with Pakistan during the tenure of Jagat Mehta as secretary of the ministry of foreign affairs. Even when thirty years of Congress Party rule ended in March 1977, the new Janata government also supported a strong international policy built around nonalignment. There were some hopes that the new G-77 (the Group of 77 developing countries organized under the U.N. Conference on Trade and Development—UNCTAD) and the NIEO—accompanied by a declining focus on security inspired by the new detente between the United States and Soviet Union—could reorient international affairs around the key economic and social issues that Nehru had initially stressed. In 1977, India demonstrated its renewed engagement with the United Nations by playing constructive roles in both the General Assembly and the Security Council. In the Assembly, it played a key role in reforming the scale of member states' contributions to the United Nations. It brokered a compromise that called for the OPEC states to pay higher rates while lowering the assessments of the least developed countries. That same year, India was elected to a two-year term on the Security Council in 1977, and when Indian ambassador Rikhi Jaipal served his one-month term as the Council's president that October, he was able to broker an agreement between African states and the permanent members of the Security Council that resulted in the Council, for the very first time, imposing economic sanctions under Chapter VII of the U.N. Charter, against South Africa.[48] U.S. acrimony, Indian engagement, and Third World hopes all clearly influenced the power dynamics within the United Nations specifically and international relations generally throughout the 1960s and 1970s, but significant changes were on the horizon.

Changing dynamics in the United Nations, 1980–2000

The 1980s started with ominous portents. On the eve of the new decade, Vietnamese troops crossed into Cambodia to stop the Khmer Rouge's genocide of its own people; the new Islamic government in Iran took fifty-two Americans hostage; and the Soviet Union invaded neighboring Afghanistan, executed the sitting president, and installed its own puppet government. All of these conflicts reverberated throughout the decade. A new U.S. president, Ronald Reagan, was elected in 1980, reignited the Cold War, and openly criticized the United Nations, which experienced its own share of challenges. China vetoed Secretary-General Waldheim's effort to secure an unprecedented third term on sixteen separate occasions. When Javier Pérez de Cuéllar, a veteran Peruvian diplomat who had served at the United Nations, took the organization's top job in 1982, his first annual report focused on the organization's weaknesses. The combative Jeanne Kirkpatrick served as the U.S. ambassador to the United Nations in Reagan's first term, where she defined her job as aggressively defending the United States against the unholy alliance of the Non-Aligned Movement and the Soviet Union, which came in for condemnation especially in the wake of the Soviet downing of Korean Airlines flight 007 on August 31, 1983. Nor did the United States respond well to the French and Mexican criticisms of its October 25, 1983, invasion of the tiny Caribbean nation of Grenada.[49]

By 1985, the United States was threatening to stop paying large portions of its dues to the United Nations in an attempt to establish a weighted voting system for budget matters in the General Assembly that would model that already found in the U.N. financial institutions (the International Monetary Fund and the World Bank). Political conservatives in the United States considered leaving the organization entirely, and the United States did leave the U.N. Educational, Scientific and Cultural Organization (UNESCO) in 1984, dealing the organization a significant blow (the United States returned in 2003 but halted funding of the organization in 2011 when it granted full membership to Palestine). However, America rejoined the International Labour Organization, which it had left in 1977, in February 1980. But the very fact that the United States was opting in and out of U.N. agencies was not promising. Even Ambassador Kirkpatrick's faith in the Security Council was so low that she was bewildered about why the British sought its mediation of the British dispute with Argentina over the Falkland Islands in 1982, and she failed to even attend the resulting emergency session.[50]

However, at this low point, new leadership emerged in the Soviet Union in 1985 that helped rejuvenate the United Nations as an important venue for international diplomacy. Mikhail Gorbachev was eager to reform his country's economy, which led him to scale back commitments in places like Afghanistan and to seek greater accommodation with the United States and Israel. And when the war between Iran and Iraq started spilling over into the Persian Gulf and involving the tankers that carried much of the world's oil, the United States worked through the United Nations to help bring a resolution to that conflict. However, given the preceding turmoil and acrimony, it took months of coffee and cookies at the British ambassador's residence for the permanent members of the Security Council to reestablish trust and the quality of relationships needed to help broker that peace with Secretary-General Pérez de Cuéllar in 1987.[51]

As U.S.-Soviet relations thawed and a former U.S. ambassador to the United Nations, George H. W. Bush, was elected president of the United States, the U.N. Security Council increasingly sought to resolve a number of regional conflicts that had been smoldering for most of the decade or even longer. It dispatched cease-fire observers to both Nicaragua and El Salvador to assist in disarming the Contra rebel forces that the United States had previously funded, and in January 1990, it began to work toward a solution to the conflict in Cambodia (discussed further in Chapter 6).[52] That summer, the Security Council undertook its most ambitious mission, when its resolutions provided the architecture for a military mission against Iraq in the wake of its invasion of neighboring Kuwait, which was followed by a significant investigation of its weapons of mass destruction and a strenuous regime of economic sanctions that is described in greater detail in Chapter 7.

Oddly enough, the issue of colonialism resurfaced in the 1990s, with the decade being designated the International Decade for the Eradication of Colonialism. Imagining that the time was right to complete the task that the Declaration on Independence had established in 1960, the Committee of 24 worked toward starting the new millennium on the right foot. A key area of focus was the strategic trust territories held by the United States since the Second World War, most of which gained their independence in 1990. In fact, the U.N. Trusteeship Council's mandate ended with the independence of Palau in 1994. Perhaps encouraged by these developments, the Committee of 24 held a Pacific regional seminar in Fiji from June 16 to 18, 1998, encouraged the elimination of all military bases in non–self-governing territories, and sent visiting missions to the remaining handful of non–self-governing territories. Although the decade did not reach its goal and a Second International Decade for the Eradication of Colonialism was established for the first decade of the new millennium, the fact was that there were now very few people living in colonial areas that lacked indigenous leadership.[53] By this time, the Non-Aligned Movement seemed to have lost the moral authority that it had had in the 1950s and 1960s when it had trumpeted an end to imperialism and racism and sought the triumph of self-determination and economic development. Even its calls in the 1970s for a New International Economic Order (NIEO) sought to improve the quality of life of large swathes of humanity on the globe. But as the economic crises and structural readjustment of the 1980s weakened the Third World and high-profile nationalist leaders devolved into little more than dictators, the movement lost much of its steam, and it seemed that the Security Council, especially with the ebbing of the Cold War, sought to pick up the mantle of leadership.

On December 21, 1991, the Soviet Union ceased to exist, breaking into its constituent republics. However, there was no debate or discussion about the Soviet Union's permanent seat on the Security Council; it simply shifted to Russia, despite strong legal arguments that an amendment to the Charter was more appropriate. But any such amendment would have raised unwanted questions about changing (and expanding) the composition of the Council. When Boris Yeltsin, president of the Russian Federation, tried out Russia's Security Council seat on January 31, 1992, he was greeted by the heads of state of the other Council members, a first in its history. And there was a new secretary-general, Boutros Boutros-Ghali, a Coptic Christian and career diplomat from Egypt, who was tasked with defining the mission of the organization in the new, post–Cold War world. *An Agenda for Peace* imagined a U.N. peacekeeping force at the ready, able to respond to the Council's orders on extremely short notice. Additionally, the Security Council was working intensively on a number of nation-building missions in Namibia, Angola, and Cambodia. But the expanded possibilities of the immediate post–Cold War world quickly faded as genocide unfolded in the former Yugoslavia and then Rwanda and chaos erupted in Somalia.[54]

The United Nations struggled to respond effectively as Yugoslavia began to break apart in June 1991, following Slovenia's declaration of independence. The Serb-dominated army tried briefly and unsuccessfully to reunite the breakaway province. When Croatia similarly declared independence, the large minority of ethnic Serbs there joined with the Yugoslav army to seize control of largely Serbian areas and to drive others out, prompting a September 1991 Security Council arms embargo of the entire former Yugoslavia, which had a disproportionate impact on the victims of Serb aggression. When an 8,000-person U.N. Protection Force was dispatched to Croatia in February 1992, the Serbs turned their attention to driving non-Serbs out of large swathes of eastern and northern Bosnia. Large-scale fighting followed the Bosnian declaration of independence in April, and the Security Council extended the scope of its Protection Force to include Bosnia. This force involved significant numbers of troops from the permanent members of the Council (a post–Cold War change) and was undertaken against the advice of the secretary-general, who believed that the conditions for successful peacekeeping (especially an agreement and the consent of the contesting parties) were absent. Once in the field, the differences between Council members about the ultimate purpose of the mission emerged, and despite passing more resolutions about the conflict in the former Yugoslavia than any other conflict in its history, the Security Council seemed unable to stop the ethnic cleansing and violence. As the permanent members disagreed, the non-permanent members (especially André Erdos of Hungary and Diego Arria of Venezuela) came to the fore, educating their fellow Council members about the region, including briefings from NGOs, arranging for a "field trip" to the conflict zone, and developing the idea of "safe areas" that would be protected by the U.N. troops (the first was the town of Srebrenica in April 1993). But the U.N. forces failed to lift the Serbian siege of Sarajevo and ultimately were unable to protect the Bosnians in Srebrenica, where thousands were rounded up and systematically executed by Serbian troops in July 1995. One analyst has attributed part of the failure to an ingrained history of U.N. impartiality that makes it averse to distinguishing between the perpetrators and victims of violence and therefore unable to intervene effectively.[55]

The secretary-general became irate when the Security Council did not appear equally eager to intervene in Somalia, which he saw as a situation analogous to Yugoslavia. In the wake of the overthrow of Siad Barre's dictatorial rule in 1991, no one group was able to govern the nation, which largely became a failed state. Council resolutions imposing an arms embargo in January 1992 and calls for negotiations yielded no change in the situation, and when the Somali people began to die from malnutrition and disease that spring, the Council delayed the dispatch of 500 U.N. troops to safeguard the delivery of food. But in the fall of 1992, the outgoing administration of President Bush decided to send almost 20,000 American troops into Somalia in coordination with a U.N. force. This mission was undertaken without the consent of the Somalis, making it the Council's first armed humanitarian intervention. By the summer of 1993, warlord Mohamed Farah Aidid's forces attacked Pakistani peacekeepers, killing twenty-four, which prompted a Security Council resolution calling for Aidid's capture. But American forces attempting to carry out this mission found themselves isolated and under fire on October 3; ultimately eighteen U.S. soldiers and hundreds of Somalis died in the fighting. The images of dead American soldiers being dragged through the streets of Mogadishu prompted U.S. withdrawal and the collapse of the U.N. mission there.[56]

Given the United Nations' lack of success in Yugoslavia and Somalia, the Council lacked the confidence needed to decisively intervene as the Rwandan genocide quickly unfolded in the spring of 1994. The small (4,000-member) U.N. Assistance Mission in Rwanda under Canadian General Romeo Dallaire, whose mission was to assist the Hutu-dominated government in making peace with the Tutsi-led Rwandan Patriotic Front, warned the United Nations in January 1994 about the accumulation of arms and plans for massacres, but he was denied permission to launch operations to seize these arms caches. The April 6 downing of the plane carrying Rwanda's president, Juvénal Habyarimana, was the starting point of the genocide, which included the killing of ten Belgian peacekeepers on the first day. The next day, the peacekeepers' primary responsibility was to guard the airport so that European nationals could be safely evacuated from the country, as the Security Council called ineffectually for an end to the violence. By April 21, there were only 270 U.N. troops still on the ground, and the Council would not even use the word "genocide" in its description of what was happening in Rwanda lest it trigger legal requirements for action. Ultimately, it was the Rwandan Patriotic Front—not the United Nations—that stopped the killing, seizing control of much of the country by June, but the United Nations did move to punish those who had perpetrated the genocide (discussed in Chapter 8). The Security Council's shortcomings in Rwanda and Srebrenica led the United States and NATO to take a more aggressive stance in protecting the population of Bosnia from Serbian aggression, including a 12,000-person force with greater ability to call in air strikes. This action, undertaken outside of the Council framework, started with waves of bombings in late August 1995 and brought both a Russian veto of further sanctions against its Serbian ally and the Dayton Peace Accords of November 1995.[57]

The divisions within the Security Council over Yugoslavia made it increasingly difficult for the Council to maintain its supervision of Saddam Hussein's regime in Iraq. Russia, France, and China sought formal action to partially lift economic sanctions in early 1995, but the United States and the United Kingdom saw them as largely permanent. In the meantime, the Security Council did not do well in regulating oil sales from Iraq through the oil-for-food program, which eventually became the target of a corruption investigation. On December 16, 1998, U.S.-led air operations against suspected weapons sites in Iraq ended the U.N. weapons inspection process, angered the Chinese ambassador, and saddened Secretary-General Kofi Annan, who had sought to mediate and bring about a peaceful resolution to the situation. The permanent members of the Security Council also disagreed on how best to respond to the conflict between ethnic Albanian militias and Serb-dominated security forces in Kosovo in early 1998. While the NATO countries sought U.N. sanction for its action there, the Russians and Chinese saw the proposed military action as a violation of Serbian sovereignty. NATO forces moved ahead, initiating bombing on March 24, 1999. Ultimately, Russia approved and China abstained on a U.N. plan to end the crisis in June of that year.[58] So while the end of the Cold War opened up new opportunities for U.N. Security Council activism, underlying conflicts of interest between the permanent members remained and became increasingly prominent in the new millennium.

The pivot to security after 9/11

While much of the United Nations' focus in the 1990s had been on peacekeeping and peace-building activities, the terrorist attacks on the World Trade Center in New York City on September 11, 2000, brought the Security Council and much of the world together to condemn the terrorist attacks and to develop stronger international mechanisms to combat this transnational danger. Security Council Resolution 1373 later that same month required states to cut funds to any terrorist organization, extradite or punish terrorists in their jurisdictions, and share information to combat global terrorism, and it created its own counterterrorism committee to supervise member states' adherence to these measures. This was the first time the Council had sought to prescribe national legislation, but it hoped these efforts would help the international organization address the real dangers of transnational terrorism as well as help curb unilateral U.S. action in the wake of the attack. The United States did not seek U.N. approval of its invasion of Afghanistan the next year. Citing its right to self-defense, it attacked the Taliban forces in that country in October 2001. However, the United Nations sought to participate in the rebuilding of the country, so in December the Security Council unanimously authorized an international security force for Kabul.[59]

The United Nations was more central to the next step in U.S. President George W. Bush's "war on terrorism"—regime change in Iraq. British Prime Minister Tony Blair's support of this goal helped to ensure that those within the administration worked through the United Nations as far as possible in pursuing their goal. As late as November 2002, the United States had agreed to a Security Council resolution that restarted the U.N. weapons inspection process, but over the next four months, the permanent members repeatedly disagreed about whether or not the Iraqis were complying with the terms of the resolution. U.S. Secretary of State Colin Powell's presentation before the Security Council in February 2003 was meant to garner support from the American people, to shore up support for Blair in Great Britain, and perhaps to sway the other permanent members of the Council. While the first two objectives might have been reached, ultimately the "coalition of the willing" led by the United States and Britain that invaded Iraq on March 20 lacked the legitimacy that a further Security Council resolution could have bestowed on the operation. Anglo-American resentment meant that after the ground war had ended the United Nations was tasked with coordinating humanitarian, economic, and political matters in postwar Iraq but was not given the authority needed to carry out this mandate. Some believed that the standoff in the Security Council bolstered the prestige of that body, which had seemingly refused to be railroaded into supporting the Anglo-American war.[60]

The Security Council also worked to address issues of nuclear proliferation directly in the mid-2000s. When the International Atomic Energy Agency (IAEA) brought Iran's nascent nuclear program to the Council's attention in February 2006, no resolution moved forward as both Russia and China were loath to endanger the lucrative energy and technology ties they had developed with that country. Similarly, when the U.S. representative on the Council pushed for an immediate condemnation and sanctions in response to North Korea's July 2006 launch of several ballistic missiles into the Sea of Japan, Chinese opposition resulted in only words of condemnation. But when North Korea undertook a small atomic test that October, the Chinese and Russian delegates were persuaded not to veto the Security Council resolution condemning the test and imposing new restrictions on trade with the country. But on the day the resolution passed, Russia's ambassador passed the American representative a note from the new Russian foreign minister: "Iran will not be this easy." Indeed, it took until the summer of 2015 to hammer out a nuclear agreement with Iran that brought its program under the U.N. inspection process.[61]

I hope this quick overview of the ever-changing dynamics of international relations that unfolded in the United Nations from its founding up until recent times has already given you ideas about what aspects of the United Nations you would like to research on your own. Subsequent chapters will provide more depth on the themes of human rights, peacekeeping, and economic and social issues—among others—and will take you deeper into case studies in various parts of the world.

CHAPTER 4
PREVENTING WAR AND PROMOTING PEACE THROUGH SOCIAL AND ECONOMIC PROGRAMS

As we saw in Chapter 2, the successful work of the League of Nations in the social and economic fields inspired the Bruce Committee to propose that such endeavors become the League's primary focus. When the Second World War precluded this possibility, delegates from China and Brazil—which had greatly benefited from the work of the League of Nations Health Organization—successfully advocated for the U.N. Economic and Social Council (ECOSOC) at the San Francisco Conference. In some ways, ECOSOC has lived up to the dream of these early promoters. It is the largest principal organ of the United Nations, overseeing all of the diverse work of the fifteen U.N. specialized agencies in addition to its own nine functional and five regional commissions. It is also the first and largest forum for U.N. interactions with nongovernmental organizations (NGOs; there were more than 3,200 registered NGOs in 2015). But the work of ECOSOC has frequently faced criticism about the "usefulness" of some of its work, and the sprawling nature of this endeavor has led to frequent calls for reform aimed at ensuring greater efficiency.

Like the League, the initial impetus behind ECOSOC's creation was the desire to prevent the type of social and economic dislocation that seemed to be linked to national chauvinism and war—in other words, to treat the root causes of war. Not surprisingly, this discourse on "root causes" changed over time; as the Cold War competition between the United States and the Soviet Union set in, competition between the superpowers for the loyalties of the emerging Third World and the agenda of the Non-Aligned Movement (discussed in Chapter 3) led to a broader focus on many of the same things but was relabeled as the process of "development." In many ways, the work of national economic development has been the centerpiece of ECOSOC's work, bringing together the diverse expertise and the expansive resources of its wide array of specialized organizations, commissions, and the affiliated NGOs. And while this discourse of development has persisted, issues of population, human rights, and environmental sustainability have significantly altered it over the decades. Many of these new issues have been introduced in large-scale, high-profile global conferences since the 1970s, many of which will be mentioned in this chapter and in the next. Given the complexity and centrality of "development," it has earned its own chapter (which follows this one), while the present chapter will endeavor to provide the reader with a broad overview of ECOSOC's work, introducing the main categories of actors and focusing on their work. Given the number and diversity of the NGOs engaged in ECOSOC's work, there is not one discussion of them; rather they are inserted throughout the text where they become particularly important to the narrative, but even when they are not in the foreground, they were constantly shaping and influencing debate within the United Nations by their information-gathering, their membership, their presence, and their passions to build a better world.[1]

Returning to our analogy of the U.N. borderland, the ECOSOC borderland is probably the most populous and well-traveled area within the larger borderland of the United Nations—perhaps equivalent to Main Street. Even though ECOSOC has limited governmental representation,[2] it deals with everything from agriculture, narcotic drugs, women, and health to aviation, population, human rights, public administration, and education. Given this broad scope of work and wide range of actors, it is difficult to imagine the aspiring scholar not finding something to her or his liking or not finding sufficient primary sources from which to write an original research project. Frequent meetings give rise to a plethora of documentation. The Commission (working in conjunction with the U.N. Secretariat to develop and organize its program of work for the year) holds regular meetings throughout the year—an organizational meeting at the beginning of the year, a yearly spring meeting with the World Trade Organization (WTO) and the Bretton Woods institutions (discussed in greater detail later) since 2002, and a month-long "substantive" session each July (which alternates meeting between Geneva and New York) with the work being divided between five different segments: high-level (often attended by top-level national policymakers), coordination, operational activities, humanitarian affairs, and general. Recently, the high-level segment has also included an Annual Ministerial Review and a biennial Development Cooperation Forum focused on themes from the U.N. Millennium Development Goals (MDGs). Additionally, since 1990, ECOSOC has also organized a series of roundtable discussions with academics and NGOs prior to the substantive sessions to engage with the key issues to be discussed. Each of these meetings generates its own rich documentation about the global conversation related to the world's pressing economic, social, and environmental concerns. Of course, each of the specialized agencies, NGOs, and ECOSOC commissions and conferences also generates its own records, periodicals, and archival records.[3]

Despite the significance of ECOSOC and the richness of its sources (or perhaps because of them), the literature on its work is largely fragmented between its many parts, and ECOSOC's work as a whole seems to have attracted far less scholarly attention than peacekeeping or the debates of the General Assembly and the Security Council, despite the fact that its work directly affects the lives of many more of the world's people; additionally, it currently oversees approximately 70 percent of the total budget and staff resources of the United Nations. This lack of scholarly attention may be due to the fact that ECOSOC makes nonbinding resolutions—unlike the Security Council; has limited national representation—unlike the General Assembly; has no mandate clearly outside of the work of the other principal organs; and oversees the work of specialized agencies, which prefer to maximize their freedom of action. In addition, the Non-Aligned Movement has primarily sought to introduce what it sees as the most important changes in the international realm of social and economic relations to the General Assembly, which generally receives greater attention. As a result, much of the literature about the Commission is especially focused on what are perceived to be needed reforms and its future. Nonetheless, its debates are perhaps richer (or more candid) for their nonbinding nature and much more varied given the integration of NGO, U.N. specialized agency, and other expert voices in its deliberations. If we return to the idea of ECOSOC as borderland, it is one with a relative shortage of "sheriffs" policing the area. Guatemalan economist, former ECOSOC president, and U.N. Secretariat member Gert Rosenthal has summarized it in this way: "Many states have viewed ECOSOC as an impartial and objective meeting place where different positions and approaches can be contrasted, and implications of alternative policy prescriptions can be analyzed." Turning to the development enterprise, Rosenthal concluded that this has resulted in "successes in promoting the development debate, identifying emerging issues, and offering guidelines for policymakers."[4] So in the next two chapters, we will explore this populous, contentious, multipolar ECOSOC borderland.

To provide just one recent example of ECOSOC's effectiveness and managerial expertise, we can turn to its ministerial declaration in July 2000 on the importance of information technology to the process of development and the resulting creation of the Information and Communication Technologies Task Force in November 2001 (whose members were appointed by U.N. Secretary-General Kofi Annan). This ECOSOC task force provided catalytic global leadership for an issue first raised by the G-8's Digital Opportunities Task Force (an intergovernmental group from the world's eight largest economies that started meeting in November 2000) and the Digital Divide Initiative of the World Economic Forum (a nonprofit foundation established in 1971). The ECOSOC task force included U.N. personnel, global telecommunications chief executive officers (CEOs), governmental personnel, and leaders of NGOs to provide top-flight technical advice to governments and international organizations on how to integrate information technologies into development processes. It organized its work through working groups, global fora, regional nodes and meetings, publications, and high-level roundtables on linking information and communication technology (ICT) to the Millennium Development Goals (MDGs, discussed fully in the next chapter). The highlights of these processes were showcased through its two World Summits on the Information Society (WSIS) in Geneva in December 2003 and in Tunisia in November 2005 before its mandate expired the next month. Following the work of the task force, the Global Alliance for ICT and Development (GAID), a more informal and open forum for "Information Society" stakeholders, continues as a locus for discussion and suggestions on the ways in which information technology and economic development need to be integrated to promote twenty-first-century development. This quick snapshot is meant to provide a short example of the ways in which ECOSOC seeks to organize and manage its complex work and nexus of stakeholders across the planet.[5]

In the pages that follow, I will introduce you briefly to each of the parts of ECOSOC, but we will pause and have a longer conversation with some of them. For those that receive only cursory introductions, you will find information, historiography, and primary sources in the endnotes and in the online guide for further research if you want to get to know these organizations more deeply. And I will end the chapter with an example of the work that ECOSOC did around the issue of global population in the 1960s and 1970s as another case study of its work.

Wartime relief efforts

Even as the Second World War raged, the United Nations (which is what the Allies formally called themselves during the war) began organizing collective, international relief operations. The first was the U.N. Relief and Rehabilitation Administration (UNRRA), officially established on November 9, 1943, to "plan, co-ordinate, administer or arrange for . . . the relief of victims of war in any area under the control of any of the United Nations through the provision of food, fuel, clothing, shelter and other basic necessities, medical and other essential services" (Articles 1 and 2). It grew out of the earlier work of the U.S. State Department's Office of Foreign Relief and Rehabilitation Operations (est. November 21, 1942) and the Inter-Allied Committee on Post-War Requirements (the Leith-Ross Committee, est. September 1941). A director-general oversaw the day-to-day management of a staff that expanded to some 20,000 members and two headquarters (Washington, DC, and London). A central committee representing "the Big Four" (the United States, the United Kingdom, the Soviet Union, and China) made policy decisions between meetings of the Council, on which each member government had a representative (it met in six sessions from November 1943 to December 1946). Although UNRRA suffered the expected difficulties of creating from scratch such a large organization in the midst of war (especially in recruiting competent staff and distributing its aid), it nonetheless distributed some $3.7 billion in humanitarian aid (the equivalent of approximately $40 billion today), improving the lives of many vulnerable people. Appeals from UNRRA officials about how its aid could serve the West's long-term interests and about how feeding the hungry was simply the right thing to do failed to win over the support of the U.S. Congress (the source of 80 percent of UNRRA funding) needed to continue the organization. Active UNRRA operations ended in 1947, with some of its budget reallocated to the World Health Organization Interim Commission, which used these funds to dispatch multinational missions to Ethiopia, Greece, and China with the goals of training auxiliary health personnel and taking basic precautions to prevent the spread of epidemic disease. Other parts of UNRRA's work, especially assisting displaced persons, shifted to the International Refugee Organization (est. 1946, subsequently the Office of the U.N. High Commissioner for Refugees).[6] There was a similar effort by the United Nations to assist during the Korean War, which gave birth to the U.N. Korean Reconstruction Agency (UNKRA) that experienced difficulties very similar to those that UNRRA had in trying to carry out humanitarian and reconstruction work in an active war zone.[7]

Longer lived but springing from the same roots was UNICEF (the United Nations International Children's Emergency Fund). Created as the result of a U.N. General

Assembly resolution on December 11, 1946, UNICEF responded to the urgent needs of an estimated two million displaced and refugee children in the wake of the Second World War, most of whom were in Eastern Europe. Unlike the other specialized agencies being created at the time, however, UNICEF remained a semiautonomous fund of the General Assembly. Its executive board consists of U.N. member states who oversee its activities and provide the bulk of its funding (though a significant amount is raised through its national committees and fund-raising efforts), but it otherwise enjoys a "loose" relationship with the rest of the United Nations and has therefore developed very differently. As the immediate postwar crisis waned and the Cold War set in, efforts to wind up UNICEF's work stalled, unlike the earlier UNRRA closure. Seeing the efficacy of its work, poorer countries successfully lobbied the 1950 General Assembly session to expand its mandate to meet the needs of children in underdeveloped countries. UNICEF therefore began a focus on improving the health of mothers and children in general, with specific foci on fighting disease and improving nutrition. Given the overlap between this mission and that of the World Health Organization (WHO, est. 1948), the two developed a clear division of labor. The WHO supplied the technical expertise and personnel, while UNICEF supplied material aid to individuals in the field. This fieldwork developed into an extensive network of contacts in the countries it served and generated an organizational focus that "supports and facilitates things that have to happen on the ground." In subsequent years, UNICEF also began advocating for the rights of children that had first been enunciated at the League of Nations and then were developed into the 1959 Declaration of the Rights of the Child and the 1989 Convention on the Rights of the Child (see Chapter 8). Recognizing that children were often the most direct and helpless victims of economic underdevelopment, poverty, and armed conflict also led UNICEF to advocate for the antipoverty focus of the United Nations' MDGs (see Chapter 5).[8] Although beginning with the task of relief through organizations such as UNRRA and UNICEF, the United Nations quickly moved to constructing what it hoped would be a lasting foundation for future peace by addressing the root causes of war through the U.N. specialized agencies.

Oversight of the U.N. specialized agencies

The construction of the U.N. system was a bit haphazard. Existing organizations from the League-of-Nations days and earlier—such as the International Labour Organization and the Universal Postal Union—persisted and were joined by entirely new organizations—such as the International Monetary Fund. Also in the mix were organizations that had previously existed but were now rebranded under the United Nations—such as the WHO (growing out of the League Health Organization). And the United Nations proper—the General Assembly, Security Council, and Secretariat—developed only after some of the specialized agencies had already been created. Therefore, there was a bit of a debate about what the exact relationship between the new specialized agencies, the extant organizations, and the United Nations should be, and it took several years and some wrangling to work out a livable relationship between all the members of the U.N. family (if indeed it now exists). Additionally, ECOSOC has added additional concerns to its agenda over time—including the environment, climate change, and tourism—which have resulted in even more organizations. Altogether, they constitute the fifteen current U.N. specialized agencies, whose work ECOSOC tries to coordinate and manage. This section of the chapter will give you a brief introduction to each of them, with a slightly longer description of the World Meteorological Organization (WMO) and the U.N. World Tourism Organization (UNWTO) to give you a sense of the richness and interconnections that exist in the study of such U.N. agencies.

Early specialized agencies

A significant share of ECOSOC's initial work came with integrating the preexisting international organizations and the U.N. specialized agencies created before its own founding. The International Telecommunications Union, the International Labour Organization, and the Universal Postal Union (Chapter 2)—all well-established international organizations housed in neutral Switzerland during the war—transitioned to being U.N. specialized agencies relatively easily. Others were rebranded as U.N. specialized agencies. For example, the Food and Agriculture Organization of the United Nations (FAO) was the first U.N. specialized agency, created at the 1943 Hot Springs Conference. Its mission was to realize the Atlantic Charter's call for a postwar world where "all the men in all lands may live out their lives in freedom from fear and want," specifically in terms of food, which was exactly the focus in American artist Norman Rockwell's painting depicting this wartime aspiration. The FAO replaced Rome's International Institute of Agriculture, but its headquarters returned to Rome not very long afterward (1951) from racially segregated Washington, DC. Under the leadership of Scotsman John Boyd Orr, the organization's first director-general (leading FAO from 1946 until 1948), the FAO worked to alleviate the immediate postwar food shortage and developed an ambitious plan for international buffer stocks of all key agricultural commodities meant to increase prices and ensure stable supplies, but this ambitious World Food Board ran into immediate opposition from both the United States and the United Kingdom and therefore remained only an idea. The next two directors-general focused on gathering agricultural statistics and providing technical assistance before the FAO elected the first Third World national to head a U.N. organization. Indian B. R. Sen (who served from 1956 until 1967) brought NGOs actively into the organization's work as part of its Freedom From Hunger Campaign, which sought to make small, grassroots changes to agricultural production with the goal of promoting local food security, a vision that did not fit well with the U.S. food surplus disposal program.[9]

Even after the immediate postwar crises had wound up, it was clear that the structural work of alleviating the root causes of war persisted. In the case of "freedom from want" specifically, an interrelated series of global food and economic crises hit the Saharan countries of Africa in the early 1970s and prompted the General Assembly to convene a 1974 World Food Conference, which in turn resulted in the creation of the International

Fund for Agricultural Development (IFAD, est. 1977), which worked and was housed with the FAO. IFAD was an instrument for financing agricultural development projects (through grants and low-interest loans) to "developing countries and in particular in the least developed and most seriously affected among them." A significant portion of its funds came from OPEC (the Organization of Petroleum Exporting Countries) and the European members of the Organisation for Economic Co-operation and Development (OECD). IFAD quickly came to understand that food insecurity and famine were tied to the structural problems related to rural poverty. Therefore, its current stated goal is to enable poor rural people to improve their food and nutrition security, increase their incomes, and strengthen their resilience. It also acts as an advocate for poor rural women and men. Its multilateral orientation provides a strong global platform for discussing rural policy issues and increasing awareness of why investment in agriculture and rural development is critical to reducing poverty and improving global food security. The 1992 International Conference on Nutrition and the 1996 World Food Summit similarly sought to refocus attention on the interrelated issues of agricultural development, nutrition, and health. Much of the language of the food summit reappeared later in the United Nations' MDGs.[10] Initially established to ensure "freedom from want," the ECOSOC bodies working on agriculture, hunger, and food issues are now much more focused on issues of poverty, economic development, and the environment, but the underlying rationale and goal of this work has not changed.

UNESCO (the U.N. Educational, Scientific and Cultural Organization, est. 1945) grew out of a strong reaction against the Nazi and fascist methods of actively using culture and education to implant and spread their ideology. It also had deeper roots in the work of the League of Nations Committee on Intellectual Co-operation (est. May 1922). This League committee had always struggled to attract the funds and attention needed to carry out its threefold mission of improving the livelihoods of intellectual workers (equivalent to the work the ILO was performing for industrial workers); increasing international contacts among artists, authors, scientists, teachers, and members of other intellectual professions; and engaging teachers at all levels and in all countries in the work of promoting international cooperation and peace. Among the diverse items it set for its agenda were the regulation of archaeological exploration, the establishment of student and faculty exchanges among universities, and the protection of intellectual property rights. This work gained additional support from the French government, which partnered with the League to establish the International Institute of Intellectual Co-operation in Paris in 1924.[11] After the Second World War had engulfed the European continent, the Allied Ministers of Education gathered in 1942 to begin planning for the postwar reconstruction of their educational systems; they quickly turned to broader, more international issues as more countries joined the work, ultimately laying the groundwork for establishing UNESCO in Paris in November 1945. The preamble to its constitution rather famously declared "that since wars begin in the minds of men, it is in the minds of men that the defenses of peace must be constructed." While some have characterized this language as idealistic, it was actually a pretty realistic response to the questions that its practitioners had received in the interwar period about why this work was important. The signatories to the UNESCO constitution went on to assert their belief "in full and equal opportunities for education for all, in the unrestricted pursuit of objective truth and in the free exchange of ideas and knowledge." Concretely, in the 1940s it recommended all member states make primary education both compulsory and free; in the 1950s, its intergovernmental conference adopted the Universal Copyright Convention to supplement the earlier Berne Convention; in the 1960s, UNESCO began its work of preserving historical structures; in the 1970s, it helped establish the United Nations University in Tokyo and adopted a Declaration on Race and Racial Prejudice; in the 1980s, UNESCO promoted histories centered in indigenous cultures; in the 1990s, it developed (and the United Nations endorsed) the Universal Declaration on the Human Genome and Human Rights; and in the twenty-first century, UNESCO convened a World Education Forum in Dakar, Senegal, to commit to a framework for achieving its goal of Education for All by the year 2015.[12] This very brief chronology offers the reader some tidbits about the broad range of UNESCO's work that might lead the curious investigator to deeper study.

An organization that functionally undergirded the growth of transnational exchange after the Second World War was the International Civil Aviation Organization (ICAO, est. 1944), which built on the interwar work of the International Commission for Air Navigation (ICAN) in regulating transnational airplane traffic under the auspices of the League. When ICAO's foundational Chicago Convention (drafted in 1944) entered into force in 1947, it took over the global standardization job of developing the "Standards and Recommended Practices" (SARPs) and "Procedures for Air Navigation Services" (PANS) that guide member states in developing their own national civil aviation regulations. Much like the earlier technical organizations, the pressure to conform comes from the fact that the global system—which currently supports close to 100,000 flights each day—pretty much only works if everyone is using the same language and procedures. Therefore, much of the technical work of the organization is done by the Air Navigation Commission, currently nineteen qualified professionals "in the science and practice of aeronautics" who act in their personal capacity to develop the SARPs and PANS. Although headquartered in Montreal, Canada, ICAO has regional offices all over the world that built upon ICAN's earlier tradition of regional meetings.[13]

Another functional member of the United Nations ensuring transnational exchanges is the Inter-Governmental Maritime Consultative Organization (IMCO, est. 1959, which became the International Maritime Organization [IMO] in 1975), which was rooted in the earlier League Communications and Transit Organization.[14] The organization promotes governmental cooperation on all technical matters related to international ocean shipping, especially to ensure safety, efficient navigation, and prevention of marine pollution from ships. With such universal aims, the IMO includes non-U.N. members (like Switzerland), who can join the IMO by a two-thirds vote of the membership. Early efforts to have the organization deal with the economic aspects of international shipping met significant resistance from the membership, which has confined the organization to technical issues. Nonetheless, the IMO members have adopted more than forty formal conventions and protocols covering everything from establishing international shipping routes and a maritime satellite network to promoting ship safety and preventing marine pollution (especially spills of oil and hazardous substances). In addition, it has made hundreds of nonbinding recommendations, which fall below the level of an international treaty but (like ICAO's SARPs and PANS) provide guidance for framing national legislation and regulations. With the growth of piracy in the late 1980s and early 1990s, the IMO established a long-term, antipiracy project in 1998 that included assessment missions as well as regional seminars and workshops and that resulted, for example, in a sixteen-nation Regional Cooperation Agreement on Combating Piracy and Armed Robbery against Ships in Asia (ReCAAP) in November 2004. Also as part of that work, the IMO has worked in the Red Sea and Gulf of Aden area to coordinate the work of multilateral military forces, to support U.N. development efforts, and to provide training to reduce the incidence of piracy in the area. It has similarly worked with the U.N. High Commissioner on Refugees (UNHCR) to improve existing treaties in order to deal with the legal aspects arising from the increase in "asylum-seeking boat people"—an issue back in today's headlines. The goal of this joint UNHCR-IMO work (which resulted in the 2004 amendment to the 1974 IMO Convention for the Safety of Life at Sea) was to strengthen the legal obligation of governments to allow such people to disembark regardless of whatever claims they might subsequently make about their status; this lightens the burden on ship masters rescuing refugees on the high seas (in other words, ship captains picking up people from ships about to sink can drop these people at the ship's next port of call). While the IMO has dealt effectively with the growth in international merchant shipping over its life span (e.g., reducing the number of oil spills and the number of collisions between ships through its traffic separation schema), its work continues to evolve, to present new challenges, and to face criticism (e.g., environmentalists have criticized the slow pace of its work in protecting the oceans).[15]

Also rooted in an earlier League organization was the World Health Organization (WHO). It grew out of an initiative of the ECOSOC and only came into being in 1948, but its structure united several prewar health organizations, including the League of Nations Health Organization, the Pan American Sanitary Bureau, and the European-based Office International d'Hygiène Publique. The WHO also expanded on this earlier work by creating a network of regional offices (there is great research to be done on these, I think) to implement its new, proactive strategy of attacking disease at its source rather than using the defensive techniques of tracking disease (epidemiology) and then treating it. Using the wartime technological advances of antibiotics, a new tuberculosis vaccine, and a new insecticide called DDT, the WHO now fought venereal disease, infection, tuberculosis, malaria, and yellow fever at their source. A similar focus on prevention informed its early work plan, which aimed to improve maternal and child health, environmental sanitation, and nutrition (another outgrowth of the League's earlier work). Governments around the work embraced this work, especially India, which raced to establish the organization's first regional office in New Delhi. But the allure of completely eradicating malaria in the 1950s and 1960s (and the money the campaign attracted) helped distract from a more personal and individual focus on health improvement and ultimately failed (unlike its later smallpox eradication campaign, which declared success on May 8, 1980). The structural adjustment programs implemented in many developing countries as a result of the debt crises of the 1980s (Chapter 5) decimated many national public health services. The resulting shortcomings of national and international systems of health care have been glaringly exposed by recent, widespread outbreaks of HIV/AIDS, avian flu, ebola, and the Zika virus.[16]

The Bretton Woods institutions: Regulating the global economy

The Allies created two new U.N. specialized agencies during the war to manage and develop the global economy. At the 1944 Bretton Woods Conference, they established the International Monetary Fund (IMF) and the International Bank for Reconstruction and Development (IBRD, but more commonly the World Bank) that eventually grew to six separate agencies. The IMF's mission was to ensure an "objective" method of determining exchange rates between currencies, something that the Nazi regime had manipulated in the prewar period and something that the gold standard alone was no longer capable of doing in the postwar world. To create this system that tied exchange rates to both gold and the American dollar, the IMF needed significant monetary reserves (contributed by members) and had a weighted voting system tied to each country's contribution to this reserve.[17] The World Bank had a similar system of reserves and weighted voting, but it did not generate as much attention at the Bretton Woods Conference. After a relatively rocky start, the organization shifted to the "development" portion of its function in the wake of the 1948 Marshall Plan. To carry out its development work, the World Bank sold its bonds on Wall Street (with its reserves serving as collateral) in order to finance economic development projects, initially in India and Latin America and more broadly as decolonization took hold (Chapter 5).

The World Bank quickly developed a set of subsidiary agencies to help carry out this work in the field of economic development. The International Finance Corporation (IFC, est. 1956) was meant to be an incubator for private enterprise investment in the Third World. The International Development Association (IDA, est. 1960) was the direct result of efforts by the Non-Aligned Movement (Chapters 3 and 5) to establish a large fund in the United Nations to promote development (SUNFED or the Special United Nations Fund for Economic Development). The United States was not interested in such a program but wanted to appear responsive to these needs; putting the fund under the weighted voting of the IBRD was its answer. Additionally, the success of early World Bank lending made this possible. Since the Bank was receiving more money in loan repayments in the early 1960s than it was able to disburse through new development loans, it could finance IDA, which made long-term, low-interest loans for social as well as economic development. These loans had to meet the Bank's same exacting project standards but did not meet its traditional standards of creditworthiness. In 1966, the Bank established the International Centre for Settlement of Investment Disputes (ICSID), which was an organizational recognition of the work that the Bank had done in trying to settle various disputes between international investors and states (including stockholders in the Suez Canal Company in the wake of the 1956 nationalization of that canal). Rather than a traditional "international organization," ICSID is an arbitral service within the Bank that "provides facilities for conciliation and arbitration of investment disputes," putting the responsibility for making any monetary awards to investors on the contracting state or government, under the oversight of ICSID. The last to join the "World Bank Group" was the Multilateral Investment Guarantee Agency (MIGA) in 1988; it provides "political risk insurance" to foreign investors with the goal of promoting direct private investment abroad in order to promote development. Over time, it has focused its lending on the world's poorest countries, those emerging from conflict and war, and projects that focus on energy efficiency and climate change.[18] Collectively, the "Bretton Woods institutions" primarily defined economic development issues in the 1950s and provided much of the funding for development through the 1960s and 1970s, before coming in for sustained criticism during the 1980s and 1990s, all of which will be discussed in the following chapter.

The World Meteorological Organization: Weather to climate change

The WMO was another new U.N. specialized agency (formally established in 1951) with a long history. At this point, I would like to provide a short profile of this organization to enrich your understanding and provide some ideas about the types of research topics that analysis of a single specialized agency can give rise to. The WMO's first organizational identity was as the International Meteorological Organization (IMO, est. 1873), primarily a network of national weather observatories and services lacking formal regulatory power that grew out of the first International Meteorological Conference held in Brussels in 1853.[19] In 1947, the IMO's membership unanimously approved the convention to transform itself into the WMO, which came into force on March 23, 1950. The new agency's mission—"coordinating, standardizing, and improving world meteorological activities and . . . encouraging an efficient exchange of meteorological information between countries"—continued to grow and expand over time—just as the IMO's original mountain-top and shipboard observatories to improve weather forecasts had expanded to gather more upper-atmosphere data by and for airplanes. The postwar WMO's work encompassed not only improving global weather forecasts but also understanding and publicizing the effects of ozone depletion and of carbon dioxide emissions on global warming.[20]

The very nature of this work required a cooperative ethos, as the organization sought to harness scientific, governmental, and international resources to understand and predict the interaction of water and air around the planet. An early example of this was its co-sponsorship with the International Council of Scientific Unions (ICSU)[21] of the 1957–58 International Geophysical Year (IGY). The director of the National Science Foundation in the United States called it "the greatest single act of cooperation among the scientists of the world," as it brought together the human, economic, and physical resources of fifty-five countries to study and make simultaneous observations of the aurora, the ionosphere, meteorology, solar activity, geomagnetism, glaciology, oceanography, seismology, gravity, and the upper atmosphere and to collaboratively learn more about the planet than ever before.[22] A later example of a similarly broad initiative was the WMO's role in the International Polar Year (IPY) of 2007–08, again cosponsored by the ICSU and coming on the fiftieth anniversary of the IGY. This polar year built on a long history of internationally coordinated study of the polar areas marked by the first (1882–83) and second (1932–33) IPYs. But unlike its predecessors, this year focused on the polar areas as laboratories for understanding how small changes related to global warming "can produce dramatic consequences for polar ecosystems, for inhabitants and for the global climate itself" and for crafting "an integrated understanding of geophysical-ecological-social systems." This work began by bringing together scientists from a variety of disciplines who hailed from sixty-three different countries in 2004 to collaboratively develop a research agenda and "themes" to give the year's research coherence. Ultimately 228 projects were formally branded as IPY activities addressing its six themes, and these also created an ongoing "legacy of observing sites, facilities, and systems to support ongoing polar research and monitoring as the basis for observing and forecasting change."[23]

This motif of cooperation also permeated the WMO's work throughout the 1960s and 1970s on the prediction of global weather—especially of destructive storms—which, in turn, transformed into the study of global climate change in the 1980s. Weather forecasting, of course, was at the core of the WMO's work and led to the 1963 creation of the World Weather Watch, whose goal was to gather and combine data from national observation systems, satellites, and data-processing and forecasting centers to disseminate the best possible weather information to all countries in order to safeguard public safety and welfare. Hoping to bring additional resources to bear upon this task and building upon the successful collaboration of the IGY, the WMO and ICSU again collaborated to launch the Global Atmospheric Research Programme (GARP) in 1967, which was an early adopter of satellite and computer technologies in weather prediction. Lending urgency to this work was the 1970 Bhola Cyclone that hit East Pakistan (now Bangladesh) on November 12 at lunar high tide with winds of 225.3 km/h and a storm surge of 6 meters that killed 300,000–500,000 people who had no way to learn of meteorological predictions, making it the deadliest tropical cyclone in recorded history and contributing to the Bangladeshi fight for independence in 1971 (see Chapter 3 for more). In response, the 1974 GARP Atlantic Tropical Experiment (GATE) sought to better understand the tropical atmosphere and its role in the planetary atmosphere's circulation in order to extend daily weather forecasts to two weeks. GATE utilized forty research ships, twelve research aircraft, and buoys from twenty countries reaching across the tropical Atlantic Ocean from South America to Africa. Interestingly, a U.S. scientific director and a Soviet deputy scientific director oversaw the work together. Follow-ups included the Global Weather Experiment and Monsoon Experiments of 1978–79, which prompted a redesign of the operational work of the World Weather Watch.[24]

The WMO's role in studying the atmosphere also led it, early on, to study and publicize the effects of ozone depletion, starting in 1957, when it established the Global Ozone Observing System. Subsequently, in 1976, it issued its first international assessment of the state of the global ozone layer; these assessments laid the groundwork for the

1985 Vienna Convention on the Protection of the Ozone Layer and the 1987 Montreal Protocol on Substances that Deplete the Ozone Layer. It also began annual assessments and studies of ozone depletion to raise awareness of the issues.[25] The ability of the WMO in this case to move from the science to relatively quick and consensual international action to remedy the identified problem stands in stark contrast to its current work on climate change, which directly effects every human being on the planet and requires a vaster scale of involvement and change.

The climate science agenda grew as a result of the WMO's earlier work on weather and the atmosphere and led the WMO, ICSU, and U.N. Environmental Programme (UNEP) to organize an international workshop on climate issues in 1978, hosted by the International Institute for Applied System Analysis. This laid the groundwork for the 1979 World Climate Conference that brought together three hundred scientists from fifty countries to examine scientific evidence, confirm the long-term significance of carbon dioxide levels in the atmosphere, and analyze the role of the oceans in seasonal and annual climate variability. A turning point in the organization's mission and life, this first World Climate Conference led the WMO to establish an Intergovernmental Panel on Climate Change (IPCC), the World Climate Programme (which replaced the GARP), and the World Climate Research Programme (est. 1980 in cooperation with the ICSU to determine the extent of human influence on climate and to determine the scientific boundaries for climate prediction). The resulting IPCC Assessment Reports (1990, 1995, 2001, 2007), the second World Climate Conference (1990), the International Decade for Natural Disaster Reduction (the 1990s), the Intergovernmental Negotiating Committee on the U.N. Framework Convention on Climate Change (est. 1991), and the Global Climate Observing System (est. 1992) all laid the scientific foundation for the 1992 Earth Summit and its language of sustainable development. But all of this effort has not yet been able to secure governments' adherence to an international agreement to limit the so-called greenhouse gases and slow the rate of climate change. Although the IPCC received the Nobel Peace Prize in 2007, the lack of a comprehensive international climate agreement "threatens irreversible and dangerous impacts" according to its most recent report.[26]

Later U.N. specialized agencies

After the initial spate of U.N. specialized agencies were created or rebranded, ECOSOC settled into the work of managing and trying to harness these organizations to a common purpose. The first goal was to rebuild the human, agricultural, and physical infrastructure destroyed or damaged by the war as a way of beginning to address the "root causes" of war, but before long, the goal of promoting economic development became the driving force in the life of ECOSOC and the U.N. specialized agencies. This early Cold War period was not a propitious time for consensus about new international organizations. However, with the lessening of these tensions (at least temporarily), the changing nature of the global economy, and ECOSOC's experience with the enterprise of development, it became clear that there were areas that needed new U.N. agencies. I have already introduced you to the newest parts of the World Bank (MIGA) and the Food and Agriculture Organization (IFAD), both created during this period of new institution-building. Next, I will provide short introductions to the other organizations elevated to specialized-agency status during this later period—the United Nations World Tourism Organization (UNWTO) and the World Intellectual Property Organization (WIPO), while leaving discussion of the United Nations Industrial Development Organization (UNIDO) to Chapter 5's focus on economic development.

The UNWTO became a U.N. specialized agency in 1970 in order to promote and manage a growing and increasingly significant sector of the global economy that was having numerous impacts on a variety of economies. Its international history was more recent than most of the earlier U.N. specialized agencies, growing out of the short-lived International Union of Official Tourist Propaganda Organizations (est. 1934) and the postwar International Union of Official Travel Organisations (IUOTO, est. 1946). IUOTO began by establishing a headquarters (1947) and gathering statistics in order to know and disseminate information about the importance of this sector of the economy (through its Study Commission on International Travel Statistics, which began publication of its *Digest of Tourist Statistics* to establish and publicize national statistics on tourist arrivals and travel payments)—in a pattern very similar to other early international organizations. This work grew and expanded with the 1950 establishment of a permanent IUOTO Research Commission that gathered data from its new regional commissions in Europe (1948), Africa (1949), the Middle East (1951), Central Asia (1956), and the Americas (1957). In 1957, it elected its first secretary-general, and by 1963 it had developed enough clout through its statistical work to convene a U.N. Conference on Tourism and International Travel in Rome, which differentiated between the statistical definitions of "visitor" (who does not stay overnight in the country) and "tourist" (who does), simplified international travel regulations, and issued a general resolution on tourism development that called for greater technical cooperation, freedom of movement, and elimination of discrimination. Building on this momentum, IUOTO (along with the U.N. Conference on Trade and Development—UNCTAD) catalyzed the United Nations' declaration of 1967 as International Tourism Year, with the slogan "Tourism: Passport to Peace." The General Assembly elaborated on international tourism's role in "fostering better understanding among peoples everywhere, in leading to a greater awareness of the rich heritage of various civilizations and in bringing about a better appreciation of the inherent values of different cultures, thereby contributing to the strengthening of peace in the world," while UNCTAD highlighted the ways in which tourism "can and does make a vital contribution to the economic growth of developing countries." Appreciation of the many facets of tourism led the 1969 U.N. General Assembly to press for an independent, intergovernmental organization on tourism. The very next year, a special meeting of IUOTO adopted the Statutes of the World Tourism Organization on September 27, 1970 (after 1979, this day became known as World Tourism Day).[27]

Five years later, the first World Tourism Organization General Assembly took place in Madrid, electing its first secretary-general and establishing its headquarters in the host city. The work of this new secretariat was to promote a form of global tourism that met the economic, environmental, and cultural ideals of the international community. It was to promote "tourism as a driver of [inclusive] economic growth" that would also be environmentally sustainable and "universally accessible." To this end, it became an executing agency of the U.N. Development Programme for carrying out technical cooperation with governments in this field. In a series of World Tourism Conferences, the World Tourism Organization moved toward international tourism norm-setting with its Manila Declaration on World Tourism (1980) and its Acapulco Document (1982), which laid the groundwork for its 1985 Tourism Bill of Rights and Tourist Code. Seeking to publicize these principles, the organization worked with the Inter-Parliamentary Union to jointly organize the 1989 Inter-Parliamentary Conference on Tourism, which adopted the Hague Declaration on Tourism. The 1989 World Tourism Organization General Assembly meeting in Paris marked a watershed for the organization. While still doing the type of work on which it had established its reputation—approving the recommendations of the International Conference on Travel and Tourism Statistics and adopting "Recommended Measures for Security in Tourism"—it was also looking forward. It elected its first non-European secretary-general, Antonio Enríquez Savignac of Mexico, and adopted recommendations on how to create opportunities for potential tourists with handicaps. In the 1990s, the organization worked cooperatively with a number of groups to make its agenda more central to the overall work on the United Nations. It worked with UNESCO to develop culturally sensitive tourism in developing areas, evident in the 1994 joint Samarkand Declaration on Silk Road Tourism and the 1995 Accra Declaration that introduced its joint cultural program, "The Slave Route." In 1995, it partnered with the Earth Council to jointly produce "Agenda 21 for the Travel and Tourism Industry" as a follow-up to the Earth Summit in Rio. That same year, the World Tourism Organization's General Assembly also adopted its Declaration on the Prevention of Organized Sex Tourism. Pulling all of this work together was the Global Code of Ethics for Tourism (approved by the World Tourism Organization General Assembly in 1999 and the U.N. General Assembly in 2001) with the goal of maximizing tourism's role in achieving the U.N. Millennium Development Goals (MDGs) of reducing poverty and fostering sustainable development. The year 2002 was the International Year of Ecotourism, when it hosted the World Ecotourism Summit and a Forum for Parliaments and Local Authorities.[28]

Having demonstrated its ability to make itself central to the U.N. agenda, in 2003, the World Tourism Organization formally joined the U.N. system as UNWTO, the specialized agency for tourism. It focused on the pressing issues of the environment and climate change by hosting the first International Conference on Climate Change and Tourism (2003), unanimously adopting the "Sustainable Tourism—Eliminating Poverty" program in 2003 (followed by establishment of a foundation in Seoul in 2005 to undertake this work), and presenting the 2007 Davos Declaration, which constituted the tourism sector's response to the challenge of climate change. During the first decade of the new millennium, a variety of UNWTO meetings considered new ways in which international tourists determined and interacted with their destinations: the

First World Conference on Sport and Tourism conference leading up to the Barcelona Olympics (2001), the first meeting of the World Committee on Tourism Ethics (2004), the International Conference on Tourism and Handicrafts (2006), and the International Conference on Tourism, Religions and Dialogue of Cultures (2007). Less imaginative but equally necessary were its responses to the global economic crises in 2004 and 2008, especially its 2009 "Roadmap for Recovery." The year 2012 marked the first time in history that more than one billion international tourists traveled in a single year, and it was the first time that tourism was included as part of the United Nations' environmental agenda (presented by the RIO+20 outcome document of the U.N. Decadal Conference on Sustainable Development). The UNWTO's priorities for 2013 were a blend of its historical goals—to build public-private partnerships and to foster knowledge and education about and capacity within the tourism industry—and its work within the U.N. system—promoting sustainable tourism and advancing tourism's contribution to poverty reduction and development.[29] Interestingly, I could not find any clear intersection between the literature on the UNWTO and some of the new scholarly literature about the impacts of tourism, so this too could be a fruitful field for future researchers.[30]

Much like the UNWTO's straddling of the economic and cultural realms, the World Intellectual Property Organization (WIPO, est. 1967 and a U.N. specialized agency in 1974) sought to protect the economic rights of those who produced new inventions or creative works. It united the Paris Union for the Protection of Industrial Property (est. 1883 to safeguard patents, trademarks, and industrial designs) and the Berne Union for the Protection of Literary and Artistic Works (est. 1886 as a result of a campaign by French writer Victor Hugo to uphold international copyright) with a number of other smaller unions protecting intellectual property. WIPO's guiding principle is that by safeguarding the investments of those who innovate and create, the fruits of these ideas will drive human progress for the benefit of all. To this end, it works to harmonize patent law across national borders (e.g., establishing a uniform minimum term or duration for patents) and to combat counterfeiting of trademarked goods. It has also worked to make the protection of intellectual property a key aspect of the work of GATT (the General Agreement on Tariffs and Trade) and now the World Trade Organization (WTO). Its WIPO Arbitration and Mediation Center (est. 1994) also provides a cost-effective alternative for those whose trademarks are being violated. Demonstrating the way in which WIPO also advocates for consumers, WIPO members met at Marrakesh, Morocco, in 2013 and adopted a new international treaty to increase the proportion of books accessible to those with visual impairments (since currently less than 5 percent are available in Braille or digitized audio versions). A lot has been written about the WIPO in the contexts of economic development, law, and even indigenous rights; but most of it is recent, and little of it embraces a historical perspective. It seems a particularly ready target for an analysis that would combine the insights of the "new" history of capitalism and other histories of the international economic system.[31] And collectively, the work of the U.N. specialized agencies—each with its own, accessible archive—has the potential to fuel many a research project.

ECOSOC functional commissions

Below the level of specialized agency (which brings its own organizational constitution, general autonomy within the U.N. structure, and a separate budget), ECOSOC also carries out a significant portion of its work through its functional commissions, which are largely analogous to the committees that existed within the League of Nations Secretariat. To give the reader a sampling of the work of these functional commissions, I will provide an introduction to the work of the Commission for Social Development and the Commission on the Status of Women (CSW), both of which have evolved significantly since their 1946 creation, which have been the focus of important global megaconferences, and which have helped to define and redefine key issues at the intersections between economic development and human rights. A shorter section will then examine the work of the Commission on Narcotic Drugs and the Commission on Crime Prevention and Criminal Justice, which share many commonalities. The functional Commission on Population and Development is mentioned in the case study at the end of this chapter, and you will find information on the Commission on Science and Technology for Development, the Commission on Sustainable Development, and the U.N. Forum on Forests integrated into the next chapter's discussion of U.N. development efforts. At the end of this section, I will also discuss the Statistical Commission, which is rather unique among the functional commissions, insofar as most of its work is in a supporting role of providing expertise across ECOSOC.[32]

Commission for social development

At its founding in 1946, ECOSOC created a Social Commission to advise it and member states on those areas of social relations not under the purview of one of the U.N. specialized agencies. While that general mission has survived, the Commission and its work have evolved and changed significantly over the years in the face of numerous efforts to reform the organization and its large, unwieldy mandate. In 1966, the Social Commission was renamed the Commission for Social Development, and since the March 1995 World Summit for Social Development in Copenhagen, Denmark, it has been primarily responsible for overseeing implementation of the program of action developed there (which was reviewed at the Social Summit+5 in the year 2000). Its original membership of eighteen has expanded several times, most recently in 1996, when it reached forty-six members. The Commission meets annually (usually in February) to help determine ECOSOC's work for the coming year in the main fields (currently) of aging, civil society, cooperatives, disability, employment, family, indigenous peoples, poverty, social integration, social protection, and youth.[33]

The Copenhagen Declaration on Social Development, drafted in the aftermath of the debt crises and economic adjustment programs of the 1980s (Chapter 5), sought to put "the needs, rights and aspirations of people at the centre of our decisions and joint actions." It therefore focused on "the significance of social development and human well-being for all" and sought to give "these goals the highest priority both now and into the twenty-first century" in the work of the United Nations. The declaration gave pride of place to "democracy and transparent and accountable governance and administration in all sectors of society" as the "indispensable foundations for the realization of social and people-centered sustainable development," but it also acknowledged key roles for peace, human rights, environmental protection, and equality and equity between women and men. The attendees at the Copenhagen Summit were positively inspired by the fiftieth anniversary of the United Nations and the end of the Cold War to try to bring together the work done by the earlier conferences of that decade (the Rio Conference on Environment and Development in 1992, the World Conference on Human Rights in 1993, the Global Conference on the Sustainable Development of Small Island Developing States in 1994, and the International Conference on Population and Development in 1994). The signatories of the Copenhagen Declaration and Programme of Action committed themselves to (1) providing "a stable legal framework" that promoted human rights, eliminated all forms of discrimination, and created "an enabling economic environment," (2) eradicating global poverty, (3) promoting full employment, (4) promoting the social integration needed to create "stable, safe and just" societies centered on the protection of all human rights, (5) "achieving equality and equity between women and men," (6) providing education and access to primary health care for all, (7) accelerating development in Africa and the least developed countries, (8) including social development goals in all structural adjustment programs, (9) devoting more resources to social development, and (10) strengthening the multilateral framework for social development. It is not terribly surprising that the follow-up summit five years later was unable to note much progress.[34] With a slightly more focused program, the Commission on the Status of Women (CSW) has been able to attain some measure of progress during its existence.

Commission on the status of women

Although there were only four women who signed the U.N. Charter at the 1945 San Francisco Conference, they helped make sure that that Charter included women, discarding the sense that "man" had universal connotations. After committing themselves to saving "succeeding generations from the scourge of war," the second point in the Charter's preamble reaffirmed "faith in fundamental human rights, in the dignity and worth of the human person, in the equal rights of men and women." This equality between the sexes was not an immediate U.N. priority, but including the principle in the Charter provided a foundation for much of the subsequent work to improve women's lives that flowed through and from the United Nations. Half of those female signatories were from Latin America—Minerva Bernardino of the Dominican Republic and Bertha Lutz of Brazil—and were veterans of the interwar work done by the Inter-American Commission of Women (IACW, est. 1928), the first intergovernmental body devoted entirely to women's issues. Women's organizations had successfully lobbied the Pan-American Union (later renamed the Organization of American States) to create this pioneering body devoted to removing all barriers to women's full civil and political rights. Members of the IACW lobbied the League of Nations, organized the 1933 Montevideo Convention on the Nationality of Married Women, and drafted their own 1938 Lima Declaration in Favor of Women's Rights that sought to ensure women's full civil and political equality but also to protect mothers and women in the workplace. But the unequivocal assertion of equality between men and women in the U.N. Charter and in Article 1 was a step beyond anything that had preceded it, and it was the delegations from Brazil, Mexico, the Dominican Republic, and Chile who led the charge, backed by representatives from some forty-two nongovernmental organizations (NGOs) who were also attending the conference.[35]

Women's issues were also integrated into the work of the United Nations as a subcommission of ECOSOC in February 1946 to prepare reports and recommendations about women's movement toward political, social, economic, and educational equality. Bodil Begtrup of Denmark, who had fought in the resistance during the Second World War, chaired the subcommission and immediately set to advocating for ECOSOC to move toward making the words of the preamble a reality by extending the right to vote to the women of all member states (only thirty of the original fifty-one had already done so). Ironically, she also led the fight against Eleanor Roosevelt, who believed that women could work toward full equality most efficiently if they worked as part of ECOSOC's Commission on Human Rights that she chaired. Begtrup disagreed, arguing that a commission tasked with the important task of improving the status of half of the world's population should not be subsumed under another commission. She also thought the idea that women's issues could be most effectively addressed under the neutral rubric of human rights absurd. ECOSOC agreed and elevated its status to a commission, rather than simply a subcommission. But the fifteen-member Commission on the Status of Women (CSW) also worked to ensure within a year that there was also a Section on the Status of Women within the Human Rights Division, working to ensure that women's issues were integrated into the work of as many U.N. bodies as possible. To this end, the CSW invited representatives from the International Labour Organisation, the U.N. Educational, Scientific and Cultural Organization (UNESCO), UNICEF (the U.N. International Emergency Children's Fund), and the Commission on Human Rights' Subcommission on the Prevention of Discrimination and Protection of Minorities to sit in on its meetings and took advantage of the reciprocal invitation. CSW members also regularly attended meetings of the Commission on Human Rights as it drafted the Universal Declaration on Human Rights (discussed in more detail in Chapter 8) to ensure that its language, like the Charter, specifically included women. In these ways, CSW members sought to ensure both that women's issues were raised and integrated into the work of many U.N. bodies and that there was a specific place within the bureaucracy where women could formulate and advocate women-specific policies.[36]

In the late 1960s and 1970s, the seeds that the CSW had earlier planted began to bear fruit. The Commission drafted the 1967 Declaration on the Elimination of Discrimination Against Women that led to the Convention on the Elimination of All Forms of Discrimination Against Women, which was adopted by the U.N. General Assembly in December 1979 (both are discussed further in Chapter 8). During this same period, the International Labour Organization helped conceptualize ways to "see" and "count" the work of poor women around the world. These laid the foundation for the first World Conference on the Status of Women held in Mexico City in 1975, which the United Nations had designated as "International Women's Year." Women headed 85 percent of the delegations, and the parallel NGO forum—the International Women's Year Tribune—brought together some four thousand participants.[37] The discussions of the Tribune clearly showed differences between women's priorities based on existing North-South and East-West divisions; in broad brush strokes, Eastern bloc women emphasized women's roles in promoting peace, Western women emphasized gender equality, and women from the developing countries were primarily interested in economic development issues. Ultimately, the final documents from the conference recognized that "under-development imposed upon women a double burden of exploitation," but everyone at Mexico City recognized that further dialogue was needed, leading them to urge the General Assembly to designate 1976–85 as "the United Nations Decade for Women." The primary goal of the decade was to open a global dialogue on gender equality "that would involve deliberation, negotiation, setting objectives, identifying obstacles and reviewing the progress made." By the end of the Women's Decade, "127 Member States had responded by establishing some form of national machinery, institutions dealing with the promotion of policy, research and programmes aimed at women's advancement and participation in development," and the United Nations had established the International Research and Training Institute for the Advancement of Women (INSTRAW) and the United Nations Development Fund for Women (UNIFEM) "to provide the institutional framework for research, training and operational activities in the area of women and development."[38]

When 145 member states convened in Copenhagen in 1980 to assess progress since the Mexico City conference, they noted with approval the General Assembly's adoption of the Convention on the Elimination of All Forms of Discrimination Against Women in December 1979, but conference participants recognized a growing gap between rights that had been legally secured and women's ability to exercise these rights, which it attributed to a veritable laundry list of factors including "insufficient political will" and "overall lack of necessary financial resources." Copenhagen therefore focused the attention of the world specifically on securing women's "equal access to education, employment opportunities and adequate health care services." But in this contentious forum, women's advocates also called for "stronger national measures to ensure women's ownership and control of property," "improvements in women's rights to inheritance and child custody," and "an end to stereotyped attitudes toward women."[39]

When the world's women gathered for a third time in Nairobi, Kenya, in 1985 in both the 157 delegations to the formal world conference and 15,000 representatives at the parallel NGO forum, U.N. data showed that a decade of work had resulted in gains for "only a small minority of women," with "improvements in the situation of women in the developing world" being "marginal at best." This conference's recommendations (unlike Copenhagen) were adopted by consensus by the 157 participating delegations. At this point, the conference decided that progress would come only with the full integration of women's issues into all issues, making "women's participation in decision-making" a "social and political necessity that would have to be incorporated in all institutions of society." The document enjoined governments to promote equality in three basic categories: constitutional and legal rights; equality of social participation; and equality in political participation and decision-making. And it called on the United Nations "to establish, where they did not already exist, focal points on women's issues in all sectors of" its work. This focus on the need for women as equal partners in the decision-making process was evident in the conferences on development, the environment, human rights, population, and social development of the early 1990s.[40]

At the fourth World Conference on Women in Beijing, China, the focus was on gender and on an analytical approach to conducting a reevaluation of "the entire structure of society, and all relations between men and women within it" and then fully empowering women "to take their rightful place as equal partners with men in all aspects of life." This was seen as "a strong reaffirmation that women's rights were human rights and that gender equality was an issue of universal concern, benefitting all." This was the response to the finding in the conference's preparatory reports that more women lived in poverty than in the previous decade and that that poverty was more systematic. The conference "drew unprecedented international attention" and resulted in the Beijing Declaration and Platform for Action, which was unanimously adopted. The platform expanded upon earlier such documents in laying out twelve critical areas of concern that seemed to constitute the main obstacles to women's advancement.[41]

Although there was a special session of the U.N. General Assembly in 2000 to provide a five-year review of the Beijing Declaration and its platform for action, the CSW and other leaders of the global women's movement believed that little more could be accomplished through such conferences.[42] Instead, they continued their work on integrating and highlighting women's issues across the entire United Nations. We see an example of that in the work of the functional Commission on Crime Prevention and Criminal Justice, which has worked steadily on the crime of trafficking of women and children in order to provide greater punishments for the criminals responsible for such actions and greater services to the victims of trafficking.

The commissions on narcotic drugs and on crime prevention and criminal justice

The League of Nations had worked to track and suppress various aspects of the drug trade throughout its history, and ECOSOC picked up that work from the beginning with its Commission on Narcotic Drugs, which took up monitoring and reporting on nations' compliance with the previous treaties as well as updating them. Additionally, in the early 1960s, it began dispatching technical assistance to help both with enforcement but also with assisting Iranian poppy-growing farmers, for example, to transition to alternative, legal crops. One commentator found such a useful program to be a great "rebuttal to many of the ill-considered criticisms that have been hurled at the UN charging it with manifesting an unrealistic attitude in its efforts to alleviate adverse social conditions."

In 1988, the United Nations opened for signature the Convention against Illicit Traffic in Narcotic Drugs and Psychotropic Substances meant to encapsulate and update earlier conventions; to maximize efficiency in the complex web of law enforcement, it urged signatories also to conclude bilateral treaties to complement the overall convention.[43]

Over time, much of the work of international narcotics control bled over into the mandate of the Commission on Crime Prevention and Criminal Justice, which grew out of the earlier work of the International Penal Commission (est. 1872, and renamed the International Penal and Penitentiary Commission in 1929).[44] In 1955, ECOSOC absorbed its work of hosting an international conference every five years related to issues of criminal justice and of maintaining a secretariat in between that helped keep up with aspects of U.N. criminal policy (included in at least four thousand U.N. documents by 1985) and that gathered comparable international data every five years through its U.N. Survey of Crime Trends and Operations of Criminal Justice Systems. Over time, these conferences have evolved along with the field of criminology, moving from a more traditional and academic criminological approach in the 1950s to a more practical and policy-oriented approach that sees crime within a vast web of national and international social, cultural, political, and economic relationships. Part of this expansion has meant incorporating additional voices, not only from the other U.N. specialized agencies and INTERPOL (the intergovernmental organization coordinating national central police bureaux) but also from international experts, civil society NGOs, and regional organizations. The 1995 congress was hosted, for the first time, on the African continent in Kampala, Uganda, and included workshops on environmental law, the use of computers to create criminal justice systems, and mass media and crime prevention, among other topics.[45] By 1998, the Commission on Crime Prevention and Criminal Justice was working to draft a binding and comprehensive international convention against transnational organized crime (and its various practices, including trafficking in women and children, endangered species, firearms and ammunition, and migrants as well as money-laundering), as the next step following the 1994 Naples Political Declaration against Organized Transnational Crime and its call for closer alignment of national laws to address these challenges. Although that declaration purposefully linked such organized crime to terrorism, these linkages have generally not been able to sustain a comprehensive anti-money-laundering regime capable to undermining terrorism.[46]

Statistical commission

Established in 1946, the U.N. Statistical Commission is rather unique among the ECOSOC functional commissions, since it primarily provides the data and tools for analyzing those data that the United Nations and its member states use. As such, its statistics range from agriculture to international commodities and from international war crime tribunals to population figures—to name just a few. The Commission initially leaned heavily on the expertise of the U.S. Division of Statistical Standards, but it also had a long international history of statistical analysis on which to draw. Its initial goal was to work toward internationally comparable data, so the Commission advises on national statistical policies and programs with an eye to both helping each country derive the information it needs and to developing international statistical standards. For example, when it sought to conduct the first world population census in 1950, it realized that its goal exceeded the capacity of many Third World governments, so it developed a technical subcommission in order to develop a standardized sampling method that could be used in such cases. Although its job was "just" to figure out how to develop the statistics, such work had significant impacts across the United Nations. In this case, the 1950 world census warned of an impending "population explosion" and triggered the convening of one of the first U.N. conferences, the World Population Conference that ran from August 31, until September 10, 1954. Additionally, over time the Non-Aligned Movement and women (among others) began asking different questions of traditional statistics, which, for example, tended to mask women's contributions to the economy throughout the Third World.[47]

ECOSOC's regional economic commissions

ECOSOC, worried about the economic and physical devastation of the Second World War, quickly established the Economic Commission for Europe (ECE) and the Economic Commission for Asia and the Far East (ECAFE) in the summer of 1946. Although they had not experienced the same level of wartime destruction, both the Middle East and Latin America subsequently argued that they needed similar commissions in order to help their regional economies recalibrate after the war and to promote economic development in the area. Although the Middle East commission did not immediately come to fruition following the establishment of the state of Israel, the Economic Commission for Latin America (ECLA) was established in 1948. Then a decade later, the Economic Commission for Africa (ECA) aided the newly independent countries on that continent, and in 1973, the Economic Commission for Western Asia finally brought together the Arab countries of the Middle East. Collectively, these commissions have established a regional identity for the United Nations as well as doing the concrete work of developing comparable economic data and drafting consensual regional economic plans.[48]

The ECE was headquartered in Geneva, Switzerland, and played an intriguing role in the life of Europe, helping to preserve that central and unified idea even during the Cold War. Initially established to aid with European reconstruction, the ECE continued to meet and work throughout the Cold War period as the only intergovernmental European organization linking the two sides of the iron curtain, a feat facilitated by the fact that it ruled only by consensus. Led initially by Swedish economist Gunnar Myrdal, the ECE quickly developed a reputation for technical expertise and for its ability to broker effective working relationships between Western and Eastern European countries. Early on, it took over the work of the European Central Inland Transport Organization, conducted comprehensive economic research, standardized economic statistical procedures, arranged a $120 million exchange of Eastern European timber for

Western European machinery through the World Bank, restored inland waterways, and standardized traffic signs and signals, among other things.[49]

The ECAFE—headquartered in Bangkok, Thailand, and headed by Indian economist P. S. Lokanathan—had a much slower start and a more difficult time in seeking to integrate the economies of its vast region, which stretch south from the Soviet Union to Australia and east from Pakistan to the Philippines. Unlike the ECE, ECAFE lacked an earlier history of economic cooperation and a coherent regional identity, so it began modestly by hosting a series of regional meetings throughout 1947 and 1948. Membership issues dominated the agenda of the first meeting. India wanted the colonial areas (which were to be associate members) to be able to vote in order to give Asiatic countries a majority on ECAFE, but the majority opposed this. The economic commission was also asked to choose between the membership applications of the Dutch and the Indonesian Republic, but it simply procrastinated until the military conflict in that area was settled (see Chapter 3). ECAFE's early work included drafting plans for economic development in the area, improving the quality of the area's statistical and economic documentation, and establishing its Bureau of Flood Control. Later initiatives similarly focused on both developing greater economic development capacity (through the Asian Development Bank and the Asian Institute for Economic Development and Planning) and on some concrete improvement projects (such as the Asian Highway), and in 1974, it changed its name to the Economic and Social Commission for Asia and the Pacific (ESCAP), a reflection, in part, of the broadening definition of economic development during that period.[50]

Although its economic situation and needs were different from the first two regions, Chile began to push for a U.N. economic commission in July 1947 to further Latin America's postwar economic adjustment and to lay the foundation for further growth. The ECLA (est. 1948), headquartered in Santiago, Chile, began its work under the leadership of Mexican economist G. M. Cabanas. ECLA developed into a particularly strong and cohesive regional institution under the charismatic intellectual leadership of long-time executive secretary, Dr. Raúl Prebisch of Argentina. He diagnosed the economic difficulties of Latin America (and indeed the entire "developing world") as being rooted in the steady deterioration of its terms of trade with the First and Second Worlds. In other words, the Third World's exports of primary goods (agricultural commodities and raw materials) and import of manufactured goods from the First World caught it in a vicious cycle of debt and economic dependence. To combat the situation, ECLA promoted a doctrine of regionally balanced economic growth meant to ensure more equitable trade and development, and this work yielded some tangible results, due in part to the fact that there was a significant exchange of economists between ECLA and governmental finance ministries throughout the 1950s and early 1960s. Prebisch later sought to expand these ideas globally as the first executive director of the U.N. Conference on Trade and Development (UNCTAD, discussed in the next chapter).[51]

The Economic Commission for Africa (ECA) was established in Addis Ababa, Ethiopia, in 1958 with the same goals as the earlier commissions of gathering and standardizing regional data to lay the groundwork for economic and social development and regional cooperation. However, in the case of Africa, ECA was not drawing on well-established national infrastructures, since most of the governments on the continent were new; this also meant that ECA's work was especially needed to form the basis for technical assistance requests. Specific institutions arising from ECA's work include the African Development Bank and the African Institute for Economic Development and Planning as well as five regional offices, but one early member of the secretariat touched on a more ephemeral, but important, point of its work: "The Economic Commission for Africa is in a real sense the United Nations in Africa. It is Africa's own Commission and common tool for unity." To develop a more concrete sense of unity, ECA began working with the U.N. specialized agencies to develop an integrated African telecommunications union, to nationalize African air transport, and to promote a trans-Saharan road system.[52]

The success of the regional commissions led the United Nations to make them centers for the regional planning of economic development that was jump-started by the designation of the 1960s as the Development Decade (see next chapter for more on this). This "vote of confidence" was based on the work that the commissions had already done in promoting trade cooperation, integrating markets, training development personnel, and facilitating the transfer of technology. Indeed, some of these regional activities laid the groundwork for adoption of similar projects on a larger scale by the United Nations as a whole. The work of these regional economic commissions will be a focus of the next chapter's discussion of economic development, which became a primary focus of the United Nations' work by the 1960s, but first, I would like to provide you with a different case study that will show you the ways in which the many different actors within the ECOSOC borderland interacted around the issue of global population in the 1960s and 1970s, showing its strengths and its weaknesses in mobilizing global public opinion and action.[53]

A case study of ECOSOC coordination and management: Population

To begin to understand how all of these diverse organizations under the umbrella of ECOSOC work together, we will now turn to the issue of global population. This was something that the United Nations began studying through its Population Commission in 1946. Like most international efforts, it began with a relatively straightforward search for accurate and comparable data through its regional population bureaux and by hosting a World Population Conference in Rome in 1954 for academicians "to exchange scientific information on population variables, their determinants and their consequences." However, the "population problem" burst onto the global and U.N. stage in the 1960s. That decade's emphasis on economic development had led to some concerns that the rate of economic development would be eclipsed by the rate of population growth so that, much like a person running up an escalator going down, more and more would be invested by the international community to achieve less and less in terms of measurable growth, especially in gross domestic product.[54]

This pairing of concerns also emerged from the effort in the 1950s to promote malaria eradication through the World Health Organization (WHO) as a means of promoting economic development (by increasing worker productivity and allowing cultivation of lands previously uninhabitable due to the high incidence of the disease). When that eradication campaign began facing difficulties and when population figures started to increase as fewer (especially babies) were dying from malaria, international development planners largely abandoned malaria eradication and turned to the new, inexpensive, artificial birth-control methods that were increasingly available. The United Nations' second World Population Conference in Belgrade in 1965—called by ECOSOC's Population Commission—gave full voice to the fear that population growth was threatening development. Specifically, this led to the creation of a Commission on Population and Development within the Population Commission. Additionally, old Malthusian arguments about food supply not being able to keep up with population growth and resulting in famine combined with new ecological and environmental concerns about the planet's "carrying capacity"—how many people the planet could support. Adding to this volatile mix were eugenic arguments that the "wrong type" of people were reproducing too often, new birth-control technologies, the Vatican's announcement that it was studying the issue of birth control's morality, and significant monies for population control efforts from the Rockefeller Foundation.[55]

If we go back to our image of ECOSOC as a borderland, these ideas about population arrived and originally settled on the periphery of town, but eventually (bolstered by external resources) they made a power play to take control of much of the agenda and discourse of the organization—to become sheriff, if you will, of this volatile borderland. In other words, a set of international players came together and sought to refocus the previous discourse of development around the issue of population control—that is, you could not have economic development without intensive and immediate efforts at population control. And this coalition developed new institutions, such as the U.N. Fund for Population Activities (est. 1969, now the U.N. Population Fund) to promote the new agenda. In some ways, the population discourse also sought to reconfigure the emerging language of "rights"—a country's right to economic development and the reciprocal responsibility of richer countries to provide development aid and resources through the United Nations—to one of "responsibilities," in which the country seeking economic development first had a responsibility to control its population growth before it was deemed "worthy" of aid. And the question of women's rights cut both ways during this early period of the population debate. While some women embraced the empowerment that came with the possibility of consciously spacing one's children, other women—especially in the Third World—found themselves the victims of coercive state measures and blamed for the failures of their countries' development enterprises.[56]

This effort to reassert traditional global power and gender relationships was nowhere more naked in its intentions than the policy of U.S. President Lyndon B. Johnson (LBJ) toward the new Indian Prime Minister Indira Gandhi. While founding father Jawaharlal Nehru had enunciated a policy of nonalignment and an independent path toward development that relied on Soviet-style five-year plans and mass infusions of Western aid, Gandhi found herself in a position in which her country faced potential famine (with the failure of monsoon rains in several areas), while LBJ followed a "short tether" policy of releasing grain shipments only as he saw what he judged to be "progress" by India in committing to population control if not an entire set of pro-Western policies (including making peace with Pakistan, ending its independent nuclear program, and ceasing its anti-Western rhetoric in international fora such as the United Nations).[57]

Despite this shoot-out at high noon, the efforts of the new sheriff to focus all of the border area's monies, energies, and discourse on "population" failed pretty spectacularly. The war against women and the poor that emerged in India under the guise of population control, the implicit racism of the eugenicists, and the slap-dash approach to mass insertions of intrauterine devices (IUDs) at camps by mobile teams that ignored a lack of medical infrastructure and traditional doctor-patient relationships succeeded in mobilizing a coalition of stakeholders in the U.N. borderland to stand up to the new, bullying sheriff. Additionally, scientists and social scientists soon found that the numbers undergirding the population control movement just did not add up. Rates of population growth, which had already started to decline in a number of areas by the early 1960s, seemed to resist efforts at population control and responded instead to rates of female literacy specifically and economic development in general. This laid the groundwork for new fights to control the discourse of development, as women laid claim to being the key to development and vied with the environmentalists over what "sustainable" development might look like.[58]

I would like to focus your attention on two historians who have written excellent, new international histories of different aspects of this fight over issues of population that emerged in the 1960s—Matthew Connelly's *Fatal Misconception: The Struggle to Control World Population* and Thomas Robertson's *Malthusian Moment: Global Population Growth and the Birth of American Environmentalism*. Connelly's multinational and multiarchival history weaves together the various histories of the key actors in the population debate, including many U.N. organizations, a variety of national governments, the Vatican specifically and the Catholic Church generally, NGOs (most notably Planned Parenthood and the Rockefeller Foundation), a cast of international population "experts," and collectively the many people impacted (usually negatively) by this rush to control population (especially in India and China). He points out how concerns over "quality of life" led a host of international actors to seek to control the "quantity of life" that presumably threatened this qualitative aspect, which was expressed in terms of economic development on a national level as well as personal prosperity on the individual level. But curious alliances emerged to resist these arguments, including the Catholic Church (which instructed the faithful against using the new, "artificial" forms of birth control) and some national leaders who saw these new arguments as eugenic efforts to control people of color and therefore argued against "race suicide." Ultimately Connelly's book does reveal that this population control effort—despite its public rhetoric of eradicating poverty and saving the planet—was primarily an effort to plan the families of other people and therefore exhibited some of the worst aspects of neocolonialism and neo-Malthusianism.[59]

Robertson's *Malthusian Moment* looks at roughly the same time period and topic but from a very different perspective. He examines the ways in which the international milieu of population growth, especially in India and the Third World generally, shaped American fears and concerns and therefore influenced both domestic policy and U.S. foreign policy. As a result, the president and federal government are key actors, but even more so are the books (most famously Paul Ehrlich's *Population Bomb*) that cultivated the atmosphere of fear that fed into a broad and urgent demand that something be done (very similar to Connelly's argument). Robertson points out the diffuse ways in which this urgency expressed itself—from the invention of Earth Day and calls for more wilderness preservation to the governmental effort to provide greater access to birth control, especially among minority and poor populations. And again paralleling Connelly's argument, these actions led to push-back from the targets of this action, especially in the growing feminist movement and the continuing Civil Rights Movement (including among the Black Panthers). Perhaps most interestingly, Robertson also points out how conservatives, led by U.S. President Ronald Reagan, also pushed back—arguing that the science on population was wrong and sought to cripple the U.S. greatness—and created a political legacy that continues to plague international environmental politics in the United States.[60]

The United Nations also played a key role in wrapping up the population "crisis." Its 1994 Cairo Conference on Population and Development centered and publicized the ways in which promoting the rights of women and girls were far more crucial than birth control to promoting meaningful economic and human development. The confluence at Cairo of the work of the Commission on the Status of Women (CSW), the Commission on Human Rights, and a broad range of NGOs "placed individual dignity and human rights, including the right to plan one's family—at the very heart of development." The resulting program of action reprioritized human beings over numerical targets.[61]

Both Connelly and Robertson look at the intriguing and challenging intersection between global, national, and local actions and actors, but they also bring individuals, their most intimate personal relationships, and their sexual activities into this nexus. Historian Laura Belmonte, in a later book in this same series, will similarly analyze the ways in which the AIDS/HIV epidemic that started in the 1980s quickly catalyzed local, national, and international social movements for debates and conversations in the United Nations and other venues that complicated traditional narratives about public health and human rights and that continue to redefine the relationships between the personal, the political, and the international.[62] The next chapter, on the development enterprise, will similarly seek to bring together the diverse cast of national, international, and local actors as they defined, redefined, and contested what it might mean to live in a modern and developed world.

CHAPTER 5
THE DEVELOPMENT ENTERPRISE

In this chapter, I have done what historians do—I have looked at the relatively long and messy history of what the United Nations has done to promote development in the period following the Second World War and have tried to divide it into discernible periods, each with a dominant philosophy. It is important for you to understand that a different periodization is certainly possible and that within each period there were contending narratives and different intellectual currents bubbling up. But my goal in this chapter is to provide an understandable and accessible entry point for you to begin to develop your own understanding and interpretation of U.N. efforts to promote economic development.

As postwar relief work wound down and the Cold War heated up, the United Nations rather quickly focused on the promotion of "development." U.S. President Harry S. Truman's commitment to funneling some American development aid through the United Nations, which he enunciated most famously as "Point IV" of his 1949 inaugural address, created the U.N. Expanded Program for Technical Assistance (EPTA) that supplemented the budgets of the specialized agencies and focused their work on development efforts. But the transition to development was nowhere as dramatic as in the International Bank for Reconstruction and Development (more commonly, the World Bank). With its reconstruction role largely usurped by the United States' Marshall Plan, the Bank, under the leadership of President Eugene R. Black (who served in this role from 1949 until 1963), shifted to the work of identifying economic infrastructure projects in the developing world (primarily India and secondarily Latin America at this time) that could meet the high lending standards of the Bank, that would materially contribute to these countries' economic development, and that would help make the recipient governments better able to borrow in open financial markets in the future. Given this liberal internationalist model of development, the Bank was therefore very much part of the early Cold War with its promotion of a gradual, capitalist model of economic development battling the revolutionary, communist model (a process facilitated by the fact that the Soviet Union and its Eastern European satellites had chosen not to join the World Bank after their initial participation in the Bretton Woods Conference). New states emerging from colonial rule generally preferred multilateral aid through the United Nations and its specialized agencies to bilateral aid from a single country, which seemed to come with more "strings" attached (such as demands for strategic raw materials in exchange) and seemed to threaten their jealously guarded sovereignty (by tying their economies to specific, bilateral economic relations that resembled the colonial period). But this Bank-led, investment loan-focused, and technical aid-driven model could not retain its dominance as decolonization brought a major influx of new "Third World" countries into the United Nations, as dependency theory and the Non-Aligned Movement provided a theoretical counterpoint to the prevailing economic development model and as the Cold War between the Soviet Union and the United States shifted in the 1950s to a fight for the loyalty of the Third World.

At the end of 1961, the 1960s belatedly became the United Nations' "Decade of Development." The decade was certainly one that witnessed significant challenges and conflicts around the globe. The same can be said of the United Nations, which saw its General Assembly majority shift to the developing countries, who in turn became increasingly critical of previous economic development efforts and sought new avenues for growth and development. Pressure from the Non-Aligned Movement resulted in the establishment of the International Development Association (IDA, est. 1960 within the World Bank to provide low-interest economic development loans and grants), the U.N. Conference on Trade and Development (UNCTAD, est. 1964 with the goal of renegotiating international terms of trade to the benefit of the Third World), and the United Nations Development Program (UNDP, est. 1965 to expand and coordinate U.N. development funding in aid-recipient countries).

When it became clear that one decade was not sufficient for this global effort of promoting development, the United Nations tried again, designating the 1970s as another "Decade of Development." The Non-Aligned Movement renewed its efforts to reorganize development efforts and global trade patterns to address historical inequalities through its proposed New International Economic Order (NIEO), which was the focus of special sessions of the U.N. General Assembly. More new U.N. agencies also originated with the decade, most prominently the International Fund for Agricultural Development (IFAD, est. 1974 within the Food and Agriculture Organization [FAO]) and the United Nations Industrial Development Organization (UNIDO, est. 1975). Alongside these new institutions for agricultural and industrial development was also a growing emphasis on the role of women and the environment in the development process.

The 1980s was simply a disastrous decade for Third World development by almost any measure. "Structural adjustment" programs by the World Bank and the International Monetary Fund (IMF) in response to crushing Third World debt (accrued primarily through the development efforts of the previous decades) and the subsequent danger of default led to social crises in much of the developing world, as governments were forced to slash government programs, especially for public services. The international community reacted with a renewed emphasis on the social, noneconomic, human dimensions of development with new foci on poverty alleviation, and the environment. Significant changes to the dominant models of economic development came with the United Nations' focus throughout the 1990s on improving the status of women worldwide as a prerequisite for economic and social development and on the need to create new, environmentally sustainable models of development moving forward. All of this helped to lay the groundwork for the Millennium Development Goals in 2000, which drew on the collective, decades-long experience of the United Nations with the development enterprise.

Introduction to development

The origins of the United Nations' efforts in promoting development came primarily from the League of Nations. The League engaged in two key activities that later came to be associated with modern development efforts—first, it sent technical missions to several countries (at their request) to assist with the development of public health or financial services, and second, under the League of Nations' Mandates Commission, it gathered and charted statistics on the health and nutrition of "native populations" and compared those to the ideal nutritional standards that it had helped to develop and publicize. This work in health, nutrition, and economics was at the core of the 1939 Bruce Report, which saw the future of the League as expanding and coordinating this work—something that ultimately had to wait until the end of the Second World War and the creation of the U.N. Economic and Social Council (ECOSOC, the focus of Chapter 4). The financial support for this League work came from private foundations in the United States, such as the Rockefeller Foundation (which had worked with the League of Nations Health Organization to promote medical education in China and with the Pan American Sanitary Bureau to reduce rates of yellow fever throughout Latin America). But the ideas of both the Rockefeller Foundation and the League of Nations about how best to "help" or "assist" these countries were informed by a longer history of European colonial administration as well as by American notions about how best to manage the problems it saw emerging in the postwar world.[1]

Models of economic development (more commonly called imperialism) had already been under discussion and had been practiced for centuries in Europe. Historian Joseph Hodge's recent book does an excellent job of surveying the new historiography on the intersections between early ideas of development and these colonial administrations before launching into his own analysis of the significance of British Colonial Office efforts, primarily in sub-Saharan Africa, from the turn of the century until the 1960s. He sees the ideas of development that are the focus of this chapter emerging from "efforts to manage the social, economic, and ecological crises of the late colonial world" that were particularly exacerbated by the Great Depression (which crushed agricultural commodity markets and colonial wages and set off widespread social disturbances) and by the postwar needs of the colonial powers that triggered a wholesale reorientation of the colonial mission to focus on a variety of state interventions meant to produce additional resources. But this was certainly not an uncontested imposition; Hodge also points to the literature documenting the ways that people under colonialism shaped, resisted, and influenced these debates and practices as well.[2] To address the colonial powers' needs and to try to contain unrest from the subjugated populations, European colonial administrations in the period from the turn of the century through 1960 greatly increased the number and authority of specialist advisers, scientific researchers, and technical experts, who organized themselves regionally and professionally and then rather seamlessly seem to have integrated themselves into the new United Nations and other development bureaucracies (such as the World Bank, UNESCO, FAO, the Commonwealth Development Corporation, and the British Overseas Development

Administration) to continue the work that they had begun under the guidance of the British empire.[3] Not surprisingly, the rise of this new scientific corps caused tensions within colonial administrations that struggled between an older generation who valued local knowledge and a younger generation who seemed to privilege scientific knowledge. Collectively, these colonial administrators strove to cushion the socially disruptive realities of colonial territories' entry into a global capitalist economy more than seeking to "modernize" colonial lands and peoples. In fact, Hodge argues that colonial development efforts were spurred more by "the specter of colonial and third world poverty and population growth, which . . . might lead to increasing conflict over global resources," than any "optimism regarding modernity as the destiny of mankind."[4]

And this leads us directly to historian Nick Cullather's definition of development as "the species of politics that speaks to humanity's greatest ambitions for progress and welfare and to its greatest fears of social collapse," which the postwar United States developed into a "new style of diplomacy" that revolved around food and that was meant to address the dangers of communist expansion, nationalist revolution, and rising expectations that it faced in Asia. In its focus on food, the United States was drawing on its own historical experience and expertise, which was institutionalized in its land-grant college and extension system as well as the U.S. Department of Agriculture and its efforts during the Great Depression/New Deal in the form of the Agricultural Adjustment Administration. For American policymakers, this food focus seemed a significant and appropriate contrast to the Soviet Union's model of industrial development, and it fit with the British imperial system's focus on agrarian and rural development.[5] Hodge argues that the legacy of the British model was "the depoliticization of poverty and power achieved by recasting social and economic problems as technical ones that could be fixed by rational planning and expert knowledge." So when U.S. ideas about development came together with European models and Third World aspirations in the borderland of the United Nations (as well as outside of it), development manifested itself as an aspirational and idealistic rhetoric, as a dizzying "interchange of figures" managed by technocrats in a presumably apolitical manner, and as a way of managing the careening road toward a capitalist globalization for both the new nations and those trying to shape international relations.[6] But I would add to Nick Cullather's characterization that the new wrinkle in the United Nations was that the discourse on development was also an effort to define the respective rights and responsibilities of the "developed" and the "developing" nations. In the chronological narrative that follows, I will try to trace the ways in which these four aspects of international development efforts changed over time.

Before we get too far along the path of describing the history of development, we should define some of our terms. As we have seen earlier, development has a relatively long and diffuse history, but Truman's inaugural address popularized the term. However, commentators have since noted how that same address immediately established a dichotomous hierarchy in which some countries were "developed" (with the accompanying adjectives of "modern" and "advanced") while others were "underdeveloped" or "undeveloped." Over time the language shifted to "developing countries," and more recently these countries have variously called themselves the Third

World, the Non-Aligned Movement, the G-77, and the global South.[7] I will generally use the historical terms that these countries called themselves and that the U.N. literature used most often during the specific time period, both for word variety and because these historical terms are useful to have in mind as you are conducting keyword research.

The meaning and measurement of "development" have changed over time just as what the "developing world" has called itself has changed. Starting in the immediate postwar period, the term "development" was synonymous with economic development, which was primarily gauged by macroeconomic measures such as gross domestic product (GDP) and/or production numbers (such as gross agricultural or industrial output). This definition of development established a responsibility of the United Nations and the developed countries to provide the technical assistance and infrastructural lending needed to help developing nations establish the preconditions for development, which included both national planning for development as well as creating an open, capitalist economy that welcomed investment. The first major critique of this system came from the United Nations' Economic Commission for Latin America (ECLA) in the late 1950s and early 1960s, which focused on a different macroeconomic indicator—trade balances (the number and value of exports vs. imports)—to best explain why the countries of Latin America (and other nations that were on the periphery of the world economy and that focused on primary commodity production) had been unable to break out a cycle of economic dependency on the First World and poverty for the majority at home. Such a reckoning put more responsibility on the developed world to change some of the global economic imbalances that had been favoring them, and new U.N. bodies were charged with carrying out this mandate, including UNCTAD and the International Development Association. In the 1960s and early 1970s, women effectively argued that traditional economic statistics literally counted them out—that women's work in the informal sectors of the economy (such as child care, domestic service, and household production) were not included in development experts' calculations on how to promote economic growth. The International Labour Organization (ILO) did important work in ferreting out ways to count women back in, and the Second U.N. Development Decade in many ways focused on how to build women into development programs, which required significant changes in the developing country to remove impediments to women's access to the nation's political, social, economic, and educational life. Recognizing that national development required the active participation of women helped the U.N. system in the 1970s to widen its focus generally to other people and factors that had also been overlooked in the earlier macroeconomic measures. Policy shifted as a result. For example, we see a change in the World Bank's loans from primarily infrastructural funding to a focus on poverty alleviation measures such as disease eradication, agriculture, education, and population planning under the leadership of World Bank President Robert McNamara and his Policy Planning Department director, Mahbub ul Haq (former chief economist of Pakistan's National Planning Commission). At the same time, within the U.N. General Assembly, the G-77 (or group of 77 developing countries) pressed—in UNCTAD and a series of special Assembly sessions—for the development of a New International Economic Order (NIEO) that was meant clearly to shift the responsibility to the developed countries to promote the economic independence of the new states, just as it had worked in the previous decade to ensure a new international political order through the independence of the non-self-governing territories that was discussed in Chapter 3. Additionally, the 1972 Stockholm Conference introduced "the environment" as a key focus of development thinking and further tasked the First World with assisting the Third World to develop in such a way that poverty was alleviated and the environment was protected.

Significant changes in the international economy and the ascendancy of aggressively conservative leadership in both Britain and the United States in the 1980s sought to effectively reengineer the international development discourse. Responsibility for development was placed squarely on the shoulders of Third World leaders, and the same economic schema employed in the developed world—wholesale privatization of state enterprises and deep cuts to social service programs meant to significantly decrease federal budgets—were applied to the developing world under the rubric of the "structural adjustment" programs of the World Bank and the IMF. Justified as a response to the "debt crisis" of the 1980s that saw a number of countries on the verge of defaulting on the development loans they had accrued since the 1940s, structural adjustment also catalyzed a fundamental rethinking about what development was and how to measure it, which was summarized in the new Human Development Report series of the U.N. Development Programme (UNDP) that ul Haq innovated in 1990. His goal was to establish people as both the agents of change and the beneficiaries of development, so the measurements that went into his Human Development Index included not only individual income but also indicators of a country's political, environmental, social, educational, and physical health, including how it treated women, minorities, and the environment. In many ways, this expansive equation of human development sought to share the responsibility between the aid-disbursing and the aid-recipient countries by measuring recipient countries' work toward developing the type of society (progressive, egalitarian, transparent, and productive) that disbursing countries said they wanted to see and also by pointing to their needs for further assistance. This formulation was expanded in the Millennium Development Goals (MDGs), but these have fallen short in almost every category by the time of this writing.[8] In other words, in the shifting definition of development we see change over time—the history—of what rhetoric was used to justify the disruptive interventions of development (both its goals and who was primarily responsible for its realization) as the global economy accelerated toward globalization, which was also reflected in the figures or statistics that were gathered to measure progress toward development.

I have entitled this chapter "The Development Enterprise" in an effort to capture the complexity of the efforts that have been lumped together under the name of "development." National governments developed plans for economic development that encompassed agriculture and industry as well as the related area of human resources—that is, ensuring that the people were prepared for work in both sectors through minimum levels of health, education, and nutrition. These national development plans were then underwritten (or not) by funds (loans or grants) and personnel (both technical experts and overseas volunteers) who might come from some organization within the United Nations or from another national government or coalition of governments (such as the Organisation for Economic Co-operation and Development [OECD] or the British Commonwealth's Colombo Plan).[9] Development aid also came from nongovernmental organizations (NGOs) that ranged in size and scope from private foundations like the Rockefeller Foundation disbursing millions of dollars and a cohort of experts to a group of students engaged in a study-abroad project under the supervision of a university. The implementation of these plans "on the ground" in a specific country then involved not only the task of monitoring and coordinating aid in its many forms from a variety of sources (which is sometimes coordinated by the UNDP's resident representative in each country) but also understanding the political and social dynamics within the communities receiving such aid and their receptivity to it (this last part is the segment of the development enterprise that is least studied in the current literature). In this very simple outline of the key elements of a development program, I hope that you begin to see the layers and complexity within the development process that will be discussed further within this chapter.

There is a very large scholarly literature on "development" that emanates from economists, political scientists, sociologists, other social scientists, and historians in addition to a huge number of U.N. reports, studies, and histories as well as other primary sources by practitioners (both governmental and from private foundations and other NGOs) and contemporary commentators. Many of these works tend to either criticize the development enterprise or to at least implicitly support it and/or its intellectual presuppositions. Another work has similarly divided the historiography into those "optimistic [critics] who think that international organizations should do far more in fostering global development, and the pessimistic ones who have become disillusioned by their inability to deliver on this mission."[10]

In many ways, the argument comes down to one about modernity—it is good or not? Is it sustainable or not? Again, as I have done throughout this book, I will urge the reader and the would-be researcher to avoid such moralistic dichotomies and instead see the United Nations as the borderland where all of these arguments—about the global economy, about the planetary environment, about human beings and their rights, about international equity and fairness, about the shape of the world as it is and as we might hope it to be—play out. It is a place where pretty much all are represented—governments from East and West and North and South as well as NGOs in the thousands seeking to give voice to any number of concerns and/or subpopulations. These are ongoing debates, which often seem to tempt scholars to weigh in with their opinions, their plans for reform, and/or their visions for the future. This can be an uncomfortable place for many historians, who would prefer to study something that is over and done, events in which all the participants are long dead. But this author, who specializes in contemporary history, would urge you not to shy away from this area of study. Much more solid historical scholarship is needed on the ideas and actions of this period to show how these ideas have changed over time, what drove particular programs at particular times, and perhaps most importantly, what the consequences of these actions and programs have been.[11]

This will allow us to understand more clearly how these currents of thought and action have shaped the entire postwar world and also give scholars a place in the conversation about how we human beings have gotten to this point in our history so that we might make clearer decisions in the future about where we would like to go from here.

The eras and philosophies of development

The postwar era of technical assistance

As the immediate need for postwar relief faded and the U.N. system got its feet under it, development immediately rose to the top of the organization's agenda. Newly independent countries—especially India—and those in Latin America identified economic development as a key area of interest, and U.S. President Harry S. Truman announced in 1949 his plan to funnel millions of dollars of American aid through the United Nations into what came to be called the Expanded Program of Technical Assistance (EPTA). This Point IV program (because it was the fourth point in his inaugural address) laid the groundwork for the U.S. foreign aid program that has persisted to this day and for the later U.N. Development Programme (UNDP). Significantly, it posited a responsibility by wealthy countries like the United States to aid in the development of poorer countries by providing such aid. Given these origins, the World Bank, EPTA (which funneled funds to the various specialized agencies), and Western experts largely defined the terms of the development enterprise in this first period. This was also the early period of the Cold War—the competition between the United States and the Soviet Union—that played out in places like Greece, Turkey, and Korea, but there was little actual competition with the Soviet Union over development efforts in this immediate postwar period, allowing the United States to promote its model of capitalist economic development (as opposed to the communist development model that had brought an agrarian Russia to superpower status by the end of the Second World War and that was eagerly embraced by Mao Zedong's victorious Chinese communist forces). But there was also a clear undercurrent during this period, which became the dominant paradigm of the next, that was clearly expressed by Indian Prime Minister Jawaharlal Nehru's call for a movement among the newly independent countries that eschewed alignment with either superpower and that attracted other leaders of newly independent nations such as Indonesia's Sukarno and Ghana's Kwame Nkrumah. Similarly Egyptian leader Gamal Abdel al-Nasser's seizure of the Suez Canal and subsequent acceptance of Soviet aid to build the Aswan High Dam (the keystone of his economic development program) signaled a willingness of this new Non-Aligned Movement to welcome communist funds and expertise to balance, if not replace, Western and U.N. aid.

The emergence of technical assistance and aid monies for economic development was also a recognition on the part of the West that a larger restructuring of the global economy through the proposed International Trade Organization (ITO) would not happen. While the United States, the United Kingdom, France, Canada, and the Benelux countries had developed a consensus (with which the Indian delegate disagreed) that they wrote into the draft charter for the proposed organization, the thirty-three delegations attending the U.N. Conference on Trade and Employment at Havana in 1947 insisted on also including commodity agreements (since the bulk of their export trade at that time was in commodities such as sugar and coffee). These countries also wanted to discuss issues such as balance-of-payments disequilibria, access to technology, and restrictive business practices that had significant impacts on their economies. The clear divide that emerged at Havana was that the developed countries were seeking primarily to address what they had identified as the key trade issues that had contributed to the outbreak of the Second World War and that would contribute to reconstruction after the war, while the other countries present identified the issues that they had faced and would continue to face as they sought to elevate the quality of life of their citizens in the wake of the war. The inclusion of commodity arrangements and early formulations of development were factors that resulted in the ITO's fall from favor among the Western governments that had drafted the much more narrow preparatory draft. As a fallback, they utilized the General Agreement on Tariffs and Trade (GATT, which was the 1947 compilation of the trade chapter of the ITO charter and the result of more than one hundred bilateral tariff negotiations that came into force on January 1, 1948, as an interim step toward the ITO) in order to achieve the more circumscribed trade goals they desired at that time (until they sought a broader organization, the World Trade Organization [WTO], in 1995). Although the ITO did not come into existence, the issues—which later became known as "development issues"—remained the focus of much discussion in the U.N. borderland, as we will see in this chapter, especially given GATT's general inability to effectively handle trade issues in a way that was responsive to Third World development needs.[12]

Development thinking throughout the 1950s and early 1960s was particularly tied to the economic history of the United States and the recent example of the Marshall Plan. In the U.S. model, external European investment had transformed a seemingly underdeveloped economy that had initially focused on the export of raw materials (especially lumber, naval stores, food, and cotton) to an exporter of manufactured goods as well; and in the postwar period, America emerged as the leader of the global capitalist economy. With this as a model, the focus was on external private investment to develop infrastructure, which had presumably laid the foundation for the development of a national—and subsequently an international—market in which each area could specialize in the production of its own particular specialty (be it iron ore, coal, corn, or meat production) and receive relatively inexpensive manufactured goods in exchange. The Marshall Plan seemingly illustrated similar lessons, so there was a decided emphasis in early aid efforts on external investment in infrastructure (in this case, which had been destroyed by the war) and the removal or lowering of trade barriers between countries, which was the primary work of the GATT. These were the two key elements undergirding the World Bank's lending in the immediate postwar period, and the Marshall Plan directly gave rise to the OECD, which had initially been the European organization through which Marshall Plan aid flowed. This Organisation for European Economic Co-operation was transformed into a broader coalition with the December 14, 1960, addition of the United States and Canada and took on the mission of strengthening "the tradition of co-operation" that had evolved among them to promote economic strength and prosperity among the member states, to help attain the purposes of the United Nations, to preserve individual liberty, and to increase general well-being.[13] In the European reconstruction period, there was also an emphasis on helping professionals on the continent to reconnect with their international professional communities and to get up to speed on wartime scientific developments, which were many. As a result, there was significant focus by the United Nations during this early period on fellowships and study tours. This rather naturally also carried over into early development efforts, which focused on the transfer and development of expertise in this early technical assistance model of economic development. Throughout the period of the EPTA, we see the specialized agencies of the United Nations sending experts to various countries to consult on key economic issues.[14]

The British Commonwealth's Colombo Plan followed very similar lines. Initiated by Sir Percy Spender, the Australian minister for external affairs, at the January 1950 Commonwealth Conference on Foreign Affairs, the representatives of Australia, Canada, Ceylon (now Sri Lanka), Great Britain, India, New Zealand, and Pakistan committed to furthering the economic and social development of South and Southeast Asia (later expanded to Asia and the Pacific and including twenty-six nations). Like Truman's inaugural, it stressed the dual needs of capital and increased skill levels. Starting on July 1, 1951, early Colombo Plan lending built infrastructure (like airports, dams, cement factories, and steel mills) and developed skills through new universities and training programs.[15]

In addition to technical assistance, the early development thinkers and doers in the United Nations saw the need for a transfer of resources and the creation of a set of global institutions to coordinate and direct this important work of creating a new international system that was based on a "pragmatic solidarity," as professionals, leaders, and peoples in other countries worked together toward the same goal of improving the lives of citizens in all countries in order to build a planet in which a third world war would not happen. As a result of the availability of EPTA funding (which was provided voluntarily by governments and organizations and which supplemented existing U.N. budgets) and then after 1958 of U.N. Special Fund monies, the U.N. specialized agencies largely reoriented their work toward economic development programs based in technical assistance. The resulting set of experts who did short-term contract work with these organizations therefore created a large network of people who developed close professional relationships with their counterparts in other countries and whose international experience had deepened their professional perspective. As we will see later in this chapter, EPTA eventually combined with the U.N. Special Fund to form the UNDP in 1966, which continued to coordinate development through a large network of professionals in partnership with the governments and peoples of countries seeking such aid for development. In assisting newly independent nations, the UNDP especially sought to quickly build the capacity of the new national administrations to take over key aspects of the public sector—such as postal systems, public health organizations, and airports.[16]

At the same time that EPTA was focused on the transfer of expertise and the World Bank worked on building new infrastructure, an alternative analysis of the obstacles that faced the Third World—and therefore an alternative model for "economic development"—emerged from ECLA under the leadership of Raúl Prebisch (who headed the Commission from 1949 until 1963, when he moved to UNCTAD). Collectively his *The Economic Development of Latin America and Its Principal Problems* and ECLA's *Economic Survey of 1949* argued that the failure to address trade issues through the ITO meant that the Latin American countries (and by extrapolation the other newly independent countries reliant on commodity exports) got further and further into an economic hole as trade inequities continued to erode their relative position, power, and strength in the global economy. This trade gap, by implication, meant that developing countries could never get to "development" without significant changes in the terms of trade. This theory is variously called structuralism (for emphasizing the structural impediments to Latin American economic development) and dependency theory (for emphasizing the dependence of the developing economies of the periphery on the core, industrialized economies). Therefore, ECLA stressed the need for developing economies to industrialize, which generally required an initial period of protectionism and might require regional economic collaboration (as it pursued among five Central American economies in the late 1950s and early 1960s). It also called for state-centered and state-directed development (to both spur industrial growth and ensure that the benefits of economic growth were equitably distributed across society) and some external assistance to develop these new industrial capacities. While Prebisch was theorizing about such an approach, Argentina was using its wartime economic reserves to develop a program of import-substitution (domestically manufacturing the goods that had previously been imported) and to purchase its infrastructure from foreign private enterprises.[17]

At the same time, the newly independent countries of India, Indonesia, and Egypt were also seeking to chart their own way out of colonial trading patterns and to meet the urgent needs of their people. India's Nehru and Indonesia's Sukarno had previously met in 1927 in Brussels, Belgium, at a Congress of the Oppressed Peoples, and as we read in Chapter 3, Nehru organized a 1948 All-Asia Conference in response to the West's efforts to quash the fight for Indonesian independence. Not surprisingly, given the solidarity the two men had developed while fighting for independence, they then convened—along with Burma, Ceylon, and Pakistan—a conference in Bandung, Indonesia, in April 1955 to develop a common international agenda that highlighted both development and decolonization and to mobilize the new nations of Asia and Africa to press collectively for action on these fronts. The conference's final communiqué specifically mentioned the need for additional development funds from international sources (such as the World Bank) and the stabilization of commodity prices through bilateral and multilateral agreements. Historians often use Bandung as a marker for the emergence of the Non-Aligned Movement—the effort by countries emerging from colonization to avoid being caught up in the Cold War rivalry between the United States and the Soviet Union and to develop a set of international relations that met the needs of their people. Although some nations, like the newly independent Indonesia, pursued a nonaligned or independent foreign policy but readily accepted most forms of U.S. aid, the nonaligned nations of India and Egypt generally pursued a slightly different model of nonaligned aid policy. India adopted a pro-industrialization and centrally planned economy that featured five-year plans and initially struck many Americans as being inspired by the communist model (though it largely foreshadowed much of ECLA's development prescription). The new nation also welcomed aid from the Soviet Union. As we saw in Chapter 3, Nasser's Egypt—when rebuffed by the withdrawal of U.S. and British aid for the Aswan High Dam—turned to nationalization of the Suez Canal that, when combined with Soviet aid, provided the resources needed to build the dam. And the unease with the prevailing model of World Bank–funded large infrastructure projects as well as the sense that something different was needed was not confined to the Third World.[18]

American Paul Hoffman, who led EPTA after his work in administering the Marshall Plan, found similar skepticism among his staff, most notably his Saint Lucian deputy, W. Arthur Lewis, who drew his conclusion from his extensive network on the ground in the developing countries and by listening to the concerns of the governments moving along and/or resisting this path. At the very least, more had to be done to promote development, and different methods were likely needed if the developing countries—which swelled to a majority of U.N. members very early in the 1960s as a result of decolonization—were to make significant and needed economic progress.[19] The United Nations' first "Development Decade" proffered an initial response to these perceived needs.

The First Development Decade

Speaking just one week after the tragic and unexpected death of U.N. Secretary-General Dag Hammarskjöld, U.S. President John F. Kennedy addressed the U.N. General Assembly on September 25, 1961. His speech struck a tone halfway between a eulogy for the fallen U.N. leader and his own inspirational inaugural just eight months prior. He started, "We meet in an hour of grief and challenge. Dag Hammarskjold is dead. But the United Nations lives. His tragedy is deep in our hearts, but the task for which he died is at the top of our agenda." Kennedy then went on to talk about disarmament and peace issues (including an atmospheric nuclear test ban) and dismissed the idea that the office of secretary-general should be run by a committee rather than a single person before turning—very briefly—to the issue of economic development:

> Self-determination is but a slogan if the future holds no hope. That is why my Nation, which has freely shared its capital and its technology to help others help themselves, now proposes officially designating this decade of the 1960's as the United Nations Decade of Development. Under the framework of that Resolution, the United Nations' existing efforts in promoting economic growth can be expanded and coordinated. Regional surveys and training institutes can now pool the talents of many. New research, technical assistance and pilot projects can unlock the wealth of less developed lands and untapped waters. And development can become a cooperative and not a competitive enterprise—to enable all nations,

> however diverse in their systems and beliefs, to become in fact as well as in law free and equal nations.

He then quickly moved on to international crises in Southeast Asia (Laos and Vietnam) as well as Berlin in this address, which is much more notable for its traditional, dichotomous Cold War rhetoric than its commitment to new initiatives in development.[20] Nonetheless, the assembled delegates took it as a signal that the world's largest donor was willing to think about new approaches and make new investments in economic development and therefore quickly followed up with a December 19, 1961, General Assembly resolution that sought to provide a specific goal of economic development to be achieved during this "Development Decade." After general language about the need of both developed and developing countries to "intensify their efforts" to bring about "in each under-developed country a substantial increase in the rate of growth," it set the goal of seeing each developing country hit "a minimum annual rate of growth of aggregate national income of 5 percent at the end of the Decade." To accomplish this, it primarily sought additional funding commitments to EPTA and the Special Fund, with the goal of reaching an annual average of 1 percent of the combined GDP of the developed nations. The Special Fund, working with the United Nations' regional economic commissions, set up institutes for economic development and planning to train the government officials who would carry out the work of the Development Decade.[21]

A "Development Decade" was exactly the type of large initiative that the Kennedy administration seemed to embrace (it had already established the Peace Corps, reorganized foreign aid in the newly rebranded U.S. Agency for International Development, and launched the decade-long Alliance for Progress aid program to Latin America that same year). Additionally, it had already been taking steps to increase the amount of international monies available for development. It had worked through the Development Assistance Group/Committee of the newly renamed and expanded Organisation for Economic Co-operation and Development (OECD)[22] to gain a commitment to a higher level of aid from a broader section of the developed world at its meeting of March 27–29, 1961. At that same meeting, an OECD study showed that the United States provided more than 40 percent of the total official aid then flowing to the developing countries, with Britain and France collectively making up another third. The organization became famous for figuring each country's level of Official Development Assistance (ODA, which was a ratio that compared a country's GDP to its private and public capital transfers to the Third World) that it then used to motivate those at the bottom of the list to become more generous. Between the calls of the United Nations and the OECD, 1961 saw the emergence of a significant number of new governmental agencies to distribute aid, including the Kuwait Fund for Arab Economic Development, the Japanese Overseas Economic Cooperation Fund, the Swedish Agency for International Assistance (renamed in 1965 the Swedish International Development Authority), the Canadian International Development Agency, and official development-aid coordination bodies within the French, German, and Swiss governments. But there is another side to this positive view of the OECD as motivating higher levels of giving; it was also developed as a tool of the Cold War and as a forum for the Atlantic powers to negotiate and make decisions on aid away from the United Nations, in which it no longer held a majority after the 1960s.[23]

In this development work, the Kennedy administration sought, much like the earlier, Democratic Truman administration had, to make the United Nations a vital part of U.S. foreign policy. He also consciously sought to differentiate himself from the Republican Eisenhower administration by taking on the Soviets and the Eastern bloc much more directly in the United Nations when they taunted the U.S. government about the policies of Jim Crow and racial discrimination. This was one part of his effort to more fully engage with and win the loyalty of the emerging Third World, and a second part of this engagement strategy was to more fully move away from the "trade, not aid" orientation of the previous administration. Kennedy instead initiated the Alliance for Progress aid program with Latin America (which ultimately had little to show for itself in terms of economic development). These policy initiatives were also a response to external pressures. Soviet Premier Nikita Khrushchev had taken a much more activist approach to courting the Third World in the United Nations by providing substantial development aid, in addition to his much more activist foreign policy that resulted in the building of the Berlin Wall and the installation of nuclear weapons in Cuba (see Chapter 3). In other words, the Cold War had decidedly shifted to a fight for the loyalty of the Third World, and the area of development was a key arena in that battle. And there were many more Third World countries to compete for, as they made up the majority of the General Assembly by the end of the decade.[24]

It was within this international context that the new, Burmese U.N. secretary-general, U Thant, presented his *The United Nations Development Decade: Proposals for Action to ECOSOC* in July 1962, which focused more on planning for development than on actual economic development (much like the OECD during this period). He called for systematic surveys of available development resources in the Third World (which were generally carried out by the ECOSOC regional economic commissions), the creation of national development plans undergirded by a sufficiently robust bureaucracy to carry out the plans, and a redirection of some of the science and technology research and development taking place in the developed world to take account of challenges in the emerging nations. Additionally, he sought an increase in the developing world's export earnings and more development capital on suitable terms—both of which would require significant action from the donor countries. As the U.N. system increasingly organized its work around promoting and planning economic development, ECOSOC established in 1966 the Committee for Development Planning as a subsidiary body to organize and coordinate this work with the goal of establishing best practices for this relatively new field of action. Its first reports warned governments away from comprehensive plans that might overestimate their ability to shape the private economic sector or to overcome the political difficulties inherent in such plans.[25]

The growing number of Third World delegates in the U.N. General Assembly pressed throughout the decade for new and different types of aid and different conversations about aid. They recognized that the development infrastructure of the United Nations that had emerged since the end of the Second World War was one based around development loans and technical assistance. EPTA and its funds for technical assistance primarily prepared countries to apply for World Bank loans, which had to be repaid in full with interest, which meant that they were available only (or certainly primarily) for projects that would be remunerative; large infrastructural projects—such as ports, highways, and dams—would generate the income to repay these loans. In addition to the increased competition for such loans that resulted from the growth in the number of independent, less-developed countries, the Third World in the United Nations pushed for concessional aid or grants—monies that would come for development purposes but either did not have to be paid back or carried extremely low interest rates. Although the proposed Special United Nations Fund for Economic Development (SUNFED) did not come to fruition, the World Bank, as a direct result of this push, did develop the International Development Association (IDA) in 1960 as a subsidiary organization of the Bank to make such concessional loans.[26]

While the United States opposed the creation of SUNFED, it actively supported the creation of a new World Food Programme established inside of the FAO to repackage American agricultural surplus disposal as an effort to assist economic development. In 1960, Eisenhower had suggested to the U.N. General Assembly that it create "a workable scheme" for providing emergency food aid through the U.N. system, an idea that U.S. Food for Peace Director George McGovern followed up on with the FAO in 1961. The United States hoped that such laundering of its agricultural surpluses through the United Nations would at least not anger other countries and could potentially garner international goodwill. Since the FAO had increasingly focused its program of work on helping the people in the developing world to increase their own capacity for food production and distribution with its Freedom From Hunger Campaign, it was not particularly interested in administering such a program. As a result, the FAO and the United Nations passed parallel resolutions creating the World Food Programme on a three-year experimental basis. Its governing body, the Intergovernmental Committee, held its first session in February 1962, and it was soon ready to help meet the needs of Iranian earthquake survivors, Thai hurricane victims, and the five million refugees that Algeria was working to resettle in the wake of its hard-won independence. The World Food Programme's life was extended indefinitely with parallel resolutions in December 1965 in the United Nations and FAO, and its annual budget (including the value of donated food) rose from $100 million in 1963 to almost $1.5 billion in 2000. But it became even more focused on relief than development over time, with 86 percent of its 2000 budget going to relief and just 14 percent to development assistance.[27]

A key Third World organizational innovation during the First Development Decade grew out of analysis by the ECLA and GATT secretariats about the deteriorating terms of trade that served to keep most export-dependent economies in a state of underdevelopment. These ideas came together in the new U.N. Conference on Trade and Development (UNCTAD), established in 1964 and led throughout the decade by Raúl Prebisch, who had previously been the moving force behind ECLA. Reflecting Third World nations' discontent with GATT and the lack of progress in trade issues up until this point, UNCTAD emerged, not as a specialized agency of the United Nations but as a regular conference of the General Assembly, where the Group of 77 (G-77) developing nations could exercise greater power in renegotiating trade terms than was available to them in GATT, the IMF, or the World Bank, all of which had been established before a majority of these countries had gained their independence. UNCTAD convened every four years as a forum for trade negotiations and consensus-building between the G-77 and the Western powers (the communist powers played little effective role in UNCTAD's early work). UNCTAD's secretariat assisted in these negotiations by providing research studies developed between sessions, and in the original vision for the organization, UNCTAD's Trade and Development Board would create and implement the policies agreed upon at each conference. Perhaps just as important, each conference was a global media event meant to provide the Third World with a bully pulpit to air its collective grievances against the world trade regime and to put the First World on the spot.[28]

The first conference in 1964 (known as UNCTAD I) resulted in a set of fifteen general and thirteen special principles that had been framed before the conference by Prebisch and that the majority held should govern international trade relations in order to craft policies that would help promote economic development. The principles stressed the importance of trade (not simply aid) to the development process, the need for greater coordination at the national and international levels between trade and aid policies broadly conceived, the interdependence of the global economy that made Third World development a benefit to the advanced economies, and the responsibility of developing countries to guide their own development policies (especially since national conditions differed widely) as well as the reciprocal responsibility of the international community to facilitate such development. UNCTAD I also recognized and sought to propose codes of behavior for private actors such as the multinational corporations that were so influential in global trade. The end goal of these principles was greater economic equity between developed and developing countries by promoting, for example, global commodity agreements and a system of preferences that would foster the development of Third World manufacturing.[29]

However, moving toward this goal in the 1960s proved to be highly problematic in practice. While the G-77 had hoped that operating as a bloc would give it greater coherence and collective bargaining power, negotiating as a single bloc with the bloc of industrialized, capitalist countries instead created a relatively inflexible system. Within this system, the unique needs of the new countries were largely submerged, the socialist countries felt no compunction to act (since they defined themselves as outside of the capitalist system that UNCTAD sought to reform), and the developed countries (feeling a bit bullied by the majority votes of the G-77 and socialist countries) defined UNCTAD as a deliberative body and dodged any efforts to move toward implementation procedures through the Trade and Development Board, preferring instead to take any actions related to international trade through the GATT mechanism. Nonetheless, UNCTAD's secretariat continued to conduct research during the First Development Decade that focused on commodities, shipping, and technology, three key areas related to economic development that seemed potentially amenable to change given sufficient research; it also sought to work with the World Bank, IMF, and FAO to develop some sort of funding mechanism that would compensate commodity exporters for wild swings in global prices.[30]

Another Third World–led institutional effort to change the international terms of trade came when the U.N. General Assembly on November 17, 1966, established the U.N. Industrial Development Organization (UNIDO) as an autonomous body under the leadership of Ibrahim Helmi Abdel-Rahman of Egypt to promote and accelerate the industrialization of developing countries. However, the organization did not come into its own during the first or even during the Second Development Decade (DD2). Despite a 1975 U.N. General Assembly Resolution and UNIDO Conference recommendation that it be converted into a specialized agency (as part of the NIEO discussed in greater depth later in this chapter), it took four years until a new constitution was adopted and six more years until it entered into force in 1985. The preamble to that constitution declared industrialization to be "the sovereign right of all countries" and "essential to rapid economic and social development, . . . the improvement of the living standards and the quality of life of the peoples in all countries, and to the introduction of an equitable economic and social order." The shift to specialized agency and the appointment of its first director-general outside of North Africa did not solve the organization's woes, as it went through additional organizational overhauls well into the 1990s.[31]

Recognizing the need for better coordination of U.N. aid to more effectively assist Third World development during the Development Decade, the United Nations merged EPTA and the U.N. Special Fund in January 1966 into the UNDP to partner with governments in supporting their development goals. Its initial funding (much like that of its predecessors) focused on capacity-building and pre-investment financing—that is, preparation of the country and its institutions for the larger-scale projects that development funders like the World Bank might undertake. The monies to undertake this work came from voluntary donations from member states as well as from bilateral agencies and foundations. Donating member states constituted the Governing Council that held ultimate decision-making responsibility for the program's work, which it reviewed every three years. But the new program was meant—in line with the Development Decade—to partner with each recipient government in helping to implement the plan of economic development that the government had developed, oftentimes by coordinating the many actors involved in the so-called country program through the UNDP resident representative in each country. These "res reps" could approve on their own authority "small projects" (originally $100,000 or less) and make adjustments within the ongoing operational program in consultation with the host government, especially based on a continuous system of evaluation and follow-up as the country program developed. This level of decentralization was a significant shift from its predecessor programs, but it allowed each representative to learn about the country in which she or he was posted, to build trust with the folks on the ground and in the government, and thereby to effectively coordinate the nation's development plans/priorities with available resources. Within the overall scope of UNDP's work, the focus was very much on these country-level programs; regional and even global projects were envisioned and approved, but no more than 18 percent of the total budget could be devoted to them originally. Over time, these resident representatives earned the trust of a broad spectrum of types of governments and have become either the de jure or the de facto coordinators of all external assistance flowing into a particular country (United Nations, bilateral, multilateral, and NGO) and a global booster promoting the needs of her or his resident country. All of this led one political scientist, in examining UNDP, to ascribe its significance to the way it did things as much as to the actual things that it did in terms of promoting development. He ultimately called UNDP "a way of conducting relations among peoples and nations."[32] As such, UNDP resident representative records would be an extremely rich primary-source trove for those interested in studying the history of pretty much any "developing" country in the postwar and postcolonial period.

The United States, as the primary donor to the UNDP, sought to exercise some control over this new U.N. program, reserving to itself the right to appoint the UNDP administrator (until 1994). Paul Hoffman, former president of the American Studebaker car company whose work in administering the Marshall Plan had laid the groundwork for economic integration and the current-day European Union (E.U.), seemed perfect for the job of coordinating such a complex, multinational job and for at least seeming to meet the demands of the Third World for a Marshall Plan–like development effort. Although the early UNDP had far fewer resources available on stricter terms than the Marshall Plan, the program did prioritize those countries with the most urgent needs and imposed lower requirements for counterpart funds and local costs from those nations that were least developed. In this early period, UNDP yearly pledges grew from $146 million in 1965 to $225 million in 1969, with more being donated to pre-investment activities than technical assistance. Throughout the period, the United States was the largest single donor, but it limited its role to no more than 40 percent of the total. Sweden, Britain, Canada, and Germany were the other top contributors respectively; India was the largest contributor among the developing countries, who donated as much or more than the Soviet Union (at 2 percent). UNIDO and UNCTAD were included in the work of the Development Programme in response to Third World demands, but funding for agricultural development continued at higher levels than industrial development and public utilities. UNDP also became the coordinator for a new program of United Nations Volunteers, launched on January 1, 1971, to create an international corps of volunteers equivalent to groups like the U.S. Peace Corps.[33]

Despite this burst of institution-building, U.N. Secretary-General U Thant's May 1966 interim report on progress during the Development Decade was not good. Although some commentators have sought to put the best possible spin on this by pointing out that the U.N. Secretariat and specialized agencies now increasingly focused on the development enterprise in a coordinated manner, that both the United Nations and member nations had increased their ability to gather and analyze development data, and that the entire organization had begun to learn the complexities of this enterprise in the growing number of countries it was called to serve—the harsh reality was that Third World countries now faced worse terms of trade than they had before the decade started. Adding insult to injury, there was also less development aid available in 1964 than there had been in 1962. As a result, GDP in the Third World was actually lower for the first five years of the 1960s than it had been in the previous decade. This report—in many ways—laid the groundwork for the demands of the Third World that emerged fully in the plan for a New International Economic Order (NIEO) in the 1970s. Reflecting on the lack of development in the Development Decade, Thant's report downplayed the intent of the original resolution, calling it an "instrument of persuasion," and began planning the Second Development Decade (DD2) from the presumed lessons of the last effort. Specifically, the interim report called for a focus in DD2 on the development of human resources—especially the young, who made up almost half of the population in much of the Third World. This was also a nod to the rapid population growth of the 1960s (discussed in more detail at the end of Chapter 4). Thant also posited that science and technology might play a larger role in accelerating the pace of economic development in DD2. Additionally, there was a push for greater integration and evaluation of the effectiveness of U.N. development efforts.[34]

The second conference of UNCTAD in 1968, held in New Delhi rather than Geneva, picked up on many of Thant's themes and put them before a global media audience. The conference's president, Dinesh Singh (India's minister of commerce), opened the meeting by characterizing the job of the present session as providing a bridge between the "aroused expectations" of the first session and a future beyond the present "morass." U.N. Secretary-General U Thant picked up on the theme of "frustrated hopes" and gently chided the capitalist countries for the progress made in the recent Kennedy round of the GATT and in the IMF, which were not matched by similar efforts to adjust the international economy in ways that would benefit the developing world. He also called for them to invest in the future through higher levels of development aid. UNCTAD Secretary-General Raúl Prebisch's opening address to UNCTAD II identified three main obstacles to development—"the trade gap, the savings gap, and the external vulnerability of the developing countries"—and identified the remedies as greater access in the First World for Third World export products, higher levels of international aid, and regional market integration (very similar to his earlier ECLA prescriptions). Comments from the representatives of the G-77 countries generally followed the Charter of Algiers, issued by the leaders of those states meeting in October 1967 ahead of UNCTAD II. That charter decried the lack of progress in implementing the prescriptions of UNCTAD I, which had led to a deteriorating situation for the majority of the world's population in the developing world. As such, they identified the international community's "obligation to rectify these unfavourable trends [deterioration of trade and decline in aid monies] and to create conditions under which all nations can enjoy economic and social well-being, and have the means to develop their respective resources to enable their peoples to lead a life free from want and fear" as part of "a global strategy for development." To make progress toward such a global strategy, part two of the Charter of Algiers laid out a program of action that included commodity policies, trade liberalization, the expansion of Third World exports of manufactured and semi-manufactured goods, increases in development financing, rationalization of international shipping, and special measures to assist "the least developed among the developing countries." The "representatives of the developed market-economy countries," on the other hand, spoke of the "substantial" achievements of recent years, urged the delegates to exhibit "realism" in their choices, and warned that it was "unrealistic to expect a rapid increase in the flow of aid in the immediate future."[35]

One can only imagine that following these comments, the remarks of the socialist representatives—who "declared their readiness to continue their efforts in expanding their trade with the developing countries"—were much better received. The session president optimistically declared at the end of the opening remarks that "a broad consensus had emerged . . . recognizing economic development as a matter concerning all nations [and as] an international responsibility," but by the conclusion of the conference "basic issues of substance" remained unresolved due to "remaining differences of opinion." However, UNCTAD II could point to one achievement. The U.S. administration of President Lyndon B. Johnson (seeking to make a good impression) decided to back the call in Resolution 21 for "a mutually acceptable system of generalized, nonreciprocal and nondiscriminatory preferences" for Third World countries that largely replaced GATT's most-favored nation status for such countries. But it took several years for the United States to formally adopt such a measure, following in the wake of GATT and the European Economic Community's 1971 decisions to adopt this measure. So issues of trade (especially in commodities), development aid, and how best to assist the least developed countries (LDCs) remained prominent, largely unresolved issues heading into DD2.[36]

The Second Development Decade

In many ways, DD2 belatedly participated in the intellectual and creative ferment of the global social movements of the 1960s and early 1970s, as it focused increasingly on women's issues, the environment, and the concerns of those peoples who had previously been oppressed. The United Nations struggled to keep up with all of the emergent trends and to overcome the identified shortcomings of the First Development Decade, but it created new institutions and innovated through its new global conferences, which brought together governments, international civil servants, and NGOs to discuss the most pressing global questions of the decade. Alongside this creative impulse, the U.N. bureaucracy also sought to become better at promoting development and achieving measurable progress in this Development Decade, which included clear policy objectives and targets. But the objectives and targets increasingly defined "development" differently, especially trying to understand how and if development might result in an increased quality of life for those who lived in the emerging nations. The director-general of the ILO, for example, in his 1969 report drew attention to issues of unemployment and poverty. The ILO responded by drafting a World Employment Programme, and this concern for a more human-centered pattern of development found its way into the agenda of many U.N. groups and into DD2's goals in employment, education, and health. This was part of the general concern with equity among different socioeconomic groups that animated DD2 and gave rise to a number of new approaches.[37]

In preparation for DD2, the United Nations convened two expert panels to help plan the decade. The United Nations as a whole created the Commission on International Development, chaired by Canadian Lester Pearson (and therefore more commonly called the Pearson Commission), which highlighted the domestic politics and international resources needed to accelerate economic development within a generation. But in terms of impact, more important was the study of the needs and capabilities of developing countries conducted by Sir Robert Jackson, an Australian serving in the UNDP, at the urging of the U.S. delegation. Presented to the June 1969 UNDP Governing Council session, it found that needs were far greater than anticipated UNDP resources. Perhaps most damning, Jackson commented:

> For many years, I have been looking for "the brain" which guides the policies and operations of the UN development system. The search has been in vain. Here and there throughout the system there are offices and units collecting the information available, but there is no group (or Brains Trust) that is constantly monitoring the present operations, learning from experience, grasping at all what science and technology has to offer, launching new ideas and methods, challenging established practices, and provoking thought inside and outside the system. Deprived of such a vital stimulus, it is obvious that the best use cannot be made of the resources available to the operation.

The Jackson study recommended UNDP become the "brain" of the U.N. development effort, uniting the entire development system, conducting annual reviews to inform the country program, and then moving to formulate, implement, and evaluate projects. It was also to combine a variety of development funds as part of the effort to double UNDP resources over a five-year period. To make the organization more receptive to national needs, Jackson also urged UNDP to empower its resident representatives to assist governments to create (by providing indicative planning figures) and implement (by helping to coordinate aid resources) five-year development programs. Collectively, this set of reforms is called the "1970 Consensus," because that was the year in which both the UNDP Governing Council and ECOSOC reviewed and approved the study's recommendations. But by the mid-1970s, changes in the global economy brought on by the oil shocks and a sense within the donor nations that UNDP had become too closely aligned with the Third World meant that the Programme lacked the resources to carry out its ambitious plans to accelerate development. These changes were symptomatic of the challenges facing the entire Second Development Decade.[38]

The developing countries—which held a commanding majority in the U.N. General Assembly during DD2—sought to restructure international relations to devote time, energy, and attention to the pressing global economic issues about which they were most concerned. This resulted in plans for a New International Economic Order. The 1970s appeared to be the decade during which the global South could seize the initiative and fundamentally change things. The power of OPEC was highlighted in the wake of the 1973 war in the Middle East when oil prices quadrupled in just a couple of months, bringing huge numbers of so-called petrodollars to oil-producing countries while simultaneously exposing the vulnerabilities of the European and Japanese economies. At the same time, the Vietnam War and the U.S. abandonment of the gold standard in August 1971 called into question the ability of the United States to shape the global economy and even its own foreign policy. And the independence of Portugal's African colonies (Angola, Guinea-Bissau, and Mozambique) also seemed to indicate that momentum was on the side of the G-77 and their desire for fundamental change in international relations.[39]

While the NIEO as a whole made little concrete progress, some parts of its agenda prompted change in the United Nations during the decade. As we have seen in the previous section, the G-77's Charter of Algiers had already called on the international community to develop new ways to assist what came to be known as the "least developed countries" (LDCs) during the 1970s. These nations faced profound poverty; fundamental weaknesses in their economic, institutional, and human resources; and geophysical handicaps (such as being landlocked or a small, island economy) that made their economic development even more difficult, meaning that it would have to be promoted primarily on a grant rather than a loan basis. Such countries and their needs attracted increasing attention throughout the decade, resulting in the first international conference on LDCs in September 1981. The resulting "Substantial New Programme for the 1980s for the Least Developed Countries" linked guidelines for domestic action with commitments of international support, but the relative overall economic position of the LDCs continued to deteriorate.[40] Another area of Third World concern that prompted new attention was the role of transnational corporations in the global economy, especially given the hostility of International Telephone and Telegraph (ITT) toward the government of Salvador Allende in Chile. This concern bore fruit at the intersection between G-77 demands and the interest and expertise of a member of the international secretariat—Philippe de Seynes of France, Under-Secretary-General of the U.N. Department for Economic and Social Affairs. A 1972 ECOSOC resolution led to reports by the U.N. secretary-general as well as the Group of Eminent Persons to Study the Impact of Transnational Corporations on Development and on International Relations as well as the hosting of a special ECOSOC intersessional committee on transnational corporations to consider this body of work. Therefore, ECOSOC was ready in 1974 to create an intergovernmental Commission on Transnational Corporations (to advise ECOSOC and to keep the issue of possible regulation and supervision of transnational corporations on its agenda), which evolved over time into the U.N. Centre on Transnational Corporations (UNCTC).[41] In sum, historians examining DD2 should acknowledge both the frustration as well as the creativity that characterized the decade's efforts, which were thrown into high relief by the distinctive change in international politics that characterized the 1980s.

Institutionally, we see innovation and concern for equity in development coming from a number of different arenas. Interestingly enough, the "basic needs" approach emerged first from the World Bank, which had previously argued that poverty alleviation was best tackled by reallocating a share of the proceeds of the economic growth that came from development ("redistribution from growth" in the short-hand of the time). But World

Bank President Robert McNamara (who held office from 1968 until 1981) innovated the basic needs approach, which he initially termed "essential human needs," and began making loans specifically for such programs. Additionally, women emerged forcefully into the development debate in the mid-1970s, arguing that previous measures of economic development disregarded their contributions and that no success would take place in development programs until they were designed with women's economic roles clearly in mind (see Chapter 8 for a full discussion). And concern for the environment as a separate actor/victim in the economic development process also first emerged during DD2. However, these new ideas had few concrete results to show for themselves by the end of the decade. Although they changed the discourse and some of the thinking about development, they did not have a direct impact on the lives of the people who lived in the Third World, especially since such changes had the potential to challenge a variety of entrenched interests and required significant legal and institutional change to become a reality.[42]

Environmental concerns: The 1972 Stockholm Conference

Concerns about the environment—couched in a variety of terms—had emerged forcefully onto the world stage and in the United Nations in the later 1960s. Secretary-General U Thant's 1969 report to the General Assembly opened with a warning: "For the first time in the history of mankind, there is arising a crisis of worldwide proportions involving developed and developing countries—the crisis of the human environment." He pointed to the increase in atmospheric carbon dioxide that the World Meteorological Organization had been tracking (Chapter 4) as well as land erosion, deforestation, extinction of plant and animal life, and air, land, and water pollution. Without significant, coordinated international action, such trends could endanger life on earth, Thant warned. This report helped prepare the ground for the upcoming 1972 World Conference on the Human Environment in Stockholm. This was the first of the "megaconferences" that the United Nations used to catalyze interest in and garner attention for key global issues in the coming decades.[43]

However, the secretary-general had not convinced everyone of the importance of this issue; in the lead up to the conference, heavy criticism came from both the developed and developing world. Third World nations did not rank this issue on a par with pressing economic issues, like development, which they feared could be derailed by an environmental agenda. The leadership of Canadian Maurice F. Strong helped to win over key constituencies. He put together a panel of twenty-seven experts in June 1971 to review the pertinent issues and concerns; the resulting Founex Report argued that a comprehensive form of economic and human development was absolutely key to preservation of the global environment. This focus on promoting human development helped Strong win the support of Indian Prime Minister Indira Gandhi, who made a key speech during the conference that linked the two themes:

> Even though our industrial development is in its infancy, and at its most difficult stage, we are taking various steps to deal with incipient environmental imbalances, the more so because of our concern for the human being—a species which is also

> imperiled. In poverty he is threatened by malnutrition and disease, in weakness by war, in richness by the pollution brought about by his own prosperity.

And she ended by pointing out that only a cooperative global effort could attain the goals laid out by the conference:

> If there is to be a change of heart, a change of direction and methods of functioning, it is not one organization or a country—no matter how well intentioned—which can achieve it. While each country must deal with that aspect of the problem which is most relevant to it, it is obvious that all countries must unite in an overall endeavour. There is no alternative to a cooperative approach on a global scale to the entire spectrum of our problems.[44]

The Stockholm Conference established both a unifying declaration of principles and a set of organizations to carry on the work of global environmental conservation. The "Declaration on the Human Environment" identified humankind as the creators and molders of their environment on an unprecedented scale in contemporary times and pointed to both the natural and the man-made environments as being essential to "well-being and to the enjoyment of basic human rights—even the right to life itself." It then laid the responsibility for protecting and improving the human environment at the feet of "all Governments." Positing faith in science and technology, the declaration envisioned them, "if used wisely," bringing "all people the benefits of development and the opportunity to enhance the quality of life." Elaborating on this theme, the declaration argued that "in the developing countries most of the environmental problems are caused by under-development," and therefore the Third World should focus on implementing development (while keeping an eye on the environment) and the First World on funding that development. It mentioned the challenges posed by population growth before calling for "an enthusiastic but calm state of mind and intense but orderly work" throughout the world. To accomplish this work, it called on "citizens and communities . . . enterprises and institutions at every level" to share "equitably in common efforts" to preserve and improve "the human environment for the benefit of all the people and for their posterity." The Stockholm Conference then elaborated upon this declaration with twenty-six principles before making its recommendations for action, which included the creation of national organizations to manage environmental concerns and the establishment of the U.N. Environment Programme (UNEP) and a voluntary fund to finance environmental protection programs. Underlining the importance of environmental concerns to the Third World, Nairobi, Kenya, was the home of the new UNEP, the first "Southern" institution of the United Nations.[45]

Stockholm began a long process of elevating and integrating environmental concerns into all aspects of the work of the United Nations and of individual countries. The U.N. Conference on Human Settlements (Habitat I), which followed Stockholm in 1976, similarly stressed the connections between development and environment. The momentum continued as environmental concerns continued to hold the attention of policymakers, local activists, and scientists and led to both the Earth Summit (officially the 1992 Rio Conference on Environment and Development) and the 2002 World Summit on Sustainable Development in Johannesburg. While sometimes treated as just one more thing to be considered, some world systems historians have argued that Stockholm played a catalytic role in initiating a fundamental challenge to the world system by rejecting "the commodification of nature as a whole and [adopting] a holistic view (the ecosystem) rather than a national one."[46]

The New International Economic Order

More controversial was the effort during the Second Development Decade to promote greater equity between the developed and developing countries through the NIEO. The goal was to force a real consideration of Third World grievances about the current economic system that it had enunciated since at least the Havana Conference on the ITO right after the Second World War. The NIEO called for specific measures to ensure more sovereignty over national resources and economies; an increase in the level of appropriate types of foreign investment; stabilization or increases in primary commodity export prices; the opening of First World markets to Third World exports; facilitation of technology transfer; higher levels of development assistance (at least 0.7 percent of GDP in overseas development aid); reductions in developing countries' debt burden; and greater decision-making power for the developing nations in the Bretton Woods institutions specifically and the United Nations generally. These debates and discussions took place in several fora and across a broad range of issues. Scholars have identified these demands as fundamentally conservative and keeping with the major norms of the international system at that time, but many contemporary observers in the First World saw them as fundamentally radical.[47]

The NIEO agenda dominated North-South discussions throughout the U.N. structure for the rest of the decade, especially during the 1972 and 1976 UNCTAD rounds and in special sessions of the U.N. General Assembly in 1974 and 1975 dedicated to this work. In some ways, this was a vote of confidence by the Third World in the capacity of these international arenas to serve as the most effective means for contesting the ongoing globalization that materially affected their sovereignty in terms of their ability to regulate the international flow of capital and commodities that they were dependent on and which were often seemingly beyond their grasp (international trade grew at an average rate of 6.6 percent between 1958 and 1970). The United Nations, after all, was a global forum that provided a space for new nations (which often had limited ability to create embassies abroad) to develop a collective agenda and to press that agenda in those bodies where they held a majority through discourse, knowledge, moral pressure, and the development of public outrage. U.N. Secretary-General Kurt Waldheim (who served from 1972 until 1981) also embraced the United Nations' role at the center of key global debates. Another way in which developing countries pressed for the NIEO was through their own economic policies—for example, President Julius Nyerere's "African socialist" plan of self-reliance for Tanzania within the interdependent global economy that he laid out in the Arusha Declaration of 1967. Practically, this meant that Nyerere's ruling Tanganyika African National Union began to nationalize dozens of international companies and focused on rural (rather than industrial) development efforts within the country's borders; internationally, it worked through the NIEO in an attempt to negotiate an international regulatory framework that would limit commodity fluctuations and overcome some of the structural inequities of the global free market. Nyerere could only imagine Tanzania being able to exert the influence needed to negotiate such trade terms and gain true sovereignty (economic as well as political) within a global forum like UNCTAD in which his small country could exert pressure through the G-77, which he called a "trade union of the poor." Indeed, Nyerere became a noted spokesman for UNCTAD's work, gaining a voice and influence well beyond what would have otherwise been available.[48]

The 1972 UNCTAD III meeting in Santiago de Chile featured a global "Charter of Economic Rights and Duties of States" (proposed by Mexican President Luis Echeverría), a critique of multinational corporations, and bitter clashes between the First and Third Worlds. Starting with a call to "remove economic cooperation from the field of good faith and move it to the legal sphere," Echeverría called on the delegates to "transfer the accepted principle of solidarity among men to the area of relations among countries" and then laid out the charter's key ideas: national sovereignty over natural resources; the freedom of each country to choose its own economic system; domestic legislative control over international capital flows; prohibitions against multinational corporations' interference in domestic affairs; elimination of commercial practices that discriminated against the exports of the developing world; creation of international commodity price-stabilization agreements; preferential commercial arrangements based on level of economic development; quicker transmission of key technologies and scientific advances to the developing world; and more unfettered development aid. In the wake of UNCTAD III, the "Charter of Economic Rights and Duties of States" was drafted in 1973 and adopted at the 1974 General Assembly meeting by a vote of 120–6–10. More concretely, Sicco Mansholt, the Dutch president of the European Commission from 1972 until 1973, pushed for action that resulted in the 1975 Lomé Convention that gave a bloc of African, Caribbean, and Pacific countries' agricultural and mineral exports preferential access to the European market, created a price-stabilizing mechanism for twenty-nine export commodities, and guaranteed European aid to their less-developed trading partners.[49]

The G-77 hosted its first special session of the General Assembly from April 9 until May 2, 1974, to consider problems related to raw materials and economic development. The session was notable for its "Declaration on the Establishment of a New International Economic Order" and its accompanying Programme of Action, which reiterated many of the ideas developed over the previous decade and promoted in UNCTAD. The leaders of Algeria, Iran, Mexico, and Venezuela played prominent roles in the conceptualization of these NIEO documents and in many ways became their public face, perhaps to emphasize the growing power of the G-77 since all four came from oil-producing countries. As they had in UNCTAD, most of the First World nations resisted the direction of the NIEO, although the Netherlands, Norway, and Sweden exhibited some flexibility.[50]

The next year's special session (1975) took place within the context of the OPEC embargo, which had seemingly put the West on the defensive. In response, Valéry Giscard d'Estaing, who served as the president of the French Republic from 1974 until 1981 and portrayed himself as "a conservative who likes change," sought to foster a more civil and flexible discussion of outstanding issues through his North-South Dialogue project hosted at the Conference on International Economic Cooperation in Paris. The tone of UNCTAD IV in 1976 was more conciliatory, with U.S. Secretary of State Henry Kissinger, addressing the meeting and stressing the common ground between the First and Third World blocs by emphasizing the need for multilateral solutions to the world's economic problems. Perhaps the economic difficulties that the United States had been experiencing made the Nixon administration attach more political importance to this conference. In the wake of the meeting, the UNCTAD secretariat increasingly focused on understanding international trade as a whole and functioning as the "think-tank" for the global South in its ongoing (but more fragmentary) trade negotiations outside of the UNCTAD framework (such as those that had resulted in the Lomé Convention during the previous year). This fragmentation resulted from the increasing realization that "the Third World" shared little in common beyond its colonial past and certainly did not collectively share the same economic status or goals (especially as the gulf between the oil-producing and oil-consuming nations expanded). Such fragmentation also served to minimize the number of concessions that First World governments and companies had to make in their ongoing globalization efforts.[51]

As this indicates, the gains from the NIEO agenda were relatively small and fragmentary, well short of the global and equitable regulation of world markets that it had aimed for. For example, OPEC countries did receive an increase in their number of voting shares in the World Bank and IMF, but the Bretton Woods institutions' governing boards simultaneously increased the size of the majority needed to move a resolution forward. And in place of a global regulatory regime for multinational corporations, the NIEO could only claim to have catalyzed the voluntary code of conduct that the OECD countries instituted. Rather than comprehensive reform of global commodity markets, agreements were reached to stabilize the price of sugar, cocoa, and rubber. Other scholars have argued that the NIEO mobilized NGOs, like Oxfam, which became increasingly concerned with trade and development issues and conducted public relations and fair trade campaigns in Western Europe that sought to address—on a small scale—some of these macro-issues. As DD2 drew to a close, contemporary observers felt that the moment when global reform within the U.N. framework had seemed possible had passed.[52]

Women, development, and the 1975 Mexico City Conference

The 1970s saw a fundamental rethinking (or even thinking for the first time by many in the U.N. bureaucracy) about the role of women in the field of development. While the Commission on the Status of Women (CSW) within ECOSOC had been gathering information on women's status and working to codify women's legal and civil rights since the founding of the United Nations (see chapters 4 and 8), that work had not necessarily penetrated the development enterprise. Nor had the CSW initially been eager to take up questions of economic development (when asked to make a report on the topic by the General Assembly in 1962), which it saw as a diversion from its key work on securing women's equality. Increasingly, however, the Commission began to see the ways in which economic barriers to women (such as lack of access to land ownership and credit) constituted barriers to their advancement generally, as it began the preliminary research for a long-term plan for the advancement of women at the initiative of Secretary-General U Thant. Looking at the work of the U.N. specialized agencies, regional commissions, and member states, it became strikingly evident that very little of the economic development work then under way was "trickling down" to have positive impacts on women; in fact, the Commission found that poverty disproportionately affected women. Already, the ILO had recommended as early as 1965 that provisions to reconcile women's family and working obligations would benefit all workers and the economy as a whole.[53]

In 1966, the CSW sponsored a Regional Seminar on the Advancement of Women in Manila, Philippines, that helped frame its proposed "Long-Term Program for the Advancement of Women." This long-term program included goals that aimed particularly at advancing women's economic status, including compulsory elementary education for the world's girls as well as new educational opportunities for women and the creation of national commissions on the status of women that would consciously integrate women's abilities and needs into national plans for economic development. This work found its way into Resolution IX—"Measures to Promote Women's Rights in the Modern World"—of the International Conference on Human Rights in Tehran in 1968. This "magical amalgam" of women's economic development and their legal equality was an important intellectual milestone for the CSW. At the same time, ECOSOC's Economic Commission for Africa had incorporated an item on women's roles in development as part of its 1968–69 work program, at the initiative of Kenyan Margaret Kenyatta (who had organized both the All Africa Women's Conference and the first Women's Seminar in 1962).[54] But women's importance to economic development became a key concept in the work and planning of the United Nations as a whole only during the Second Development Decade.

The year 1970 saw the publication of two key documents about women and development that fundamentally refuted the previous notion that women would be the passive recipients of the benefits that would presumably emerge from economic development—substituting instead the idea that women needed equal rights to resources and opportunities so they could partner with men fully and equally in promoting national development. Jamaican Gloria Scott of the U.N. Department of Economic and Social Affairs ensured that the phrase "the full integration of women in the total development effort" was included in DD2's planning document. This built, in part, on the work of Danish economist Ester Boserup (who had worked with the Economic Commission for Europe), whose 1970 book—*Women's Role in Economic Development*—utilized official

U.N. statistics to begin the work of revealing women's vital contributions to national economic productivity. She also illustrated how most of the current models of economic development—which focused on industrialization or the cultivation of cash crops—hurt women's economic status, since in much of the Third World women's work focused on the cultivation of food crops for domestic consumption. Boserup's work clearly identified women as contributors to national economies, thereby warning policymakers in the United Nations, national governments, and development funding agencies that ignoring women's work could damage efforts to promote economic development generally. While sometimes criticized for "instrumentalism" (arguing for women's advancement on the basis of their role in the economy rather than from a position that women simply had the right to be treated equally), Boserup's work launched an entirely new focus on women in development as one of the key ingredients to a successful overall plan for economic development. Throughout the Second Development Decade, the CSW lobbied for women's education, training and employment, health and maternity protection, and full participation in public life as key ingredients in any successful program of economic development.[55]

The U.N. Commission on the Status of Women rolled out these ideas to a broader audience at its 1972 "Interregional Meeting of Experts on the Integration of Women in Development," which was organized by Egyptian Aida Gindy (chief of the U.N. Social Affairs Section and formerly of the Economic Commission for Africa) and whose working document had been drafted by Boserup. These experts stressed that women's exclusion from economic development programs had been a significant factor in the rapid growth of population, illiteracy, malnutrition, poor health, and poverty—all key obstacles to development. As a corrective, the meeting emphasized the need to integrate women into the overall planning of development initiatives at the regional, national, and global levels, rather than a focus on "women-only" initiatives. Jumping on this conclusion, the Economic Commission for Africa (ECA) created a women's program within its secretariat that very same year. The 1974 world conferences on population (Bucharest) and food (Rome)—both of which included women in the preparatory stages—affirmed the key role of women in both of these areas, and the new U.N. Fund for Population Activities that grew out of Bucharest provided funds to the programs of ECA, UNICEF, and FAO that promoted women's roles in economic development. All of these initiatives indicated a significant and systemic shift in thinking about the role of women in development; now national and international policymakers increasingly understood the essential role that women could play in promoting economic development.[56]

These ideas became one of the focal points for the first World Conference on the Status of Women held in Mexico City in 1975, whose participants received Gloria Scott's report, "Integration of Women in the Development Process as Equal Partners with Men." Indeed, the discussions showed that women from the developing countries were primarily interested in development issues and saw male biases in development planning and practice as a key factor in women's inferior economic position through much of the Third World. As a result, the final conference document recognized that "under-development imposed upon women a double burden of exploitation" and called for the elimination of all obstacles preventing women's "full integration into national development."[57] The subsequent General Assembly "World Plan of Action" established the U.N. Decade for Women (1976–85), including guidelines for achieving minimum targets in "the integration and full participation of women in development." By the end of the Women's Decade, many member states had established some form of national machinery to advance women's participation in development, and the United Nations had established both the International Research and Training Institute for the Advancement of Women (INSTRAW) and the United Nations Development Fund for Women (UNIFEM). Their work, in turn, generated the need for additional information and research on women's issues. In 1979, a Brazilian research institute (the Instituto Universitário de Pesquisas do Rio de Janeiro) convened its Seminar on Women in the Labor Force in Latin America, which brought together demographers and women's rights activists from across the region with the goal of improving the quality of data on women's work in order to improve development planning. This work eventually included representatives from Africa and Asia as well, which grew into the global network Development Alternatives with Women for a New Era (DAWN). Ultimately, new research from the United Nations and other sources determined that women's global work generally was characterized by more intermittent participation in formal work, a greater contribution to productive activities that did not generate cash and therefore were less visible to traditional economic statistics, and a mixture of production for consumption in the family and for the market.[58]

By the time that delegations from 145 member states reconvened in Copenhagen in 1980 to assess women's global progress since Mexico City, however, the topic of economic development was largely submerged under discussions of the barriers for women to adequate education, employment, and health care. The final conference document only reiterated the Mexico City point that governments needed to commit to "equal and full participation of women in economic and social development," including the "systematic and sustained linking of efforts to integrate women into national development planning."[59]

A new leader for the UNDP, 1976

As the program of the United Nations became broader and more inclusive of the concerns of women and the environment and as the Third World became more assertive about its needs through the NIEO, the largest development funders, especially the United States, became resistant to the expanding agenda and its costs. The UNDP was certainly among the programs initially facing difficulties, but Frank Bradford "Brad" Morse, who became the third UNDP administrator in 1976, helped to turn its fortunes around. As a six-term Republican Congressman from a traditionally Democratic district in Lowell, Massachusetts, who had assumed Ralph Bunche's position as U.N. under-secretary-general for Political and General Assembly Affairs in 1972, he knew both Republican-party and U.N. politics. After being appointed to the UNDP administrator's position by U.S. President Richard Nixon, Morse sold the organization's limousine and booked coach-class tickets as he flew to the world's capitals to drum up record pledges for the fiscally ailing organization he now headed. But he increased fiscal support for the organization and its mission without limiting any of the diversity of UNDP programs, which in fact helped to incubate the UNIFEM program among others.[60]

Morse understood and navigated through the sources of anti-Third World feeling that had sprung up among Republicans and other fiscal conservatives in the U.S. government and that had affected its support for the UNDP. The traditional conservatives (some of them isolationists) were strongly anticommunist and resentful of Third World leaders who were not clearly aligned with the Western democracies and who had inflicted significant damage on the U.S. economy with the oil shocks. In addition, realists like Nixon and Kissinger were unsettled by the new Third World efforts to destabilize the status quo. Morse's work proceeded incrementally and in reaction to a variety of constituencies in order to allay concerns in the United States. This gave him room to work creatively (and ultimately successfully) with communist China, Vietnam (following America's war there), Iran under the Ayatollah, black nationalists in southern Africa, and the Palestinians (discussed in Chapter 7), which allowed realists in the United States to see how the UNDP could help bring these states into the global economy and status quo while simultaneously being responsive to the interests of UNDP's Nordic and Dutch funders and to the growing assertiveness of Third World interests.[61]

Morse, who had already developed a passion for Africa while working for the U.N. Secretariat, was delighted that UNDP's Governing Council in 1974 had resolved that the program would treat national liberation movements that had been recognized by the Organisation of African Unity (OAU) as partners in its work. He opened a UNDP Liaison Office with the OAU in Addis Ababa in 1977 that allowed it to work with many of the black nationalist groups, providing technical assistance, training programs, fellowships to other African countries, and even opportunities to travel to New York to visit the General Assembly. Specifically, it worked with South Africa's African National Congress (ANC) in Tanzania, and in Lusaka, Zambia, the UNDP helped fund the U.N. Institute for Namibia (UNIN), which provided services from 1976 until Namibian independence in 1990, when UNIN's director, Hage Gcingob, became prime minister. In addition to providing other senior governmental leaders, UNIN also provided assistance in structuring the new nation's governmental and legal structures.[62]

But it was at the New York headquarters of the United Nations that UNDP experienced one of its great surprises in 1978. Morse's courtesy call to the Chinese mission that year revealed that under Deng Xiaoping's new economic policy, China had chosen to work with UNDP to promote its economic development and integration into the global economy. Throughout the 1990s, the U.N. agency assisted China in developing and adopting a set of twenty-two economic laws that laid the foundation for its market economy and accompanying "social security" program. On the basis of this fruitful partnership, since 1996, UNDP has also worked with the Chinese government on some poverty reduction and cultural programs with Chinese minorities.[63] Despite the hopeful developments in the UNDP, the 1970s—marred by political and economic upheaval on a planetary scale—brought much more conservative regimes to the primary development funding countries, who were very assertive in their rejection of the idea of redistribution of wealth through governmental structures and in their trumpeting of free-market economies and "trickle down" wealth both at home and abroad.

The 1980s and 1990s: The debt crises, the Washington Consensus, and the backlash

Following the election of Margaret Thatcher of the Conservative Party as British prime minister in 1979 and conservative Republican Ronald Reagan as U.S. president in 1980, this Anglo-American power couple dominated the decade, calling for accountability in the U.N. system as a whole for the funds already invested in development and rejecting at the 1981 Cancún Summit the previous decades' global negotiations under the U.N. umbrella about issues of finance, investment, and trade in favor of free-market, neoliberal globalization. Even before the Thatcher and Reagan elections, at the end of GATT's Tokyo Round in 1979, the First World economies had begun working toward stronger protections for intellectual property rights and fewer obstacles to transnational services (including advertising, computing, financial, and telecommunication services), both of which would benefit the most advanced economies and were actively pursued in the subsequent Uruguay Round of 1986–94, which laid the groundwork for the World Trade Organization (WTO). While the United Nations had adopted a Third Development Decade Strategy in 1981 that included detailed social goals and had a focus on human development and poverty alleviation that it inherited from DD2, there was no Third Development Decade.[64] The Mexican debt crisis in 1982 was the first of a number of "dominos" to fall to balance-of-payment difficulties. A "Washington consensus"[65] developed during these debt crises that put the World Bank and IMF on center stage, where they demanded neoliberal economic policies of structural adjustment and economic stabilization that slashed public-sector funding and privatized state industries as the best route to financial health. Increasingly too, the Western powers (organized through the OECD or the even more elite G-7 or G-8) developed common macroeconomic policies and positions that largely marginalized the United Nations in terms of decision-making on broad economic issues.[66]

The unraveling of communism also emboldened neoliberal policies. With the fall of the Berlin Wall in 1989 and the dissolution of the Soviet Union in 1991, there was seemingly no Soviet/communist development alternative, especially as even China started moving toward a freer market model for its economy. As Eastern European nations and parts of the former Soviet Union emerged from communism, they experienced such neoliberal policies directly. The abrupt transition from communism to free-market capitalism—dubbed "shock therapy"—had uneven results. While Poland and some of the Baltic nations did well, the former Soviet Union saw many of its previous state industries distributed to organized crime and former government officials, while fully one-third of the population fell into poverty.[67] With command-economy communism largely gone from the scene, globalization increasingly seemed to be a juggernaut.

Seeking ever greater economies of scale and larger markets, the 1990s witnessed a push toward regional economic integration. In 1992, the Association of Southeast Asian Nations (ASEAN) created a free trade area for its members. The next year the Maastricht Treaty created the European Union that furthered the development of a single market for the free circulation of goods, services, people, and financial services, which was further strengthened by the 1999 adoption of the euro as a common currency. Third World economies continued their efforts to gain increased access to this expanding market through the Cotonou Agreement in June 2000, which updated and expanded upon the previous Lomé conventions (which the United States had successfully challenged through the WTO). Cotonou generally called for the Asian, Caribbean, and Pacific countries to provide the same duty-free access to their markets that their exports enjoyed in the European Union.[68]

At the same time that the European Union was born, Mexico joined the United States and Canada in signing the North American Free Trade Agreement (NAFTA) in 1993, abandoning the important leadership role it had previously played in the NIEO and joining the OECD in 1994. But Mexico also seemingly became an early victim of globalization, as it catalyzed a new set of financial crises with its 1994–95 peso crisis, which resulted from weaknesses in the regulation of the country's banking system, changes in U.S. monetary policy, and sudden shifts in external investors' sense of the desirability of Mexican investments. The resulting economic free-fall only ended with a $50 billion U.S. bailout (complemented by the World Bank and IMF) in 1995, which primarily benefited American banks that were very heavily invested south of the border.[69]

Despite increasing regionalism and the debt crises, globalization seemed to roll on with the Marrkesh Ministerial Declaration of 1994 that launched the WTO the next year. The WTO superseded the GATT, handled a broader array of types of trade, and had much greater power to ensure that national trade policies conformed to the norms of the new world economy, even when these conflicted with efforts to protect the environment. At the same time, the position of UNCTAD secretary-general stood vacant for all of 1994 and much of 1995; its North-South bloc politics seemed increasingly outdated, and the U.S. willingness to use its power of the purse to withhold contributions from U.N. organizations it did not want to support had a significant impact on UNCTAD. Nonetheless, under the new leadership of Brazilian Rubens Ricupero, it reorganized, and at its 1996 conference (UNCTAD IX), it focused primarily on helping developing countries adapt to the globalized economy. Specifically, it armed the Third World with negotiating strategies in the new WTO. UNCTAD first provided technical guidance in the negotiations on the General Agreement on Trade in Services (GATS), but its signature contribution was the 1997 Positive Agenda for Trade Negotiations, which provided each developing country with a sound technical and legal basis from which to develop its own specific, proactive ability to develop a negotiating position tailored to its economy. As a result, almost half of the proposals submitted to the Seattle WTO ministerial meeting in 1999 came from the developing world. In addition to this new vision of its role, UNCTAD retained its sense of historical mission. In its reorganization, it created an ombudsman to advocate for the needs of the least developed countries (LDCs) within the organization and welcomed NGOs into the mix as equal partners for the first time.[70]

The high-water mark of the neoliberal globalization movement came at the fall 1997 joint meeting of the IMF and World Bank, which actually approved an amendment to the IMF Articles of Agreement that sought to ban any type of capital control. Although that amendment has never been implemented, it was a clear indicator of the type of momentum that globalization had gathered by the mid-1990s. Also in 1997, the OECD abandoned its negotiations for a "Multilateral Agreement on Investment" and shifted those negotiations to the WTO. While the WTO was gaining prestige and power in the global arena, the traditional U.N. development agencies came under attack. In the name of efficiency, a proposal was made in 1997 to merge UNICEF, the World Food Programme, and the U.N. Population Fund into the UNDP. Instead, Secretary-General Kofi Annan opted for closer coordination through the U.N. Development Group.[71]

But just as globalization seemed triumphant in 1997, the Asian financial crisis hit when the Thai currency (the baht) lost almost half of its value in just a couple of days, despite governmental efforts to head off the crisis. Given Thailand's integration into ASEAN, the financial crisis quickly spread to its neighbors. Investors, worried about the value of other Asian currencies, began selling off Indonesian, Malaysian, Philippine, Singaporean, and South Korean currencies as well. Stocks and exchange rates followed the currencies in a downward spiral that then spread to Argentina, Brazil, and Russia before Wall Street stocks experienced a 7.2 percent drop in October 1997 due to fears about the spreading economic crisis. More than 150 Asian financial institutions went out of business, were nationalized, or were placed under IMF control, and the leaders of Indonesia and Thailand left office; but Washington decision-makers argued that the crisis was the result of corruption and greed rather than being a structural characteristic of the new, integrated, global economy.[72]

Alternative currents in the 1980s and backlash in the 1990s

Despite the strength and seeming momentum that the Washington Consensus had developed through the 1980s and mid-1990s, the U.N. system continued to offer alternative views of development that focused on the needs of the LDCs, women, and the environment among others. The 1985 Nairobi Conference, convened to review and appraise the achievements of the U.N. Decade for Women, declared that all issues were women's issues, an ethos that further integrated women's issues into the United Nations' work. The next year, the UNDP adopted an official program of advocating for the needs of women as well as minorities, the poor, and other disadvantaged people in its work with governments in crafting and implementing their development strategies. It also sought to institutionalize such advocacy through a focus on sustainable development and democratic and transparent planning processes, which were measured and tracked in its annual human development report. In the broader U.N. system, the emphasis on women as equal partners in the decision-making process was also evident in the early

1990s' conferences on development, the environment, human rights, population, and social development.[73]

But the first overt attack on the World Bank and IMF's structural adjustment programs came from UNICEF. In its role as the global advocate of children, it publicized the human and social costs of structural adjustment programs with its 1987 publication *Adjustment with a Human Face*. UNICEF Executive Director James Grant (who headed the organization from 1980 until 1995) then turned his organization's focus toward intensive, pro-health, antipoverty programs that both critiqued structural adjustment and planted the seeds for the subsequent Millennium Development Goals (MDGs).[74] But this was just the first volley in the U.N. offensive against the Washington Consensus. UNCTAD led the charge against the economics of structural adjustment, while other specialized agencies and a set of U.N. conferences sought to regain the focus on the social aspects of development that had emerged in the 1970s.

Given its history, it is not surprising that UNCTAD's secretariat was skeptical of the new globalized economic order. This skepticism led to extensive research on the 1980s' debt crises that helped clarify the ways in which this new order—by its very nature—would be characterized by more frequent and destructive currency and financial crises. UNCTAD studies also documented how the structural adjustment programs tended to worsen inequalities and imbalances both between and within countries. It then drew the conclusion that a more diversified approach to the struggles of the Third World, coupled with a focus on human development was the most appropriate way forward.[75]

By the time the WTO hosted its third ministerial meeting in Seattle, Washington, in the United States in 1999, the broad array of people and organizations opposing the almost exclusive focus on neoliberal globalization grabbed the spotlight. Protests outside the meetings and the growing assertiveness of the developing world inside the meetings resulted in deadlock. The head of UNCTAD has argued that the primary reason for this (as well as a lack of progress at the fifth WTO ministerial meeting in Cancún in 2003) was a disagreement over development, primarily over creating space within the global economy for an expansion of Third World exports. Ricupero has also characterized the resistance of the developed world to deal with agriculture—even as it pushes intellectual property issues—as "smack[ing] more and more of power politics and less and less of a movement guided by the principles of sound economic doctrine." Therefore, he worked throughout his tenure at UNCTAD (which stretched from 1995 until 2004) to develop a new, constructive commercial policy that linked trade and development in a way that was responsive to the global South. However, the high hopes for the success of his "Development Agenda for Trade Negotiations" and meaningful changes to promote global development at the Doha Development Round (the first under the WTO), which started in 2001, were largely dashed. The seven-year round of talks was the first not to end in an agreement of some sort, as a new Third World trade bloc (calling itself the G-20 and led by Brazil, China, India, and South Africa) deadlocked with the First World economies on almost all of the key trade issues (agricultural trade, competition, customs, government procurement, and investment).[76]

In an effort to make social—or human—development measurable in the same way as economic development, which would in turn allow funders to hold aid recipients accountable for making process in these areas, the UNDP published its first human development report in 1990, which analyzed 130 countries' progress in social development through the 1960s, 1970s, and 1980s. The initiative of former American businessman-turned-UNDP administrator William H. Draper III, and the creation of Pakistani Mahbub ul Haq in 1986, the human development reports measured the social, political, and economic environments in both the developing and the developed countries. These reports both responded to criticism about UNDP's work with oppressive governments and formalized a structure for its work in advocating steps toward democratization and the promotion of global norms that it had already undertaken in its work. UNDP also put its money into these tasks, using its grants to help countries transitioning to democracy (such as Palestine and South Africa) to develop new, democratic institutions—such as election bureaux, parliamentary systems, and political parties. Over time, the human development reports have added measurements—for example, the 1995 publication (laying the groundwork for the fourth U.N. World Conference on Women in Beijing) included both a gender-related development index and a gender empowerment measure to measure both women's capabilities within the social system and their ability to take advantage of these opportunities. Over time, the UNDP reports have shown developing countries' significant social progress, even as the income gap between the rich and poor countries has expanded. This work has also revealed the need for subsidies to both the poorest nations in the global system and to the poorest segments of national populations in order to create and sustain significant social development.[77]

The UNDP's human development reports were indicative of a larger trend within the United Nations to focus on social development issues during the 1990s and the first decade of the new millennium. The United Nations' global conferences focused on this social dimension of development. For example, the September 1990 U.N. Conference on the Least Developed Countries focused on the need for human-centered, broadly based development measured by, among other things, the degree of decentralization, democratization, and transparency in all decision-making processes related to development. The 1995 World Summit for Social Development similarly put the social dimension of development squarely in the spotlight, and the presence of some 2,315 delegates representing 811 NGOs was meant to reinforce international support for such an agenda. The summit convened to bleak news: the gap between rich and poor countries had expanded in the previous decade, more than one billion human beings were living in abject poverty, and global patterns of consumption and production were environmentally unsustainable and threatened to become more so given continued population growth. Creating a people-centered framework for social development under such conditions called for commitments from both aid donors and recipients, so the summit called on donors to set aside 20 percent of their overseas development aid for social development programs and for recipient governments to match this with 20 percent of their national budgets. NGOs also labored throughout the decade to highlight the inequities of globalization, most famously in the 1997 international shaming of Nike for reaping incredible profits while its female workers in Indonesia, Vietnam, and China labored under inhuman conditions. Even the World Bank shifted toward a greater focus on poverty alleviation and good governance in the 1990s in the wake of criticisms that culminated in tens of thousands protesters turning out in the streets around its annual meeting in 2000.[78]

By far, the U.N. conference that made the biggest splash as the millennium approached was the June 1992 Conference on Environment and Development in Rio de Janeiro, Brazil, more frequently called "The Earth Summit" or the "Rio Summit." With almost 10,000 journalists on site, the summit's "Agenda 21" received intense global media coverage of its interlocking initiatives on forests, climate change, biological diversity, and the interrelationship between development and the environment—which collectively were meant to promote sustainable development worldwide. The Earth Summit also birthed a set of organizations to put this agenda into action: the U.N. Forum on Forests, the Commission on Sustainable Development, the Inter-Agency Committee on Sustainable Development, and the High-Level Advisory Board on Sustainable Development. Similar to the previous Stockholm Conference, Rio emphasized the ways in which both poverty and excessive consumption were dangerous to the planetary environment; and oddly akin to the Nairobi conference on women, Rio essentially declared that all decisions were environmental decisions. This sentiment was reflected in both the 1994 International Conference on Population and Development and the 1994 Global Conference on the Sustainable Development of Small Island Developing States as well as the integration of environmental measures in the UNDP's human development reports.[79]

Efforts to reduce "greenhouse gases" and global warming also earned follow-up international meetings. The 1997 Kyoto Protocol set targets for reducing greenhouse-gas emissions by 2010; but the United States (which accounted for more than 36 percent of such emissions before 1997) ultimately did not ratify the agreement, and neither China nor India signed on. Subsequent conferences in Montreal (2005) and Copenhagen (2009) pledged undefined reductions in emissions that were characterized as failures of the international community to deal with the accelerating effects of climate change. The results of the Copenhagen Climate Change Conference were deeply disappointing, especially given the mobilization by environmental NGOs preceding it. But this is a case when initial news reports—which tended to blame the Obama administration for the conference's shortcomings—were fundamentally misleading. Instead it was China that effectively blocked a more ambitious deal and cleverly worked with G-77 spokespeople to place the blame elsewhere. The movement to limit climate change regained momentum with the December 2015 U.N. Climate Change Conference's "Paris Agreement" to limit the planetary temperature increase to 1.5 degrees Celsius, which has been signed (at the time of this writing) by countries producing 56.87 percent of global greenhouse gas emissions and went into effect on November 4, 2016.[80]

Conclusion: The Millennium Development Goals, 2000–15

With the coming of a new millennium, the U.N. General Assembly hosted, in September 2000, the largest-ever summit of the world's leaders, which adopted the United Nations Millennium Declaration and committed the organization to pursuing progress on a set of measurable MDGs that integrated much on the previous decade's work on social development and poverty alleviation. For example, the Millennium Development Goals (MDGs) called on the international community to cut by 50 percent the proportion of the globe's people living on less than one dollar a day, to increase to 100 percent the proportion of boys and girls completing elementary-level schooling, and to halt the spread of HIV/AIDS and malaria—all by 2015. Secretary-General Kofi Annan's subsequent "Road Map toward the Implementation of the United Nations Millennium Declaration" recognized that a combination of political will and significant, additional material resources were needed to achieve this ambitious agenda. While U.N. organizations and conferences did their best to promote the MDGs and despite some hopes that a post-9/11 world would see a greater commitment to development as the surest way to prevent "failed states" and terrorism, there was little measurable improvement to report by 2015. The 2007 subprime mortgage crisis in the United States soon precipitated a global credit shortage. Coupled with a mid-2008 spike in gasoline prices and the collapse of Iceland's national finances (due to extreme banking speculation), the First World did not feel equipped to also handle the vast global commitments needed to realize the MDGs. As a result, wide disparities continued to grow both within and between countries.[81]

In a process very similar to the First Development Decade, the United Nations tried—as the deadline for the MDGs approached—to conceptualize a brighter future by collating the more than five million responses to its global online survey, "The World We Want," and developing a new set of global goals. But the reality was that the U.N. could only develop the rhetorical frame. It could not manufacture meaningful improvement in the lives of those most hurt by the speeding of globalization. In this way, we can see significant continuity between the earliest and the most recent U.N. efforts to promote development. All these efforts were cast as a type of presumably apolitical politics "that speaks to humanity's greatest ambitions for progress and welfare and to its greatest fears of social collapse" and define poverty/development as a socioeconomic problem that can be fixed by the appropriate application of rational planning and expert knowledge. While this new form of global politics was certainly not limited to the United Nations, the intergovernmental organization was the central borderland where development's aspirational and idealistic rhetoric, its dizzying array of statistics, and its politics occupied center stage.[82]

CHAPTER 6
MAKING AND KEEPING THE PEACE: U.N. PEACEKEEPING AND REFUGEE ASSISTANCE OPERATIONS

Jeanna Kinnebrew and Amy L. Sayward

As we have already seen in earlier chapters, the primary and most difficult responsibility assigned to the United Nations was keeping the peace; the League of Nations had failed in this responsibility and had been dissolved as a result. Maintaining "international peace and security" was the first purpose listed in the first chapter of the U.N. Charter. Encompassed within that definition were taking "effective collective measures for the prevention and removal of threats to the peace," suppressing "acts of aggression or other breaches of the peace," and bringing "about by peaceful means, and in conformity with the principles of justice and international law, adjustment or settlement of international disputes or situations which might lead to a breach of the peace." While the organization's founders believed that this job would be carried out by the Security Council, we saw in Chapter 3 that the members of the U.N. Security Council—especially during the Cold War—disagreed frequently about what did and did not constitute a "breach of the peace." As a result, the organization as a whole had to be creative to deal with situations.

In this chapter, we will take up the question of what happened when U.N. peacekeeping troops arrived at their destinations. Additionally, we will see how the United Nations has developed a variety of types of peacekeeping forces over time to meet the ever-changing demands of the world. It has stationed military observer groups in places like the Middle East, Kashmir, and Cyprus to monitor truces; peacekeeping forces have actively participated in combat, most prominently in Korea and Kuwait; and especially after the Cold War, newly rebranded "peace-building" troops helped maintain law and order as regimes torn by civil conflicts transitioned through elections in places like Cambodia and South Africa.[1] However, even before the end of the Cold War, the international community saw U.N. troops as instrumental in developing "an atmosphere which makes active peace work possible," in the words of the 1988 Nobel Peace Prize committee. Secretary-General Boutros Boutros-Ghali made peacekeeping the central focus of his post–Cold War agenda for the United Nations, with the goal of using such troops to contribute to the overall "peace process." He centralized and accentuated these operations by establishing the U.N. Department of Peacekeeping Operations in 1992 (these operations had previously fallen under the umbrella of the U.N. Office of Special Political Affairs), and the work of the U.N. High Commissioner on Refugees (UNHCR) was also brought under this operation, recognizing that part of the peace-building mandate required the repatriation of refugees who had been driven from their homes by the previous civil conflict. Integrating these many thousands of previous refugees into a society struggling to redefine itself magnified the challenges but also offered the skills of a resilient and committed group to the process.[2]

The task of caring and advocating for the world's refugees—unlike military peacekeeping activities—had not been foreseen by the founders of the United Nations. In fact, despite the massive numbers involved, the United Nations sought to handle both the displaced persons (DPs) of the Second World War and the Arab refugees displaced in the 1948 war that established Israel's independence (Chapter 7) as transitory challenges that required only temporary organizations. As a result, the December 14, 1950, General Assembly resolution establishing the office of the UNHCR provided for just a three-year organizational mandate. However, the onset of the Cold War and the many wars of colonial liberation quickly showed that there was not a single refugee crisis to be resolved but an ongoing set of crises that required an agile organization that could quickly and effectively organize and coordinate the provision of food, clothing, shelter, and protection at any point on the globe. Unsurprisingly, international political realities often played a decisive role in the ability of the high commissioners to protect, care for, and repatriate or settle the refugees elsewhere—especially since they lacked significant resources of their own or the power to enforce their mandate. As a result, the person and office staff of the UNHCR have had to combine the moral authority of the office with equal measures of education, diplomacy, persuasion, and public relations in order to convince governments to follow the regulations laid out in the 1951 Refugee Convention and to mobilize public opinion and monies to carry out the tasks at hand. And these tasks have changed significantly over time. While it was easier to settle refugees from communist states during the Cold War (due to their propaganda value to the West), refugee operations in the Third World had to be integrated into development plans. The work of the high commissioner's office and the rest of the United Nations have become increasingly enmeshed, and greater and greater cooperation between agencies has been needed to minimize the environmental impact of refugee camps, to protect the human rights of those who have been displaced, and even to work with those in the U.N. system seeking to prosecute those responsible for genocide and massive human rights violations. With the end of the Cold War and the increase in the number of refugees being forcibly displaced, U.N. member states have become increasingly reluctant to see these people resettled in third states and have become focused more and more on the need for repatriation rather than resettlement. At the time of writing, the refugees from the Syrian conflict are running headlong into Western Europeans' perceptions that they are being overrun by a combination of "economic refugees" and "political refugees" and that they simply cannot absorb any more people into their cultures and economies. But for the 9,300 UNHCR staff members working in 123 countries, the Syrians are just one group among the forty-three million individuals they are currently assisting—a scale and scope that the United Nations' founders could not have fathomed.[3]

Historiography

Historians, political scientists, scholars of international law, and those studying refugees have similarly struggled with the scale and scope of the United Nations' work in peacekeeping and refugee assistance. Any number of works mention this work peripherally in their descriptions of civil wars and international conflicts, although sometimes the victims of these conflicts and those who seek to help them remain invisible, and oftentimes the work of peacekeepers is mentioned in passing in a conclusion or as a tangent. In part, this absence in the literature may reflect the fact that refugees and peacekeepers do not fit easily into narratives focused on nation-states. And much of the scholarly literature seems to be focused on contemporary crises, rather than on historical analyses of longer-term trends and patterns. The UNHCR has generated relatively few institutional histories—perhaps because its historical record includes some spectacular failures and many qualified successes; on the other hand, U.N. peacekeeping operations have lacked a single organizational structure to generate such histories.[4]

The literature on U.N. peacekeeping seems particularly presentist and/or fragmented. There are chapters on peacekeeping in a variety of edited volumes on general topics. Focusing specifically on peacekeeping, the United Nations Peacekeeping website simply lists the past and present operations without any effort to synthesize the meaning and significance of this work that has now stretched over seven decades. The most recent scholarship comes predominantly in the form of edited volumes in which each operation is similarly treated separately by different authors, but in these cases, the volumes' editors do make some effort to sketch out overarching themes in the books' introductions or conclusions. The most promising works to date are by political scientists striving to point out what is working in U.N. peacekeeping.[5]

Supplementing the handful of institutional UNHCR histories is a small literature by and about those who have worked for and led the organization and those who have been refugees. Interestingly, in the 1980s, the multidisciplinary academic field of refugee studies emerged, with the University of Oxford developing its Refugee Studies Centre in 1982 within its Department of International Development. Like the study of international development, refugee studies emerged with a goal of improving policymaking and international service-delivery in order to materially improve the lives of those being served. As the field has developed, some scholars have become more interested in and concerned with the lives of specific groups of refugees, their experiences, and their challenges, while others have adopted postmodern frames in order to understand the ways in which the UNHCR, its camps, and its professionals function and the ways in which refugees are stripped of identity and voice as they are named and treated as "refugees."[6]

For the aspiring scholar, there seems to be much work to be done in integrating the stories of peacekeepers and refugees into the state-centered histories of wars and conflicts. Additionally, looking at the ways in which the immigrant experience and the refugee experience compare with one another and the ways in which both intersect with national political, economic, and social histories could be very fruitful. The same could be said for integrating the history of peacekeeping into the histories of the national militaries who undertake these duties and the roles of these militaries, in turn, in shaping domestic perceptions about conflicts abroad. Additionally, histories of U.N. peacekeeping that take a longer view of the work and that seek to synthesize the long-term meaning and significance of this work would significantly deepen the current literature.

Dealing with Europe's displaced persons (DPs): From UNRRA and the IRO to the UNHCR, 1943–55

Even before the United Nations Organization was created, the wartime Allies formally pledged on November 9, 1943, to create the U.N. Relief and Rehabilitation Administration (UNRRA) to provide basic necessities and services to the victims of war. Part of the impetus behind this early planning was the lesson the international community had learned from the mass displacement of people during and in the wake of the First World War. In addition to the work of the League of Nations Health Organization in combating the spread of epidemic disease among these populations, the League had appointed, in 1921, Norwegian Fridtjof Nansen to serve as its first high commissioner for refugees; he served Armenians fleeing war and genocide in Turkey and white Russians fleeing the communist revolution and state in the new Soviet Union. During the 1930s, Nansen developed the first international refugee convention, which allowed his office to provide refugees with travel documents, legal protection, and a small amount of social assistance; the high commissioner's office administered the convention and sponsored reintegration programs during the late 1930s that assisted about half a million people. Building from this experience, the Allied nations that participated in UNRRA underwrote its budget through voluntary contributions, but as the vast majority of aid came from the United States, the organization was based in Washington, DC (with field offices throughout Europe and the Pacific) and was led by three American directors until it ceased operations in 1948.[7] In addition to caring for the immediate physical needs of the citizens of occupied countries and the DPs present in those areas, UNRRA also helped repatriate the vast majority of DPs back to their countries of origin after the cessation of hostilities, but a number remained as the organization wound down its activities.

As a result, the United Nations established a new organization—the International Refugee Organization (IRO)—in February 1946 to handle a special subset of the DPs not repatriated by UNRRA. The IRO defined a "refugee"—as opposed to a DP—as a "pre- or postwar victim of Nazi or fascist regimes or of racial, religious, or political persecution," and it specifically excluded from assistance Soviet citizens who refused to return home (these were forcibly repatriated) and "persons of German ethnic origin," except for those who could prove they had been persecuted by the Nazi Party. The IRO dealt especially with those who had been released from German concentration camps, many of whom were Jews with no interest in returning to the countries that had supported or facilitated the Holocaust. As a result, the new organization focused on resettlement in third countries—unlike UNRRA's focus on repatriation. This also ensured, as the Cold War heated up, that these refugees could find new homes outside of the Soviet sphere. Ultimately, the IRO resettled more than a million people between 1948 and

1952 and helped normalize the notion that large numbers of displaced people required international assistance so that they could be dispersed and assimilated.[8]

Despite the IRO's efforts, thousands of wartime refugees continued to languish in camps, leading the United Nations take steps at the end of 1949 to establish a new office, that of the High Commissioner for Refugees (UNHCR). In its Resolution 319, the General Assembly directed the secretary-general and the Economic and Social Council (ECOSOC) to prepare a charter and a budget for the new UNHCR, which would begin work on January 1, 1951, to protect the remaining refugees and provide for their final dispensation during its three-year mandate. Given its temporary mandate, the new office received no regular budget allocation and initially could not even seek governmental or private support without the explicit permission of the Assembly. The 1951 Convention Relating to the Status of Refugees (along with its later updates) provides UNHCR's legal mandate. It defines a "refugee" as someone who "owing to well-founded fear of being persecuted for reasons of race, religion, nationality, membership of a particular social group or political opinion, is outside the country of his nationality [or lacks a nationality] and is unable or, owing to such fear, is unwilling to avail himself of the protection of that country." It specifically excludes war criminals, but the change from the IRO to the UNHCR now afforded protection—and potentially asylum—to those fleeing communist persecution, enmeshing the high commissioner from the beginning in the international politics of the Cold War. The convention also charges the UNHCR with protecting the legal rights of the refugee, which include freedom of religion, the right to gainful employment, property rights, the right of nonrefoulement (meaning that a refugee cannot be forcibly repatriated), and the right to be treated as any other foreign national in a host country—which collectively marked an important advance in refugees' human rights. The high commissioner acted under the guise of the convention, which did not fully enter into force until 1954; more challenging was the fact that countries that were not party to the convention were not bound by it. Initially, the convention also only applied to European refugees fleeing the circumstances of the Second World War. From the beginning, therefore, the high commissioners often had to rely on the moral and normative force of their office—rather than a strictly defined legal authority—and on their ability to mobilize resources to carry out their work, a situation that continues to this day since a number of countries have still not ratified the convention and its subsequent protocols.[9] By the end of 1953 (when its original authority was set to expire), it was clear that the refugee problem was not something that could be solved so quickly. Not only was it difficult to resettle the remaining wartime refugees (many of whom were elderly or disabled), but new refugee crises also sprang up both within and outside of the borders of the European continent during the rest of the 1950s.

Peacekeeping's first major test: The United Nations and the Korean War, 1950–53

In the past decade, historians writing about what was once termed "the Forgotten War" now see the Korean War as "the turning point in the globalization of the Cold War." Certainly, the United Nations' involvement in the Korean War was, in many ways, a turning point for the ways in which it thought about itself and its role in promoting and maintaining international peace. The United Nations' role in the conflict embodied the ability of the Security Council to respond with force to aggressive actions taken by or against member states and stood in stark contrast to the League of Nations, whose system of collective action—which relied entirely on individual countries to act—had failed to stop the aggressive fascist states. In addition, U.N. involvement in a regional East Asian dispute signaled that the Cold War was a global conflict, not one merely confined to Eastern Europe. This was a problematic development for the United Nations, because the idea of political neutrality was the basis for much of its international legitimacy. In some ways, the boldness of its response in 1950 led to the withdrawal of full support for U.N. peacekeeping for the rest of the Cold War, as some governments saw its actions in Korea as a negation of its neutral stance. However, U.N. peacekeeping actions on the peninsula, particularly in its usage of Article 51 to justify armed response to conflict, set the standard for future peacekeeping operations.[10]

The causes of the Korean War, like those of the preceding crisis in Berlin, were directly tied to the immediate aftermath of the Second World War. Japan had ruled the Korean peninsula since 1905. As the Second World War wound down, U.S. President Harry S. Truman negotiated the temporary division of Korea at the 38th parallel to facilitate the disarmament of the Japanese soldiers there. The Soviet Union occupied the area north of that line, and the United States occupied the southern zone. Although intended to be a temporary occupation, both the Soviet Union and the United States recognized the benefits of remaining in control of a strategically significant portion of East Asia. With the Cold War heating up in Eastern Europe, the temporary division between North and South Korea became increasingly fixed. In 1948, a distinctly noncommunist state, the Republic of Korea (ROK), formed in the south under the leadership of Dr. Syngman Rhee and with the blessing of the United States. The Soviet Union, in turn, established the communist Democratic People's Republic of Korea (DPRK), led by Kim Il Sung. Both leaders claimed their government was the legitimate leader of all of Korea and called for reunification.[11]

Another East Asian conflict played an important role in catalyzing war between North and South Korea. Back in 1927, conflict had broken out in China between the communist People's Liberation Army (PLA) and the nationalist Kuomintang. Struggle for control of the country continued until 1949, when the PLA took full control and established the People's Republic of China (PRC). The Kuomintang fled to the island of Taiwan, where it established itself as the Republic of China (ROC). The United States supported the ROC and argued that the government of Taiwan—not the communist government in Beijing—should maintain China's permanent seat on the Security Council. The Soviet Union argued that the PRC should take the Security Council seat. The Soviet Union, in protest of U.S. support of the Kuomintang, rang in the new year of 1950 by boycotting the United Nations, including its seat on the Security Council.[12]

On June 25, 1950, North Korea invaded South Korea and pushed quickly south, beginning the Korean War. Truman, in addressing both the American people and the United Nations, framed the events as an act of Soviet-inspired aggression that required a strong U.S. response to contain the spreading communist threat. China had fallen to the communists, and Truman argued that South Korea was next. Historians throughout the 1960s and 1970s supported this viewpoint. The general consensus during this time was that North Korea, working with the full knowledge and support of Moscow and Beijing, had invaded South Korea in order to establish a reunified, communist state. Not until the revisionist historians of the 1970s and 1980s were the roots of the Korean War situated more clearly within the context of pre-1950 tensions between the ROK, DPRK, China, the Soviet Union, and the United States. Historians accessing declassified U.S. materials as well as some captured Korean documents came to understand that in reality North and South Korea had been fighting a civil war, characterized by frequent but low-impact border skirmishes, since at least the summer of 1948.[13] And another wave of scholarship has revealed new aspects of the origins of the Korean War, as the end of the Cold War brought Soviet documents and archives to light. These reveal that Stalin, although certainly concerned about a potential military threat from South Korea, repeatedly refused North Korean requests to invade the South. Eventually, however, these same documents show that Stalin did play a part, "albeit reluctantly," in the invasion. The scholarly consensus at this point about the origins of the Korean War is that the conflict is best understood as an "international civil war"—that is, it was, at its root, a civil war between the two Koreas, but that war quickly drew in additional powers, making it a truly and frighteningly international conflict. Regardless of its roots, it quickly escalated given the Soviet representative's absence from the Security Council.[14]

Truman pressured the United Nations to intervene militarily in the Korean conflict, portraying such intervention primarily as a peacekeeping action. On June 25, the U.N. Security Council passed Resolution 82, defining North Korea's invasion a "breach of the peace" and calling for full withdrawal of DPRK forces north of the 38th parallel. At the time, the North Koreans were moving south quickly, and many feared that South Korea would not hold out long enough to receive U.N. assistance. Two days later, the follow-up Resolution 83 noted that North Korea had not responded to the earlier resolution and recommended that "members of the United Nations furnish such assistance to the Republic of Korea as necessary to repel the armed attack and to restore international peace and security in the area." Though the Soviets' U.N. boycott had been crafted as a symbolic gesture in support of communist China's representation on the Security Council, their absence meant that—rather than being vetoed—both resolutions passed and the United Nations was now on its way to war.[15]

Citing Resolution 83, Truman quickly sent air and sea troops to assist South Korea. The Soviet Union, via diplomatic channels, protested, arguing that American military participation in what the Soviets classified as a civil conflict was tantamount to a declaration of war on North Korea. Throughout the summer of 1950, Truman continued to supply South Korean forces with troops, materiel, and assistance with a naval blockade. U.S. forces helped the South Korean government maintain itself within what came to be called the "Pusan perimeter," but southern forces lacked the troop strength to push the invading North Koreans back any significant distance. On September 15, 1950, a United

Nations force (composed of U.S., British, and ROC troops) landed at Inchon, close to the North Korean border, and closed in on the 38th parallel. Moving north of the parallel, China warned, would spark Chinese and Soviet retribution. In the meantime, the Soviet Union retook its seat on the Security Council, intending to veto any future resolutions supporting South Korean military operations.[16]

Stymied in the Security Council, the United States convinced the majority of the General Assembly to adopt a resolution titled "Uniting for Peace." This resolution, passed on November 3, 1950, redefined the U.N. Charter's Article 51—member states' right of individual or collective self-defense—to allow for direct American military intervention in the Korean conflict. The resolution stated that if the Security Council could not come to a unanimous vote among the five permanent members on a question of "international peace and security," the General Assembly would be justified in considering the question itself. Essentially, the resolution offered the United States an end-run around potential Soviet vetoes of military action. This new power drastically enlarged the potential possibilities of U.N. peacekeeping forces, as they could now be directed by the General Assembly even in the case of a dispute within the Security Council. In the Korean case, the nature of the war changed drastically with the intervention of communist Chinese forces (starting in November 1950) that pushed the U.N. forces south; fighting continued but largely stalemated along the 38th parallel. American fervor for the war waned, and the United States and the United Nations came under increasing criticism. After President Dwight D. Eisenhower took office in 1953, he supported a U.N.-led effort (led by India) that led to an armistice being signed by China, North Korea, South Korea, and the United States on July 27, 1953.[17] The war was over, but the United Nations' work as an international peacekeeping force had just begun.

Prior to Korea, U.N. peacekeeping forces had only mediated and monitored cease-fires, observed border conflicts, and ameliorated belligerent activity through a show of force and not necessarily the use of force. They carried out these missions by and large with the consent of all parties in conflict, and a substantial portion of the United Nations' authority rested on the fact that all governments agreed to abide by its mediation efforts. By accepting American arguments that Article 51 justified the use of force, the General Assembly and Security Council showed themselves willing to embrace a broader definition of peacekeeping in response to urgent problems.[18]

UNKRA and American Cold War refugee policy

In the midst of the Korean War, the United Nations (at the initiative of the Canadians) worked not only to conduct the war effort but also to assist the refugees of that war and to begin reconstructing the southern part of the war-devastated peninsula. Although the U.N. Korean Reconstruction Agency (UNKRA) faced many difficulties working in an active war zone that was controlled by the U.S. military (which was entirely focused on security concerns), this organization sought to aid the Koreans displaced by the conflict (who might or might not have fit the legal definition of "refugee," depending on whether or not one recognized the border between the northern and southern parts of Korea as an international border at that time), primarily by reconstructing the infrastructure needed for them to settle back into civilian life.[19]

Despite the strategic interests present in this situation, entrusting this work to UNKRA—rather than to the UNHCR—was part of a larger pattern in the early Cold War in which the United States clearly enunciated its view that refugee issues were too important to evolving U.S. Cold War policy to be left to the United Nations. Just as the United States held up the negotiations on the Korean cease-fire agreement over the issue of repatriating Korean prisoners of war to the communist north, Americans enshrined the idea that people fleeing the evils of communism would be welcomed with open arms through two other multilateral organizations that it established outside of Korea and outside of the U.N. framework. Terming those fleeing communist persecution "escapees," who "voted with their feet" on the merits of the respective superpowers, the United States created its Escapee Program as well as the 27-nation International Committee on European Migration (ICEM, which began operations on February 1, 1952) to facilitate the granting of asylum to those from the communist bloc; both were also much more generously funded with American dollars than the High Commissioner's office. ICEM's goal was to resettle European migrants from "overpopulated" areas (some 570,000 by 1957), which functioned to provide new homes for some refugees from communism as well as for the influx of Dutch citizens displaced by Indonesian independence (Chapter 3).[20] The United States also supported a different organization to care for the Palestinian refugees of the 1948 war in the Middle East (see Chapter 7)—the U.N. Relief and Works Agency for Palestine Refugees in the Near East (UNRWA), which also had a temporary mandate. The UNHCR, however, quickly realized that a durable, nimble organization would be needed to deal with ever-evolving global circumstances.

The High Commissioner develops his office's autonomy in the 1950s

Despite this narrow American vision of the mission of the UNHCR, Gerrit van Heuven Goedhart of the Netherlands, who first held this post, secured his office's permanency—and a degree of autonomy—by using the Cold War dynamics to his advantage. The UNHCR's care of refugees from communist East Berlin and Hungary made his organization useful to the West in the Cold War, which gave it the autonomy needed to globalize its mandate in ways that the West frequently resisted—especially in its care of refugees from the French efforts to quash the fight for Algerian independence. The Dutchman's success in navigating the Cold War currents to best serve the interests of the refugees also earned his organization the 1954 Nobel Peace Prize. And by 1958, when the United Nations named June 1959–May 1960 as World Refugee Year, the organization had proved itself essential to the international community in caring for refugee communities in ways that were more effective and more broadly supported than efforts outside of the High Commissioner's office (viz. the work of both UNRWA and UNKRA).[21]

Goedhart—as a lawyer, journalist, and active member of the Dutch resistance during the Second World War, who had also contributed to its government-in-exile in London—had a set of skills that allowed him to provide refugees with the legal protections offered by the 1951 Convention, to publicize the plight of the world's refugees and gain the support of international public opinion, and to navigate international relations in a way that maximized his office's freedom of action prior to his sudden death in 1956. His first step was to obtain permission from the General Assembly in February 1952 to independently raise funds for the office's work through the new U.N. Refugee Fund; in doing so, he gained Assembly recognition of the need to provide material assistance to refugees—for legal protection without food, clothing, and shelter was little comfort. Although it acknowledged the need, the General Assembly provided no additional funds to meet these material needs, and donations to the U.N. Refugee Fund lagged behind the need.[22]

However, a $2.9 million grant from the Ford Foundation in 1952 (though far short of the $10.5 million requested) cemented the high commissioner's relationship with the World Council of Churches, the National Catholic Welfare Conference, the American Joint Distribution Committee, and the Lutheran World Federation (its service providers) and equipped the UNHCR to play a leading role in addressing an early 1953 refugee crisis in West Berlin. Although West Germany had struggled since the Second World War to effectively handle refugees within its borders, early 1953 witnessed a huge increase in the number of refugees entering it monthly (28,276 came in January, and the number peaked at 48,000 in March). Although this population fell outside of the high commissioner's mandate, he recognized the need and cabled sixty U.N. members requesting assistance—specifically to create prefabricated homes near industrial centers for the predominantly young, skilled refugees. Switzerland and other nations responded, and the West German government and banks matched every external dollar with four of its own to meet the crisis as well as the needs of the population that had been living in refugee camps for years.[23] Having demonstrated how it could effectively orchestrate governmental and nongovernmental support during a refugee crisis when it had sufficient funding, UNHCR subsequently headed up the response to the 1956 Hungarian refugee crisis.

The UNHCR's experiences in Berlin and its growing capacity both to address emergency situations and to develop permanent solutions for refugees made it ready to answer the secretary-general's call to act as the lead agency (despite American qualms) dealing with some 200,000 Hungarians fleeing to Austria and Yugoslavia in the wake of the unsuccessful uprising against the communist government in 1956. The high commissioner determined that the crisis fell under his office's mandate, since the refugees were fleeing communist persecution, and another Ford Foundation grant helped fund the settlement and care of these refugees into some 250 camps in Austria; Western governments, fearing the danger of the refugees to unsettle Austria's government and hoping to maximize the propaganda value of these newest refugees, soon pitched in as well. For example, 25,000 Hungarian refugees settled in Great Britain, the United States admitted 38,000 in a special dispensation from its regular immigration regulations, and Canada also welcomed thousands, but none received an unreservedly warm welcome from the local population.[24]

Just as the UNHCR might have been pigeonholed as being an anticommunist propaganda vehicle, the new high commissioner, Auguste Lindt of Switzerland, showed his independence and his absolute commitment to refugees in general by repatriating those who wished to return to their homes behind the "iron curtain." Mediating between East and West, the high commissioner ultimately worked to repatriate almost 10 percent of the Hungarian refugees under his care, which earned him the umbrage of the United States, for whom repatriation to a communist country came as a severe propaganda blow. In the words of Gil Loescher, the preeminent historian of postwar refugee issues, the high commissioner's actions "underlined the capacity of the UNHCR to have an independent influence on events at the centre of world politics."[25]

Lindt also expanded the geographical scope of his office in dealing with the refugee crisis in Tunisia and Morocco emerging in 1957 (embodied by some 260,000 Algerians) from Algeria's war for liberation from France. Wanting to escape the perception that he served only as "High Commissioner for European Refugees," Lindt leveraged both the international support and goodwill that his office had earned from the Hungarian refugee crisis and the language of UNHCR's original mandate to fashion a response to the Algerian refugee crisis. He correctly gauged the need for a broad spectrum of international goodwill (that included the Soviet bloc as well as the emerging Third World) and for his office to develop the capacity to respond to similar crises of decolonization in the future. Although the French government initially denied UNHCR's authority to deal with what it considered a domestic matter and saw it as just another effort by the rebels to internationalize the conflict, Lindt's diplomacy, international public opinion, and the urgent requests for international assistance coming from neighboring Tunisia and Morocco in 1958 eventually overcame French objections (in part the concession came because the Algerians were not officially identified as "refugees" nor the French regime, by implication, as the source of persecution). Starting in May 1959, UNHCR coordinated the aid effort, which took place primarily in Tunisia, itself a relatively poor country. Unlike the previous Hungarian crisis, there was little desire on the part of the refugees to be resettled elsewhere; they primarily sought to survive until the revolution had been completed and they could return home. The fact that more than half of the refugees were children helped to mobilize popular support for the relief measures needed, which came from a wide spectrum of governments—including the Soviet Union, Egypt, and the United States—as well as from the International Red Cross and Red Crescent societies. At the end of the conflict in 1962, UNHCR worked to repatriate most of the Algerian refugees. Given this success, the office now effectively had a global mandate that it lived up to in the coming decades.[26]

Just as the UNHCR prepared to intervene in North Africa, the high commissioner—catalyzed by a small group of British journalists and politicians—promoted the idea of a World Refugee Year that would bring international attention and monies to the world's refugee challenges—not just those under his mandate but also those in Hong Kong and the Middle East. In response, the General Assembly named the period from June 1959 to May 1960 as "World Refugee Year." Specially commissioned postage stamps, plays, documentaries, exhibits of photographs, advertising, and an "All-Star Festival" organized by actor Yul Brenner helped to raise both sympathy and funds. Simulated "refugee camps" in Geneva, London, and Manchester were immensely popular. Ultimately, the year opened up new emigration possibilities, directly resulting in a decrease in the number of refugees in Europe, including 2,200 individuals with physical handicaps. New funds were used to hire a mental health adviser to work with the long-term refugees to find them the most appropriate, individual path out of the camps. Although some of the funds raised also went to UNRWA in the Middle East, UNHCR saw both an increase in funds and a significant change in the sources of its funding. Previously almost 90 percent of UNHCR funds had come directly from governments, but World Refugee Year contributions saw private contributions surge, making up a full half of the $8.78 million pledged in that period.[27]

The high commissioner used some of these funds to expand his work, using his "good offices" to contribute to the relief of refugees from the Chinese communist revolution who had fled to the tiny canton of Hong Kong and further break down the barriers between his legal mandate and the effective mandate of his office. The year also helped to normalize the idea that an international organization was needed to protect and care for refugees, a task far too heavy for any single country to tackle. In fact, until the 1980s, most governments relied on the UNHCR to screen refugees for asylum and deferred to the Office's interpretations of international law as it related to refugees.[28]

Peacekeeping in the shadow of decolonization: The United Nations and the Republic of the Congo, 1960–64

U.N. peacekeeping efforts in the early 1960s were not as successful as the efforts to resettle refugees. Intervening in the conflict in Congo left its reputation battered and bruised. The Congolese conflict can best be understood as a series of civil wars within a larger decolonization conflict. In the 1950s, Africans across the continent had rightly clamored for independence, and the Congo was no exception. Located in the sub-Saharan center of the continent and endowed with valuable natural resources (including rubber, coal, and diamonds), the Congolese people had suffered horrendously as the personal colony of King Leopold II of Belgium from 1885 until wholesale atrocities against the local population forced him to cede control to the Belgian government in 1908, which had done very little to prepare the aspiring nation for independence by the time that Brussels had agreed to a six-month transition period preceding independence and elections (scheduled to take place in May 1960). Congolese voters elected Patrice Lumumba as prime minister, and the Democratic Republic of the Congo officially became independent on June 30, 1960. But only days later, troops serving in the national army mutinied, leading to general disorder across the country as long-standing tensions between native Congolese and approximately 100,000 Belgians still residing in the country exploded. Citing the need to protect Belgian nationals, Brussels sent troops to the Congo without the new government's permission. Belgian soldiers engaged with Congolese troops still loyal to the state army as well as minor insurgent forces. Various forces within the Congolese government competed for power, and one Congolese leader announced the secession of his province, Katanga (especially rich in natural resources), which prompted threats of secession from other provinces.[29]

On July 12, 1960, the Democratic Republic of Congo appealed to the United Nations for military assistance to protect itself against the Belgian troops and to maintain a unified Congo. A unanimous Security Council vote approved this assistance and called on Belgium to withdraw its troops. However, U.N. troops were unable to prevent the conflict between the Congo and Belgium from devolving into a morass of violence and a "vivid reminder of what could go wrong" in both independence struggles and peacekeeping operations.[30]

In response to the Congolese appeal, the United Nations established the U.N. Operation in the Congo (known by its French name and acronym, Operation des Nations Unies au Congo, or ONUC), which ran from July 1960 until June 1964. At its height, ONUC consisted of an extraordinarily large peacekeeping force of approximately 20,000 troops as well as a multinational group of civilian leaders and observers. ONUC's mandate was to "restore and maintain the political independence and territorial integrity of the Congo; to help it maintain law and order throughout the country; and to put into effect a wide and long-range programme of training and technical assistance" to ensure the new nation would be able to maintain itself after the cessation of hostilities. Secretary-General Hammarskjöld stressed the United Nations' neutrality and repeatedly refused to publicly take a political side in the crisis. In practice, his peacekeepers struggled in their mission to hold Congo together and to protect themselves, the Congolese, and Belgian settlers from both internal and external threats. The secretary-general's political neutrality notwithstanding, Congo's central government and the U.N. leadership both saw Katanga's return to the republic as vital to the continued success of the country, leading to repeated clashes between the U.N. force and the Katangese army. Additionally, foreign mercenaries—many of them white supremacists and opponents of African independence—took up arms on behalf of Belgium and conducted guerrilla warfare against U.N. peacekeepers, who prevented massacres of civilians, rounded up and jailed mercenaries, and policed arms shipments into the country—in other words, they carried out a "massive intervention in the guise of non-intervention." The January 1961 assassination of former prime minister Patrice Lumumba, executed in Katanga province, only served to fan the flames.[31]

In September of 1961, Hammarskjöld himself perished in a plane crash on his way to peace talks with Congolese leaders in neighboring Zambia. His death, the growing cost of ONUC, and U.N. efforts in other areas lessened international attention on the Congo crisis. The new secretary-general, U Thant, coordinated Katanga's surrender in late 1962, but armed clashes and unrest continued for several years. U.N. peacekeeping forces left the country finally on June 30, 1964, having fulfilled their costly mandate to keep the Congo whole. The United Nations had spent some $408 million on ONUC, but multiple member states—including the United States—refused to pay their share until the International Court of Justice ordered them to do so in 1962. In addition to far exceeding its financial budget, the United Nations had overextended its political capital during the Congo crisis; its peacekeeping forces had clearly entered the conflict as participants with defined objectives, fighting troops, and political preferences. Although U.N. forces had also fought in Korea, this set of peacekeepers in the Congo was directed by the secretary-general, and their attempt at neutrality ensured, as one historian put it, "at one point or another every Congolese political faction considered ONUC the enemy." Additionally, many saw the further expansion of the hazy "self-defense" duties under Article 51 of the United Nations Charter—which were now used to justify U.N. troops using preemptive force to achieve and enforce peace in the Congo—as unacceptable. The ultimate result of ONUC's financial and mission overreach was a decade-long hiatus in new peacekeeping missions.[32]

New refugee challenges in the developing world, 1960s–1970s

Just as the Congo crisis pulled the U.N. peacekeepers more deeply into the process of decolonization in Africa, the high commissioner's earlier experience in Tunisia with the Algerian refugees was just the first of many experiences for his office in working on the African continent. Throughout the 1960s and 1970s, UNHCR and its allied voluntary agencies assisted many refugees fleeing wars of liberation or conflicts following independence, which constantly challenged them to expand their capacities. As early as 1961, several thousand fled Ghana for neighboring Togo, and 150,000 fled Angola; by 1965, the high commissioner was involved in fifteen different refugee situations on the continent. To meet the growing need, the nongovernmental charitable organizations that had an established track record with his office organized themselves in March 1962 into the International Council of Voluntary Agencies to better coordinate their efforts. The largest—Catholic Relief Services, the World Council of Churches, the Lutheran World Federation, and the Young Men's Christian Association (YMCA)—were best able to expand further and meet the refugees' varied needs on the ground; while the Danish Refugee Council and Oxfam focused on raising funds to meet each new crisis. As there were more—and more complex—refugee operations in Africa and elsewhere, the high commissioner's work in coordinating them became increasingly visible and important, and he increasingly integrated the expertise of the World Food Programme, the Food and Agriculture Organization, UNICEF, the International Labour Organization, and UNESCO into refugee operations. In response, the office's budget increased by $200,000 each year from 1965 until 1969, when the total number of African refugees under UNHCR care numbered just short of a quarter-million. Support for these significant annual budget increases came from the United States, which worried that the instability caused by large refugee influxes could serve as an entré for communism in these emerging states. Nonetheless, an analysis of UNHCR aid to Africa from 1963 until 1981 showed that the number of refugees played a larger role than political factors in the funding received by the high commissioner.[33]

Throughout this period, High Commissioners Felix Schnyder of Switzerland (who served from 1960 until 1965) and Prince Sadruddin Aga Khan of Iran (who headed the organization from 1965 until 1977) worked diligently to gain the new African governments' adherence to the 1951 Convention and to encourage them to grant aid and assistance to refugees. Such adherence also enhanced these new countries' international profile and legitimacy, as it made them eligible to serve on the UNHCR Executive Committee (which grew regularly throughout the decade) or serve as an observer to the committee. By the end of the decade, High Commissioner Sadruddin had parlayed that goodwill into agreement from the Organisation of African Unity (OAU) on a new regional convention on refugees in 1969. The "Convention Governing the Specific Aspects of Refugee Problems in Africa," signed by forty-two governments, expanded the definition of refugee to provide protection for those who had been fighting for independence in their home countries and for those fleeing civil wars, and it provided specific protections for ethnic minorities who lacked a nationality and were forced to flee persecution. Additionally, as the new African and Asian countries organized themselves into the Non-Aligned Movement, they worked through the United Nations to expand the high commissioner's purview to include a variety of types of people displaced by conflicts.[34] But UNHCR did not have the luxury to focus entirely on the growing challenges on the African continent.

In 1971, the U.N. secretary-general asked UNHCR to serve as the lead agency in coordinating the international effort to care for some 10 million refugees who had taken refuge in India while Bangladesh (formerly East Pakistan) struggled to gain its independence from Pakistan (originally West Pakistan). India, which had previously granted asylum to more than 40,000 Tibetan refugees fleeing Chinese occupation and was facing significant economic strains due to its own high rate of population growth, insisted from the beginning that it would only temporarily care for the refugees until they could be repatriated. The massive UNHCR operation included housing some 6.8 million refugees in 896 camps and feeding an additional 3 million. Bangladesh's independence in 1972 brought with it the world's largest repatriation effort (7 million in just three months), in which the two governments worked together under the coordination of the high commissioner to provide transportation, two weeks of basic rations, en route housing, and some assistance to bide the refugees over as they reestablished their homes. High Commissioner Sadruddin, basking in the success of this herculean effort, could well imagine that he had succeeded in making his office the most important international humanitarian organization on the planet—a far cry from the narrow mandate present at its founding.[35]

New refugee challenges in the 1970s and 1980s

High Commissioner Sadruddin had indeed overseen a period in which his office made significant and impressive contributions to the stability of the international system and the safety of millions of refugees. However, a number of challenges lurked just below the surface of these successes. As the nature of refugee crises in Africa shifted from wars of decolonization to civil wars, the 1969 OAU convention became less relevant and refugee situations became more protracted and less productive. Even his achievement of repatriating millions of Bangladeshis soon paled as thousands of "boat people" took to the seas to escape the violence and instability of Indochina in the wake of the Vietnam War. And one of the office's fundamental principles—that of maintaining safe havens for civilians fleeing war and violence—came under attack with the new phenomenon of "refugee warriors." Within a decade of Sadruddin's departure, the U.N. High Commissioner for Refugees faced its most significant financial and philosophical challenge since its founding period.

Refugee warriors

The internationalization of regional conflicts in Afghanistan, Central America, the Horn of Africa, Indochina, and southern Africa during the 1970s and 1980s created a new phenomenon—the "refugee warrior." The dominant model of the refugee camp in the previous quarter century had been people seeking refuge and asylum from the violence in their home country; now, however, refugee camps became places where rebel forces—often supported by the superpowers—recruited additional troops and staged new, cross-border attacks on their previous home nation. Specifically, during the 1970s, refugee camps in Mozambique, Tanzania, and Zambia supported the liberation efforts against the apartheid regimes of South Africa and Rhodesia. And then during the 1980s, Afghans used camps in Pakistan to attack the Soviet-dominated government with American and Saudi support; the Khmer Rouge used refugee camps along the border with Thailand to continue its fight against the Vietnamese forces occupying Cambodia; and the "contras" used refugee camps in Honduras to continue attacks against the leftist government in Nicaragua. As a result, refugee camps came to be seen as legitimate military targets, and international humanitarian support—by supplying food, medical care, and shelter to rebels—helped to prolong a number of international conflicts. Since the United States was actively supporting the anticommunist refugee warriors and was the largest donor to the high commissioner, Poul Hartling of Denmark (who succeeded Sadruddin in 1978 and left office in 1985) lost much of the Third World goodwill and the international reputation for impartiality that his predecessor had garnered.[36] However, a closer examination of one of these refugee warrior situations—along the Thai-Cambodian border—shows the complexities and difficulties that faced any humanitarian organization seeking to relieve human suffering in this extremely bloody and protracted conflict.

Cambodia had suffered a series of political upheavals during the U.S. war in neighboring Vietnam. The country's king had been overthrown by Lon Nol with backing from Washington, but he, in turn, was overthrown in 1975 by the Maoist Khmer Rouge, which proceeded to empty the nation's cities, reeducate millions, and slaughter an estimated 1.7 million of their compatriots (21 percent of the total population) before Vietnam invaded to end the genocide in December 1978. Some 800,000 Cambodians fled to Thailand; about 100,000 of them settled in UNHCR refugee camps and sought resettlement, but the majority stayed in camps along the Thai-Cambodian border that served as a safe haven, tax base, and reserve force for Khmer Rouge troops who continued to harass the Vietnamese government across the border. These border camps—overseen by the U.N. Border Relief Operation created by Secretary-General Kurt Waldheim in January 1982—ultimately received some $1 billion of support from the United States, Japan, and China that sustained the Khmer Rouge for fifteen years. The high commissioner, however, limited his office's role in Thailand (for example, only aiding those who maintained their residence in a refugee camp) in an effort to uphold time-honored distinctions between refugees and members of the military and other norms that his office had promoted for the previous two decades—a position that earned him vociferous, public criticism from the United States and from some humanitarian agencies. American officials caricatured UNHCR as legalistic, rigid, and unable to effectively dispense aid in dangerous environments. Similarly complicated dynamics prevailed in refugee camps in Pakistan and Honduras in the 1980s and in Zaire in the mid-1990s and led some to call for international humanitarian agencies to withdraw from the provision of aid in such circumstances.[37]

Indochinese "boat people"

The mass exodus of hundreds of thousands of Vietnamese, Laotian, and Cambodian refugees by boat elevated the unstable situation that had prevailed in Indochina since the end of the American war in Vietnam into an international humanitarian crisis. Despite the dangers such refugees faced at sea (frequently being on overloaded or unseaworthy vessels), ships' captains were reluctant to assist for fear they would not be allowed to disembark such persons when they reached port. Some countries instituted "shoot on sight policies," and some ships that reached their Asian ports were "pushed off." Many of what came to be termed "boat people" also faced extreme danger from pirates who increasingly preyed upon the vulnerable refugees. Cumulatively, these dangers—which the media came to term an "Asian holocaust"—finally motivated the United States and other countries to receive unprecedented refugee flows from Southeast Asia.[38]

Although some Vietnamese and Laotian refugees had begun fleeing reeducation and relocation efforts as early as 1976, they did not grab UNHCR attention until 1978, when thousands drowned and the remainder met with extreme hostility throughout Southeast Asia. The high commissioner faced great difficulties in protecting refugees in this part of the world, because none of the refugee-receiving countries in Southeast Asia (except the Philippines) were signatories to the 1951 Convention; therefore they had no legal obligation to provide any protection or services to the refugees. This meant the high commissioner had to utilize all of his "soft power" to arrange for the protection and resettlement of these refugees. He channeled funds to all of the refugee-receiving countries to assist in the care of the refugees, hoping in this way to indirectly improve their care. To provide one extended example of his work, in Singapore, UNHCR created a system starting in 1978 that provided such refugees rescued at sea by passing ships with Belgian visas; in 1979, UNHCR expanded this Disembarkation Resettlement Offer when eight more countries also offered visas, which removed the disincentive for ships' captains to rescue boat people in imminent danger of drowning.[39] But such efforts were inadequate as the magnitude of the crisis grew.

Despite the high commissioner's efforts in Singapore and elsewhere, the crisis got much worse before there was any improvement. In the second half of 1978, Vietnam privatized trade and expelled the country's sizable Chinese ethnic minority, resulting in some 160,000 traveling overland and crossing China's border before it was closed in July 1978. Following the border closure, 2,829 refugees reached neighboring Asian countries in August; these numbers quickly expanded to 8,558 in September, 12,540 in October, and 21,506 in November, as the Vietnamese government systematically encouraged such emigration contingent on substantial bribes. This exodus quickly drowned any goodwill that the Southeast Asian countries had held toward the refugees. Those not turned back to the open sea were confined to tiny camps with inhumane conditions. When Vietnam invaded Cambodia and then China invaded Vietnam in 1979, the number of Indochinese refugees expanded further: March saw 13,423 refugees, which grew to 26,602 in April, 51,319 in May, and 56,941 in June. A joint communiqué from Southeast Asian leaders on June 30, 1979, declared that they would allow no more refugees to enter and would expel those already in camps within their borders. This announcement—combined with thousands of deaths as the boat people drowned, fell prey to Thai pirates, and died of hunger, thirst, exposure, or disease—finally prompted the United States (which had been trying quite unsuccessfully to "internationalize" an issue that most of the global community felt strongly was an American responsibility) to accept more than 750,000 Indochinese refugees as part of a thirty-nation international plan hammered out in Geneva in July. Ultimately, the United States accepted as many refugees during the period between 1975 and 1980 as the rest of the world combined. Despite completing "one of the most elaborate and expensive programmes in UNHCR's history," problems lingered in the region until adoption of the Comprehensive Plan of Action for Indo chinese refugees in 1989.[40]

Crises and repatriation

The crisis of the boat people as well as the increasingly protracted care and maintenance programs for African refugees caused the UNHCR budget to balloon at the end of the 1970s and ultimately precipitated a financial crunch at exactly the same time that governments in Europe and North America were increasingly resistant to refugee flows (given their own economic and political difficulties). Collectively, these challenges precipitated a crisis within UNHCR and a pivot in its emphasis from resettlement and asylum to repatriation. The high commissioner's budget had doubled from 1978 to 1979 and again in 1980. As relations between the Soviet Union and the United States grew increasingly frosty in the early 1980s, international solutions to many of the planet's long-lasting refugee situations (which were largely responsible for the budget crisis) seemed increasingly distant. Nor were the prospects for resettling these refugees improving. In fact, the advent of "jet age" refugees, who flew directly to the country in which they sought asylum, both created an asylum crisis (in which these countries made it increasingly difficult to qualify for asylum) and undermined the position of the high commissioner as the primary mediator between the refugee and the asylum-granting countries of Europe.[41]

Seeking a new approach to international refugee issues, the international community turned to a new high commissioner, Jean-Pierre Hocké of Switzerland (who served only three years, from 1986 until 1989), who focused the office addressing the "root causes" of mass exoduses and pursuing repatriation of refugees as "the only realistic alternative to indefinite subsistence on charity." While one historian has termed his ideas ahead of their time, they were likely built on the repatriation experience of the UNHCR with Chile during the period from 1982 until 1985. Though still under the regime of General Augusto Pinochet (who had seized power in Chile on September 11, 1973, and whose campaign against those who opposed the regime included murder, "disappearances," and exile), in the mid-1980s Chile cooperated with UNHCR to develop a system to determine which of the 200,000 Chileans in exile were eligible to return. Additionally, the high commissioner created more than twenty safe havens in Chile (owned by the Catholic Church and placed under the diplomatic aegis of Switzerland) where refugees could safely reenter the country and reclaim their nationality and where other Chileans could seek safe passage and resettlement abroad (especially those who had been jailed for political crimes). And the end of Hocké's tenure was marked by his office's participation in the U.N. Transition Assistance Group (UNTAG)—the United Nations' first comprehensive peace-building operation put in place as South Africa withdrew from Namibia. In that situation, the high commissioner helped repatriate some 40,000 refugees from southern Angola by September 15, 1989—in time to register for that country's first democratic election. Regardless of whether or not the high commissioner's ideas fit his time, donor nations revolted, prompting both a major financial crisis for the office and Hocké's resignation by the end of the decade, on the cusp of major changes in the international system.[42]

The end of the Cold War and the rise and decline of "peace-building" activities

As we have seen in Chapter 3, the end of the Cold War in the early 1990s fundamentally changed international relations and opened up new avenues for the United Nations to take the lead in resolving long-standing regional crises that had largely been the victims of superpower gridlock. The United Nations' diplomatic success in Cambodia and military success in Kuwait (as well as success in South Africa, which is discussed in Chapter 8) helped buoy hopes for a new, peaceful, post–Cold War order. However, as the period's conflicts became increasingly intrastate rather than interstate conflicts, the United Nations struggled to find viable and sustainable solutions to the human suffering and international instability created by such "civil" conflicts. Even though the Security Council was willing to adopt an expansive interpretation of its duties under Chapter VII of the U.N. Charter (which two political scientists characterize as "strikingly intrusive") and commit resources to "peace enforcement" missions in Bosnia and Somalia, such operations quickly showed the limits of what the global organization could accomplish. By the time of the Rwandan genocide, the international community in fact started to despair about its ability to effectively intervene, even in the face of genocidal intentions.[43]

Previous U.N. secretaries-general might have envied Kofi Annan's ability to summarize the organization's post–Cold War mandate as "Our job is to intervene." Seemingly overnight (from 1987 until 1994), the number of Security Council resolutions quadrupled, the number of peacekeeping operations tripled (which added more than 60,000 new troops sporting the blue beret/helmet), the number of economic sanctions imposed increased by a factor of seven, and the annual peacekeeping budget skyrocketed from $230 million to $3.6 billion (which was three times the regular operating budget of the United Nations). Secretary-General Boutros Boutros-Ghali's 1992 *An Agenda for Peace*, which had been written at the request of the Security Council, laid the groundwork for this expansion. In it, he had called for a new era in which the United Nations engaged in "preventive diplomacy" and was prepared to undertake "peace enforcement" measures—with or without the consent of the parties involved. Such measures would, in his opinion, make the Security Council's many calls for cease-fires far more effective. He imagined a larger role for peacekeeping forces, who would build confidence between the conflicting parties during peace negotiations, and a new emphasis on the postconflict reconstruction efforts needed for a durable peace. His thinking combined "in a radical way instruments of warlike enforcement and peacelike negotiation that were once kept separate and that evolved separately."[44]

The members of the Security Council were increasingly willing to intervene in what had previously been defined as domestic affairs within the sovereign purview of the state in order to provide international protection for human rights. The precedents for such actions could be seen in the United Nations' earlier condemnations of colonialism, apartheid, and genocide, but only in this new international context could most observers imagine a United Nations intervening to protect vulnerable populations in Iraq, Somalia, and Yugoslavia and defining an international responsibility to protect such peoples. And the Security Council could legitimately claim to be the voice of the international community since any such action required nine affirmative votes and no veto from a permanent member, which would mean some level of consensus between representatives from both large and small countries, from capitalist and command economies, from democratic and nondemocratic governments, and from several cultures, races, and religions. This period of Security Council–led "assertive multilateralism" (a term coined by Madeleine Albright) stretched from the end of the Cold War, through the First Persian Gulf War, and up until the death of U.S. soldiers in Mogadishu, Somalia, on October 3, 1993.[45]

The rise of "peace-building": The United Nations in Cambodia, 1979–93

In one of its longest and most complicated peace operations, the United Nations spent more than a decade successfully restoring civil rule to Cambodia. Significantly, the U.N. mission to Cambodia was the first in which negotiators sought to build a lasting peace within the country, not just protect a cease-fire or stanch civilian bloodshed. Continuing the expansion of powers seen in U.N. participation in the Korean and Congolese conflicts, the Cambodian peace effort reflected an increased role for the U.N. as an agent as well as guarantor of peace.

U.N. peace-builders entering Cambodia found a country suffering from two generations of civil war, genocide, and societal breakdown as a result of the spillover from the American war in Vietnam, the Khmer Rouge's seizure of power and subsequent genocide, the Vietnamese invasion, and then the ongoing conflict between the Vietnamese and the "refugee warriors" along the Thai border. Although the General Assembly had immediately called for the withdrawal of invading Vietnamese forces in 1979, U.N. peacekeepers made little progress until the mid-1980s. Beginning in 1985, Secretary-General Javier Pérez de Cuellar made several trips to the region to meet with the parties involved, and in 1988, he presented several proposals for achieving peace as well as for reestablishing civil rule. In April of 1989, Vietnam announced it would withdraw its forces from Cambodia, and on October 23, 1991, all parties signed the official "Agreements on a Comprehensive Political Settlement of the Cambodia Conflict" in Paris, which ended the conflict and paved the way for the United Nations Transitional Authority in Cambodia (UNTAC).[46]

UNTAC (officially established in February 1992) heralded a previously unheard-of development in U.N. peacekeeping operations. For the first time, the United Nations assumed control of an entire country in order to carry out its mandate to "supervise the cease-fire, the end of foreign military assistance and the withdrawal of foreign forces; regroup, canton and disarm all armed forces of the Cambodian parties and ensure a 70 percent level of demobilization; control and supervise the activities of the administrative structures, including the police; ensure and respect . . . human rights; and organize and conduct free and fair elections." In practice, this mandate meant that UNTAC needed to reestablish Cambodian defense, foreign affairs, finance, communication, and public safety structures; educate millions of voters—most of whom had never participated in an election—while organizing the election of a 120-person assembly that would then draft a new constitution; and develop a human rights program in a country scarred by genocide. UNTAC and the office of the U.N. High Commissioner for Refugees were also expected to repatriate the 350,000 Cambodians living on the Thai-Cambodia border and resettle 170,000 internally displaced persons (IDPs) and up to 150,000 demobilized soldiers.[47] All of these efforts built toward the same overall goal: the creation of a new and peaceful Cambodia.

This vision was part of Secretary-General Boutros-Ghali's "peace-building" agenda, and Cambodia was the showcase for its potential. In May 1993, UNTAC oversaw elections in which over 90 percent of registered voters cast ballots; UNTAC declared the elections fair and oversaw the establishment of a new government in September 1993. As part of this process, UNTAC employed approximately 50,000 Cambodians on its electoral staff, which both established a corps of Cambodian civilians with experience in conducting elections and helped rebuild relationships between civilians and their government. Additionally, the Paris peace accords of 1991 required that Cambodia recognize its responsibility, pursuant with the U.N. Convention on Genocide, to prosecute human rights abuses promulgated by the government. All of these UNTAC efforts were part of the overall mission of establishing a long-term, sustainable peace. But, of course, the peace-building work of UNTAC and the United Nations has not been an unqualified success. In addition to the difficulties in prosecuting those responsible for the Cambodian genocide (see Chapter 8), there has been a general lack of reporting of human rights abuses since UNTAC withdrew in 1993. Following withdrawal, there were sporadic armed conflicts between the Khmer Rouge and the government, followed by a coup in 1997, and under the rule of the Cambodian People's Party and Prime Minister Hun Sen, Cambodia has struggled with both law and order and democracy. Nonetheless, UNTAC's mandate in Cambodia was undoubtedly a groundbreaking departure from previous U.N. peacekeeping missions in Korea and Congo, marking a dramatic shift in the world's concept of peacekeeping, peace-building, and the role of the United Nations.[48]

While the difficulties involved in Cambodia might have been the most challenging, the United Nations also intervened successfully in several other areas in the wake of the Cold War. In addition to the Namibian case already mentioned earlier, the United Nations was also able to broker peace in El Salvador, Guatemala, Mozambique, Croatia (more recently Eastern Slavonia), and East Timor (in Indonesia). The key to "success" in each case seems to have been building consent among the rival parties and crafting a peace agreement that provided for the creative use of transnational authority to foster the needed transitions in the war-torn societies.[49]

Military peace-building: The First Persian Gulf War, 1990–2003

The United Nations' first major, post–Cold War peacekeeping test came when Iraq invaded its neighbor in the Middle East, Kuwait (see Figure 7.1). In many ways, this conflict resembled the Korean conflict forty years before: one state invading another, with the potential to destabilize an entire region, and significant U.S. and Soviet interests at stake. However, the United Nations drew on decades' worth of experience in peacekeeping successes and failures and did not make the same mistakes in Kuwait that it had in Korea.

On August 2, 1990, Iraq invaded its neighbor to the south, the constitutional emirate of Kuwait. The invasion surprised not only the Kuwaiti people, but also the United Nations, the United States, and the rest of the world. Bordering Iraq, the Persian Gulf, and Saudi Arabia, Kuwait stood as one of the most liberalized Arab countries. It had held its first parliamentary election in 1963, and its citizens enjoyed a high standard of living supported by the country's many oil wells. Kuwait had maintained a cordial relationship with its neighbors as well as with the United States throughout most of the 1970s and 1980s. However, after the Iran-Iraq War ended in 1988 (see Chapter 7 for more details), relations between Kuwait and Iraq fractured. Although Kuwait had supported Iraq in its war against Iran, the emirate refused to forgive Iraq's multibillion-dollar war debt. Iraq responded by accusing Kuwait of stealing its oil through "slant drilling" on the Iraq-Kuwait border. Although the two countries bickered publicly throughout a series of negotiations sponsored by the Egyptian government, Kuwait—and the rest of the world—did not anticipate Iraqi leader Saddam Hussein's order to begin bombing Kuwait City on the evening of August 2, 1990. Iraqi tanks and infantry, hastily massed near the Kuwaiti border, crossed into the country shortly thereafter. Within a day, Kuwait fell to Iraqi forces.[50]

The United Nations reacted quickly to this turn of events. Kuwait's representative to the United Nations, along with the U.S. ambassador, obtained a Security Council resolution condemning Iraq's actions on the same day that the bombing started. Four days later, on August 6, 1990, the Security Council passed Resolution 661, imposing economic sanctions and a trade blockade against Iraq. When sanctions failed to convince Iraq to leave Kuwaiti territory, Security Council Resolution 678 (passed on November 29, 1990) authorized member states to use "all necessary means" to restore international peace, which laid the groundwork for a military coalition of twenty-eight member states, led by the United States, that utilized air and land forces to expel Iraqi forces from Kuwait by February 28, 1991. Following these successful military operations, the Security Council established the United Nations Iraq-Kuwait Observation Mission (UNIKOM) to monitor and police the demilitarized zone on the border between Iraq and Kuwait (it disbanded in October 2003). For the first time, all five permanent Security Council members agreed to provide military observers to UNIKOM.[51] While this unanimity among the permanent members helped UNIKOM to be successful in its mission, this now seems to have marked the high-water mark of support for "peace-building."

In evaluating U.N. peacekeeping work, academics, policymakers, U.N. officials, refugees, and regular people start from the foundational agreement that civil wars are harmful (at least in the short term). Even discounting the considerable death and displacement they cause within their borders, scholars have also found that they lead to an overall deterioration of health and economic growth levels throughout the region long after such civil wars have ended. We also know that such civil disputes have made up the vast majority of new armed conflicts since the end of the Cold War. As a result, the number of civilian deaths has greatly increased (they made up 90 percent of all war-related deaths in 1990), with millions displaced as refugees or internally displaced persons (IDPs). Agreement on the magnitude and seriousness of the problem has not, however, led to easy solutions for the international community. As we have seen in Chapter 3, U.N. efforts to enforce peace in Bosnia and Somalia—unlike the more traditional military action against Iraq in Kuwait—quickly went awry and served to dash the Security Council's enthusiasm for engaging in similar situations. In fact, it largely abstained from action in Rwanda, with the result that more than 700,000 Rwandans (both Tutsis and moderate Hutus) died in the resulting genocide.[52]

Political scientists Michael W. Doyle and Nicholas Sambanis, in examining the circumstances in which U.N. interventions have succeeded and failed, find that the interrelationships between the level of hostility between the factions, the extent of local postwar capacities, and the amount of international assistance are the three sides of the "peace-building triangle." So, the greater the hostility and the destruction of local capacity, the higher the level of international aid needed to craft a durable peace. They have also found that a U.N. peace-building mission that has been well-crafted and well-funded to handle the unique circumstances of a particular case increases the chance for peace as a society transitions from war to peace even more than the military victory of one side in a civil war. Key to such successful operations seems to be the capacity to rebuild an economy (and therefore provide employment) and to provide security while new domestic institutions are crafted. Doyle and Sambanis have also found that the United Nations is particularly well equipped to mediate between different factions, mobilize needed resources, and provide legitimacy to what are, by definition, intrusive operations.[53]

Post–Cold War realities for the world's refugees: Repatriation and another asylum crisis

The post–Cold War transitions in international relations also had profound effects on the ways in which the high commissioner handled the resulting refugee crises. UNHCR experienced remarkable successes marked by the repatriation of hundreds of thousands of refugees back to their homes in ways that fostered genuine hope in Cambodia and South Africa, and a philosophical emphasis on "human security" as a key U.N. principle seemed to offer a more comprehensive mission in which the UNHCR would play a key role. Additionally, the international political environment after the Cold War and the terrorist attacks on the World Trade Center on September 11, 2001—which cast refugees as potential threats and certainly as destabilizing influences—also led to innovation meant to prevent mass exoduses, including multinational interventions during the 1990s to stem such population flows in Albania, East Timor, Haiti, northern Iraq, Kosovo, Liberia, Sierra Leone, and Somalia. In this shift toward intervention and intrastate conflicts, the high commissioner was increasingly called upon to assist internally displaced persons (IDPs) and to address the "root causes" of mass exoduses, thereby preempting refugee crises.[54] This focus on IDPs and repatriation was oftentimes less about hope and more about an international community (North and South) that was unwilling to fund protracted refugee situations and unwilling to have such refugees resettled within their borders, leaving the high commissioners with few choices other than to put the best possible face on the limited range of options now available to them. And thousands and thousands of refugees—from the genocidal crises of the 1990s in the former Yugoslavia and Rwanda to the Syrian civil war and Daesh's violent religious persecution of the 2010s—have been caught in the middle, feeling imperiled and unwelcome as they shift from place to place in an effort to find hope for themselves and their families amid the rough currents of international politics and donor fatigue.

Ever since the end of the Cold War, the international community has pressed the UNHCR for speedy repatriation, often regardless of the uncertainties and dangers facing the returning refugees. This became more of the norm as the office operated in conjunction with larger U.N. peace-building operations and dealt increasingly with IDPs. UNHCR work with "war-affected populations" in Bosnia was just one example of the redefinition of the high commissioner's work that increased the number of people under the office's purview from fifteen million in 1990 to some twenty-six million in 1996 (only half of whom were refugees). Such actions have brought intense criticism from scholars of international law and from human rights activists, who argue that the high commissioner has largely abandoned refugees' fundamental freedom from forced repatriation (spelled out in the 1951 Convention), has consequently endangered the lives of the refugees, and has traded these valuable protections simply in the name of political expediency.[55]

The phenomenon of refugee warriors and the subsequent military targeting of refugee camps carried over into this new period as well, and the UNHCR struggled to maintain the integrity and security of its facilities in Albania, Congo, northern Iraq, Macedonia, Sierra Leone, and northern Uganda. At the same time, there were increasingly fewer alternatives for housing such refugees. Western governments became increasingly reluctant to grant such refugees asylum, a pattern that the global South soon emulated. Where the need was especially pressing, Western governments provided only "temporary protection" in place of asylum to those fleeing war and ethnic cleansing and became increasingly assertive in repatriating those who were temporarily housed. Gil Loescher argues that by the end of the twentieth century, "refugees became a symbol of system overload, instead of a symbol of what was always best in the Western liberal tradition."[56] In the Third World, the economic, environmental, social, and security costs of such refugee flows similarly led governments to take steps to exclude refugees entirely or to press for their repatriation as soon as possible (and often sooner than advisable). In the 1990s, the lack of alternatives—added to significant changes in Afghanistan, Cambodia, and Mozambique—played a role in pushing up the number of refugees returning home to twelve million (with or without help from the UNHCR). While acknowledging the shortcomings in the high commissioner's historical record, the most comprehensive history of the organization offers this summation:

> The UNHCR functions with an imperfect mandate, under circumstances necessitating competition with other agencies for limited resources, in political environments that are inhospitable to crisis management and refugee protection. The Office is frequently expected to work within exceedingly complex and insecure situations with little or no backing from the international community.[57]

These complexities and challenges have not lessened since the millennium. In fact, additional attention has been devoted to the needs of IDPs, whose numbers (first measured in 1982) have risen from 20 million in 1997 to 33.3 million in 2013 (of whom 23.9 million received protection and/or assistance from UNHCR). Humanitarian NGOs pushed for the means to protect and provide for this new population, prompting U.N. Secretary-General Boutros-Ghali in 1992 to appoint Dr. Francis Deng to serve as the first representative of the secretary-general on IDPs. One of his first mandates was to develop a framework in collaboration with the U.N. Commission on Human Rights that defined the rights of IDPs and the responsibilities of states (and potentially the international community) in protecting these rights. The Human Rights Commission and the General Assembly both approved in 1998 the nonbinding "Guiding Principles on Internal Displacement" that resulted.[58] These principles identified IDPs' freedoms from discrimination, from arbitrary or extralegal displacement, and from violence (when not involved in the hostilities); the document also affirmed their rights to life, dignity, liberty, security, and property. Additionally, it voiced the special needs of displaced women and children for security and protection and enunciated the right of the international community to freely and safely provide humanitarian assistance. However, several states—worried about the potential these guidelines had for eroding the absolute nature of their national sovereignty—began to question them at U.N. fora, starting with the July 2000 ECOSOC meeting and including the 2001 General Assembly session. And the interconnections between human rights, the work of UNHCR, "failed states," international law (including international maritime law), humanitarian action, and protection of refugees from organized criminal organizations (especially traffickers) grow stronger with the passing years. Perhaps the increasing number of people under the protection of the UNHCR and the increasing complexity of that office's work is what finally prompted the General Assembly in 2004 to end its process of periodically renewing UNHCR's mandate, opting instead to authorize it "until the refugee problem is solved."[59] A similar mix of determined realism and optimistic faith in the ability of the international community to care for the endangered has marked the United Nations' seven decades of work toward building and maintaining the peace and toward caring for those displaced by armed conflicts.

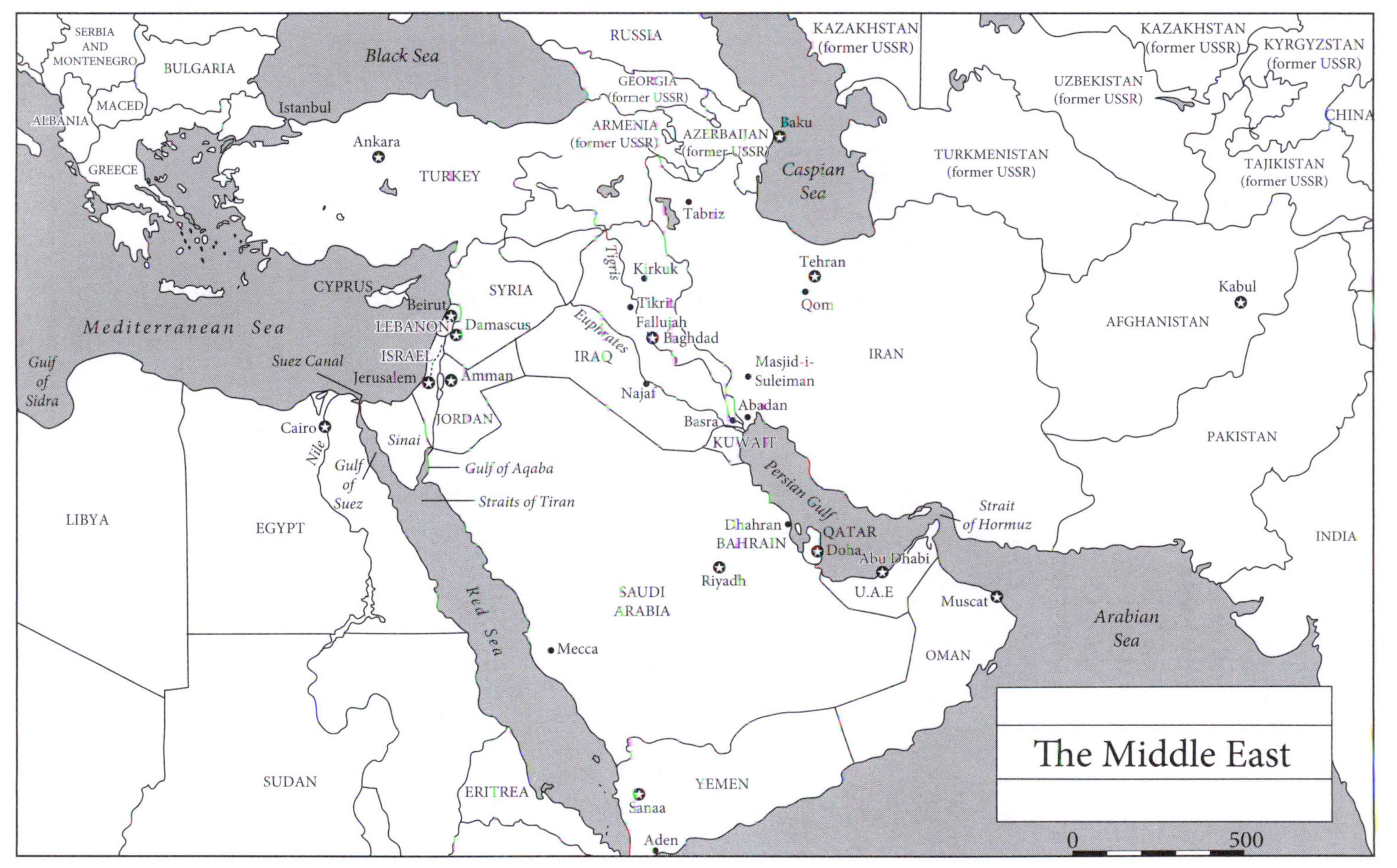

Figure 7.1 Map of the Middle East.

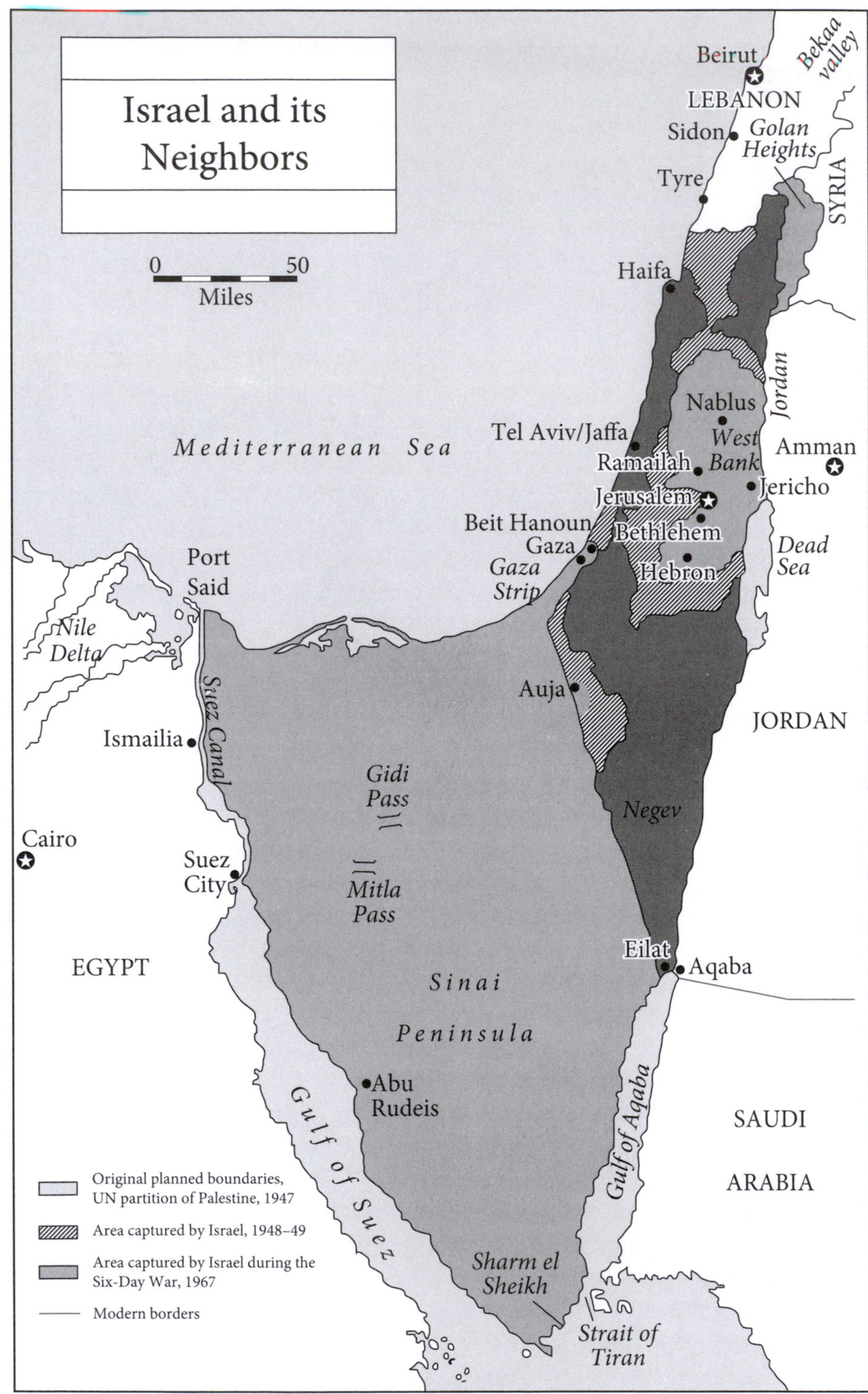

Figure 7.2 Israel and its neighbors.

CHAPTER 7
THE MIDDLE EAST AND THE UNITED NATIONS

What is commonly called the "Middle East" (although the World Health Organization refers to it by the less Eurocentric term "Eastern Mediterranean") is a borderland between the continents of Asia, Europe, and Africa whose history has been shaped by a variety of civilizations that have at various times sought to control this vital global crossroads (see Figure 7.1). Additionally, the region is home to significant oil reserves and the religious traditions of Judaism, Christianity, and Islam, so it is unsurprising that conflict marks the area. It is equally unsurprising that the United Nations—as an international organization that itself operates very much as a borderland of ideas, peoples, and civilizations—has been so enmeshed in the borderland of the Middle East.

As a part of the world that has witnessed significant human tragedy and where many vital issues are involved, much of the writing on Middle Eastern history has been influenced by its ongoing conflicts—especially the Arab-Israeli conflict—and can tend toward clearly siding with one group or the other. Given this, examining the work of the United Nations in the Middle East—its work, its people, and its examinations of the situations—probably comes the closest to trying to balance the different sides and therefore can be a helpful entry point for the student beginning to study the region for the first time. For the student worried about navigating the difficult, tragic, and highly politicized currents of these contemporary histories, you could usefully read the introduction to a recent international history of the Palestine Liberation Organization (PLO), in which Paul Chamberlain laid out his position as a historian wading into these waters:

> I agree with the prevailing precepts of international law that Israel has a right to exist and that the Palestinian people have a right to a sovereign state in the West Bank and Gaza Strip. . . . [Historically, both] groups faced what they believed were threats to their existence as nations; both groups behaved ruthlessly in defense of their claims and were responsible for acts of terrible violence against civilians. . . . Neither side's actions were the product of irrational hatreds or sectarian bloodlust. Rather, violence in the Israel-Palestine conflict was the result of considered—though at times misguided—strategies that the various parties followed in the hopes of maximizing their chances for national survival in a dangerous environment. These points should not be read as justifications for the bloodshed, nor do they imply some sort of judgment about the moral balance between the two

> sides. Instead, they serve as explanations that are essential for understanding the history of the conflict.[1]

This position—of a historian examining historical phenomena rather than making moral judgments—could certainly be extrapolated to studies of the other dynamics within the Middle East in the postwar period and indeed, as I have argued throughout this book, to the United Nations' relations with the world after the Second World War.

Once we have overcome any trepidation about dipping our toes in the study of this region, it entices us into deeper waters with the complex cast of actors in this borderland. We see all of the major state actors (the United States, the Soviet Union, Great Britain, and France) engaged in high-stakes efforts to influence the region's politics, often unsuccessfully given that the regional powers are the primary shapers of area politics. Spicing up this mix are new nation-states (Israel) and nonstate actors (the PLO, Hamas, Daesh, and others) vying with one another on both regional and global stages. And we see "small" states like Denmark, Japan, and Sweden playing crucial roles at significant points in the area's conflicts. Then, in the middle of it all, we see the United Nations in its great variety—its Security Council and General Assembly, its secretaries-general and their representatives, its specialized agencies, and its collaborations with nongovernmental organizations (NGOs)—acting, reacting, interacting, and trying to build the conditions for peace. As such, I designed this chapter as a "laboratory" for the aspiring researcher to begin examining the dynamics within the United Nations and between it and this broad variety of state and nonstate actors. This examination may lead you into a deeper examination of the Middle East, or it may lead you into your own examination of U.N. work in other parts of the globe with a fuller understanding of the complexity of the dynamics at work.

And as always, there is a wealth of primary sources for you to explore and base your own interpretations on. In the endnotes and online "Guide to Further Research," http://www.bloomsbury.com/us/the-united-nations-in-international-history-9781472510600/ you will find links to these as well as to secondary sources that will give you a deeper examination of the issues briefly covered in this chapter. Before the start of this chapter, there are two maps on pages 147 and 148 to provide a bit more background and context for those who are less familiar with the region and its history.

The United Nations' failed Palestinian partition plan and its aftermath

When the British announced to the General Assembly on September 3, 1947, that they were returning the Palestinian mandate (received from the League after the First World War) to the United Nations, the Security Council ducked the issue, but the organization as a whole sought a peaceful way forward that would allow the Jewish and Arab populations to coexist peacefully in the territory. The Assembly appointed a committee, which could not come to consensus, but in August 1947, a majority recommended partition. U.N. General Assembly Resolution 181 on November 29, 1947, therefore endorsed partition of the territory into an Arab state that would be home to some 725,000 Arabs and 10,000

Jews and into a Jewish state that would be home to some 498,000 Jews and 497,000 Arabs (90,000 of whom were nomadic people). The city of Jerusalem and its environs—with their religious significance to Jews, Christians, and Muslims—would be administered by the United Nations and contain approximately 105,000 Arabs and 100,000 Jews (see Figure 7.2). The partition plan also included a mechanism for economic unity, and a U.N. commission would oversee this entire arrangement until both were ready to join the United Nations as member states. The Jewish leadership in Palestine supported the resolution (which promised it future political independence), but the Arab leadership did not (as the division seemed both inequitable and unjust, taking land they considered their own to establish a Jewish state). News of the resolution and the impending British withdrawal set off large-scale fighting and rioting in Palestine that led the U.N. Security Council in April 1948 to create a truce commission that sought to establish buffers between the two communities to restrain the violence.[2]

The Jewish provisional government declared its independence at the moment that the British formally terminated their mandate on May 15, 1948. Within minutes, U.S. President Harry S. Truman extended de facto recognition to the new Jewish State of Israel, and within days the Soviet Union became the first country to extend de jure recognition. But the declaration of independence also immediately brought Israel war with its Arab neighbors who sought to quash the upstart state. Fighting finally wound down by July 18, 1948, with some assistance from two Security Council cease-fire resolutions. As the dust settled on the battlefields, Israel emerged as a larger state than it would have been under partition, the violence displaced hundreds of thousands of Palestinians, and the U.N. partition plan became a moot point.[3] The United Nations, having failed in its state-making role, now shifted to a mediating role. The new U.N. mediator was to use his good offices to ensure that essential public services remained in operation, the Holy Places were protected, and there was a peaceful adjustment to the new status quo in Palestine. Count Folke Bernadotte, a Swedish diplomat who had previously assisted with efforts to rescue Jews during the Holocaust, assumed the difficult role of trying to implement the U.N. Security Council's successive cease-fire resolutions as well as building out from the resolution a framework for handling the previously unforeseen task of caring for the population of largely Arab Palestinian refugees who had fled their homes during the war. Bernadotte first sought to gain assurances from the new state of Israel that the refugees had the right to return to their homes when conditions warranted. Failing at this, he sought immediate aid to feed the multitude. The reasons that the Palestinian refugees fled remains hotly debated and bitterly disputed (with the main lines being that they were pushed out of their homes by Jewish terrorism and threats of violence or that they were pulled from their homes by Arab leaders who sought military advantage in the war); nonetheless, the United Nations' initial insertion of itself into the area as the new mandatory power of Palestine (under the partition resolution) and its subsequent care for the refugees created the sense that the refugees were the responsibility of the United Nations. This has caused them to hold the organization responsible for securing their right to return to their original homes and in the interim to provide for the care of themselves, their children, and subsequently their grandchildren and great-grandchildren. The neighboring Arab states generally held similar beliefs and resisted efforts to permanently settle the refugees in their own countries and seemingly release Israel from its responsibility to resettle this population.[4] This is the basic starting point for the United Nations' continuing role in seeking to settle the conflict between Israel, the Palestinian refugees, and the neighboring Arab states.

Bernadotte and Bunche's efforts to aid the refugees and negotiate peace

The plight of the refugees came to the forefront with the end of the fighting. Azzam Pasha, the secretary-general of the Arab League, appealed to U.N. Secretary-General Trygve Lie for help with the Arab refugees, and Bernadotte requested on July 21, 1948, that Lie appoint a high-ranking member of the U.N. Department of Social Affairs to make a rapid survey of conditions on the ground with an eye to recommending the development of some type of relief mechanism. After an abortive attempt to pass the job off to the International Refugee Organization, whose mandate was to resettle those displaced by the Second World War, Lie dispatched Sir Raphael Cilento (an Australian public health administrator who had previously worked with UNRRA) along with an officer of the League of Red Cross Societies. Bernadotte, however, was far from giving up on the idea of repatriating the refugees and approached Israeli Foreign Minister Moshe Sharett on July 26, 1948, with a proposition to repatriate, with international assistance, a limited number of refugees (excluding men of military age). Sharett rejected that proposal four days later, arguing that it "would relieve the aggressor States of a large part of the pressure exerted on them by the refugee problem" and would "most seriously handicap the war effort and war readiness of Israel, bringing into its territory a politically explosive and economically destitute element." He argued that settlement of the refugee issue had to be tied to an overall regional settlement that would recognize the existence of the Israeli nation-state and establish peaceful relations between the neighboring states. While Bernadotte remained convinced that a General Assembly–backed proposal could still achieve some type of comprehensive settlement, his attention nonetheless turned to the refugee crisis.[5]

Throughout August 1948, missionary and educational groups who had already been working in the Middle East sought to feed the refugees with assistance from the Arab governments. But the Cilento survey—completed on August 7, 1948—starkly established that this was insufficient. Bernadotte worked feverishly to bring needed aid into the region. He appealed to UNICEF for supplies (which resulted in an initial grant of $411,000) and developed a working arrangement with the Red Cross, which took on an increasing portion of the work that fall. Facing the threat of famine and starvation among the refugee population, on August 16 and September 1, 1948, the Swede also directly telegraphed fifty-three U.N. member states and nonmember states, urgently requesting that they divert foodstuffs then on the high seas to his headquarters in Beirut to address the developing humanitarian disaster. This emerging structure became official with the September 11, 1948, establishment of the U.N. Disaster Relief Operation in Beirut (directly attached to the mediator's office) under Cilento's leadership. This office then negotiated agreements with Egypt, Syria, and Transjordan to ensure that relief supplies could enter their ports free from tariffs and then be warehoused and transported under the direction of the new supply and liaison officers, who would coordinate the distribution of supplies to the voluntary groups (both international aid organizations and local Arab committees) carrying out the actual relief work. By September 13, 1948, twenty-five nations had responded to Bernadotte's telegraphic appeals.[6]

Still seeking a comprehensive solution to the situation in Palestine, Bernadotte made a comprehensive report on the situation to a meeting of the General Assembly on September 16, 1948. He continued to view the refugees primarily as a U.N. responsibility and recommended creation of a "long-range" program to register the refugees and ensure their most basic needs for the next year. Ultimately, however, he believed their fate was tied to the political situation in the region. He therefore recommended that the United Nations create a conciliation commission to settle outstanding issues of contention. He argued that the conditions for peace would bring an end to fighting, a recognition that the state of Israel existed, the establishment of clear boundaries based on ideas of homogeneity and integration, a recognition of the Arab refugees' rights to repatriation and compensation for property, a separate treatment of Jerusalem, and international guarantees of both the boundaries and rights of the Arabs. The so-called Bernadotte Plan received enthusiastic support from the U.S. State Department but little support from the Arab states or Israel. In fact, it appalled the Israeli press, and the next day Israeli extremists in Jerusalem assassinated the Swedish diplomat and his accompanying French U.N. observer, Colonel André Sérot, just four days before the opening the U.N. General Assembly meeting in Paris. While the State Department tried to use this shocking event to garner international support for the Bernadotte Plan over the next month, the Israeli army pursued another offensive on 15–21 October to secure the northern Negev; a similar offensive to secure the southern Negev followed in December, on the pretext that Egypt had refused to make peace (see Figure 7.2). Although the United States pushed for the U.N. cease-fire that took effect on January 7, 1949, that resolution did not call on Israel to give up any of these territorial gains.[7]

In the meantime, American Ralph Bunche had inherited Bernadotte's unenviable role of seeking a political settlement and caring for the refugees in Palestine. The U.N. specialized agencies stepped up and played an important role in assisting the refugees; most importantly, on October 28, 1948, UNICEF made an additional grant of $6 million, half of the residual assets it had received from the dissolution of UNRRA. This aid became more formalized with the General Assembly's unanimous resolution on November 19, 1948, to create the U.N. Relief for Palestine Refugees (UNRPR) program, led by an ad hoc advisory committee of seven countries (selected by the president of the General Assembly) to advise the secretary-general on issues related to policy and principle. UNRPR was meant to assist half a million refugees over the next nine months at an estimated cost of $32 million, $5 million of which would be forwarded as a loan from the U.N. Working Capital Fund until the in-kind and cash contributions from governments could be received. U.S. ambassador to Egypt Stanton Griffis became UNRPR's director on December 6, 1948, and worked to develop the infrastructure for the new program (whose mandate was later extended to May 1, 1950), including special U.N. planes and a radio network to connect the aid stations. The World Health Organization provided a medical director, the International Refugee Organization donated blankets, the Food and Agriculture Organization surveyed the refugees' dietary needs, UNESCO provided an initial appropriation to start schools for refugee children, and a Scandinavian team tested and vaccinated a quarter-million refugee children against tuberculosis. But most importantly, the International Red Cross and the American Friends Service Committee (AFSC, the Quakers) agreed to assume full operational responsibility for the program's work in the field. While fifty-six AFSC personnel oversaw efforts in the Egyptian-occupied Gaza Strip, 143 Red Cross employees worked in Israel, Iraq, Jordan, Lebanon, Syria, and the Israeli-occupied areas and Jordanian-occupied areas of the former Palestinian mandate. In addition to the difficulties of having fewer than two hundred people managing services for hundreds of thousands of refugees, the supply lines often traversed difficult terrain, and the number of people to be fed grew more quickly than governmental donations to the UNRPR, which therefore had to be supplemented by local governments, national Red Cross groups, and UNICEF. Ultimately, the operation of the mass feeding program led the voluntary organizations to the conclusion that it contributed both to "erosion of the soul" of the refugees and to growing distrust of all international organizations. Nonetheless, it also established an early model of effective NGO-U.N. cooperation.[8]

The same General Assembly that created the UNRPR also established the U.N. Conciliation Commission (on December 11, 1948) consisting of appointees from the French, Turkish, and American governments. Its goals were to assist Bunche in resolving the outstanding issues in the Middle East. Paragraph 11 of the resolution asserted that those refugees "wishing to return to their homes and live in peace with their neighbours should be permitted to do so at the earliest practicable date." In the meantime, the International Refugee Organization was moving in the opposite direction. Its January 25–29, 1949, special meeting in Geneva lifted its earlier (May 18, 1947) restriction on aid to Jewish immigrants to Palestine (over strong British opposition) and now earmarked $4 million for such travel. The resulting pattern of new Jewish immigrants (first from postwar Europe then from Iraq and other areas of the world) settling in Israel in the areas where Palestinians had previously lived and farmed helped to complicate the issue of repatriation immeasurably in the coming decades. Nonetheless, some small measure of progress was seen in Bunche's successful negotiation of a bilateral armistice between Israel and Egypt on February 24, 1949, and with Lebanon on March 23, just after the Conciliation Commission took up another round of talks.[9]

But the prospects for a comprehensive settlement dimmed in subsequent months. In the spring of 1949, the Conciliation Commission met with the Arab governments in Beirut and consulted with the Israeli government and representatives of the refugees. The Arab governments made Israeli repatriation of the refugees the first step in any process, while Israeli Prime Minister David Ben Gurion made their return contingent on peace with the Arab countries and clearly preferred their settlement elsewhere. However, the prime minister did indicate that Israel would be willing to accept the approximately

270,000 Arab residents and refugees in the Gaza Strip (the portion of the former mandate controlled by Egypt along the Mediterranean and the southwestern portion of Israel) in exchange for control over this area, a proposal—not surprisingly—rejected out of hand by the assembled Arab states. The only forward movement came after the conclusion of the talks when Transjordan's King Abdallah signed an armistice with Israel in April 1949 and took de facto control over the portion of the former mandate of Palestine that had been retained by his Arab League forces during the earlier conflict, including the Arab-held sections of Jerusalem. The Conciliation Commission reassembled in the summer of 1949, and while there seemed an opportunity to move forward early on—when the Israeli delegation was willing to consider the refugees as the first item on the agenda and to consider readmitting no more than 100,000 refugees (although not having them return to their original homes), the Commission and the Arab delegations found the proposal generally unsatisfactory. And even that slight concession was the result of strong U.S. pressure on Israel and quickly undone by the negative reaction of the Israeli press and Knesset (parliament). But all sides had agreed on August 15, 1949, to an economic survey of the area and the refugees' situation (encouraged by the prospect of international aid), resulting in the establishment of the Economic Survey Mission on August 23, 1949. Coupled with the conclusion of the final bilateral armistice between Israel and Syria on July 20, 1949, the Commission might have felt that some small measure of progress had been made.[10]

The failure to bring about a political solution that would fundamentally resolve the misery of the Palestinian refugees paired with the establishment of the Economic Survey Mission and the desire to foster stability among the displaced Palestinian population laid the foundation for the new, semipermanent U.N. Relief and Works Agency for Palestine Refugees in the Near East (UNRWA). In December 1949, the U.N. General Assembly charged UNRWA with taking over the work of the voluntary agencies and adding a health program, but it was also to create jobs for the refugees (such as building roads, clearing brush, digging wells, developing irrigation systems, and planting trees) with the goal of bringing about their permanent settlement. At this time, UNRWA was serving one million refugees. Political scientist Benjamin Schiff, who specializes in the study of international organizations, describes UNRWA as a particularly challenging borderland in which the many players are rather dysfunctionally codependent. Describing UNRWA as "tightly bound into the web of relationships that define the Arab-Israeli-Palestinian conflict," he sees the U.N. agency as a vehicle that has allowed the Great Powers to put off "solving" the crisis in the Middle East, that has provided key material resources to regional powers, and that has served as "a political symbol and tool for Palestinians," all while rather successfully carrying out a complex humanitarian mission plagued with "difficulties traceable to a unique mandate, structure, and environment" and whose every action carries significant political ramifications.[11]

While UNRWA was settling into what became its long-term work with the refugees, the U.N. Truce Supervision Organization (UNTSO, originally the Truce Commission) took up a similar mandate for monitoring the armistice agreements between Israel and its neighbors that Bunche had negotiated. The unarmed UNTSO military observers' mandate was to oversee the agreements and report any violations to the U.N. Security Council; this first U.N. "peacekeeping" or peace-monitoring mission is still a work in progress today.[12] While such an unending mission could be seen as a failure, as we will see later in this chapter, the ongoing presence of the UNTSO has given the United Nations the ability to dispatch highly trained military observers to other "hot spots" in the Middle East on short notice. And ideas about U.N. peacekeeping would evolve from this starting point, as we have seen with the Korean War in Chapter 3 and other peacekeeping missions in Chapter 6.

Israel's membership in the United Nations

Israel was eager to become a member of the United Nations, first applying on November 29, 1948, and finally achieving its goal on May 11, 1949, just short of its one-year celebration of independence. It had acutely realized the shortcomings of not being a full member of the body in the previous year, as its Arab neighbors had been full members able to freely and fully air their concerns to the international organization. Additionally, full membership brought with it the promise of a share in its collective security mechanisms. But the U.N. Security Council had viewed its first application as premature, given the unsettled state of affairs between Israel and its neighbors. However, on the day that Israel and Egypt signed the General Armistice Agreement (February 24, 1949), the Security Council voted 9–1 in favor (with Egypt, a nonpermanent member, voting against). At the beginning of the next General Assembly session, the ad hoc Political Committee conducted an extensive investigation of Israel's application that extended over four days but ultimately was approved. Israeli Minister of Foreign Affairs Moshe Sharett told the Knesset that this resolution "brought Israel back into the community of nations. It conferred upon the Jewish people regathered in their ancient land equal rights with all free nations."[13] But the hope in this proclamation soon dimmed.

Tel Aviv had hoped that membership would help it to regularize its international relations, especially through participation in the technical work of the U.N. specialized agencies. Before the year had closed, it was already a full member of the Food and Agriculture Organization, International Civil Aviation Organization (ICAO), International Labour Organization, International Telecommunication Union, UNESCO, Universal Postal Union, and World Health Organization; World Meteorological Organization membership followed shortly, and Israel became a member of the International Monetary Fund and World Bank in 1954. But membership often did not mean normalization or integration into the region on an equal basis with its neighbors. The case study of Israel in the Eastern Mediterranean Regional Office (EMRO) of the World Health Organization (WHO) illustrates the challenges. EMRO, including Israel and its Arab neighbors, had met together in Geneva in 1949 and in Turkey in 1950, but following the Arab League's decision in September 1950 to boycott any meetings that included Israel, the WHO struggled to find a way to develop an EMRO agenda and budget within the organization. Given that WHO member states may choose which regional organization to join (e.g., Pakistan chose to join EMRO rather than the Southeast Asian Regional Office headquartered in rival India), the Arab states suggested that Israel join the European Regional Office (which also included the French North African colonies at that time), but Israel fought to be represented in EMRO, a decision generally backed by the World Health Assembly, which refused to allow Israel's exclusion from EMRO on political grounds. The director-general, trying to develop a coherent regional health program, then tried to carry out EMRO's work by correspondence or by having two different regional "committees" meet. When neither of these strategies worked, the Arab members of EMRO simply started meeting in 1954 without Israel and without the WHO director-general's approval, then simply proffered its "opinion" to the World Health Assembly. Three decades following its effective exclusion from EMRO, Israel requested membership in the European Regional Office.[14]

Membership in the ICAO was a bit easier, as Israel joined before its Arab neighbors; but the region's politics soon affected its role in the Montreal-based specialized agency as well. ICAO, charged with ensuring the coordination of international civil aviation to protect the safety of passengers around the globe, was keenly interested in safeguarding the airspace over the Middle East, which sits under the main air routes connecting Africa, Asia, and Europe. But in the wake of the Arab League boycott, the Egyptians barred the Israelis from the Cairo regional ICAO office, and therefore no flight information was disseminated from the office about any flights going into or coming out of Israel. In addition, there was no communication between the airports in Cairo and Tel Aviv. ICAO recognized the dangers inherent in this situation and sought in 1952 to create an Eastern Mediterranean Flight Information Centre at Nicosia, on the island of Cyprus, that would "provide complete and non-discriminatory service to the aircraft" of all ICAO states, but the project collapsed due to lack of funding. The international organization's council similarly failed to prevent Arab discrimination against Israeli aircraft, which was clearly in violation of the Chicago Convention governing the organization, declaring that "although the situation had technical aspects, it was part of a larger political problem outside of the purview of ICAO."[15] In sum, Israel's hopes that U.N. membership and participation in the specialized agencies would integrate it into the Middle East "encountered profound disappointment" in the face of Arab states' concerted effort to ostracize the Jewish state within these international organizations. Nonetheless, Israel did benefit from U.N. membership, drawing on the resources of UNICEF and the Expanded Program for Technical Assistance in its early days.[16] Ultimately, there was no nonpolitical issue in the United Nations when it came to the ongoing conflict between Israel and its neighbors.

The stalemate of the early 1950s

Just as Israel realized that its participation in intergovernmental organizations would not automatically resolve the issues it had with its neighbors, the United Nations itself settled into something of a stalemate, as its efforts to advance and improve the situation in the

Middle East made little, if any, progress. When the fall 1951 Conciliation Commission's meeting made clear that the two sides were further than ever from a settlement of the refugee crisis, it decided to tackle the issue of Israel's compensation for Palestinian refugees' property within its borders (as laid out in the 1948 U.N. Resolution 194). The commission's refugee office had already begun the work of estimating the value of Arab refugee property in Israel in May 1951. Both sides rejected a September 1951 commission proposal that Israel forego any claims for wartime reparations against the neighboring Arab states in return for cancelling its debts for wartime destruction of Palestinian property. When the final 1957 U.N. report estimated the value of immovable Arab refugee property in Israel at 100 million Palestine pounds and the movable property at 20 million (collectively the equivalent of $336 million at the time), it prompted establishment of a Reintegration Fund, and at various points it was imagined that Israel would contribute to this fund (to be administered by UNRWA) as a method of paying these reparations. Obviously, such a large amount would have to be funded over a number of years, but even an August 1955 offer of American assistance in doing this failed to move the negotiations along. The Commission also considered the issue of blocked bank accounts, which a mixed committee of experts had explored in the summer of 1949 and recommended that they be paid in pounds sterling. Although this resulted in agreement, the first release only came in 1953. By the end of July 1965, Israel had paid Palestinians with blocked bank accounts some £3.5 million, the Commission's single monetary achievement.[17]

The Conciliation Commission made similarly slow progress in reuniting Palestinian families that had been divided by the armistice lines resulting from the war. It had developed the procedures under which Israel agreed, in the first phase, to allow wives and unmarried children under fifteen years of age to rejoin their husbands/fathers in Israel. The second phase, which ended in March 1953, allowed for the entry of fiancées, sons up to seventeen years old, a limited number of older children who had been studying abroad, and 150 Arab husbands under hardship conditions. By the beginning of 1957, approximately 8,000 such officially approved reunions had occurred.[18]

However, the vast number of Palestinian refugees were, by 1952, rather firmly entrenched as wards of the United Nations. UNRWA had developed a clear definition of who was a Palestinian refugee and an accompanying registration system.[19] However, its efforts to shift the refugees from the relief rolls to paid employment by creating 100,000 jobs in forestation, irrigation, and road-building by 1951 had fallen flat. The goal of this effort was not only to reduce the relief rolls but also to help integrate the refugees (both economically and perhaps politically) into the host countries, but the host countries and refugees quickly sussed out these motives and resisted. Additionally, the higher costs of these works programs, compared to relief, led to reluctance on the part of the donor countries as well. UNRWA did create 12,000 jobs by 1954, far short of its goal. As half of the entire registered population were children, education emerged as an increasingly urgent UNRWA priority. As it built hundreds of schools and hired thousands of teachers, it offset the investment by cutting food aid to the refugees (with the exception of feeding programs for infants and free lunches for schoolchildren). A combination of unemployment, uncertainty about the stability of aid, the exhaustion of personal savings, and the mental stresses of being refugees resulted in what one commentator called an increasing number of "professional refugees, without hope or desire to work again."[20] Despite the difficulties of caring for the Palestinian refugees and of monitoring the armistices in the Middle East and the discouragement that came with the sense that progress had stalled in remedying the aftermath of the 1948–49 war, these issues paled in comparison with the new challenges posed by a new outbreak of hostilities in 1956.

The U.N. role during the Suez Crisis

The outbreak of war in the Middle East in the fall of 1956 had been brewing for some time, despite efforts by the chief of staff of the U.N. Truce Supervision Organization (UNTSO) and Secretary-General Hammarskjöld. Egyptian restrictions on Israeli shipping through the Suez Canal and the Strait of Tiran (at the entrance of the Gulf of Aqaba—see Figure 7.2), Egyptian-supported raids by Palestinians against Israel from Gaza, reprisals by Israeli forces, and a regional arms race were capped off by Egyptian nationalist leader Gamal Abdul al-Nasser's July 26, 1956, nationalization of the Suez Canal, which connected the Mediterranean and Red seas and therefore served as a vital transportation link between Europe, the Middle East, and Asia. Nasser's action was intended to bring him the foreign exchange resources he needed to build the Aswan High Dam across the Nile River in his country (the keystone to his economic development plans) following the withdrawal of U.S. support for plans to obtain World Bank funding of the dam project on July 19, 1956. In the meantime, the secretary-general worked behind the scenes with all parties and worked out the six general principles for a settlement of the "Suez question" that were incorporated into Security Council Resolution 118: free and open transit through the canal, respect for Egyptian sovereignty, apolitical operation of the canal, jointly agreed upon tolls and charges, an equitable apportionment of all collected fees to Egyptian development, and fair resolution of all disputes through arbitration. But while Hammarskjöld was preparing for peace, Israel, France, and Great Britain had been preparing for war. UNTSO Chief of Staff Major-General E. L. M. Burns of Canada reported the Israeli violation of the Egyptian border on the Sinai Peninsula in the early hours of October 30, 1956, and called upon the encroaching troops to cease their fire and pull back to their side of the border. President Eisenhower was incensed at the aggression, which distracted from the recent uprising against the communist regime in Hungary and came just before the presidential election. The United States called an emergency session of the Security Council and condemned the action; the session was interrupted by news that the French and British had issued ultimatums to the warring parties (which Nasser rejected, according to plan, providing the pretext for Anglo-French intervention). When the Council reconvened that evening, France and Britain vetoed a resolution condemning Israel and calling on all states to avoid the use of force (this was the first U.K. veto in the Security Council). The United States responded by calling the first emergency special session of the U.N. General Assembly, which met on

November 1, 1956, one day after the British Royal Air Force began bombing Egyptian airfields. It was certainly remarkable that the United States was now using the same tactic—taking a key issue out of the Security Council to get around the use of the veto—against its traditional allies that it had earlier used against the Soviet Union in garnering ongoing support of the Korean War effort.[21]

The emergency session adopted Resolution 997 the next day, which condemned the use of force and called for an immediate cease-fire, separation of all troops behind armistice lines, and the reopening of the canal (Australia, France, Israel, New Zealand, and the United Kingdom voted against). Lester Pearson, Canada's Secretary of State for External Affairs, abstained from the vote, objecting that the resolution called only for a temporary cessation of hostilities; he wanted to see the United Nations develop a lasting peace settlement. At this point in the crisis, Canada—relying on the reputation it had built as a country that listened to all sides at the United Nations—played a decisive role in developing a creative solution to the complex issues facing the Assembly. On November 3, 1956, Pearson proposed giving the secretary-general the power to create a peacekeeping force to secure and supervise the cessation of hostilities, which became the U.N. Emergency Force (UNEF). The idea of a peacekeeping force in Sinai that would actively secure and supervise an end of the fighting—rather than just observe (like UNTSO)—was an innovative effort to help the United Nations develop a way to carry out its fundamental task of maintaining international peace and security in a world and a United Nations divided between the superpowers—a world in which the original idea of Great Power cooperation was largely a dead letter. One commentator has noted that Pearson's experience with the League of Nations in Geneva in the 1930s was crucial to his commitment to seeing the United Nations develop a viable way to keep the peace in the postwar world.[22]

Even as the United Nations scrambled to assemble its peacekeeping force, French and British paratroopers landed in the canal zone on November 5, 1956. Eisenhower was livid that his closest allies had developed this plan behind his back. Such blatant Western intervention to reverse the nationalization of the canal (which was wildly popular in the Middle East), especially when carried out in partnership with Israel, threatened to strengthen Nasser further and create more opportunities for Soviet influence in the area. So the president worked with the Soviet Union through the Security Council to reverse the Anglo-French-Israeli aggression. In addition, Eisenhower applied political and financial pressure to his erstwhile allies on November 6 to ensure their compliance with the U.N. cease-fire (they complied but fought up to the last minute before the cease-fire took place at midnight on the evening of November 7).[23]

As the hours ticked toward the anticipated cease-fire, Hammarskjöld presented his plans for the peacekeeping force to the emergency session of the General Assembly on November 6. He recommended that Burns (the commander of the UNTSO) be appointed to command a multinational force (which was to be recruited from member states other than those who were permanent members of the Security Council) and be responsible to the General Assembly and/or Security Council, not any one member state—a model very different from the U.N. military action in Korea. Hammarskjöld clearly stated that there was no intent to influence the military or the political balance in the conflict. But its mission would be broader than previous observer groups—in that it would "help maintain quiet during and after the withdrawal of non-Egyptian forces" following the cease-fire—and it would not be a military force that controlled territory, working instead with local authorities and under the overarching permission of the Egyptian government. The secretary-general was not able to establish the exact length of the UNEF mission, which was only defined as temporary and "being determined by the needs arising out of the current conflict." Nor was he able to make a recommendation on the force's budget, but Hammarskjöld did indicate generally that the member state supplying the manpower for the unit would also be responsible for all of its equipment and salaries, with the U.N. administering additional costs beyond its normal budget. The seven resolutions of the emergency session had created something new—a U.N. peacekeeping force that would secure the cease-fire and withdrawal of invading forces.[24]

Hammarskjöld now scrambled to assemble a sufficient force on the ground in Egypt to carry out its mission, since the British and French made their withdrawal contingent upon the UNEF being able to effectively assume its tasks of protecting public and private property and preventing further hostilities. As Burns and a group of UNTSO observers established their headquarters in Cairo, the secretary-general ironed out final arrangements with the Egyptian government, laying the groundwork for arrival of the first of 6,000 UNEF troops on November 15. In constituting the force, the U.N. sought largely self-contained national contingents, long enough commitments to ensure some continuity, and to avoid being overly dependent on any one member's volunteers. Hammarskjöld insisted that the commander of each country's contingent would take orders only from the UNEF commander, but the national commander would be responsible for issuing all orders to his troops. The UNEF troops wore the uniforms of their respective countries and services (as they remained part of those national armed services), but their U.N. insignia (and eventually the blue berets and helmets that the secretary-general created during this mission) indicated their international allegiance. UNEF soldiers were never to initiate the use of force but were authorized to defend themselves when fired upon. Ultimately, Brazil, Canada, Colombia, Denmark, Finland, India, Indonesia, Norway, Sweden, and Yugoslavia sent troops under these conditions. Additionally, the United States provided assistance with airlifts, shipping, transportation, and supplies; Italy placed Capodichino Airport in Naples at the United Nations' disposal; and Switzerland provided charter planes for the mission. But even the deployment of Colombian, Danish, and Norwegian contingents to the Suez Canal area on November 15–16 did not secure Anglo-French withdrawal, which the General Assembly noted with regret on November 24 in Resolution 1120 (XI).[25]

The United Nations was not, however, simply sitting by and waiting for the withdrawal of Anglo-French forces; on that very same day, the World Bank loaned Egypt, under U.N. auspices, its engineering adviser (Raymond Wheeler) to direct the clearing of thirty vessels that Nasser had sunk in the canal to slow the invaders. Wheeler cooperated with Egyptian authorities and, under the U.N. flag, supervised an American, Belgian, Danish, Dutch, German, Italian, Mexican, Norwegian, Swedish, and Yugoslav crew.

Despite delays caused by futile Anglo-French insistence that their forces join the salvage effort and some Egyptian resistance, Wheeler and his crew had cleared the Suez Canal, refloated most of the ships, and repaired the canal's dredging, communications, lighting, and workshop facilities in just three months and six days and under budget (the World Bank acted as the fiscal agent for the effort).[26]

Although the Anglo-French forces were not entirely replaced by UNEF troops until December 22, the Israeli withdrawal in the wake of the Suez Crisis was even more difficult. On November 7, Israeli Prime Minister David Ben Gurion told the Israeli parliament that the armistice lines had no standing and that Israel would not yield any territory to UNEF; Hammarskjöld immediately contacted Israeli Minister for Foreign Affairs Golda Meir, pointing out that such a stance was in violation of the U.N. General Assembly's resolutions. On November 21, Israel stated that its forces had withdrawn as far as national security would allow and any further action would be contingent on Egypt's stance toward Israel and the capacities of UNEF, which were yet to be determined. The U.N. General Assembly responded with Resolution 1120 (XI), adopted on November 24, which called for Israel to withdraw behind the armistice lines; this began a long, phased Israeli withdrawal. Despite inconclusive negotiations between Hammarskjöld and Meir, she announced on March 1 that Israeli troops would withdraw behind the armistice line, and he was able to report on March 8 that Israeli forces had done so. UNEF forces then began deploying on the Egyptian side of the armistice demarcation line (lacking permission from Israel to take up positions on the eastern side of the line) and took operational control of Gaza, including staffing the airport (although UNTSO continued to have overall control of the area and the two cooperated extensively).[27]

As UNEF settled into its peacekeeping duties along the Egyptian-Israeli border, the World Bank worked toward a final settlement of the issues raised by Nasser's nationalization of the Suez Canal. After some months of negotiations, World Bank President Eugene Black successfully negotiated a July 1958 settlement of approximately $80 million for stockholders in the Universal Suez Canal Company. He followed this up with another settlement later that same year of outstanding claims by British businesses and citizens whose property had been seized by the Egyptian government. This, coupled with the restoration of relations between Egypt and the French and British governments, allowed the World Bank to make loans to the Egyptian Suez Canal Authority to deepen and widen the canal, which allowed both two-way traffic and larger ships in the canal.[28]

For the next decade (until May 1967), UNEF effectively maintained peace along this volatile 59-kilometer-long border by using a series of seventy-two day-time observation posts, night-time patrols, and regular aerial reconnaissance. Key to UNEF's success was cooperation from the Egyptian and Palestinian authorities that led to a virtual end to the infiltrations and attacks from Gaza that had helped destabilize the prewar situation. Pearson's new model of consensual and voluntary peacekeeping was key both to the initial creation of UNEF and to the shortcomings of the mission that emerged over time. A recent history of the force by diplomatic historian Michael K. Carroll points out the dueling realities of UNEF: on the one hand was the symbolic importance of this new U.N. peacekeeper—the stalwart, blue-helmeted soldier committed to international peace—and on the other hand were the bureaucratic high hurdles of coordinating a multinational (and therefore multilingual) force on a shaky-at-best budget over an indefinite period that invariably led to disharmony and disagreement and revealed the very tenuous architecture of the decade-long effort. However, the most significant international shortcoming was the failure to craft a long-term Middle East peace settlement.[29]

U.N. peacekeeping efforts, 1956–67

Lasting peace in the Middle East remained elusive. Instead, over the decade following the Suez Crisis, the United Nations primarily concerned itself with trying to keep the belligerents separated. Though it largely succeeded in doing this in Lebanon and Yemen, the tensions that led to another general war in the Middle East continued to build.

In 1958, the United Nations dispatched an observer group to determine if there was any substance to Lebanese President Camille Chamoun's May 22, 1958, complaint to the U.N. Security Council that arms and military personnel were flowing in to undermine his government at the instigation of the United Arab Republic (UAR, the political union of Egypt and Syria established on February 1, 1958, that ended on September 28, 1961). The U.N. Observation Group in Lebanon (UNOGIL)—reassigned from the UNTSO—arrived on June 12, 1958. Following initial challenges that Hammarskjöld worked diligently to overcome, by July 15, UNOGIL had obtained full access to all sections of the Lebanese-Syrian border and the right to inspect all vehicles and cargoes coming into Lebanon from the north. But international events were unfolding simultaneously that soon eclipsed the U.N. observation efforts. Following the July 14, 1958, military coup that overthrew the government in Iraq, U.S. Marines arrived in Beirut at the invitation of Chamoun, and British paratroopers arrived in Jordan to shore up these regimes that felt threatened by Nasser's growing power and influence. When General Fouad Chehab, a Maronite Christian (who was acceptable to Muslim leaders and who had commanded the Lebanese armed forces since independence and had prevented their intervention in the political upheavals of 1952 and 1958) was elected president by the Lebanese legislature on July 31, 1958, peace largely returned to Lebanon. On August 21, 1958, the emergency special session of the U.N. General Assembly ended with unanimous adoption of Resolution 1237 (ES-III); proposed by ten Arab states, it called on the secretary-general to work with both Jordan and Lebanon to facilitate the earliest possible withdrawal of all foreign troops from their countries. Hammarskjöld was happy to receive news that the U.S. Marines and British paratroopers were both scheduled to withdraw in October. On November 16, 1958, the Lebanese minister for foreign affairs requested removal of its complaint against the United Arab Republic from the Security Council's agenda in light of the cordial relations that had been established between the two countries. The next day, UNOGIL made its final report, and the last member of the group departed Lebanon on December 9, 1958.[30]

The next official U.N. observation mission in Yemen was even more circumscribed than the one in Lebanon and had a less clear-cut outcome. Yemen found itself in a difficult position in the years following the Second World War. Located on the southwestern edge of the Arabian peninsula, it occupied a strategic location, was ruled by a Shia imam who also functioned as king, and faced pressures from its much larger and wealthier Sunni neighbor to the north, Saudi Arabia. These factors contributed to significant strife in the area in the postwar period. Imam Yahya died on September 19, 1962, and was succeeded by his son, Muhammad al-Badr, who had to flee the capital just one week later as the military carried out a coup; but al-Badr and his forces continued to wage war against the new Yemen Arab Republic, and both the royalists and republicans claimed to be the legitimate representatives of the Yemeni people. Subsequently, Ralph Bunche, U.N. Under-Secretary for Special Political Affairs, negotiated an agreement that would have Saudi Arabia end all support and aid (including haven in Saudi territory) to the royalists as the Egyptian troops left Yemen (where they were supporting the republican troops); a demilitarized zone created on the Saudi-Yemen border, twenty kilometers deep on both sides with impartial observers stationed there to note whether the terms of disengagement were being followed; and other observers in the cities and ports of Yemen ensuring Egyptian withdrawal. All of this was overseen by Lieutenant-General Carl C. von Horn of Sweden, chief of staff of the UNTSO, who headed the U.N. Yemen Observation Mission (UNYOM) starting on June 11, 1963. But just as tensions eased under the watchful eyes of UNYOM by January 2, 1964, significant arms and ammunition started coming to the royalists across the unmonitored border between Yemen and the British-controlled South Arabian Federation that fueled royalist attacks in January and February 1964. Ultimately, in his September 2, 1964, report, Secretary-General U Thant indicated that no further progress could be made under UNYOM's limited mandate, and two days later the mission ended when its personnel and equipment were withdrawn.[31] Again events on the ground and Great Power intervention had superseded a U.N. military observer group.

On the other hand, there was no end in sight for the UNTSO's work along Israel's borders with its neighbors, especially with Syria. Violence flared there in 1964 when Israel attempted to farm the demilitarized zone and Syria responded by attempting to divert the headwaters of Jordan River to prevent its water from flowing into Israel, which in turn used force to prevent this. That same year, the Palestine Liberation Organization (PLO) was established—the outcome of some fifteen years of festering Palestinian resentment about their situation that gave rise to an organization determined to give Palestinians a voice in the councils that often spoke about them and frequently presumed to speak for them but rarely included them. In 1965, Palestinian guerillas based in Syria made incursions into Israel that resulted in reprisals by that country's defense forces. The cycle of violence escalated in late 1966 and early 1967 despite U.N. efforts to defuse the situation. On April 7, 1967, Israeli fighter-jets engaged Syrian jets, which triggered retaliatory violence along the northern Israeli border with Syria and threats from Tel Aviv that it would occupy Damascus.[32] Neither the threats and escalating violence along the border nor the emergence of a nonstate actor—the PLO—boded well for peace in the region.

The U.N. role in the June 1967 war (Six-Day War) and its aftermath

When further fighting broke out between Israel and Syria, the commander-in-chief of the Egyptian armed forces requested (on May 16, 1967) that the commander of the UNEF withdraw his troops. For the next two days, Secretary-General U Thant scrambled to try to maintain the buffer between the two countries; but on 18 May, Egyptian soldiers prevented UNEF troops from assuming their posts, and Israel also rebuffed a request from Thant that the force be redeployed on its side of the armistice line. On May 22, Nasser closed the Strait of Tiran (see Figure 7.2) to Israeli shipping, and at the end of that month he signed a mutual defense treaty with Jordan. Despite efforts by U.S. officials to defuse the situation, war erupted on June 5, 1967, between Egypt and Israel; it was not the limited war to reopen the straits that the White House had expected. Israeli forces quickly demolished the Egyptian air force and occupied both the Gaza Strip and the Sinai Peninsula, making the Americans "angry as hell" and prompting an inconclusive meeting of the Security Council the next morning. Jordan and Syria responded to their neighbor's distress, and Israeli Defense Forces (IDF) occupied their West Bank and Golan Heights territories, respectively. The United States agreed to a cease-fire resolution through the Security Council on June 6 but resisted a Soviet amendment that would have called upon Israel to relinquish the territory it had already gained. Israeli Foreign Minister Abba Eban addressed the Council that evening to make the Israeli case to a world audience, arguing that his country had been forced to make the preemptive attack in order to survive as a beleaguered and blockaded nation surrounded by enemies on all sides. The speech played well to the U.S. audience but also increasingly bound the Americans to the Israelis in the eyes of much of the United Nations. Washington did, however, work to broker bilateral cease-fires. Johnson pressured Israel to accept the final (Syrian) cease-fire on June 10, just as the Soviet Union severed relations with Israel, called the General Assembly into emergency session to consider the situation, and threatened the possibility of military action in the region. Nonetheless, Arab governments severed diplomatic relations with the United States, as anti-American mobs reacted to Johnson's apparent support of Tel Aviv.[33]

The UNRWA found its work significantly complicated by the war and its outcome. While UNRWA worked to provide immediate humanitarian relief to the people displaced by this new war, it also had to care for the Palestinians displaced in the previous war under new conditions. Israeli occupation of the Gaza Strip (which had previously been administered by Egypt) meant that the U.N. agency had to negotiate a new set of working relationships with a new government in order to carry out its mandate, but the Israelis generally resented UNRWA for granting the Palestinian refugees "special" status, nurturing their sense of national identity through its schools, and presumably retarding their realization that return to their previous homes in Israel was not a possibility. Israel made some early efforts to build new, competing institutions in Gaza—such as government-sponsored schools—but the Palestinians spurned them, despite the overcrowding in UNRWA schools. Israeli regulations also slowed the flow of supplies and aid into the area, and infrastructure generally declined under occupation.[34]

In the wake of the Six-Day War, the United Nations again sought a long-term political peace settlement (with the backing of the United States). The resulting U.N. Security Council Resolution 242 on November 22, 1967, established a formula that subsequently was called "land for peace" in short hand. In other words, Israel would withdraw from territories that it had occupied in June 1967 in return for Arab governments' recognition of its right to exist (and therefore presumably their intention to stop trying to destroy it). However ambiguities remained about whether recognition would come before or after withdrawal and whether some or all of the occupied territories would have to be vacated. Nasser exposed these ambiguities by offering to make peace with the Jewish state through the United Nations if Israel withdrew from all the territory it had recently occupied. Tel Aviv's rebuff showed that Resolution 242 promised no short-term improvements in the situation.[35]

Rebuffed in his gambit to make peace, Nasser then turned to the Soviet Union, which provided massive amounts of military aid in the period following the Six-Day War. U.S. Presidents Johnson and then Richard M. Nixon sold advanced military jets to Israel to try to maintain some sort of regional arms balance. By early 1969, violence between the two nations in the area around the Suez Canal escalated into what historians have termed a "war of attrition." Egyptian artillery and air strikes against Israeli troops east of the Suez Canal in March 1969 prompted Israeli air strikes that by January 1970 included strikes on Cairo intended to demoralize the Egyptians and lead to the overthrow of Nasser. But the Egyptian leader then traveled to Moscow, where he secured antiaircraft guns, surface-to-air missiles, a radar system, Soviet MiG fighters, and the services of 15,000 Soviet military advisers, including 200 pilots. The violence continued until June 1970, when Jordan and Egypt accepted the overtures of U.S. Secretary of State William Rogers, who proposed a cease-fire followed by U.N.-brokered peace talks along the lines of Resolution 242 and a final settlement of the refugee question. Rogers envisaged determining each 1948 Palestinian refugee's individual choice between repatriation in Israel (carried out in phases) or resettlement elsewhere (along with Israeli compensation for his/her lost property). Although Israel's agreement to pursue negotiations under the plan did bring the conflict to an end on August 7, Nixon sabotaged any longer-term solution by assuring Israel's new prime minister, Golda Meir, that the United States would not force her to absorb Palestinian refugees or give up any territory before a final peace treaty was in place.[36]

The PLO bursts onto the international stage

In the wake of the war of attrition, the PLO burst onto the international stage in September 1970 when it landed four hijacked commercial airliners within miles of Syrian King Hussein's palace. As Paul Thomas Chamberlain's *The Global Offensive* points out, this nonstate actor, established in 1964 and led by Yasser Arafat after 1969, exercised its own power, harbored its own ambitions, and crafted its own grand strategies and foreign policy. The PLO saw itself as part of a global offensive against white supremacy, colonialism, and the Cold War status quo and worked with the North Vietnamese, the African National Congress in South Africa, and other revolutionary movements. Like the Algerians before them, the Palestinians saw the United Nations as a key arena for gaining international attention and sympathy for their cause, which they needed to overcome opposition to their goal of an independent Palestinian nation. The PLO went beyond this, however, becoming what Chamberlain calls "the world's first globalized insurgency." The hijackings in the fall of 1970 certainly highlighted this aspect of the PLO, which subsequently reshaped both the regional order in the Middle East and "the shape of revolutionary politics in the wider world" during the 1970s and 1980s.[37]

But the Americans—especially through the Nixon Doctrine—also recognized that they were engaged in a transnational struggle against a number of small states and guerilla groups using new techniques and strategies to fight against the states and structures that gave it "superpower" status. And they too fought back in the United Nations, seeking specifically to diplomatically contain the PLO and shield Israel with its Security Council veto. But more generally, Chamberlain sees the United States taking up a defensive position in the United Nations, where it also fought along a broad front against "Third Worldism—an amorphous, left-leaning political movement among the developing nations that emphasized the North-South divide in international affairs and sought to create greater solidarity among the nations of the postcolonial world."[38]

To combat what it termed "international terrorism," the United States worked to develop greater international cooperation on security issues and to forge stronger military partnerships and international organizations to address this new brand of transnational threat. For example, the Nixon administration worked diligently to tackle airline hijacking in the late 1960s and early 1970s through the ICAO. Before the 1967 Six-Day War, hijackings had been confined to a handful of incidents of Eastern Europeans seeking to escape from the Iron Curtain or Cubans hijacking American flights in the 1950s and early 1960s. But the number of hijackings quickly escalated to thirty-four in 1968, then eighty-seven in 1969. By 1972, there had been 364 such incidents. At the September 1968 ICAO Assembly, the U.N. specialized agency took the lead (through its new, permanent Committee on Unlawful Interference with Aircraft) in drafting and disseminating new technical and legal regulations for all members to make their airplanes and airports more secure in order to deter terrorists. In the summer of 1969, the Syrian government held a hijacked TWA plane and two Israeli passengers for several months, finally releasing them only when Israel exchanged a number of Syrian prisoners for them. This prompted Nixon to call for concerted international action when he addressed the General Assembly that September, and it responded with a resolution in December calling on members to take "appropriate measures" in concert with the ICAO. The February 21, 1970, Palestinian attacks on two European flights bound for Tel Aviv elicited a strong international response and an extraordinary session of ICAO that June, which charged the ICAO secretary-general to prepare a "Manual on Security" (published in November 1971) to provide member states with guidance on improving security. Shortly after the ICAO extraordinary session ended, the Popular Front for the Liberation of Palestine coordinated a series of hijackings that resulted in four aircraft and hundreds of passengers being held in Jordan and Cairo for several days—the worst hijacking incident to that point. And although it prompted General Assembly Resolution 2645 condemning such acts and the December 1970 Hague Convention for the Suppression of Unlawful Seizure of Aircraft, a stronger international legal convention that would have required extradition of hijackers and that would have imposed serious and significant penalties upon those countries that refused, never materialized despite vigorous American efforts and the 1972 actions of Black September (which included a May hijacking and the September murder of eleven Israeli athletes at the Munich Olympics). This inaction was due, in part, to the considerable sympathy in the international community for the Palestinian cause and to the dramatic decline in hijacking incidents after 1972 thanks to implementation of new, ICAO-drafted airport security measures.[39]

That General Assembly sympathy for the PLO cause was on full display in 1974, when it invited the PLO to serve as an observer at the Assembly and its international conferences (although thirty-five states voted against the resolution or abstained) and marked the occasion by inviting Arafat to address the body. It also became routine in the General Assembly and its conferences in the mid-1970s to condemn "the unholy alliance between South African racism and zionism" and to lump zionism along with "colonialism and neo-colonialism, foreign occupation, . . . apartheid and racial discrimination in all its forms" as detrimental to "international co-operation and peace." The 1975 General Assembly's Resolution 3379 put it most succinctly: "Zionism is a form of racism and racial discrimination." The use of such language disturbed the Israeli government, which was born out of the racial discrimination against the Jews that developed into the Second World War's Holocaust. Only the American threat of withdrawing its funding of the United Nations prevented the Assembly from revoking Israel's credentials and forbidding its participation in Assembly debates like it had earlier done to South Africa. Nonetheless, between 1973 and 1983, the situation between Israel and Palestine appeared on the Council agenda more often than any other single issue, and between 1970 and 1985, the United States used its veto power seventeen times on behalf of Israel.[40]

On the ground, the PLO, largely driven out of Jordan in the early 1970s, established itself in southern Lebanon, where it destabilized relations with Israel and utilized UNRWA infrastructure to continue its work (sometimes even lobbying Arab governments to increase their donations to the U.N. agency). PLO camp committees and the Palestine Armed Struggle Command largely governed the UNRWA camps. As a result, Israeli aircraft bombed UNRWA facilities starting in 1971, and control of such facilities was often the cause of fighting between Palestinians and various Lebanese militias. UNRWA, like Sisyphus, worked to carry out its charge and rebuild its damaged facilities. But in 1975, Israeli forces cut UNRWA communications and the movement of its staff and supplies as they attacked PLO locations in southern Lebanon, prompting an October evacuation of the families of U.N. personnel, the January 1976 relocation of UNRWA offices from Beirut to Amman, Jordan, and Vienna, Austria, and the temporary staff evacuation of the office in June 1976, leaving remaining agency operations in the hands of its local personnel. An Arab summit held in Cairo in October 1976, created an Arab peacekeeping force for Lebanon composed mainly of Syrian army units who succeeded in temporarily tamping down the civil war in that country. UNRWA estimated that some thirty thousand Palestinian refugees had been displaced (many of whom relocated to Beirut), and it had lost thirty-one members of its staff between September 1975 and October 1976. Although the headquarters' staff returned to Beirut in November 1977, they returned to Vienna in June 1978 in the face of renewed fighting.[41]

The Yom Kippur War of 1973

The origins of the Yom Kippur War lay in Israel's failure to pursue peace after the Six-Day War. Rather than seeking peace through good-faith negotiations with the new Egyptian leader, Anwar Sadat, who had conditionally accepted the peace plan laid out by U.N. mediator Gunnar Jarring in 1971, Israel rejected both the proposal and a more modest one from Sadat that Israel demonstrate its willingness to move forward in the peace process by withdrawing its armed forces from the Suez Canal area. When Israeli Prime Minister Golda Meir met with President Nixon at the end of that year, she negotiated an end to U.S. efforts to promote peace in exchange for only a partial withdrawal from the Suez area. When Kissinger's talks with Israeli, Jordanian, and Egyptian officials in the fall of 1973 brought Sadat no closer to his publicly stated goal of regaining the Sinai Peninsula, the new Egyptian leader decided that only military action could secure his goals.[42]

On October 6, 1973, during the Jewish Yom Kippur holiday, the Egyptian and Syrian armies coordinated a surprise attack against Israeli forces in both the Sinai Peninsula and the Golan Heights that initially caught the Israeli Defense Force unawares. A Soviet airlift of military supplies four days into the war helped the Arab armies further their initial advances, but a similar American airlift to Israel helped the defense forces regain that ground. Kissinger sought simultaneously to prevent Israeli defeat and to lay the groundwork for a durable postwar peace by flying to Moscow to develop the terms of the U.N. Security Council Resolution that called for an October 22 cease-fire and peace negotiations based on Resolution 242. Despite having regained all the ground it had initially lost and more, the Israeli forces continued to fight past the cease-fire deadline in an effort to encircle the Egyptian Third Army. This prompted the Security Council to establish a second U.N. Emergency Force, which immediately moved between the Israeli and Egyptian armies along the Suez Canal on October 24. Combined with Sadat's complaints, Soviet Premier Leonid Brezhnev's warning that his country would intervene militarily to protect its ally, and Kissinger's diplomatic pressure on Israel, this finally ended the fighting on October 25. Although a military defeat, the Arab states believed that they had regained their honor, which had been damaged by the Six-Day War, and were now in a stronger negotiating position. This position was further strengthened when the Arab members of OPEC limited oil sales to and raised prices for the United States and other Western powers, which caused significant economic distress.[43]

The sharp spike in American energy prices lent urgency to Kissinger's subsequent "shuttle diplomacy" between the Middle Eastern capitals for more than a year between the October 1973 cease-fire and the December 1974 conference in Geneva that included representatives of the United States, the Soviet Union, Israel, Jordan, and Egypt. Geneva laid the groundwork for an Egyptian-Israeli accord on January 18, 1974, that inserted U.N. peacekeepers to separate the armies and keep the terms of the accord. That spring (in March 1974) regular oil shipments resumed between the Middle East, Western Europe, and North America. In September 1975, Egypt and Israel further agreed to widen the U.N. buffer zone to include the strategic Mitla and Gidi passes (see Figure 7.2), complete with an American-staffed monitoring and early warning system. The so-called Sinai II agreement also called on Israel to withdraw from the Abu Rodeis oil fields, for both sides to limit their tanks, artillery, and personnel near the U.N. zone, and for the two governments to work toward a peace settlement. Due to the Watergate scandal and Nixon's subsequent resignation, Kissinger did not get to see the peace process through to its conclusion, leaving it to the administration of U.S. President Gerald Ford.[44]

Kissinger concluded a similar deal with Syria on May 31, 1974, that separated the two armies and inserted the U.N. Disengagement Observer Force (UNDOF, numbering 1,218 by June 16) to ensure compliance with the disengagement agreement. The disengagement agreement called for an area of separation with mirroring zones of limited forces on both sides of the U.N. zone. The Syrian authorities govern and police the inhabitants of this demilitarized zone, while UNDOF forces (in conjunction with UNTSO military observers) patrol the area and supervise it from fixed observation posts. These U.N. forces have also provided medical assistance, cleared land mines, and assisted the International Committee of the Red Cross in their areas of operations, resulting in a long record of maintaining a strong, cooperative peace along the Israeli-Syrian border, even when political relations between the two countries have not been good. However, UNDOF forces have recently (2013) experienced difficulties as a result of the Syrian civil war (including abductions of and firing at UNDOF and UNTSO personnel) that have led to the withdrawal of two contingents of armed forces and a rethinking of UNDOF's mission.[45]

U.N. Interim Force in Lebanon, 1978–2000

The record of U.N. forces in Lebanon has not been as strong as those in the Golan Heights. When Palestinian armed elements shifted from Jordan to Lebanon in the wake of King Hussein's 1970 crackdown on the PLO, incidents of violence along the Israeli-Lebanese border increased. An especially bloody March 11, 1978, commando attack into Israel for which the PLO claimed responsibility led the IDF to cross the border into Lebanon during the evening of March 14–15. That morning, the Lebanese government appealed to the Security Council, pointing out that it had no connection to the PLO attack and declaring the invasion to be entirely unjustified. Within several days, Israel had occupied almost the entire southern part of Lebanon, and on March 19, Security Council resolutions 425 and 426 called for an immediate cease-fire and Israeli withdrawal as well as the creation of the U.N. Interim Force in Lebanon (UNIFIL) that would confirm the withdrawal and restore peace and Lebanese governance to the area. The first troops arrived to carry out this mandate on March 23, 1978, but factional fighting continued.[46]

The Israeli-Lebanese border witnessed an artillery duel between PLO forces in southern Lebanon and IDF in the summer of 1981. It prompted the United States to dispatch a special envoy (Lebanese-American Philip Habib) to broker a cease-fire, which started in July 1981. However, Israeli Prime Minister Menachim Begin soon regretted the cease-fire, since it seemed to imply some type of Israeli and American recognition of the PLO and potentially provided the organization additional time to rearm and attack again. He therefore worked with Minister of Defense General Ariel Sharon to develop a plan to launch a major invasion of Lebanon and support the leadership of Maronite Christian leader Bashir Gemayel, hoping that he would then sign a peace treaty with Israel. Using the pretext of the PLO shooting and wounding of an Israeli diplomat in London, Israel began bombing PLO targets in and around Beirut and southern Lebanon on June 3, 1982, and three days later Israel again invaded its northern neighbor.[47]

Sharon quickly exceeded the Israeli Cabinet's authorization to attack PLO targets within forty kilometers of the border when he engaged Syrian forces and pushed toward Beirut. Not even a U.S.-brokered cease-fire on June 11 slowed Sharon, whose forces linked up with Christian Lebanese militias in the north of the country and besieged PLO forces in Beirut. The Israeli forces bombarded PLO strongholds in the city and occupied the airport. Although the United States had vetoed an earlier French-sponsored Security Council resolution calling for the immediate withdrawal of Israeli forces, U.S. President Ronald Reagan was incensed as the Israeli forces shelled Beirut. On August 12, the two sides agreed to a joint Franco-Italian relocation of some 11,000 PLO fighters (including Yasser Arafat) to other Arab countries; the French and Italian forces completed their mission on September 1 and then departed from Lebanon. But in the interim, the Israelis continued to meddle in internal Lebanese matters, helping to ensure the August 23, 1982, election of Bashir Gemayel. Reagan was not happy with his ally's actions; in an address to the American people on September 1, he laid out his position that Israel had to honor U.N. Resolution 242, rejecting its claims to sovereignty over the Golan Heights and the West Bank. He also rejected claims of Palestinian statehood, hoping to create the basis for a new, comprehensive Mideast peace plan.[48]

Neither the American nor the Israeli goals came to fruition. On September 14, Lebanese President Gemayel was assassinated, and his eldest son, Amin Gemayel, succeeded him in the presidency; he was not interested in close relations with Israel and sought to reassert Lebanon's sovereignty against the Israelis, Palestinians, and Syrians. In the wake of the assassination, Sharon reoccupied parts of Beirut. Ultimately U.S. Secretary of State George Shultz brokered a deal (signed May 17, 1983) that formally terminated the war between Israel and Lebanon, called for Israeli forces to retreat to a "security zone" approximately forty kilometers wide in southern Lebanon, and introduced U.N. troops as peacekeepers in the area north of the Israeli troops.[49]

In the aftermath of the Israeli invasion, the United Nations sought to pick up some of the pieces. UNIFIL's mission shifted to providing protection and humanitarian assistance to the southern Lebanese population that found itself experiencing various levels of Israeli occupation. The Lebanese government and U.N. secretary-general supported that mission through the year 2000. UNRWA, which had maintained large Palestinian refugee camps in southern Lebanon, likewise shifted to emergency aid to the victims of the invasion. Its camps around Lebanon's largest cities saw 57 percent of homes destroyed and another 20 percent damaged, and many students started the new school year under large tents in three different shifts. UNRWA's silver lining was that the subsequent efforts of the Reagan White House to broker a peace deal (which would require some level of Arab support) led it to reverse its stated plan to reduce and ultimately eliminate its support of the agency. Instead of reducing its annual commitment from $67 million to $50 million in 1983, it increased its contribution to $84 million. The refugees continued to struggle in the aftermath of the invasion, despite international assistance. In the so-called war of the camps, the PLO-backed groups and Syrian-backed Shia groups battled for control and aid in the camps. Nor were the UNRWA staff spared the violence; between 1982 and 1988, eight were kidnapped and thirty-three were killed.[50] The situation in Lebanon remained unsettled over the next decades, and the U.N. continued its work in the country; but the world's attention soon shifted to other crises in the region, especially the outbreak of war between Iran and Iraq, which will be discussed a bit later in this chapter.

The Programme of Assistance to the Palestinian People, December 1978

The Camp David Accords that Egypt and Israel signed in September 1978 envisioned, in the first chapter of the agreement, the rapid transfer of power to a democratic Palestinian government in Gaza and the West Bank (also known since 1968 as the "occupied territories").

Recognizing that the Palestinians needed assistance to make this promise (and peace) a reality, the signatories subsequently agreed to bring in the U.N. Development Programme (UNDP) to oversee this process. Israel had consistently resented UNRWA; on the other hand, UNDP was an organization that assisted any number of countries. Israel had, in fact, received technical assistance in its early days as a state from the predecessors of UNDP and had a good working relationship with the current program. UNDP Administrator F. Bradford "Brad" Morse was committed to the new mandate, which was codified in General Assembly Resolution 33/147. He had already appointed five Palestinians to the twenty-one resident representative posts in the Arab world, and now he appointed his closest associates to oversee the new Programme of Assistance to the Palestinian People (PAPP), including John Olver (who came out of retirement and directed PAPP for its first dozen years). During the previous decade of Israeli occupation of the West Bank and Gaza Strip, poverty and unemployment among the refugees had increased while housing conditions had significantly declined. Additionally, the physical infrastructure, education system, and public health facilities had not kept pace, as UNRWA's funding level had lagged behind population growth. UNDP organized a donor campaign and started field operations in August 1980.[51]

From the beginning, UNDP's work through PAPP differed in some ways from its predominant models in other areas. While generally a UNDP resident representative works with the national government, the contestation over governance in the occupied Palestinian territories meant that the PAPP director had to work with a number of local institutions in Gaza and the West Bank as well as the Israeli government. Nonetheless, Olver was able to gain the trust of both Israel and the Palestinians and was therefore able to do things in the area that other agencies could not. As a result, it designed and implemented its own projects (such as building public health facilities, public markets, recreation facilities, roads, schools, waste-treatment plants, and waterworks) whereas it traditionally provided only technical assistance and had other agencies handle the implementation. And while UNDP generally funds its programs and projects through its budget (made up of voluntary contributions from member states), it "provides only a modest level of core support" for PAPP (to cover administrative costs), with the bulk of the funding coming from international donors.[52]

Despite PAPP's new efforts in the region, UNRWA did not go away. In 1989, UNRWA was still running 633 elementary and high schools and eight vocational and teacher-training centers as well as ninety-eight health clinics and ninety-four feeding centers for undernourished children for the 2,301,919 registered refugees they served in sixty-one official refugee camps and other areas. Despite the increase in its educational efforts (which consumed two-thirds of UNRWA's annual budget), it also still distributed relief assistance to 137,963 refugees (10 percent of the overall budget).[53] Both agencies continue to work in Gaza and the West Bank to this day, as the hoped-for transition to Palestinian self-rule imagined in the Camp David Accords still awaits fruition.

The Iran-Iraq War, 1980–88

Beginning in September 1980, the Republic of Iraq invaded the new Islamic Republic of Iran and quickly occupied a large swath of that country. However, by 1982, Iranian troops had pushed the Iraqi forces back and had crossed into Iraq. As the war dragged through much of the decade and casualties mounted to more than one million in all, the United Nations sought peace and a mitigation of the worst aspects of the war. Anti-Iranian feeling among the permanent members of the Security Council and a generally pro-Arab inclination among the Non-Aligned Movement meant that the U.N. took no action to identify Iraq as the aggressor in the conflict, which infuriated Tehran, which would communicate only with the secretary-general. But the United Nations did seek to publicize and end the use of chemical warfare during the conflict, starting in 1984. Iraq had initiated the use of chemical weapons (first mustard gas in July–August 1983 and then the nerve agent tabun in early 1984—the first use of such a compound on a modern battlefield) in an effort to offset its disadvantage in troop numbers (Iran's population was triple that of Iraq at the beginning of the war). In response to Iranian requests, a multinational U.N. investigative team issued a March 26, 1984, report to the Security Council confirming that both mustard gas and tabun had been used in areas of Iran, leading the United States, Great Britain, France, and Japan to ban the export of all precursor chemicals to Iraq. Australia took matters further, starting a multinational effort in late 1984 to identify the chemicals, biological agents, and machinery needed to produce chemical weapons and to develop common export bans on all such materials. By 1988, Iran seemed to be responding in kind to Iraq's use of chemical weapons (given that no punitive actions followed the finding that Iraq had clearly violated the 1925 Geneva Protocol). As diplomatic pressure for a cease-fire mounted, another U.N. medical investigation found patients on both sides who had been exposed to mustard gas and tabun. On May 9, 1988, the U.N. Security Council responded with Resolution 612, which condemned both and called for tighter export controls (but still no punitive action). The inability of the Security Council to take effective action and the widespread use of chemical weapons during the Iran-Iraq War formed part of the background for the Chemical Warfare Convention that entered into force in 1997 and included verification, compliance, enforcement, and confidence-building measures.[54]

The war escalated dangerously in 1988 in what some have called the "tanker war." As early as 1984, Iraq had declared a blockade of Iran and subsequently attacked its oil tankers in the Persian Gulf in an effort to compel it to sue for peace. By 1986, Iran had occupied the Fao Peninsula (strategically important because it controlled Iraq's only outlet to the Gulf and threatened the Iraqi city of Basra) and started retaliating against Iraq by using mines and speedboat attacks against neutral shipping headed toward Iraq's key supporters of Kuwait and Saudi Arabia (approximately ninety merchant vessels were attacked that year). In November 1986, Kuwait first asked both the United States and the Soviet Union to aid it by protecting its shipments through the Persian Gulf.[55]

U.N. Secretary-General de Cuellar instigated regular, informal meetings of the permanent members of the Security Council in his office at the beginning of 1987, with the goal of winding down the conflict, but in the meantime, President Reagan, in an effort to deny the Soviets an expanded role in the Gulf, opted in March 1987 to unilaterally put American flags on Kuwaiti tankers and provide U.S. Navy escorts. Although the Security Council sought to craft a peace process in July, by the end of September 1987, there were some forty U.S. naval vessels in the Persian Gulf and tens of thousands of American sailors, who were joined, by the end of the year, by about twenty additional ships from Belgium, Britain, France, Italy, and the Netherlands. Iranian attacks on tankers, U.S. shelling of unmanned Iranian oil platforms, Iranian mine-laying in the Persian Gulf, and then the mistaken downing of an Iranian commercial airliner (killing all 290 passengers and crew) by the USS *Vincennes* on July 3, 1988, made peacemaking imperative. Two weeks later, Iran accepted Security Council Resolution 598, followed the next day by Iraq. Intensive U.N. diplomacy led to agreement on a cease-fire, creation of the U.N. Iran-Iraq Military Observer Group (UNIIMOG) to supervise its terms, and direct bilateral talks between Iran and Iraq under the secretary-general's auspices scheduled to begin five days after the cease-fire. The military observers helped de-escalate tensions along the border (until the August 1990 Iraqi invasion of Kuwait). In the fall of 1990, UNIIMOG began to wind down the final stage of its mission.[56]

The intifada, 1987–92

On December 9, 1987, twenty years of Israeli occupation and forty years of refugee status boiled over into the intifada (Arabic for "shaking off"). A Gaza motor vehicle accident that day killed four Palestinians and led to street protests that quickly flared into a widespread resistance movement in all of the occupied territories in which Palestinian youths squared off against the Israeli Defense Forces (the IDF). They responded severely to the demonstrations, rock- and Molotov-cocktail-throwing, and tire burning that characterized the intifada. By mid-1992, UNRWA had counted 912 Palestinian fatalities among the 73,727 total casualties of the crisis, with an additional 17,000 (approximately) imprisoned. Some 250 suspected Palestinian collaborators were also killed by their countrymen, and about fifty Israelis lost their lives.[57]

The intifada again altered both the perception of UNRWA and its relationship with its donors and clients. No longer did it face criticism that its aid had bred passivity among the recipients. The "David vs. Goliath" dimensions of the conflict—broadcast around the globe—heightened international sympathy for the Palestinians in the occupied territories, led to condemnations of Israel's disproportionate response, and prompted temporarily higher levels of giving to the agency that allowed it to redevelop the "works" focus of its mission. Additionally, UNRWA now defined part of its role in the region as protecting the refugees as well as providing relief, which earned it the enmity of Israel, expressed through the "temporary suspension" in June of Israel's support of UNRWA operations (including the paying of port charges, warehousing, and transport of its shipments and the costs of providing water to the camps as it had agreed to do under the 1967 Comay-Michelmore agreement). The U.N. agency publicized, criticized, and advocated for a change in Israel's policies during the intifada, especially for closing schools and imposing curfews, which made it nearly impossible to provide basic public services such as garbage pick-up and distribution of food rations. Eventually, the Palestinians recognized and appreciated this new, protective role, which was institutionalized in UNRWA's new Refugee Affairs Office program.[58]

PLO leader Yasser Arafat used the intifada to help unite Palestinians under his leadership (although the intifada also gave rise to Hamas in Gaza) and to make a bold bid for nationhood. In March 1988, U.S. Secretary of State George P. Shultz, worried about the intifada's incubation of Palestinian extremism, publicly reaffirmed the American commitment to the "land-for-peace" formula laid out in U.N. Resolutions 242 and 338 and sought to launch U.S.-brokered peace talks between Israel, Jordan, and the PLO with the goal of a three-year transition to Palestinian rule in the occupied territories. But when King Hussein of Jordan renounced his country's annexation of the West Bank and proclaimed that he would no longer represent the Palestinians on July 31, 1988, Arafat's Palestine National Council voted to approve U.N. Resolutions 242 and 338 (implicitly affirming the right of Israel to exist) and to declare the establishment of the State of Palestine, with Jerusalem as its capital. In just days, twenty-seven Arab and Muslim governments had recognized the putative state, but the Israeli prime minister found these declarations far too shaky a foundation for peace. When the United States subsequently denied Arafat a visa so that he could address the U.N. General Assembly, the international organization reconvened in Geneva to hear the PLO leader on December 13, 1988, call for a U.N.-sponsored conference between Israel and its Arab neighbors and for the introduction of U.N. troops to replace Israeli forces in the occupied territories of Gaza and the West Bank. He also signed a statement saying that the PLO "undertakes to live in peace with Israel" and "condemns individual, group, and State terrorism in all its forms," and he reiterated these themes in a press conference, which prompted the Reagan administration to declare that the United States would engage in talks with the PLO for the first time. Nonetheless, the new administration of President George H. W. Bush and his secretary of state, James Baker, struggled throughout 1989 and 1990 in its efforts to bring the two sides together. Then the Iraqi invasion of Kuwait and the First Persian Gulf War (1990–91) put these peacemaking efforts temporarily on the back burner.[59]

The First Persian Gulf War

On August 2, 1990, Saddam Hussein's Iraq invaded the small neighboring nation of Kuwait and triggered a massive U.N. response headquartered in the Security Council that was in stark contrast to its response to the invasion of Iran in the previous decade. Within just eight hours of receiving the news of the invasion of Kuwait, the Council had assembled in emergency session and drafted a resolution condemning the invasion and calling for immediate and unconditional Iraqi withdrawal. President Bush, having himself served as U.S. ambassador to the United Nations, decided to manage the crisis through the Council and his ambassador there, Thomas Pickering—a professional diplomat who had gained friends and respect in New York for his willingness to listen to others and his decision to spend most of his time at the United Nations rather than in Washington, DC. Spearheading the American response, Pickering worked hard to keep the five permanent members united and Iraq front-of-mind in the Council. Resolution 661 (adopted August 6) imposed a comprehensive sanctions regime on the aggressor (the first since Rhodesia and South Africa) that would be handled directly by a Council sanctions committee. Working through the Security Council sometimes slowed the pace of U.S. action and at one point required America to cooperate with the nonpermanent members of the Council in condemning Israeli "acts of violence" toward Palestinians at Jerusalem's Temple Mount on October 8 (rather than vetoing the resolution). Ultimately, however, the Council approved the U.S.-drafted resolution authorizing the United Nations to use military force against Iraq in order to oust its forces from Kuwait, with Secretary of State Baker lobbying hard as the Council's president in November in order to garner overwhelming support for the resolution, which passed 12–2–1 (with Yemen and Cuba voting against and China abstaining). The fruit of that resolution, the first war authorized by the United Nations since Korea, started on the evening of January 16, 1991. Subsequently, the United States worked to ensure that Council discussions about civilian casualties during that air war took place behind closed doors and that the U.S.

commander on the ground would retain operational control. On February 24, in an effort dubbed "Operation Desert Storm," the coalition of thirty-four countries began its ground operations, which were successfully concluded within one hundred hours, when it occupied the capital, Kuwait City, and the last Iraqi troops had either surrendered or fled across the border.[60]

In the wake of the successful military operations, the Council passed Resolution 687 in April 1991, which established a set of monitoring procedures and sanctions that ostensibly protected Iraq's neighbors and its residents who had suffered past abuses (especially the Kurds in northern Iraq) but had the goal (from the U.S. perspective) of removing Hussein from power. Iraq's nuclear program would be inspected by the International Atomic Energy Agency (IAEA), but its other weapons of mass destruction would be monitored by a newly created agency—the U.N. Special Commission (UNSCOM)—that reported directly to and was directly funded by the Council (whereas IAEA reported to the Secretariat). Iraq bridled at these conditions but also failed to earn any trust from the Council when it missed its July deadline for declaring its inventory of weapons of mass destruction, when UNSCOM inspectors subsequently located large caches of chemical weapons that far exceeded the quantity that Baghdad claimed to have, and when in August it admitted to efforts to enrich small amounts of plutonium. This sidetracked those on the Council who had sought to lift economic sanctions that same month and instead meant that there would be a long, complicated, and problematic period of sanctions (and exceptions to the sanctions, especially the oil-for-food program) that ultimately led to both allegations of U.N. corruption and a second war against Iraq under U.S. President George W. Bush (discussed in Chapter 3).[61]

While issues of sanctions primarily occupied the decision-makers in New York, on the ground in the Middle East UNRWA scrambled to provide emergency aid and schooling to the hundreds of thousands of refugees (many of them Palestinians) who had fled the fighting, many seeking refuge in Jordan. At the same time, the needs of its longtime residents were also growing. In the wake of the Israeli soldiers' shooting of nineteen Palestinian demonstrators at the Temple Mount in Jerusalem in October 1990 that the United States had condemned in the Security Council, Israel imposed a three-week-long curfew in the territories that led to the loss of some 63,000 Palestinian jobs in Israel. Coupled with the loss of remittances from those working in the Gulf states and a decline in international funding due to Arafat's support of Iraq's Saddam Hussein, the economy of the occupied territories largely ground to a halt.[62] So, despite the seeming victory of U.N. forces on the ground in Kuwait, the larger conflict in the Middle East, and especially the plight of the Palestinian refugees, remained problematic.

The prospect of Palestinian statehood: The Madrid peace process (1991) and the Oslo Agreement (1993)

On October 30, 1991, President George H. W. Bush and Mikhail Gorbachev (leader of the former Soviet Union) convened the Madrid conference that led to the first face-to-face meeting between Israel and its Arab neighbors, including Syria, Lebanon, Jordan, and the PLO. Above and beyond this symbolism, little could be attributed to the conference. But as the Cold War ended and the Israeli government constructed new settlements in the occupied territories to meet the needs of the influx of new Russian immigrants, the Bush administration pushed back by denying foreign aid to its longtime ally. New Israeli Prime Minister Yitzhak Rabin (elected in June 1992), however, signaled his desire to change the status quo by releasing Palestinian prisoners and slowing the construction of new settlements. Despite the fragile nature of this public show of goodwill, behind the scenes Israel and the PLO conducted secret negotiations in Oslo, Norway, during the first eight months of 1993 that culminated in both sides signing a Declaration of Principles on Interim Self-Government Arrangements (the Oslo I Accord) at the White House on September 13, 1993. The deal reiterated the PLO's recognition of Israel and renunciation of terrorism, called for Israeli withdrawal from Jericho and the Gaza Strip, and opened the door to further bilateral negotiations on Jerusalem, borders, refugees, and Jewish settlements.[63]

U.N. Secretary-General Boutros Boutros-Ghali developed a task force for the social and economic development of Gaza and Jericho anchored by UNRWA, UNICEF, and the UNDP, which had been operating in the area for decades. Their and the World Bank's reports to the October 1993 Donors' Conference to Support Middle East Peace inspired the conference attendees to pledge $2.2 billion over five years to supplement the $250 million annual budget of the three U.N. agencies already working in the occupied territories. The secretary-general also appointed an interagency coordinator to facilitate the influx of funds and increase in the number of projects. Within this framework, UNRWA redirected its efforts toward supporting the peace process and transferring its duties to the Palestinian Authority, an effort it called the Peace Implementation Plan (PIP). The first, 1994 stage of PIP involved cooperation between UNRWA and the Palestinian Authority to improve the homes within the camps, to upgrade educational and health facilities and human resources, and to update water and sewage facilities. UNRWA raised $85 million from international donors by the middle of 1994 to fund these improvements, establishing new offices throughout the territories to coordinate the projects and to hire local workers to carry them out. Then UNRWA began working directly under Arafat and the new Palestinian Authority. Other funding from the international community was funneled into the area through NGOs (which grew exponentially in the early 1990s) and other U.N. agencies.[64]

UNDP's PAPP program focused primarily on building the advanced human infrastructure that the Palestinian Authority needed to carry out self-rule. It already laid claim to training the Palestinian negotiators who helped to bring about the Oslo agreement, and after that it helped establish the Institute of Law at Birzeit University and the territories' electoral system. PAPP also made use of the Palestinian diaspora through its Transfer of Knowledge through Expatriate Nationals (TOKTEN) program, which brought more than four hundred Palestinian professionals from areas such as urban planning, information technology, agriculture, and health to the territories, building both capacity on the ground and support for a strong Palestine abroad (Japan contributed some 80 percent of the total funding for these projects, but significant contributions also came from Germany, the Islamic Development Bank, the Saudi Committee for Palestine Relief, and South Korea). At the grassroots level, PAPP sought to build human infrastructure by primarily employing local companies and workers, which also helped to combat the extremely high levels of unemployment prevailing in the Palestinian territories. Another indicator of UNDP success was that four of the ministers appointed to the cabinet of Palestinian President Mahmoud Abbas after the 2005 elections had been PAPP employees.[65]

The Middle East in the early 1990s continued to witness fast-moving, positive change. Peace talks between Israel and Jordan opened in October 1993, the two states declared an end of hostilities in July 1994, and then they signed a formal peace treaty on October 27, 1994. This was followed by Israel establishing diplomatic relations with Morocco and Tunisia. Additionally, Saudi Arabia eased its economic boycott of the Jewish state. In the midst of this process, in May 1994, the IDF left Gaza and Jericho, and Arafat returned and established the Palestinian Authority to begin taking over governance of these territories. In October 1995, the Palestinian Authority and Israel signed the Israeli-Palestinian Interim Agreement on the West Bank and Gaza (also called the Oslo II or Taba Accord) that called for the withdrawal of Israeli forces from nine major Palestinian towns. Initially, it seemed that even the November 4, 1995, assassination of Prime Minister Itzak Rabin by an Israeli who opposed his policies could not slow the momentum toward peace. In the first Palestinian election on January 20, 1996, Arafat became president and eighty-eight members were elected to the new legislature.[66]

Within weeks of this historic election, however, fifty-nine Israelis were killed in four major terrorist attacks in Tel Aviv and Jerusalem, and the tide continued to turn against the peace process throughout 1996, despite some countervailing signs. Three years of efforts to encourage a peace settlement between Israel and Syria failed that year. And even before the election of Israeli Prime Minister Benjamin Netanyahu in May 1996, the resumption of building of new Israeli settlements in the occupied territories (especially East Jerusalem) led the U.N. General Assembly into special emergency session to monitor the deteriorating situation. Rioting, suicide bombings, and Israeli reprisals followed in a tragic resumption of the pattern that had prevailed before the Oslo agreements. In August 1997, Israel imposed a blockade on the West Bank and Gaza and withheld payments to the Palestinian Authority, even as UNRWA was gearing down its direct services in these areas and as donors were looking forward to the end of UNRWA's mission. By September 1998, it was facing a deficit of $62 million, and its clients in Lebanon demonstrated against the agency, feeling slighted by its focus on Gaza and the West Bank. Its budget woes continued into the new millennium.[67]

Hoping to salvage the peace process, U.S. President Bill Clinton met with Arafat and Netanyahu in October 1998 and succeeded in getting both to sign the Wye River Memorandum to move the peace process forward. Israel agreed to transfer 13 percent more of the West Bank to Palestinian control, to release some Palestinian prisoners, and to ensure the safe passage of Palestinians between this area and Gaza. The Palestinian

Authority agreed to prosecute those responsible for violence against Israel and to take measures to prevent future attacks. The two sides also discussed cooperative economic and civil enterprises and agreed to resume talks ahead of the May 4, 1999, end of the five-year interim agreement. With the failure of those talks and Arafat threatening to declare Palestinian statehood on that date, Clinton sought to put pressure on Israel by inviting Arafat to the White House in March 1999 and issuing a letter that censured Jewish settlement building. The Palestinian leader relented, and the Israeli electorate replaced Prime Minister Netanyahu with the more moderate Ehud Barak. That September, U.S. Secretary of State Madeleine Albright helped broker an agreement that committed both parties to negotiating a final Declaration of Principles by February 2000 and a final settlement by that September. Hoping to move that process forward before he left office, Clinton invited both Barak and Arafat to Camp David in July 2000 for their first meeting in person. Arafat's commitment to nothing less than Israeli withdrawal to its 1967 borders, complete Palestinian sovereignty in East Jerusalem, and Israeli recognition of the Palestinians' right to return to Israel might have been an effort to unite Palestinians behind his leadership, but ultimately it was a recipe for deadlock.[68]

September 2000 witnessed the region descending into the second (or al-Aqsa) intifada in which both sides used violence liberally against the combatants and civilians on the other side, instead of moving toward a final plan for Palestinian statehood. In February 2001, the hawkish Ariel Sharon won national elections handily to succeed Barak as Israel's prime minister. UNRWA did its best, as it had in the first intifada, to provide assistance and protection to the refugee population. It publicly criticized Israeli attacks against civilians, its holding up of the agency's emergency assistance, its mistreatment of UNRWA staff, and its misuse and destruction of the agency's educational and health facilities—all of which prompted an Israeli and U.S. Congressional campaign against the reelection of the agency's Danish commissioner-general, Peter Hansen, but increased donations from Arab countries. In April 2002, UNRWA had to contend with open combat near the Jenin refugee camp that sparked international outrage and a Security Council–endorsed fact-finding mission by Secretary-General Kofi Annan. Then in September 2002, Israeli tanks besieged Arafat's headquarters in Ramallah. Prompted by the dangerous escalation of violence, U.S. President George W. Bush promoted a three-stage peace plan dubbed the "roadmap to peace" supported by the United States, Russia, the European Union, and the United Nations. It aimed to make progress by establishing clear reciprocal steps that each side would take in the political, security, economic, and humanitarian fields. Sharon, however, adamantly refused to consider any concessions to the Palestinians and easily won reelection in January 2003. That fall, Israel threatened to expand the conflict when it bombed what it claimed to be an Islamic jihad training base inside of Syria following a suicide terrorist attack in October. However, the ongoing carnage (some 3,500 Palestinians and 1,000 Israelis lost their lives during the second intifada) that had overwhelmed more than a dozen proposed cease-fires finally brought the two sides to the table again. The February 8, 2005, Sharm el-Sheikh Summit in which President Mahmoud Abbas and Prime Minister Sharon agreed to stop all acts of violence against the other and recommitted to the "roadmap for peace" is generally considered the end of this second intifada. In August 2005, Israeli troops finally left Gaza under the control of a Palestinian civil administration.[69]

The World Bank established the Palestinian Reform and Development Plan Multidonor Trust Fund in response to the December 2007 Paris Donor Conference's Declaration on Aid Effectiveness. The trust fund funnels the collective donations of the international community on a predictable (usually quarterly) basis directly to the Central Treasury Account of the Palestinian Authority's Ministry of Finance (in arrangements approved by the International Monetary Fund and maintained by external auditors). Though the funds are transferred without ties or earmarks, the World Bank and IMF hold the Palestinian Authority responsible for using the funds to carry out its institution-building objectives in the Palestinian Reform and Development Plan (developed and funded in part by PAPP) and has quarterly consultation meetings with the donors and the Palestinian Authority.[70] But these efforts by the international financial community were a recognition that full Palestinian statehood was still a distant objective and that something had to be done to shield Palestinian finances from Israeli interdiction. In other words, the international community was reacting to the changing situation on the ground with less optimism but in a continuing effort to see Palestinian self-rule move forward.

The U.N. Interim Force in Lebanon since 2000

When the Middle East peace process had seemed to be back on track, Israel had notified the U.N. secretary-general on April 17, 2000, of its intention to withdraw its forces from southern Lebanon and started this process on May 16. By June 16, it had completed its withdrawal behind the boundary identified by the United Nations, dismantled the de facto forces it had created in southern Lebanon, and released all detainees previously incarcerated in the Al-Khaim prison. UNIFIL monitored this withdrawal on a daily basis, as Lebanese authorities shifted into the area to maintain law and order. In a 2000 report, the secretary-general reported that the situation was much improved, but conditions still fell well short of peace and had the potential to flare up again quickly.[71]

Following the Israeli withdrawal, the situation along the "Blue Line" between Lebanon and Israel remained relatively peaceful, despite continued tension and sometimes serious breaches of the cease-fire (one of which resulted in casualties among the U.N. military observer corps). UNIFIL continued to monitor sea and air violations of this border, to investigate cease-fire violations, to provide humanitarian assistance to the local population, and to clear minefields and unexploded ordnance in the region. This relative peace was broken on July 12, 2006, when Hezbollah launched several rockets and a raid across the border at Israeli targets, resulting in the capture of two Israeli soldiers, the death of three, and the wounding of another two. The Israeli counterattack included raids against numerous roads and bridges in southern Lebanon, including within the UNIFIL area of operations. The U.N. peacekeepers held their ground and continued their mission, including maintaining its military observations and humanitarian assistance programs;

as a result, sixteen U.N. personnel were injured and five died. The U.N. Security Council (in Resolution 1701) joined the secretary-general in calls for an immediate cessation of hostilities and backed it up by increasing the UNIFIL contingent from 2,000 troops to 15,000 military personnel augmented by a maritime task force. With the retreat of Israeli forces, the enlarged UNIFIL cadre accompanied and supported the Lebanese armed forces as they redeployed in the south of the country, expanded its humanitarian assistance to include ensuring the safe return of displaced people, and continued its work in monitoring the Blue Line.[72]

Conclusion

As this book manuscript was being completed, there was little indication that Palestine was moving toward true statehood or that the violence in the Middle East was winding down. However, as this chapter reveals, this global borderland has been an area of intense U.N. activity and interest at all levels. The secretaries-general and their staffs, the General Assembly, and the Security Council have all focused significant attention and work on the region. The Middle East has served as a continuous laboratory for U.N. peacekeeping efforts, which have at times provided the room and security needed for former enemies to work toward peace. UNRWA and UNICEF helped to avert a humanitarian disaster in the wake of Israel's war for independence, caring for more than a quarter-million displaced Arab refugees, whose children and grandchildren are now also served by UNDP's PAPP. Even though the Great Powers have often failed to work toward peace in the Middle East or have pursued those efforts outside the framework of the United Nations (especially the Camp David Accords), at times—especially in ending the Iran-Iraq War and in conducting the U.N. coalition war against Iraq following its invasion of Kuwait—the United Nations has been at the center of the action.

CHAPTER 8
DEFINING HUMAN RIGHTS, INTERNATIONAL JUSTICE, AND GENOCIDE

Amy L. Sayward with assistance from Alexandrea Collins

The United Nations Organization after the Second World War became a primary arena for the definition of human rights, although ideas about international justice and human rights (usually with different names) had developed earlier.[1] In what historians of human rights have termed a practical miracle, the nation-states who gathered to create the United Nations—despite their many differences of opinion—agreed that the basis of the new organization should be human rights. Not only did they think this, but they wrote it into the U.N. Charter and acted on these ideas in the postwar Nuremberg trials of Nazi war criminals. The wartime declarations of the Allied leaders similarly fed the popular notion that the postwar period would be defined by an international commitment to uphold human rights. Soon the debates about human rights in the United Nations came to reflect the central divides and social movements of the second half of the twentieth century: the Cold War divide between the East and West that derailed the human rights covenants for more than a decade, the fights over the rights to self-determination and economic development that helped define the North-South divide, the global movement of women to secure equality, and the development of civil society with its demands that the United Nations focus on the definition and preservation of the rights of the most vulnerable in international society.[2]

Also complicating the history of human rights in international history are the competing pulls of universalist moral imperatives (the idea that all human beings are entitled to specific rights regardless of location, context, or individual ability) and of specific local contexts and political needs. So on the one hand, intellectual historians have marveled at the speed with which the ideas and language of human rights have permeated the globe over the past seventy-five years. On the other hand, historians have highlighted the ways in which the goals of specific nation-states have led to a public framing of human rights that is intended for specific diplomatic or local consumption. Nonetheless, taken together, both of these forces have pushed and pulled the human rights movement in fits and starts to a point today that is far ahead of the practices that preceded the Second World War.[3] To give the reader a sense of this uneven progress, I would like to start this chapter with a quick overview of some of the key milestones of the international human rights movement. This will help you to put the case studies that follow into the context of this broader movement.

Following on the rights language of the U.N. Charter and the new international law established at the Nuremberg and Tokyo trials and at the 1949 Geneva Convention, the chief human rights achievement of the 1940s—before the Cold War became too heated—was the adoption of the Universal Declaration of Human Rights (UDHR) in 1948. This general, nonbinding statement of rights had little practical power, although rhetorically it provided an important platform for women's pursuit of legal equality through the Commission on the Status of Women (CSW) of the U.N. Economic and Social Council (ECOSOC). The binding covenant that was supposed to accompany the UDHR was subsequently first split into two covenants (one for civil and political rights and another for economic, social, and cultural rights) and then delayed for almost two decades by the Cold War rivalry between the United States and the Soviet Union. A coalition of Jamaica, Liberia, Ghana, and the Philippines helped to finally bring this work to fruition in the 1960s, building on the rights language of decolonization. But in the interim, regional treaties and conventions—such as the 1948 American Declaration of the Rights and Duties of Man and the 1953 European Convention for the Protection of Human Rights and Fundamental Freedoms—helped to provide concrete examples of how these rights might be interpreted and protected on the ground. And the 1948 convention against genocide seemed a fitting and needed follow-up to the earlier war crimes trials.[4]

The efforts to codify a set of binding, international human rights in the 1950s quickly showed that different countries and peoples held disparate definitions of what human rights were and what they should be. And each nation seemed to have its own particular blind spot(s). The United States sought to use human rights propaganda against the Soviet Union during the Cold War only to find its own policies of racial segregation and discrimination aired before the world. Britain and France—both of whom took a great deal of pride in their own histories of developing and promoting key human rights ideas—quickly found themselves in conflicts with their colonial territories, who reached back to Woodrow Wilson's promise of self-determination and forward to the rights covenants' definition of self-determination as a right. Some, like Indian leader Mohandas Gandhi, rejected the entire notion of human rights, thinking that a language of collective responsibilities was a better way for humankind to move forward in the future.[5]

The 1960s saw a variety of rights movements across the globe. The decolonization efforts throughout Asia and Africa, the anti-apartheid movement in South Africa (apartheid was an all-encompassing system of legal racial separation practiced by the white-minority government of that country), the Civil Rights Movement in the United States, and the response to the rise of neo-Nazism in Europe shared critiques of white supremacy that the United Nations echoed in the December 1965 unanimous adoption by the General Assembly of the International Convention on the Elimination of All Forms of Racial Discrimination (which entered into force on January 4, 1969). Additionally, national liberation movements throughout the Third World sought to create connections between one another, to mobilize subject populations with the language of self-determination, and to gain the sympathy of the international community by using the rights language that it trumpeted. This decade of mass protests and marches also saw nongovernmental organizations (NGOs) similarly mobilizing individuals around the planet to put pressure on governments of all sorts to respect the human rights defined in the United Nations' instruments. The most important of these NGOs was Amnesty International, founded in 1961 in Great Britain, which asked members to "adopt" political prisoners as a sign of solidarity and in an effort to shame the government into granting the prisoner amnesty. Although it has subsequently diversified its efforts, individual letter-writing remains a key component of its work as has the public naming and shaming of states engaged in human rights abuses, a substantial change from earlier diplomatic practice. Those Americans opposed to their government's war in Vietnam particularly gravitated toward Amnesty International and issues of human rights as a way of reclaiming a sense of U.S. moral leadership that had seemingly been lost in Southeast Asia.[6] To mark the twentieth anniversary of the adoption of the UDHR and advance the U.N. human rights agenda, the United Nations hosted its International Conference on Human Rights in Tehran, Iran, in 1968. But the conference organizers did not create any role for NGOs, leading Sean MacBride, Amnesty International's co-founder and chair, to bring organizations like this together at meetings in Geneva and Montreal ahead of the conference to generate recommendations for the conference. Subsequent global conferences created formal spaces for the creative work that such NGOs could contribute to the study of and action on its theme. The delegations from forty-eight countries and sixty-one intergovernmental organizations who did attend the Tehran Conference issued a proclamation that exhorted "every country [to] grant each individual, irrespective of race, language, religion or political belief, freedom of expression, of information, of conscience and religion, as well as the right to participate in the political, economic, cultural and social life of his country" before proceeding to a veritable laundry list of thirty-nine separate resolutions, including abolishing apartheid and colonialism and promoting economic development, literacy, and women's rights.[7]

The 1970s saw some modest advances in the field of international human rights. The Cold War started to thaw as the United States, Canada, the Soviet Union, and most of Europe participated in the Helsinki Conference on Security and Cooperation in Europe, which ran from July 3, 1973, until July 21, 1975. Its final act laid the framework for increased East-West cooperation in the fields of security, trade, and cultural relations. Helsinki groups subsequently sprang up to demand and to monitor compliance with the specific human rights enunciated in the final act and helped to change the Soviet Union's approach to internal human rights issues, which ultimately contributed to the end of the Cold War. International human rights ideas also influenced U.S. President Jimmy Carter (who served from 1976 until 1980), who sought to integrate them into American foreign policy, and in 1979 the Organization of American States modeled its new Inter-American Court of Human Rights on the earlier European model.[8]

But even as human rights seemed to be triumphing, some African and Asian governments pushed back against the expansive demands of the U.N. human rights system. They claimed that gender equality, tolerance for homosexuality, and sometimes the right to free speech were incompatible with their non-Western traditions and social customs. These resentments and concerns were most evident at the 1993 U.N. Human Rights Conference in Vienna, when several Middle Eastern and Asian countries (including China, Iran, Malaysia, Singapore, and Syria) decried the UDHR as an instrument of

Western imperialism. They sought to assert the primacy of national sovereignty over claims to universalist human rights and stressed the cultural specificity of regional applications of human rights. Asian intellectuals and NGOs almost immediately rebutted such claims, arguing instead that such human rights were instead rooted in a number of cultural and religious traditions. And although they acknowledged that cultural differences indeed existed, they argued against the idea that there was a unitary "Asian" culture that stood in contrast to "Western" culture and argued for the position that the rights enunciated in the UDHR were indeed applicable to all situations. Their position largely carried the day in Vienna, where the conference as a whole backed the creation of a U.N. Commissioner on Human Rights, a move that the oppositional governments had argued was simply another Western tool to interfere in their domestic affairs. In the next decade, the nations of Africa created an African Court of Human and Peoples' Rights in 2004 in Arusha, Tanzania, to enforce the provisions of its earlier 1981 African Charter. This model of embracing international norms but focusing them on regional concerns serves as an interesting counterpoint to the earlier Asian and Middle Eastern controversy and demonstrates the significant growth and development of human rights ideas and institutions that followed the Second World War.[9]

Historiography

The historiography on human rights has exploded in recent years, with new book series and a multitude of books and articles taking a wide variety of approaches to the topic, examining the legal, intellectual, and historical questions involved as well as the growing variety of types of people seeking a definition or redefinition of their human rights. Much of the literature, however, approaches the topic from a legal perspective, which can be difficult to access for a starting student or someone approaching the topic from a different disciplinary perspective. Historians paid little attention to human rights prior to the 1960s, when practitioners and scholars of international law were the main authors in the field.[10] Additionally, much of the scholarly literature on human rights understandably tends to deal with one aspect of the topic or another, leaving some "holes" in the historiography for the new researcher to tackle. Specifically, there is a shortage of non-Western perspectives in much of the scholarly writing, despite the fact that these perspectives are very much in evidence in the published proceedings of the United Nations related to human rights as well as in the many memoirs written at the intersection between the United Nations and human rights. For example, it was exactly the tenacity of a young scholar, Steven Jensen, reading through the U.N. proceedings that led to the discovery that Jamaica–leading a coalition that also included Ghana, Liberia, and the Philippines–was a key mover of the human rights covenants of the 1960s.[11]

At its core, the very idea of "human" rights—as opposed to "civil" rights or "women's" rights—implies the need for a standard that transcends the nation-state (although these countries and their governments have remained the primary executive agents charged with protecting these human rights). As such, any discussion of human rights in the second half of the twentieth century will have at its center the United Nations and its institutions. But the very strength of the rhetoric and commitment in the early U.N. documents on human rights have helped to undermine historical assessments of this work. After all, what organization could fully live up to the Charter's call in Article 1 to promote and encourage "respect for human rights and for fundamental freedoms for all without distinction as to race, sex, language or religion" or the Nuremberg trials' commitment to prevent future genocide or the Universal Declaration's call to a comprehensive set of twenty-nine specific, individual rights? Certainly not the United Nations.

As I pointed out in the introduction to this book, the literature on the United Nations generally is one that draws moral or value judgments about the organization—paying particular attention to its successes and failures, speculating about whether or not it is likely to be successful in the future, and suggesting reforms. The literature on human rights in the United Nations is even more laden with such judgments, charged as it is with narratives of literal life-and-death struggles, atrocities, genocide, and the oppression of under-represented groups. So the history of U.N. actions and declarations in this area is often judged based on whether the United Nations succeeded or failed to expand, demand, and/or enforce these human rights. Given the fact that the ideas and language of human rights have outpaced mechanisms for enforcement and that human rights abuses seem to be flourishing around the planet, most scholars and commentators have been critical of U.N. efforts. The most comprehensive treatment of the subject to date tends to encapsulate many of these tendencies. Roger Normand and Sarah Zaidi's *Human Rights at the UN: The Political History of Universal Justice*, which is part of the United Nations Intellectual History Project series, is up-front about the fact that the authors are human rights activists who are deeply disillusioned by the lack of enforcement mechanisms attached to U.N. human rights proclamations, a lack that they forcefully contrast with the World Trade Organization's enforcement mechanisms. This critical trend is also reflected in the first scholarly review of the burgeoning historical literature on human rights, which divided it into "three competing attitudes": (1) the progressives who focus on the expansion of international law and greater awareness of human rights violations, (2) those who find human rights to be a "paradox" with no ultimate resolution, and (3) those who are "angrier" due to the "wrenching chasm between the glowing words or strenuous activism and the very slim real results."[12] This was the first historiographical essay I read that defined historical interpretations by their attitude, but emotion and/or attitude indeed seem to characterize this historiography more than most. Even a decade later, human rights historian Sarah Snyder's historiographical article characterized many of the histories of the early U.N. human rights period as praising the triumph of passing the UDHR before expressing an overwhelming sense of disappointment with the lack of progress that followed. Snyder ends her piece by calling for "a more complicated and less teleological approach to the issue," a sentiment shared by historian Mark Bradley's call that scholars set aside both their skepticism and their triumphalism when examining the history of human rights.[13]

To take up this call for a less teleological, triumphal, and skeptical approach to understanding international human rights, in this chapter we will focus on the ways in which the United Nations has served as a physical and intellectual borderland where the peoples of many states and NGOs interacted and debated human rights, alongside the international civil servants who lived and worked in this liminal borderland, and ultimately created new international norms that had not previously existed. In this way, I hope to better understand how the people and ideas that came into this border space were molded, changed, recreated, and challenged and sometimes left this space with a shape and agency that influenced the way in which nation-states acted, even without formal enforcement mechanisms. This is also in line with the recommendation in a recent volume on international human rights that we see "human rights as integral to the history of globalization without losing sight of their local manifestations."[14]

To move us in this direction, I have divided this chapter into three thematic sections. The first section deals primarily with the efforts of the United Nations to define and promote "universal" human rights, most famously through its International Bill of Rights (the UDHR plus the two rights covenants). The second section then deals with the efforts of specific groups to promote and define their rights within the concept of universal human rights with case studies on children's rights, women's rights, and the rights of indigenous peoples. And finally we will look at U.N. efforts to abolish or at least deter human rights abuses, with a focus on the decades-long campaign against South African apartheid and the creation of international criminal tribunals (and their variations) that sought to prosecute those responsible for acts of genocide and, most recently, terrorism. In this way, I hope to provide an intriguing introduction to this topic that will leave the reader wanting to know more and wanting to research the other areas that do not receive as much attention.

Defining human rights in the new United Nations

U.S. President Franklin D. Roosevelt had included a defense of human rights in his 1941 State of the Union address and also included a pledge to uphold these rights in the Allied powers' 1942 statement of war aims. And while these declarations, along with the inclusion of human rights in the U.N. Charter, heightened popular hopes, they remained vague. In trying to make these human rights specific—first in the nonbinding UDHR and then in a variety of binding rights covenants—we can clearly see the United Nations as a borderland where a variety of international actors and ideas came together and sought to craft something that would change the actions of nation-states and improve the lives of the planet's inhabitants. The UDHR was the first innovation to emerge from this borderland when the U.N. General Assembly approved it on December 10, 1948. Not surprisingly, the Cold War, the fights for and against decolonization, women's efforts to gain equality, and the rise of civil society (NGOs) all had significant impacts on the human rights debates that followed the UDHR.[15]

Before and during the Second World War, the actions of the fascist powers of Germany, Japan, and Italy appalled the world and created a sense that there had to be postwar protections against such abuses. Indeed, an international commitment to human rights emerged even before the end of the Second World War in the International Labour Organization's 1944 "Declaration of Philadelphia" that proclaimed the "right of all human beings, irrespective of race, creed, or sex" to pursue "both their material well-being and their spiritual development in conditions of freedom and dignity, of economic security, and equal opportunity."[16] At the end of the war, the Allies utilized extraordinary courts (in the Nuremberg and Tokyo trials) to punish those responsible for such abuses and then acted through the United Nations to promote a positive framework for human rights under an overarching framework of national sovereignty. The Commission on Human Rights (CHR) of the ECOSOC was to give substance to the general commitment to human rights written into the U.N. Charter by drafting the UDHR. The Commission (which met for the first time in January 1947) brought together representatives of all five of the permanent Security Council members plus thirteen other governmental representatives, with former U.S. First Lady Eleanor Roosevelt chairing and with Canadian legal scholar John Peters Humphrey and his staff in the U.N. secretariat assisting with research and compiling the many proposals and drafts generated by the Commission.[17]

From the beginning, the Commission was a borderland for a variety of competing ideas about human rights. The emerging ideological battle between the United States and the Soviet Union was evident in their respective calls at the Commission's very first meeting for the creation of a Sub-Commission on Freedom of Information and the Press and a Sub-Commission on the Prevention of Discrimination and the Protection of Minorities. But even among allies, significant differences emerged. French jurist René Cassin's cherished idea of les droits de l'homme—as a distinctly European idea whose cosmopolitanism provided rights regardless of race or religion—was contested by delegates from ECOSOC's Commission on the Status of Women (CSW) who insisted that the Declaration's language explicitly include women, rather than subsume them under the category of "men." Eleanor Roosevelt also found herself fighting with the U.S. State Department to iron out a position that would facilitate completion of the declaration.[18]

Despite all the difficulties that the CHR encountered, it succeeded in submitting the UDHR to the General Assembly within two years. Forty-eight member states of diverse moral and religious traditions affirmed the twenty-eight rights enunciated in the declaration. Even though the Saudi Arabian and South African governments and the Soviet bloc abstained, global commentators rightfully celebrated its passage. Ultimately, however, the careful rhetorical papering-over of the real differences that had emerged during drafting of the UDHR could not hold for long. Questions quickly emerged about what the declaration meant by "freedom" and "self-determination." Nor was there any consensus about what the proper relationships were between the rights of the individual, the community, and the nation-state, and since the UDHR lacked any enforcement mechanism, there was no clear way forward in terms of refining and defining its general principles. The hope that the binding covenants would serve this role was quickly flattened by the increasing bitterness of the Cold War rivalry throughout the U.N. system.[19]

Examining the period after approval of the UDHR using a borderlands approach provides us with a creative way to think about the relative power of states, non-states, NGOs, and the U.N. staff that helps us realize that such power dynamics are fluid and change over time—there are no absolutes. In this formulation, we imagine the power of various players defined by "the degree to which [they] are successful in expanding their boundaries, imposing their political control . . . , and even defining the identities of those over whom [they] claim authority." For example, the United States was initially successful in extending its power over the process of drafting and passing the UDHR and then in obtaining a censure resolution from the General Assembly for its rival's practice of preventing the Soviet wives of foreigners from leaving the country, in violation of the UDHR's articles 13 and 16. It also used its power to shape the early work of the Commission on Human Rights (CHR), especially in the final decision to draft two rights covenants, rather than a unitary document. The U.S. delegation fought for one covenant on civil and political rights that would be enforceable and another covenant on economic, social, and cultural rights without such enforcement mechanisms; it succeeded by manipulating rules of procedure and threatening to withdraw from the process. But the Soviet Union during the Stalin era was also able to use human rights formulations and the United Nations as a forum to undermine American self-righteousness. Specifically, its delegates in the CHR objected to the two separate rights covenants. They argued that such a division was a violation of the fundamental unity of the Universal Declaration and was an Anglo-American invention that sacrificed true human rights. For example, Soviet Representative Alexei Pavlov stated, "There was no individual freedom for the hungry and unemployed." While Soviet hypocrisy is also clearly present in this statement (given the lack of individual freedoms for the employed and fed in the Soviet Union), the Cold War paradigm alone does not explain the debate.[20]

The Soviets were not alone in their objection to bifurcation of the Universal Declaration; they were joined by Australia and sometimes by France, by the Latin American states that had pushed for incorporating social, economic, and cultural rights into the UDHR, and later by the developing countries that read an obligation for the richer countries to aid Third World economic development into the economic human rights detailed in the declaration. Another dimension of the debate on the human rights covenants that exceeded the Cold War construct was the inclusion of the right of self-determination in both covenants, which clearly demonstrated the growing strength of the decolonization movement in the United Nations and its ability to reshape and redefine international dialogue. Self-determination—rather than the language of rights from the UDHR—was the primary currency of the postwar decolonization movement, and at the 1955 Bandung Conference and the 1960 U.N. General Assembly session, the Non-Aligned Movement used its growing clout to pass a resolution naming self-determination a right.[21]

Using a borderlands approach moves us beyond easy East-West and North-South dichotomies and reveals that various actors were competing for moral authority in this borderland of human rights, each of whom had an impact. Although the decades-long process of drafting and adopting the international human rights covenants has generally been characterized as Cold War gridlock, the historical reality was much more complicated and less teleological. At least part of the Anglo-American desire for separate covenants came from the fact that these countries defined civil and political rights as the ones that could be enforced by their domestic courts using extant mechanisms and processes. And the Soviet emphasis on economic, social, and cultural rights—especially the rights of minorities and the right to self-determination—came from its own commitment to those rights and emphasized the central role of the government in defining and providing the rights of the individual. It genuinely mattered to both sides whose national system of law was codified into international law. But, of course, there were also other, more narrow, political and diplomatic interests behind these stands as well, and other countries brought their own concerns to the table.[22] Rather than proceeding quickly from the pioneering and innovative UDHR to legally binding treaties protecting a variety of human rights for all, the reality was that the UDHR had papered over significant issues that required significant debate and discussion within the CHR.

After passage of the Universal Declaration, Anglo-American power to control the human rights debates in the CHR noticeably ebbed. During the spring of 1949, Commission representatives and the General Assembly pushed back against a British proposal for a "colonial clause" (to exempt colonial and trustee powers from being required to extend all of these rights to their territorial subjects) and an American "federal clause" (to exempt national governments from having to enforce all rights in all of their states). The colonial clause was summarily rejected, and Eleanor Roosevelt's argument that approval of a federal clause would make it more likely that governments would sign on to the covenants fared no better. The Polish representative noted that the U.S. insistence on such a clause in the constitution of the ILO in 1919 did not prove this case, as the United States had subsequently ratified just six of the ninety-eight ILO conventions.[23]

The administration of U.S. President Dwight D. Eisenhower reacted badly to the rebuff and helped stall the Commission's work for almost a decade. Facing significant domestic political resistance within his own (Republican) party and lacking commitment to a legally binding covenant himself, the president replaced Eleanor Roosevelt on the CHR with Mary Pillsbury Lord (whose primary qualification was that she had aided the president's election campaign). Lord's first job was to announce to the CHR that her country would not sign the human rights covenants then being drafted. The Indian delegate denigrated the American statement as an effort "to render valueless the work of the commission," but he and others were undeterred in their work. Lord and the Commission suffered through eight years together in which the official U.S. attitude toward its work "alternated between disengagement and obstruction." Although the draft covenants were submitted to the ninth session of the General Assembly in 1954, they were not approved until December 1966. A decade later, both finally had enough state ratifications to come into force in 1976. These time spans show that these human rights covenants had enough power to make the nation-states of the world wary of them, despite consistent criticisms that the implementation mechanism was weak (relying as it did on national self-reporting).[24]

Despite the shortcomings of the International Covenant on Civil and Political Rights (ICCPR), the Commission on Human Rights emerged in the post-covenant period as the key protector of universal human rights under this covenant, which is one of the few U.N. agreements that has created specific obligations and a method of securing compliance with those obligations. As a part of international law that expresses the reasonable expectations of much of the earth's population, it sometimes finds its way into domestic courts and into the opinions of the International Court of Justice and international tribunals. In a handful of states, like Estonia, it is the equivalent of the law of the land, and in Colombia it takes precedence over domestic law. During the thirty years in which the ICCPR has been in existence (now accepted by more than 160 governments), the Human Rights Committee has worked through some four hundred human rights reports from member states and has included its own "Concluding Observations" on more than 225 of them. Additionally, its "General Comments" on the various provisions of the covenant have developed into what international legal scholar Yogesh Tyagi has termed "a new body of 'soft law'" that does not carry the weight or rigor of international law but that nonetheless has the ability to influence state actors. Quantitatively even more impressive are the more than two thousand individual communications the Human Rights Committee has received alleging human rights abuses in more than eighty separate countries (and it ultimately expressed its "Views" on more than seven hundred of these), which demonstrates that people around the globe see the Committee as an organ that can work to address their concerns.[25]

In 1963, these achievements were still in the future, but the CHR sought to jump-start its work by bringing it more fully into the international spotlight. That year the General Assembly agreed to designate 1968 as the International Year for Human Rights, marking both the twentieth anniversary of the Universal Declaration and hoping to move the work of attaining those objectives forward. The resolution called for a global human rights conference to evaluate the progress made to date and the steps still needed. In preparation for such a score-taking, the resolution urged member states to work toward formal ratification of the Commission's genocide convention, its Convention on the Political Rights of Women, and its Supplementary Convention on the Abolition of Slavery, the Slave Trade and Institutions and Practices Similar to Slavery; toward ratification of several ILO conventions; and toward ratification of UNESCO's Convention against Discrimination in Education. That same General Assembly also opened for signature the International Convention on the Elimination of All Forms of Racial Discrimination.[26] Clearly, the issues of human rights had proliferated and were increasingly central to the United Nations as a result of two decades of debate within this U.N. borderland.

Group rights

As we have seen, the original thrust of early U.N. definitions of rights was on individual rights and embodied a conscious effort not to attribute "special" rights to groups. The decision-makers perhaps hoped that the challenges faced by minority and other groups could be remedied by the application of universal human rights (including nondiscrimination clauses), and they certainly feared the potential of group rights to undermine national self-determination and sovereignty. However, as the Cold War set in and movement toward the international human rights covenants stalled, the focus broadened a bit to recognize that there were some groups—such as children—who could not generally advocate on their own behalf, even within a world that had fully embraced the ideals of the UDHR. Additionally, given that people live in a world that falls far short of human rights ideals, the United Nations increasingly became the place where groups and individuals worked with and against their governments in an effort to secure recognition of their rights and for help to abolish those policies and attitudes that stood in the way of fully realizing those human rights, most prominently discrimination based on race and gender. The Commission on Human Rights had, as part of its mandate, the power to make recommendations and even set up subcommissions to carry out its recommendations on any special protections for minorities. As part of this work, it drafted the Convention on the Prevention and Punishment of the Crime of Genocide (or more briefly, the Genocide Convention), which the General Assembly adopted on December 9, 1948, just ahead of the UDHR. Although the Convention criminalized the systematic killing of peoples in war or peacetime and required signatories to prevent and punish genocide, it did not contain any provisions for the protection of the rights of minorities, did not prohibit cultural genocide, and interestingly combined, and to a degree submerged, the European Holocaust of the Jews into a more generalized narrative of fascist human rights abuses that catalyzed the international recognition of the need to prevent genocide. The CHR also established the Sub-Commission on Prevention of Discrimination and Protection of Minorities, which was an independent body of twelve experts (rather than government representatives). Eventually, Article 27 of the International Covenant on Economic, Social and Cultural Rights included language to protect individuals who were part of a minority group from discrimination. Only in 1971 did the CHR establish a special working group to draft a declaration of principles on the rights of minorities, which was only adopted in 1992, indicating the continuing unease in the international community with the potentially erosive effects of minority rights.[27]

To give you a sense of the complexity of this work of pursuing human rights for groups or peoples, the rest of this section will look at a series of case studies of this agitation and its results. We will start with a case study of children's rights—an area first raised at the League of Nations but significantly underdeveloped until passage of the Convention on the Rights of the Child in 1989. Women had been some of the key advocates for children's rights in the League, and they also organized internationally and worked through the League to broaden recognition of women's rights around the globe, as we saw in Chapter 2. So we will pick up that story a bit later in this section as well, with a focus on the tensions that existed between recognition of women's group rights and the full enjoyment of women's rights as part of universal human rights. And the last case study in this section will examine the indigenous rights movement. This also started with the League but became more fully realized in the United Nations, where indigenous peoples, in fact, identified themselves as a Fourth World movement. Separate from the First World of economically developed democracies, the Second World of communist governments, and the Third World of economically developing countries, they were governments and peoples within and under governments, occupying a particularly precarious situation in a century and an organization that was so focused on national independence movements and national sovereignty. Ultimately, this Fourth World movement gained recognition for its constituent members' human rights under the U.N. Declaration on the Rights of Indigenous Peoples.

There were, not surprisingly, other efforts to define and protect the human rights of groups within the United Nations that the aspiring researcher might want to explore in greater depth but which the constraints of time and space prevent this book from exploring. Racial and religious minorities have frequently been the focus of violence and other denials of their human rights. The 1948 Genocide Convention and the international criminal tribunals in Yugoslavia and Rwanda (discussed later in this chapter) have examined these abuses and sought to craft institutions and policies that would both bring perpetrators of systematic violence to justice and craft international responses that could preempt such violence in the future. Prisoners are another group whose rights have been the focus of international action within the context of human rights. The CHR early on focused its attention on what steps were needed to ensure "the right of everyone to be free from arbitrary arrest, detention and exile," and the rights of prisoners are still often discussed as negative rights, freedoms from torture, arbitrary arrest, disappearance, and a whole host of human rights abuses that this population is especially vulnerable to. The rights of refugees are discussed in part in Chapter 6 of this book, and stories about the abuses of transnational workers have heightened efforts to define and defend their human rights globally. Also in recent years, the United Nations has been a key area for defining and seeking to protect the rights of those with disabilities, those who are infected with HIV/AIDS, and those who identify as lesbian, gay, bisexual, or transgendered.[28] All of these areas are fruitful avenues for future research, as the reader can begin to see by examining the endnotes for this paragraph.

The rights of children

The League of Nations first considered the rights of children within an international framework in its brief 1924 League of Nations' Declaration on the Rights of the Child (also called the Geneva Declaration). The initiative for this action came from Eglantyne Jebb, a young woman from Britain who had responded to the suffering she witnessed in the aftermath of the Balkan wars in Macedonia by founding the NGO "Save the Children" in 1919 to feed and clothe the children in war-devastated Europe. This collaboration between Save the Children and the League resulted in an exhortation in the preamble to the Geneva Declaration "that mankind owes to the Child the best that it has to give," including both the negative right to protection from exploitation and the positive right to the conditions for both material and spiritual development (including the means to earn a livelihood and awareness of her or his need to devote his or her talents "to the service of fellow men"). Speaking to basic human needs, it also declared that "the child that is hungry must be fed; the child that is sick must be nursed; the child that is backward must be helped; the delinquent child must be reclaimed; and the orphan and the waif must be sheltered and succored." But these admonitions were simply that, and they carried no enforcement mechanism.[29]

In the wake of the Second World War, much like the earlier postwar period that had inspired Jebb, the U.N. General Assembly was moved to create on December 11, 1946, the International Children's Emergency Fund (UNICEF) to meet the needs of more than thirty million undernourished children in Europe, since the activities of the U.N. Relief and Rehabilitation Administration (UNRRA) were winding down because of the U.S. Congress' refusal to channel any further relief through it. Alarmed European delegates warned that the fate of the next generation was at stake, and the Polish delegate Ludwick Rajchman (the former longtime head of the League of Nations Health Organization) helped unite a General Assembly majority around using the residual assets of UNRRA to create UNICEF. The new organization, which relied on the voluntary donations of governments and individuals, soon developed such a strong reputation for providing humanitarian aid to children that it even survived an effort to wind down its activities as the immediate postwar emergency faded. Since its founding resolution had included the phrase "for child health purposes generally," advocates from the Third World argued passionately and effectively in 1953 that its work should be extended, even though the World Health Organization (WHO) had been created in the interim.[30]

During the late 1950s and 1960s, UNICEF reoriented itself slightly to assist development efforts in the Third World as one key way of assisting children who were in poverty. Maurice Pate, who served as UNICEF's executive director from 1947 to 1965, argued that children were most affected by poverty and therefore should be at the forefront of any antipoverty campaign. In the same period, NGOs also began asserting the need for an expanded and updated version of the Geneva Declaration, despite the fact that children were included as part of the UDHR and the 1951 Convention Relating to the Status of Refugees (since children generally make up at least half of refugee populations). The ten articles of the 1959 Declaration of the Rights of the Child applied the ideas of the UDHR specifically to children and asserted that this group needed "special safeguards" due to their "physical and mental immaturity." Reaffirming the 1924 Geneva Declaration's assertion that "mankind owes to the child the best it has to give," the 1959 Declaration then went on to assert the universality of these rights for "every child, without any exception whatsoever," and it established that children needed "special protection . . . opportunities and facilities" to enable them "to develop physically, mentally, morally, spiritually and socially in a healthy and normal manner and in conditions of freedom and dignity." UNICEF was to be the primary agent putting these principles into practice.[31]

In 1978, Poland, continuing the earlier advocacy efforts of Rajchman, proposed to the CHR that a binding covenant containing the rights of children be drafted as part of the celebration of 1979 as the International Year of the Child (which was also the twentieth anniversary of the Declaration of the Rights of the Child). Third World delegates welcomed this opportunity to update these rights to better reflect the needs of children in their countries. But the drafting committee's work transcended the task of simply accommodating various national visions of children's needs and instead elaborated a new conceptual framework for understanding children's rights that was informed, in significant ways, by the input of some thirty-five NGOs and the children's rights movement. The core innovation of the convention was that "the best interests of the child" were the litmus test for all of its provisions. In other words, it recognized children for the first time as human beings with equal value rather than being primarily treated in law as the possessions of their guardians. A direct outgrowth of this philosophy was that the Convention established children's right to actively participate in the decision-making processes impacting their lives (based on their stage of development). After a decade of work, the General Assembly adopted the Convention on the Rights of the Child on November 20, 1989, and it entered into force less than a year later (on September 2, 1990), making it by far the quickest ratification of such a binding rights convention.[32]

A cynic might argue that ratifications came so quickly because the Convention's fifty-four articles have a weak enforcement mechanism—the Committee on the Rights of the Child consists of eighteen experts serving in their personal capacity who examine the progress of states who have ratified the Convention in moving toward attainment of its goals and then report every other year to ECOSOC. But the optimist might counter that the Convention's rights have also been written into all UNICEF programs and codified in several regional contexts, much as the earlier UDHR had been. In 1990, the Organisation of African Unity (OAU) adopted an African Charter on the Rights and Welfare of the Child (it entered into force in November 1999), which affirmed the principles of the broader U.N. convention but also specified children's rights within the African context. For example, it made specific references to the dangers to children from both apartheid and female genital mutilation (FGM). The European Union also adopted the Convention on the Exercise of Children's Rights, which encourages countries to codify specific children's rights into their legal codes, much like the African Charter.[33]

Building on the momentum created by the drafting of the Convention on the Rights of the Child, UNICEF organized a World Summit on Children that met in 1990, attracting the participation of 159 countries and forty-five NGOs who adopted the Declaration on the Survival, Protection and Development of Children and its accompanying action plan. That plan specifically sought to decrease infant and maternal mortality rates and children's rates of malnutrition and illiteracy, and it aimed to increase children's access to health services, education, and clean water. In this summit, youth primarily played a ceremonial role as the governmental delegates worked on this declaration and plan of action, demonstrating the difficulties of overcoming centuries of tradition and making the new rights, especially children's rights of participation, operable. However, at the May 8–10, 2002, U.N. Special Session on Children, children (also called U-18s for under eighteen years old) were official delegates to the session and participated in programs, appeared as panelists, offered comments, asked questions from the floor, and participated in drafting the session's report "A World Fit for Children," which reaffirmed and recommitted the United Nations to meeting the goals established at the earlier summit. Their active participation was in keeping with the call for children's participation in proceedings that affect their lives.[34]

In the years since ratification of the Convention on the Rights of the Child, new dangers have come to light, and the international community has responded with new instruments. In August 1996, UNICEF and a group of children's NGOs (now known as Child Rights Connect) convened in Sweden the first World Congress against Commercial Sexual Exploitation of Children. The resulting Stockholm Agenda for Action established "a global partnership" to combat the trafficking and exploitation of children, which continued to hold meetings and to press successfully for further international legal action to protect children.[35] We see similar advocacy surrounding the issue of child soldiers, which emerged around the same time. In 1996, Graça Machel, Mozambique's former minister of education, submitted her study on the impact of armed conflict on children to the U.N. General Assembly, which led to the creation of the Office of the Special Representative of the Secretary-General for Children and Armed Conflict. On February 12, 2002, the optional protocol on the involvement of children in armed conflict became operative and found that there were more than 300,000 child soldiers engaged in armed conflict in more than thirty countries. This helped prompt U.N. Security Council Resolution 1612 in 2005, which created a monitoring system that sought to publicly shame the organizations exploiting children as soldiers and sex slaves. The 2007 report of the Special Representative documented the progress made as well as the remaining steps that were needed, and it included input from some 1,700 children and young people from ninety-two countries. The current news, however, makes it clear that this tragedy is far from over.[36]

As a result of U.N. action, children, their rights, and their participation in global decision-making have become an increasingly visible part of the U.N. agenda. Several of the Millennium Development Goals (MDGs) adopted in 2000 directly related to children's rights, and the U.N. Development Programme keeps track of and reports on each country's progress toward these goals. UNESCO has traditionally worked on advancing children's educational rights and is specifically tasked with the MDG calling for all children to complete free and compulsory primary education. In this goal, UNESCO is aided by the Working Group on Girls that grew out of the 1993 Vienna World Conference on Human Rights in recognition of the special challenges that girl children face in achieving even the most basic education in some areas of the world. In the field of child labor, the ILO launched its International Programme on the Elimination of Child Labour in 1992 and especially prioritized eliminating the worst forms; by 2005, it could report significant gains worldwide, including an 11-percent reduction in the number of child laborers. A similarly positive note was present in U.N. Secretary-General Kofi Annan's 2001 report on the status of the world's children in which he highlighted the striking progress toward eradicating polio and guinea worm and remedying the lack of iodine and vitamin A in global diets. However, until the world extinguishes poverty and war, children will continue to suffer along with their adult counterparts.[37]

Women's rights

At the founding of the United Nations, there was a clear tension between human rights and women's rights that was not new. National legislatures and earlier international organizations had debated whether women needed "special rights" and protective legislation (for maternity leave and shorter working hours, for example) or whether they were best protected under broader definitions of and better protections for workers' and human rights as a whole. For example, both Virginia Gildersleeve (the only female on the official U.S. delegation to the 1945 San Francisco Conference) and Eleanor Roosevelt (former first lady and U.S. delegate to the CHR) agreed that women's interests were best served by integrating them into the general work of the United Nations and were united in their opposition to the creation of the Commission on the Status of Women (CSW) within ECOSOC (discussed in Chapter 4). Roosevelt believed that "if [women] should be segregated in this special feminine Commission, then it might well happen that men would keep them out of other commissions or groups, saying that they had plenty of scope in their own organization." She ultimately lost this fight to Bedil Begtrup, the former Danish resistance fighter who became the first chair of the CSW as it began its work of advancing the rights of women around the globe.[38]

The women on the Commission had their work cut out for them. Many member states considered the issue of women's equality to be a purely domestic one that was outside the work of the United Nations. And although the organization's Charter referred to the "equal rights of men and women" and committed itself to upholding the human rights, dignity, and worth of all human beings, only thirty of the original fifty-one member states allowed women equal voting rights and/or permitted them to hold public office at the time. This sad state of affairs prompted the General Assembly in December 1946 to recommend that all member states grant women political rights equal to those of men. The female commissioners also successfully lobbied to make the language of the UDHR inclusive of women, and the clear and unambiguous idea in the UDHR that men and women have equal rights served as the starting point for the Commission's efforts. A similarly inclusive language appeared in both of the human rights covenants signed in the 1960s. In addition to this rights' work, the United Nations also continued the efforts undertaken by the League of Nations to quash the trafficking of women, especially for prostitution.[39]

Other U.N. organizations also took up the mantle of women's equality in these early years, most prominently the ILO. After all, labor unions had been advocating with and for women in workplaces and legislatures for decades. Therefore it was not terribly surprising when in June 1951 it adopted a Convention on Equal Remuneration. It went even further when it called for the elimination of discrimination in employment on the basis of race, color, sex, religion, political opinion, national extraction, or social origin in January 1958. The ILO and CSW had been working closely together since 1946, and in 1956, the Commission commented that "equal pay for equal work was as important to the status of women as the right to vote." Another early and long-lasting CSW ally was UNESCO, which passed its Convention against Discrimination in Education in 1960 (adopted by the United Nations in 1962). The vibrant and diverse actions taking place outside of the CHR tend to provide a historical vindication to Begtrup's initial fight to ensure that the CSW was part of the broader ECOSOC rather than simply part of the Commission on Human Rights.[40]

The signal victory of the CSW in these early years was the General Assembly's adoption of the Convention on the Political Rights of Women in December 1952, a measure that Eleanor Roosevelt was lobbying for on her last day in the United Nations. This brief but binding convention called on its signatories to ensure that women could vote, stand for election, hold public office, and exercise all other public functions on equal terms with men and without discrimination. The first state to ratify the Convention was the Dominican Republic, which had included a woman in its delegation to the San Francisco Conference and which had lobbied for the inclusion of women's rights in the U.N. Charter. After member states deposited their ratifications of the Convention on the Political Rights of Women, they furnished progress reports to the secretary-general that were periodically reported to the Assembly and were closely scrutinized by the CSW. The impetus for the convention had come directly from a 1950 U.N. questionnaire that found that while fifty-two member states provided women with equal political rights, twenty-two did not; of these, thirteen banned women from voting or holding office, and nine made women's political rights subject to conditions and requirements that differed from men's.[41]

The CSW, recognizing that equal legal rights for women were not sufficient, ventured into the more fraught territory of culture and tradition in the early 1950s. When the Commission learned from the WHO about the practice of FGM (which was then called "ritual operations"), it urged U.N. member states through ECOSOC to progressively abolish such practices. But the WHO rebuffed a subsequent effort in 1954 to have it conduct an inquiry into the practice on the grounds that it was a cultural rather than medical issue, so the issue awaited the 1970s before it became the focus of committed action. The United Nations also trespassed on cultural traditions that violated women's human rights with its Convention on Consent to Marriage, Minimum Age for Marriage and Registration of Marriage, which the General Assembly approved in November 1962 and which required signatory states to prohibit any marriage in which both parties did not consent.[42] This work helped lay the groundwork for the November 1967 approval of the Declaration on the Elimination of Discrimination Against Women (DEDAW), whose four-year drafting process had led to the conclusion that changes in women's legal status did not result in equality due to customs, practices, and prejudices that still worked to effectively circumscribe women's lives over much of the planet. Therefore DEDAW declared such customs and private practices to be an appropriate realm for

U.N. work on promoting human rights and forthrightly declared that discrimination against women was "fundamentally unjust and an offence against human dignity." Of course this declaration—like other rights declarations—was nonbinding, but at least one scholar argues that it helped to expand "the intellectual space within which women could work, and . . . the role of the UN as the arbiter of international law" and points to the Arab League's creation in 1971 of the eighteen-nation Arab Women's Commission that used DEDAW to draft its own program of action.[43]

The CSW was successful in integrating women's issues across the United Nations throughout the 1960s. It unveiled its proposal for a Long-Term Program for the Advancement of Women in 1966, which grew out of a request from the secretary-general for a way to better mobilize women's talents in the Second Development Decade (see Chapter 5). And when the first International Conference on Human Rights convened in Tehran in 1968, it adopted and endorsed these proposals, which in turn became the basis for the 1970 U.N. Programme of Concerted International Action for the Advancement of Women (whose foci were education, training and employment, health and maternity protection, and public life).[44]

Impetus for a new direction in the CSW's work came from an unexpected direction. In 1972, the Women's International Democratic Federation (WIDF) used its observer status in ECOSOC to ask that it proclaim 1975—the WIDF's twenty-fifth anniversary—as an International Women's Year. Although previous "years" had been largely ceremonial or symbolic, the CSW decided to mark International Women's Year with a global conference in Mexico City, to which it invited the women's NGOs of the world. This decision not only set the pattern for future international conferences but also helped infuse the dynamism of the global women's movement into the CSW. However, bringing five thousand women together in the conference's Tribune meetings also revealed significant fissures that divided the international women's movement between East and West (where ideas of peace vied with ideas of rights) and between North and South (where ideas of rights and freedoms vied with ideas of development and the basic needs of survival). As a result of these differences—which had not been explored and ironed out earlier due to the tight timeline for the conference—no overarching "Declaration of Mexico City" gained consensus, but the conferees drafted an ambitious World Plan of Action that included drafting a Convention to End All Forms of Discrimination Against Women that was to be presented at a follow-up conference in Copenhagen in 1980. They also called on the United Nations to proclaim the entire decade (reaching from 1975 to 1985) as the U.N. Decade for Women. The United Nations responded and also created UNIFEM (the U.N. Development Fund for Women, est. 1976) with the goal of promoting Third World women's political, economic, and social empowerment. Taken as a whole, the women of Mexico City, for all of their differences, agreed that they needed more institutional U.N. support and more time in which to "debate, strategize and organize" around the issues that they cared about most passionately. In December 1979, more than a quarter century after passing DEDAW, the General Assembly adopted the legally binding Convention on the Elimination of All Forms of Discrimination Against Women (CEDAW) with no votes cast against it (and just ten abstentions). This gave those gathered in Copenhagen a tool to examine human rights through the lens of gender and to study women's lives through the lens of human rights.[45]

In 1980 Copenhagen had twice the number of participants who had attended the Mexico City conference just five years earlier, signaling the explosion in the number and diversity of global women's groups. Although the conference featured a dramatic ceremony in which sixty-four governments signed the CEDAW and two went so far as to deposit their ratification instruments, the predominantly male governmental delegations did not share the desire of the women present to see economic development through a gendered lens. Nonetheless, the conference energized women, who lobbied effectively for the rapid ratification of CEDAW, which came into force by September 1981.[46]

The next women's conference in Nairobi, Kenya, in July 1985 attracted some 2,000 government delegates (for the first time more women than men chaired these delegations) and more than 13,000 NGO representatives from 150 different countries. They participated in 1,198 planned workshops, which NGOs supplemented with more than 300 "spontaneous discussions." The three main conclusions that the participants drew from Nairobi were that issues of nationality, region, class, and race clearly played a role in the discrimination that women faced in attaining economic security; that violence against women undermined any efforts toward peace; and that governments had to create institutional mechanisms to promote and monitor women's concerns if any progress was to be made.[47]

Amazingly enough in the wake of such energetic women's activism on the global stage, the United Nations initially planned a 1991 Conference on Human Rights in Vienna that did not list women's rights at all on the conference agenda. The Center for Women's Global Leadership, however, quickly organized the Global Campaign for Women's Human Rights to correct this oversight. This international coalition then launched its "16 Day Campaign"—the period between the U.N.-designated International Violence Against Women Day and International Human Rights Day—and ultimately gathered more than half a million signatures from women in 124 countries on its petition demanding that the United Nations "comprehensively address women's human rights at every level" of the Vienna Conference. Not only were women's issues incorporated into the agenda but the Vienna Declaration asserted that "the human rights of women and of the girl-child are an inalienable, integral and indivisible part of universal human rights. The full and equal participation of women in political, civil, economic, and cultural life, at the national, regional and international levels, and the eradication of all forms of discrimination on grounds of sex are priority objectives of the international community."[48]

The last of the international women's conferences convened in Beijing, China, in 1995, attracting more than 45,000 attendees (more than three times the number who had attended Nairobi). For a country with a poor human rights record, the notion of having tens of thousands of human rights activists in the country led the Chinese government to relocate the NGO forum to a city well outside of Beijing, which seemed to have energized the attendees. Although the conference's support of the right to abortion and family-planning services raised the ire of the Vatican and American Republicans, the tagline of the Beijing Declaration and Platform for Action came from the U.S. delegation (headed by its U.N. ambassador, Madeleine Albright, and first lady Hilary Rodham Clinton): "Women's rights are human rights." To mainstream women's rights, the platform for action pledged governments to ensure "that a gender perspective is reflected in all . . . policies and programmes." Although this was another nonbinding resolution, the United Nations similarly committed itself to the fully integrating women's issues into its programs. The MDGs included several measurable actions related to promoting gender equality and empowering women, and the U.N. Foundation made "women and population" one of its top four investment areas. Even the Security Council sought, through a set of resolutions, to declare that women and girls should be protected during times of war, especially from sexual violence, and to set up a monitoring mechanism to that end.[49]

Beijing was the last of the women's megaconferences, which had provided women from around the world the opportunity to literally get to know one another and had helped to mainstream women's concerns in national and international agendas. In fact, in looking back on this section, it almost seems as if women in the United Nations had come full circle. Eleanor Roosevelt's early contention that women's rights should be considered simply as an essential part of human rights was where Beijing had ended up. But in between, women had to be seen and heard across the U.N. bureaucracy, had to develop their own institutional capacity for launching the Women's Decade, and had to enjoy their own successes.[50]

Indigenous rights

Examining indigenous rights provides us an example of how the U.N. human rights framework treated minority rights. Many countries have long, violent, and complicated histories of interacting, fighting, negotiating, and dealing with indigenous populations, and indigenous peoples have sought international aid to preserve and restore their collective rights within national boundaries since as early as the 1920s when leaders from the Cayuga (from the United States) and the Maori (from New Zealand) unsuccessfully sought to address the League of Nations. Such petitions continued from the earliest years of the CHR but were routinely tabled for the first twenty-five years, as the dominant international narrative was one of modernization, assimilation, and national unity. The only U.N. instrument recognizing the separate identity and challenges of indigenous peoples during this early period was the ILO's 1957 convention on indigenous and tribal populations, but even then, the proposed remedy was integration into the modern national economy. But a simple reading of this issue as the international community of nation-states resisting indigenous rights would be too simplistic. The rights to self-determination and decolonization that colonial peoples worked so hard to attain in the immediate postwar period seemed threatened by the issue of indigenous and special group rights, which could (as history had already shown in Azerbaijan and Katanga) potentially be used to undermine that very sovereignty. These concerns undergirded passage of the December 1960 "Declaration on the Granting of Independence to Colonial

Countries and Peoples," which stressed the preservation of territorial integrity, limited decolonization to overseas territories, and sought to prevent secession of an oppressed group within a domestic setting from any international consideration.[51]

By the mid-1960s, however, international organizations began investigating questions of indigenous rights in response to pressures from a variety of groups, and here we see how forces external to nation-states played key roles in redefining this borderland debate. While the rights of the indigenous black population in South Africa had been a consistent issue in front of the United Nations, a broader view developed from news about how the processes of modernization threatened the cultural survival of indigenous peoples in the Amazon basin. Such concerns spawned the creation of new international organizations—the Copenhagen-based International Work Group for Indigenous Affairs in 1968 and the London-based NGO Survival International in 1969—and action by the International Red Cross.[52]

But it was a U.N. staff member who made the most lasting institutional impact. Augosto Willemsen Diaz (previously an attorney in Guatemala), recognizing that the international human rights covenants only defined the rights of individuals and therefore closed off a direct legal route to addressing the collective rights of peoples, decided to seek redress for indigenous peoples through the International Convention on the Elimination of Racial Discrimination. Although racism toward individuals was only one of many challenges these peoples faced, Diaz brought the issue before the CHR Subcommittee on the Elimination of Racial Discrimination, which in 1971 appointed a special rapporteur to study the issue—a study that took a dozen years to complete. In the interim, the indigenous peoples of North America began organizing their own groups to lobby for greater international action—the International Indian Treaty Council (est. 1974 in the United States as part of the American Indian Movement) and the World Council of Indigenous Peoples (est. 1975 in Canada). The World Council quickly drafted its declaration of principles, which served as the focus of the 1977 international NGO conference on discrimination against the indigenous peoples of the Americas. The next year's U.N. World Conference to Combat Racism and Racial Discrimination, in turn, highlighted the issue of discrimination against indigenous peoples as a global issue. Norway emerged at this latter conference as a champion for indigenous rights, symbolized by its inclusion of a member of its own indigenous community—the Sami—among its official delegation. As a result of lobbying by the World Council of Indigenous Peoples and the International Indian Treaty Council, the U.N. Human Rights Subcommission on the Prevention of Discrimination and Protection of Minorities appointed (in 1982) a working group on indigenous populations, which granted indigenous peoples their first official access to the world body and an arena to air their grievances. The next year, it received Diaz's long-awaited draft report, which concluded that self-determination was the sine qua non for indigenous peoples' enjoyment of their full fundamental rights and which asserted their inalienable right to their territory. The draft received a warm reception from the Nordic states and the U.N. Centre for Human Rights, but most governments were less enthusiastic and worked to stall forward movement on the issue.[53]

But while progress slowed in the CHR, it was moving forward in the ILO. In 1989, the ILO's gathered representatives of business, labor, and government adopted the Indigenous and Tribal Peoples Convention (ILO Convention No. 169). Its key provisions included the right to self-identify as a member of an indigenous group, governments' responsibilities to end discrimination against indigenous and tribal peoples, the right to maintain and develop indigenous institutions, the right to retain customs and customary law (including penal systems) that do not conflict with international human rights standards, rights of ownership and possession to land and natural resources, protection of indigenous and tribal peoples' traditional occupations, the right to maintain contacts and cooperation across borders where indigenous peoples have been divided by international borders, and rights to economic development, health, social security, and education. Over the next two decades, twenty countries ratified the convention, giving the international organization's supervisory bodies the ability to monitor and report on their progress toward implementation. These supervisory bodies therefore also became a vehicle for indigenous populations to raise their specific issues in an international arena and inspired further activism by and for indigenous peoples.[54]

While the U.N. Declaration on the Rights of Indigenous Peoples was making its way through the international bureaucracy at a glacial pace, it nonetheless helped to give birth to two fora for indigenous peoples and issues. In May 2002, the U.N. Permanent Forum on Indigenous Issues began meeting; its sixteen independent experts function in their personal capacity, but half of them are nominated by governments and half by regional indigenous organizations. Additionally, the CHR appointed a special rapporteur on the rights of indigenous peoples in 2001 who was responsible for promoting good practices between indigenous peoples and states, reporting on the overall human rights situations of indigenous peoples in selected countries, addressing allegations of human rights violations against indigenous people, and contributing to the overall study of indigenous rights and issues.[55]

Finally on September 13, 2007, the U.N. General Assembly adopted the Declaration on the Rights of Indigenous Peoples by a vote of 144–11–4 (the four negative votes came from Australia, Canada, New Zealand, and the United States). The Declaration "emphasizes the rights of indigenous peoples to live in dignity, to maintain and strengthen their own institutions, cultures and traditions and to pursue their self-determined development, in keeping with their own needs and aspirations." It also provided a detailed application of current U.N. rights standards to the specific circumstances of indigenous peoples and individuals. Following passage of the Declaration, the U.N. Human Rights Council created the permanent Expert Mechanism on the Rights of Indigenous Peoples (est. 2007), which took over from the Working Group on Indigenous Populations; it supports the Human Rights Council's work with studies, research-based advice, considerations, and approvals. A follow-up conference (in Durban, South Africa, in April 2009) helped indigenous peoples organize their plans to apply the rights in the Declaration to their own circumstances and integrate them into the national and state laws that shaped their circumstances.[56]

In examining how issues of indigenous rights have played out within the United Nations' human rights machinery, it is clear that an exclusive focus on any one group—be it nation-states and their affiliated politics, NGOs of various stripes, or international civil servants—would miss significant parts of this history. And a preexisting belief that indigenous rights should have already been defined and protected by the United Nations makes commentators incredulous about the continuing delays, overlooking the significant challenges that granting such self-determination would cause to the very foundation of the current international order (for better or worse).

Efforts to end human rights abuses

In addition to its efforts to promote human rights we have seen already in this chapter, the United Nations also sought to end ongoing human rights abuses and in some cases to punish those who are responsible, especially for genocide. This aspect of the U.N. human rights agenda—which had been evident in the Nuremberg and Tokyo trials—had lain dormant throughout the Cold War. However, as East-West tensions thawed, there was renewed optimism about the ability of the United Nations, and especially the Security Council, to shape global events and bring about more peaceful outcomes. The fall of the Berlin Wall on November 9, 1989, began the period of transition to an uncertain post–Cold War constellation of international relations. This raised the hopes of the world for a more peaceful global situation, and as we saw in Chapter 3, it also increased the possibilities for the U.N. Security Council to act as an active manager of global crises. At roughly the same time, the release of longtime South African political prisoner and anti-apartheid activist Nelson Mandela on February 11, 1990, came at the end of a decades-long effort by the United Nations to isolate and punish the white South African government for its racist policies. But this post–Cold War euphoria rather quickly ebbed in the face of genocides in the former Yugoslavia and Rwanda and acts of terror that highlighted the limits of the international system. Nonetheless, the United Nations does not have the option of simply throwing up its hands and quitting. The Security Council responded with a new innovation—the international criminal tribunal—in the hope that holding the perpetrators of genocide accountable for their actions can deter such acts in the future and provide some sort of healing to the victims and countries involved.

The fight against apartheid

Apartheid was one of the issues raised at the United Nations' first General Assembly on June 22, 1946, and it took about half a century of nearly continuous pressure from the United Nations and other organizations and movements (along with the courage of the leaders in South Africa) to bring South Africa's brutal system of racial violence and segregation to an end. There are many books and shorter scholarly works that deal with the many parts of this story.[57] What follows here is a relatively short summary of the key highlights of the United Nations' role in this process.

The Indian delegation brought before the 1946 General Assembly its concern about the South African government's treatment of its Indian population (which it termed "colored"). On October 24, the General Committee declined the request of the Union of South Africa that this item be removed from the agenda as an issue of domestic jurisdiction beyond the United Nations' competence, a contention that the General Assembly as a whole affirmed two days later. During the deliberations on the Indian complaint, a multiracial South African delegation headed by Dr. A. B. Xuma, the president-general of the African National Congress (ANC, which was working to abolish apartheid), came to U.N. headquarters to interact with and inform the other delegations about what was happening in his country. While the General Assembly expressed its opinion that South Africa should live up to its obligations under the U.N. Charter and its agreements with India, it was not able to muster the two-thirds vote needed to adopt a resolution on the Indian complaint. When India raised the issue again later that year, it warned that "if the belief that there is to be one standard of treatment for the White races and another for the non-White continues to gain strength . . . the future for solidarity among the Members of the United Nations and, consequently, for world peace, will indeed be dark." The General Assembly responded with a proposal for a roundtable conference of the Indians, Pakistanis, and South Africans on the issue, which ultimately fell through. That fall, the General Assembly established a commission to study the situation in South Africa and again rejected Pretoria's claim that the United Nations had no competence in this field.[58] In this initial flurry of activity, we clearly see the U.N. serving as a borderland where governmental and nongovernmental (ANC) representatives gathered, debated, and ultimately decided to use their available tools to bring outlying governments into compliance with a new set of global norms that included racial equality and laid the groundwork for decolonization. But rather than take this international criticism to heart, the government in South Africa dug in its heels—for example, withdrawing from UNESCO in 1955 when that specialized organization undertook activities against racial discrimination.[59]

The Security Council weighed in on the South Africa issue in the wake of the March 21, 1960, police shooting of some 269 peaceful, black South Africans in Sharpeville, who were protesting a law that required all black South Africans to carry and present a government identification pass at all times. Faced with the deaths of sixty-nine men, women, and children and the wounding of another 200, the Security Council deplored the policies and actions of the South African government. When the fifteenth session of the General Assembly convened that spring, an African proposal for sanctions against Pretoria failed, but an Asian resolution condemning apartheid as "reprehensible and repugnant to human dignity" passed 96–1. This marked the first time that Great Britain joined the majority, and South Africa responded by withdrawing from the British Commonwealth. But the pressure did not recede. On June 29, 1960, a majority of the membership of the ILO voted for a resolution calling for South Africa's withdrawal, and the next year the ILO Conference requested that its governing body send South Africa a request that it withdraw. When South African delegates participated nonetheless, African delegates walked out of the ILO annual assembly in 1962, and in 1964, South

Africa withdrew. Additionally, in 1966, the day of the Sharpeville "massacre"—March 21—became an annual day of worldwide protests, which the U.N. General Assembly declared as "International Day for the Elimination of Racial Discrimination," building on its December 1965 adoption of the International Convention on the Elimination of All Forms of Racial Discrimination (ICERD). Not surprisingly, India was among the earliest signatories of ICERD, played a leading role in developing the General Assembly's Subcommittee against Apartheid, and contributed generously to the U.N. funds established to assist the victims of apartheid.[60]

The arrest of prominent ANC leaders Nelson Mandela, Govan Mbeki, and Ahmed Kathrada (plus fifteen others) in July 1963 and their indictment under South Africa's Sabotage Act (which carried the possibility of a death sentence) unleashed another round of U.N. condemnations. The General Assembly asked member states to take actions meant to put pressure on the apartheid regime, and on August 7, Security Council Resolution 181 called upon all states to end the sale and/or shipment of any arms, ammunition, or military vehicles to South Africa, a resolution that was expanded and reinforced over the years.[61] Although the South African government ignored calls from the General Assembly and the Security Council to end the trials and unconditionally release the prisoners, in June 1964 the key leaders were sentenced to life in prison, rather than the death penalty, which many had feared.[62]

Having failed to have a direct effect on South Africa, the United Nations became the borderland in which much international organizing and work against the apartheid regime flourished. On November 9, 1965, the secretary-general established the U.N. Programme for the Education and Training Abroad of South Africans, and that December the General Assembly also asked him to establish a U.N. Trust Fund for South Africa to provide humanitarian assistance to those being persecuted under the system of apartheid. In August of 1966, the United Nations, the Special Committee against Apartheid, and the Government of Brazil sponsored the first of many U.N.-organized and/or U.N.-cosponsored international seminars on apartheid.[63]

The United Nations also took actions in response to South Africa's aggressive foreign policy, especially its mandate over neighboring Namibia. On October 21, 1966, the General Assembly voted 114–2–3 to terminate South Africa's mandate, placing the territory instead under U.N. administration (discussed in Chapter 3). On March 6, 1967, the CHR deplored the government of South Africa's refusal to do so as "contrary to international law and international morality." Then on January 30, 1970, Security Council Resolution 276 terminated South Africa's trusteeship of Namibia (a decision that the International Court of Justice upheld in 1971), but Pretoria simply ignored the ruling.[64]

The United Nations responded to South African intransigence with increased pressure from a variety of sources. Beginning in 1970, the General Assembly began a campaign to delegitimize the South African delegation as unrepresentative of the people of South Africa. The first challenge came at the fall 1970 General Assembly session, when a number of states successfully challenged the legitimacy of the delegation in the Credentials Committee, but the General Assembly as a whole voted to approve the delegation nonetheless. South Africa's establishment of bantustans (separate areas of the country where black Africans would live, similar to U.S. Indian reservations) and the forced removals of African people to these areas again upped the ante. On November 29, 1971, the General Assembly condemned these practices, and on February 4, 1972, the Security Council met in Addis Ababa, Ethiopia, and endorsed the entire U.N. program against apartheid.[65] On November 30, 1973, the General Assembly passed the International Convention on the Suppression and Punishment of the Crime of Apartheid; two weeks later, the Assembly session declared that the current government had "no right to represent the people of South Africa" and designated the liberation movements as "the authentic representatives of the overwhelming majority of the South African people." At the subsequent Assembly session on September 30, 1974, the majority voted to reject the credentials of the South African representatives and to have the Security Council "review the relationship between the United Nations and South Africa in light of the constant violation by South Africa of the principles of the Charter and the Universal Declaration of Human Rights." The Council took up this task in October and considered a proposal for expulsion that failed due to the negative votes of France, Great Britain, and the United States. Therefore at the 1974 General Assembly session, its president, Algerian Abdelaziz Bouteflika, led a majority that voted to bar the South African delegation from participating in the work of the organization and that called for it to be "totally excluded from participation in all international organisations and conferences under the auspices of the United Nations."[66]

In the summer of 1976, the costs of South African apartheid were fearfully demonstrated when police fired at some 20,000 students in the African township of Soweto who were protesting the government's imposition of Afrikaans (considered the language of apartheid) as the language of instruction in their schools. The death toll on that day was approximately 176, and in the violence that followed throughout the country, some one thousand died and many more were injured. The violence sped the delivery of ratifications to the International Convention on the Suppression and Punishment of Apartheid, which entered into force on July 18 of that year.[67]

That fall, South Africa's proclamation of the "independence" of the bantustan of Transkei was part of its effort to create small, "independent," black African states within South Africa so that Pretoria could then claim to legitimately represent the majority of the population left within its gerrymandered borders. The U.N. General Assembly angrily rejected this ruse on the very same day, calling on member states to reject recognition of Transkei or any future bantustan. The Assembly then adopted a comprehensive "programme of action against apartheid" for governments, the specialized agencies of the United Nations, and other intergovernmental and nongovernmental organizations. The next year it issued an International Declaration against Apartheid in Sports and declared that March 20, 1978 (the anniversary of the Sharpeville massacre), would mark the beginning of International Anti-Apartheid Year. That year saw the U.N. Special Committee against Apartheid launch the World Campaign against Military and Nuclear Collaboration with South Africa (which led the annual meeting of the International Atomic Energy Agency to expel it).[68]

Since November 5, 1982, marked the twentieth anniversary of the first U.N. resolution on sanctions against South Africa, the General Assembly marked it as the beginning of the International Year of Mobilization for Sanctions against South Africa, running very much against the "constructive engagement" policy of newly elected U.S. President Ronald Reagan, which included linking South African withdrawal from Namibia to Cuban withdrawal and therefore lengthened that conflict. Pressure did not ease with the end of the International Year: the 1983 General Assembly session adopted a new program of action against apartheid, and in December 1984, the Security Council reaffirmed its earlier arms embargo. International tensions escalated following South Africa's declaration of a state of emergency on July 20, 1985. This declaration gave police the power to detain people without charge, impose curfews, censor the media, and even control funerals (it banned public funerals for victims of unrest and political statements at any funeral). Immediately following the declaration of the state of emergency, France protested by banning investment in or loans to South Africa and by introducing a Security Council resolution calling for voluntary sanctions against Pretoria; Great Britain and the United States abstained, allowing the resolution to pass. And for the first time the Reagan administration publicly called on the government of Prime Minister Pik Botha to lift the state of emergency and release the people detained as a result of it (more than nine hundred). On July 31, 1985, Chase Manhattan Bank announced that, for economic reasons, it would stop lending to South Africa, including nonrenewal of short-term loans worth approximately $400 million. Botha exacerbated matters by taking a hard line in an August 15, 1985, speech, prompting a 20 percent loss in the value of South African currency (the rand) and speeding divestment efforts.[69]

South Africa's United Democratic Front (UDF, which was committed to nonviolence and therefore was one of the only anti-apartheid organizations that had not already been banned) resisted the state of emergency and helped further the looming financial crisis. The UDF called for a boycott of white-owned shops and then a march on August 28, 1985, in the area under the state of emergency. When the police used force to stop the march, the subsequent violence resulted in twenty-eight deaths and then in violence throughout the region, police closings of 500 schools and colleges serving black and "colored" South Africans, and a two-day strike.[70] Following the lead of Chase Manhattan, other foreign banks similarly reduced lending and refused to renew short-term loans (which constituted $11.5 billion of South Africa's total foreign debt of $17 billion) in the wake of the violence. The news took the rand to a record low on international exchanges. Pretoria's announcement on September 1, 1985, that it was instituting a temporary "standstill" on repayments and creating a two-tiered exchange system that would make it more difficult to repatriate profits from South African ventures led to limited economic sanctions that fall from the United States, the European Community, and the British Commonwealth. Under the circumstances, it was practically impossible for the South African Central Bank's governor to renegotiate the terms of his country's debt. At the end of January 1986, Botha announced that he would repeal the pass laws (which required blacks to have a government pass to enter "white" areas) on July 1, in an apparent gesture required by the banks to settle the debt crisis. Soon afterward, Fritz

Leutwiler, the Swiss banker mediating between South Africa and its creditors, worked out an interim agreement that might or might not have been connected to Botha's lifting of the state of emergency on March 4. However, these concessions soon disappeared. On June 12, 1986, South Africa declared a national state of emergency to head off anticipated protests marking the tenth anniversary of the Soweto uprising; it detained more than 1,000 people on the first day alone, which prompted additional calls for more restrictive economic sanctions. But President Reagan and Prime Minister Thatcher remained opposed, vetoing Security Council resolutions calling for sanctions in June 1986, February 1987, and March 1988.[71]

Finally, in 1989, there seemed to be some progress in the right direction. On January 16, 1989, the Security Council responded to the treaty signed by Angola, Cuba, and South Africa on December 22, 1988, that established a path for Namibian independence. Some attributed this progress to economic pressure on South Africa, so that spring and summer, pressure built around the next round of negotiations on Pretoria's debt. Changes in key leadership positions also brought new hope for change. In May, newly elected U.S. President George H. W. Bush decided to take a different tack on South Africa than his predecessor by inviting key black opponents of apartheid to meet with him, and on August 14, 1989, South African Prime Minister Botha, who had secretly met with Mandela in July, abruptly resigned and was replaced by F. W. de Klerk on the eve of scheduled national elections. The South African elections of September 1989 gave de Klerk a five-year term and his National Party the slimmest majority since the party's founding; he viewed this as a mandate for reform, a sentiment reinforced a week later when the largest legal protest march since 1959 (numbering some 20,000) took place in Cape Town. On October 10, 1989, de Klerk announced that Walter Sisulu and six other political prisoners would soon be released from prison in an effort to affirm the Anglo-American stance against additional economic sanctions and to soften creditors' stance in refinancing South African external debt. That December the General Assembly's "Declaration on Apartheid and its Destructive Consequences in Southern Africa" called for negotiations to end apartheid and establish a nonracial democracy. On February 2, 1990, de Klerk, in his speech opening Parliament, announced the lifting of its ban on anti-apartheid organizations, the suspension of the death penalty, the release of some political prisoners, and the easing of the state of emergency. The world eagerly watched when, on February 11, 1990, Nelson Mandela was released after twenty-seven years of imprisonment. The next month Namibia declared its independence, and many rejoiced that things finally seemed to be changing for the good in South Africa.[72]

The United Nations, however, remained vigilant and cautious, given its experiences with the difficulties and dangers inherent as countries transition toward democracy—a sentiment actively reinforced by Mandela, who feared that a premature lifting of sanctions could derail the dismantling of apartheid. This tone was reinforced by a U.N. fact-finding mission dispatched in June 1990 as well as Mandela's address to the Special Committee against Apartheid that same month. The Committee followed up with a July statement that the process of change was in a preliminary stage. These statements informed the General Assembly's discussions in July and September and the three days devoted to debate on apartheid in mid-December. Beginning in the spring of 1991, the U.N. High Commissioner for Refugees began working with the South African government to repatriate approximately 40,000 political exiles,[73] but the Special Committee against Apartheid's June 1991 interim report found "limited progress" toward dismantling apartheid and expressed the opinion that pervasive violence in the country made "the prospects for a speedy . . . establishment of a united, non-racial and democratic South Africa . . . less promising now than a year ago." But that same month the South African parliament repealed key parts of the legal system of apartheid and released more political prisoners.[74]

Though maintaining most sanctions, the international community also began building capacity to assist a new South Africa. A June 1991 conference cosponsored by the U.N. Special Committee against Apartheid and the Association of West European Parliamentarians for Action against Apartheid focused on "Supporting Democracy and Development" in both a post–Cold War Eastern Europe and a post-apartheid South Africa, and later that same month UNESCO and the Special Committee called an International Conference on the Educational Needs of the Victims of Apartheid. U.S. President George H. W. Bush signed an executive order doubling aid levels to assist black South Africans and terminating sanctions against South Africa, which drew international fire for being premature. Nonetheless, the secretary-general's September 4, 1991, progress report called South Africa's "halting" progress toward ending apartheid in the previous twelve months "on course." And the General Assembly that December called for the resumption of academic, cultural, and scientific relationships between the international community and nonracial organizations in South Africa. Additionally, a high-level U.N. delegation attended (as observers) the Convention for a Democratic South Africa (CODESA) when it convened for the first time on December 20, 1991, with the stated objective of bringing "about an undivided South Africa free from apartheid." Following these initial negotiations, de Klerk announced a "whites only" referendum on the issue of reforms and negotiations, which resulted in a landslide 68 percent vote calling for the continuation of the process, which happened in May 1992. CODESA II negotiations broke down on June 17, 1992, over the issue of continuing violence, in which Mandela and the ANC thought the government complicit. The U.N. Security Council spent two days in July examining the issue of political violence in South Africa before unanimously adopting a resolution that led to the appointment of former U.S. Secretary of State Cyrus Vance as the special representative of the secretary-general to investigate the circumstances and recommend measures for ending the violence so that negotiations could resume.[75] Based on Vance's advice, the secretary-general recommended a full-scale investigation of the South African security forces and political armies and created the U.N. Observer Mission in South Africa (UNOMSA) to monitor conditions on the ground.[76] Despite continuing violence, talks restarted on April 1, 1993. On May 25, World Bank Vice President Edward Jaycox tried to coax the process along by announcing that the bank had $1 billion in development projects prepared for South Africa's impoverished black population and was only awaiting the creation of a nonracial transitional government. On September 24, 1993, the South African parliament approved the creation of the multiracial Transitional Executive Council, and for the first time Mandela called, in a speech to the U.N. Special Committee on Apartheid, for an end to economic sanctions, which he credited for having "brought us to the point where the transition to democracy has now been enshrined in the law of our country." Sanctions were repealed throughout the fall as the Transitional Executive Council prepared to take power on December 6. One of its first actions was to ask the international community for observers to oversee the first inclusive and free elections in the country's history.[77]

The elections on April 27, 1994, resulted in the election of Nelson Mandela as president, de Klerk and Thabo Mbeki as deputies, and the ANC (which had won 62 percent of the vote) joining with the National Party (which had won 20 percent of the vote) to form a Government of National Unity under a new flag, which was unfurled for the first time at the U.N. headquarters in New York City, symbolizing the important role of the international organization in bringing about this largely peaceful transition. President Mandela's first State of the Nation Address announced that the country would subscribe to the UDHR and accede to the United Nations' human rights covenants. On June 23, the General Assembly approved the credentials of the South African delegation, and on June 27, the Security Council, after lifting the arms embargo it had enacted in 1977, noted "with great satisfaction" that it could now remove the question of South Africa from its agenda.[78]

International Criminal Tribunals

The end of the Cold War in many ways had the most significant impact on the United Nations' human rights fights. Now largely free of East-West gridlock, the U.N. Security Council, operating under its broad mandate "to forcibly remove threats to international peace and security," first created the ad hoc International Criminal Tribunal for the former Yugoslavia (ICTY) in May 1993 at the Hague and then the International Criminal Tribunal for Rwanda (ICTR) in November 1994 in Arusha, Tanzania. These initiatives—and those that followed—drew on the procedures and the definitions of crimes against humanity developed by the Nuremberg and Tokyo trials that followed the Second World War, but the tribunals were unprecedented in a number of ways: they prosecuted people for war crimes and crimes against humanity in the context of "domestic disputes" for the first time, they first defined rape and sexual assault as genocidal, they compelled cooperation from U.N. member states, and the Security Council successfully claimed that these tribunals trumped domestic courts in the two regions. Collectively, these innovations have been called "the first sign of a seismic shift, from diplomacy to legality, in the conduct of world affairs" and "one of the most ambitious judicial experiments in the history of humankind—a global assault on the architects of atrocities." The goal of these tribunals was to hold perpetrators internationally responsible, since the available domestic courts were unable to do so. Additionally, there was some hope that the tribunals might aid in reconstruction of these societies and/or deter future atrocity crimes.[79]

The international community and its constituent parts have been widely condemned for their inaction and/or inability to stop the Serbian ethnic cleansing (displacing, terrorizing, and killing) of Muslims as Yugoslavia fractured. In the period from August 1991 until the end of 1992, Serbs displaced tens of thousands and killed approximately 3,300 Croatians and 30,500 Bosnian Muslims. It was not until after the August 2, 1992, publication of a newspaper article about Serbian concentration camps by Roy Gutman in New York City's *Newsday* (subsequently complemented and amplified by other media reports) that first the Conference for Security and Cooperation in Europe (in August 1992) and then the U.N. Security Council (in October 1992) dispatched small teams to investigate the atrocities then happening in Bosnia and Croatia. The United States, in the middle of a presidential election and then in the interregnum between two administrations, took no action. However, the new U.S. ambassador to the United Nations, Madeleine Albright, put the issue at the top of her agenda when she arrived in New York City. But even the initial discussions about the tribunal came under fire. It was cast as a poor alternative to military intervention by the Western powers rather than a parallel decision-making process with different goals, and several efforts were made to use it as a bargaining chip to bring the Serbs into cease-fire negotiations. The ICTY was set up in 1993 in the Hague, but it took more than a year to hire a prosecutor. When Serb forces overran the U.N. "safe haven" at Srebrenica in July 1995 and massacred thousands, many questioned what good a tribunal was doing for those on the ground. Ultimately, however, the tribunal indicted 161 of those considered to be most responsible for the atrocity crimes in the dissolving nation-state, all of whom have subsequently either died or been apprehended. Once it took up its work, the International Tribunal very quickly made legal history. Its first case against Duško Tadić, a relatively minor player in the Yugoslav conflict who was charged with war crimes and crimes against humanity, established that the traditional definition of "war crimes" as atrocities committed during international armed conflicts applied equally to those crimes committed during domestic or non-international armed conflict.[80] The law developed by the ICTY was quickly applied to another genocide, this time in Africa.

Commentators were even more critical of the lack of a proactive response to the Rwandan genocide, and not without reason, given the appallingly high number of casualties and the inability and/or unwillingness of the international community to intervene to bring the killing to an end. In the 100 days that followed the assassination of the presidents of Rwanda and Burundi on April 6, 1994, somewhere between 800,000 and 1 million Rwandans died, mostly those identified as Tutsis and moderate Hutus who sought to protect their neighbors and stop the genocide. A small U.N. peacekeeping force on the ground in Rwanda had no authority to intervene in the unfolding tragedy; its mission was to monitor the fragile peace agreement between Rwanda and Burundi.[81] However, the student-researcher interested in taking a historical view of the United Nations in this situation will find that some of the assumptions undergirding the criticisms are problematic. For example, Linda Melvern says that the prevention of genocide is "the single most important commitment of the countries who join together as the United Nations." This may be her opinion, but it does not square with the historical record. While human rights were written into the U.N. Charter, as much of this chapter recounts, there was not a strong commitment among member states to enforce a universal code of human rights, especially not by military force. Rather, the key goal of the drafters of the U.N. Charter was to prevent a third world war, and most of its peacekeeping activities have sought to facilitate and maintain peace settlements and cease-fires once they are already in place.[82]

Following the Rwandan genocide (ended by the military action of the Tutsi rebel army), the U.N. Security Council established the ICTR to hold accountable those who had perpetrated the genocidal killings and other crimes that occurred throughout Rwanda. Like the Yugoslavia Tribunal, the very first case of the ICTR set an important legal precedent. The witness testimony against Jean-Paul Akayesu, the mayor of Taba during the genocide, included graphic accounts of how he encouraged and even ordered Hutu men to commit rape and other acts of sexual violence against Tutsi women in addition to ordering the deaths of numerous Tutsis. This testimony prompted Judge Navanethem "Navi" Pillay to pointedly tell the prosecution that it should consider amending the indictment to include these very serious sex crimes. They were not initially included since sexual violence during armed conflict had traditionally received little attention under international law. Nonetheless, in this case, the prosecution did amend the indictment, and Akayesu's conviction included rape and mistreatment of Tutsis as part of the genocide. The Trial Chamber defined "sexual violence" as an underlying act of genocide: "Sexual violence was a step in the process of destruction of the Tutsi group—destruction of the spirit, of the will to live, and of life itself." This marked the first of a number of charges and convictions for sexual violence as a crime against humanity. The ICTR was also the first court to hold members of the media culpable for broadcasts meant to inflame public opinion preparatory to genocide. Ultimately, the ICTR indicted ninety-three individuals for their roles in the genocide and had sentenced sixty-one by October 2014.[83]

Recognizing that genocide is not a spontaneous action but instead requires organization and resources and is usually perpetrated through the state apparatus, on the tenth anniversary of the Rwandan genocide, U.N. Secretary-General Kofi Annan outlined an action plan to prevent future genocides based around five key aims: (1) preventing armed conflict that serves as a context for genocide; (2) protecting civilians during armed conflict, which in some cases may require the use of U.N. peacekeepers; (3) ending impunity for the perpetrators of genocide through the use of national and international judicial action; (4) gathering information through the U.N. special adviser on the prevention of genocide (est. 2004) and setting up an early warning system in potentially genocidal situations; and (5) committing to swift and decisive action, including military action, to prevent large-scale genocide once it has started. Subsequently the secretary-general also established a special adviser on the responsibility to protect (est. 2008), who works under the overall guidance of the special adviser on the prevention of genocide "to further the conceptual, political, institutional and operational development of the responsibility to protect" people from the crime of genocide.[84]

In addition to the responsibility to protect, the international criminal tribunals also gave birth to several international, legal offspring. The value of the work of the tribunals in Yugoslavia and Rwanda helped to highlight the fact that many similar crimes perpetrated outside the chronological framework of the tribunals or undertaken on a "smaller" scale in other areas of the world still largely enjoyed impunity from prosecution. This realization served as the catalyst (along with the end of the Cold War and strong advocacy by NGOs) for adoption of the Rome Statute of the International Criminal Court (ICC) on July 17, 1998, which entered into force with sixty ratifications on July 1, 2002.[85] While the ICC is entirely separate from the United Nations, other courts in Sierra Leone, Cambodia, and Lebanon within the U.N. orbit were also the direct descendants of the ICTY and ICTR.

The Special Court for Sierra Leone (SCSL, est. 2002) was the first of the "hybrid" courts established by the United Nations that blended international and domestic jurisprudence in the hope of bringing justice more quickly and at a lower cost than the earlier tribunals for Yugoslavia and Rwanda. The SCSL dealt with the aftermath of the gruesome, decade-long civil war in that country (1991–2002) that primarily pitted the Civil Defense Force against the Revolutionary United Front, whose members became infamous for their use of child soldiers, amputations, and mass rape to terrorize local populations and gain control of key diamond-producing areas and who traded those diamonds for arms and training from Charles Taylor, the president of neighboring Liberia. When peace finally came in 2002, one of the first requests of the government of Sierra Leone was for a special court to try those who were most responsible for the war crimes and crimes against humanity that had devastated the country. This hybrid court's innovations included public outreach programs; its 2004 ruling that recruitment and use of child soldiers, forced marriages, and attacks on peacekeepers are prosecutable crimes under international law; and its June 4, 2007, trial of a sitting head of state, Charles Taylor of Liberia. In 2013, the SCSL also became the first international tribunal to complete its mandate.[86] The work of the Special Court for Sierra Leone was particularly successful when compared with the Cambodian effort that followed.

In 2003, the United Nations and the new Cambodian government agreed to a draft document creating another hybrid court, the Extraordinary Chambers in the Courts of Cambodia (ECCC), which included both international and Cambodian judges and jurisprudence. In this case, the court was to deal with the atrocities committed during the reign of the Khmer Rouge from 1975 until 1979, when an estimated 1.7 million died in what became popularized as the "Killing Fields." But unlike Sierra Leone, these trials took place almost a quarter century after the atrocities had been committed. It took nine years and more than $200 million before Kaing Guek Eav (Comrade Duch), chief of the infamous S-21 prison in the capital, Phnom Penh, where some 15,000 lost their lives, was ultimately sentenced to life in prison, the maximum punishment allowed. Four other indictments of elderly defendants yielded just two more life sentences in August 2014. Although the court has also been working toward indictments in two additional cases, those have stalled amid U.N. funding issues and the government's general refusal to cooperate, given Prime Minister Hun Sen's close ties with the former Khmer Rouge regime (he was a battalion commander).[87]

The Special Tribunal for Lebanon was the United Nations' first attempt to handle, in an international criminal court, a case of terrorism—the February 15, 2005, car-bombing in the capital city of Beirut that killed former Prime Minister Rafik Hariri and twenty-one others and injured 226. Since Hariri had increasingly criticized the Syrian government for its long-standing military presence and political influence in Lebanon (see Chapter 7), the assassination sparked mass protests in Beirut and anti-Syrian sentiment throughout the country. On April 7, 2005, the U.N. Security Council created the International Independent Investigation Commission and dispatched German Detlev Mehlis to lead its investigation, which implicated top Syrian and Lebanese officials and prompted Syrian denials and claims of a politicized investigation.[88] On December 13, 2005, Lebanon asked the United Nations to create an international tribunal to try those responsible for the attack.[89] This tribunal (est. March 1, 2009), like the tribunals in Sierra Leone and Cambodia, is a hybrid court—it follows Lebanese criminal code and upholds international standards of justice (including exclusion of the death penalty); it contains Lebanese jurists, but in order to ensure the independence of the court, a majority of the judges and the prosecutor are non-Lebanese; and it is paid for by Lebanon (51 percent of the court's costs) and voluntary donations. The first indictments on January 17, 2011, were followed by an expansion of the tribunal's scope to include other killings and acts of terrorism linked to the main suspects that occurred after October 1, 2004. The trial (in absentia) of five Lebanese nationals connected with Hezbollah alleged to have had a role in the Hariri assassination started on January 16, 2014, but had not reached a verdict by early 2016. While some observers have wondered if similar types of trials might be used to bring peace to this troubled region or to provide international trials for terrorists, the ten-year gap between the assassination and the trial and the way in which the tribunal has exacerbated the fraught relationship between the Lebanese government and Hezbollah are not promising augurs (at the time of this publication).[90]

Conclusion

In examining the human rights work of the United Nations, we see a microcosm of much of what is best and worst about the organization. On the positive side of the ledger, almost everyone on the planet has now heard the term "human rights" and has some sense of what this term entails, no mean educational feat. And this capacious term and the U.N. organization have sometimes provided the rhetorical and organizational space for people who have faced discrimination, persecution, and violence to have their grievances recognized, addressed, and remedied. The ideas, conferences, and NGOs arising from this U.N. human rights agenda have also motivated millions of people to take an active interest in and action on behalf of the well-being of others, with the hope of creating a better world. Certainly we can see the ways in which the United Nations helped to spur and support an international women's movement over the past seven decades as well as a global effort to end apartheid in South Africa. U.N. efforts to deal with genocide have not been particularly fruitful, but the United Nations continues to innovate—to try to find a way to avoid these horrors—through its tribunals and now in defining an international "responsibility to protect." Here at the end of the chapter we are left pretty much where we started—with the acknowledgment that the United Nations is a borderland. What happens there is important in defining human rights, but the United Nations in most circumstances lacks the tools to impose its will on recalcitrant governments. And this "failure" has led to reform of the U.N. human rights machinery. In 2006, the General Assembly voted to replace ECOSOC's Commission on Human Rights with the U.N. Human Rights Council (with forty-seven member states) that works under the authority of the General Assembly and in conjunction with the office of the High Commissioner for Human Rights.[91] Although it is too soon to judge the effectiveness of this reorganization, it does not seem likely that this newly configured United Nations body will suddenly be able to guarantee the rights enshrined in the UDHR to the planet's billions. But without a United Nations, it is difficult to imagine that international relations would be better or that human rights would be more secure.

CHAPTER 9
CONCLUSION: JOIN THE CONVERSATION!

Sometimes you start to feel old when you write about things that you remember in your lifetime. Although I had that feeling at several points in writing this narrative, I have also been energized in surveying and reflecting on all of the great new scholarship available to inform our understanding of what has happened over the past seventy years as the United Nations—for all its flaws—has sought to craft a better world than the one that emerged from the Second World War and the first atomic bomb. And while we could argue about its effectiveness or ineffectiveness, it is undeniable that the United Nations has played a crucial and wide-ranging role in the international history of the twentieth and twenty-first centuries.

Now, I invite you to join this vibrant conversation: Explore more deeply how the U.N. was able to assist in the transition to a post-apartheid South Africa or safeguard the peace in Cyprus. Compare current campaigns against human trafficking with their origins in the League of Nations or the current plight of today's Syrian refugees to their predecessors. Understand why people are concerned about the power of the World Trade Organization. Research India's U.N. diplomacy that allowed it to decisively intervene in Bangladesh's effort to gain its independence. Examine how U.N. norms on the environment, human rights, and women's equality have—or have not—had a discernible impact on the practices of its members. Immerse yourself in the history of the Middle East and the United Nations' efforts to play a positive role in the relations between Israel and its Arab neighbors. Explore the role of Tanzania, Jamaica, and Mexico in the Non-Aligned Movement's efforts to reshape global economics. Dive into the archive of a nongovernmental organization that has acted through the United Nations to better understand what it hoped to achieve. Research the ways in which a global policy or movement has shaped the experiences of a local community. See yourself as part of a planet whose seven billion inhabitants share a history of learning and striving to live equitably and peacefully with one another. Then join the conversation and make your contribution to the history.

If you join the conversation, your life will never be boring. Currently the public discourse in the United States and elsewhere discounts the value of a "liberal education" and the wisdom of students who major in history, literature, and philosophy and instead urges students to focus on "practical" areas of study—like business and the STEM fields of science, technology, engineering, and mathematics—in which the cost of their studies will be sufficiently offset by their future earnings so that they can pay off their student loans. While I would certainly not advocate abandoning such practical areas of study, I will tell you that when I was a freshman in college, I was a math major, and I was bored. After all, how many times could you do the same calculus problems in the text? But when I changed my major to history, I was never again bored. There was always another book or article to read, another realm of historical study that intrigued me and enticed me to learn more. The news came alive as I linked the events of the present to those of the past and understood the international connections between countries and regions. I wish you, my reader, the same lively interest in the world around you and the same engagement with the past and the world that my time in researching, reading, and writing about the United Nations and international history has brought to me.

GUIDE TO FURTHER RESEARCH

While there are many sources in the notes of this manuscript to assist the researcher interested in the history of the United Nations, Bloomsbury has been kind enough to create an online guide to further literature on the history of the United Nations in international history: www.bloomsbury.com/the-united-nations-in-international-history-9781472510037. This is serving in place of the traditional bibliography or note on sources at the end of a book, and it has the added advantage that I will be updating it annually, making it more of a living document than is possible with a traditional, printed bibliography.

NOTES

Chapter 1

1. Paul Kennedy, *The Parliament of Man: The Past, Present, and Future of the United Nations* (New York: Vintage Books, 2006), xiv, xv, dust jacket. Other examples are legion, but a sampling includes the heading "Successes and Failures of the ICTY and ICTR," in Richard Goldstone, "International Criminal Court and Ad Hoc Tribunals," in *The Oxford Handbook on the United Nations*, ed. Thomas G. Weiss and Sam Daws (Oxford: Oxford University Press, 2007), 467; Sydney D. Bailey and Sam Daws, "Has the UN a Future?," in *The United Nations: A Concise Political Guide*, 3rd ed. (Lanham, MD: Barnes & Noble Books, 1995), 103–12; Francis Lyall, "The Future of the ITU," in *International Communications: The International Telecommunication Union and the Universal Postal Union* (Surrey, UK: Ashgate, 2011).
2. James Barros, *The United Nations: Past, Present, and Future* (New York: Free Press, 1972); Maurice Bertrand, *The United Nations: Past, Present, and Future* (Hague: Kluwer Law International, 1997); Scott Kaufman and Alissa Warters, *The United Nations: Past, Present, and Future* (New York: Nova Science Publishers, 2009).
3. Weiss and Daws, eds., *Oxford Handbook.*
4. International Committee of Historical Sciences, "XXIInd CISH Congress, in Jinan, China, 23–29 August 2015: The Making of Histories of International Organizations: UNESCO as a Case Study," accessed February 27, 2015, http://www.cish.org/congres/SS1-Making-Histories-OI.pdf; Aalborg University, Department of Culture and Global Studies, "Routes of Knowledge: The Global History of UNESCO, 1945–75," accessed February 27, 2015, http://www.unesco.aau.dk/.
5. Thomas G. Weiss, Tatiana Carayannis, Louis Emmerij, and Richard Jolly, *UN Voices: The Struggle for Development and Social Justice* (Bloomington: Indiana University Press, 2005); Richard Jolly, Louis Emmerij, and Thomas G. Weiss, *UN Ideas that Changed the World* (Bloomington: Indiana University Press, 2009). For the UNIHP generally, see Ralph Bunche Institute for International Studies, "United Nations Intellectual History Project," last modified 2011, http://www.unhistory.org/. The website includes links to the list of publications as well as oral history interviews, a reading list, links to several relevant archival websites, and a downloadable pdf of the June 2005 summary of the project's findings, *The Power of UN Ideas: Lessons from the First 60 Years* by Richard Jolly, Louis Emmerij, and Thomas G. Weiss.
6. Mark Mazower, *Governing the World: The Rise and Fall of an Idea, 1815 to the Present* (New York: Penguin, 2012), xiii, xv.
7. Stephen C. Schlesinger, *Act of Creation: The Founding of the United Nations* (New York: Basic Books, 2004); Ilya V. Gaiduk, *Divided Together: The United States and the Soviet Union in the United Nations, 1945–1965* (Washington, DC: Woodrow Wilson Center Press, 2012); David L. Bosco, *Five to Rule Them All: The UN Security Council and the Making of the Modern World* (New York: Oxford University Press, 2009).

8. Paul Thomas Chamberlain, *The Global Offensive: The United States, the Palestinian Liberation Organization, and the Making of the Post–Cold War Order* (Oxford: Oxford University Press, 2012), 8. See also Matthew Connelly, *A Diplomatic Revolution: Algeria's Fight for Independence and the Origins of the Post–Cold War Era* (Oxford: Oxford University Press, 2002); Scott Thomas, *The Diplomacy of Liberation: The Foreign Relations of the African National Congress since 1960* (New York: St. Martin's, 1996); Matthew Connelly, *Fatal Misconception: The Struggle to Control World Population* (Cambridge, MA: Belknap Press of Harvard University Press, 2008).
9. Carol Anderson, *Bourgeois Radicals: The NAACP and the Struggle for Colonial Liberation, 1941–1960* (Cambridge: Cambridge University Press, 2015); idem, *Eyes off the Prize: The United Nations and the African American Struggle for Human Rights, 1944–1955* (Cambridge: Cambridge University Press, 2003); George Manuel and Michael Posluns, *The Fourth World: An Indian Reality* (New York: Free Press, 1974); Global Policy Forum, "Basic Information on NGOs at the UN," accessed July 2, 2015, https://www.globalpolicy.org/un-reform/ngos-9-25/31834.html.
10. The Carnegie Endowment for International Peace partnered with international institutions in the 1950s to publish (through the Manhattan Publishing Company) a series of studies about particular countries' relations with the United Nations.
11. For oral histories, see Weiss et al., *UN Voices*; United Nations International History Project, *The Complete Oral History Transcripts from UN Voices*, compact disc (New York: UNIHP, 2007). The United Nations Oral History collection within the Dag Hammarskjöld Library also maintains more than 200 oral histories conducted in conjunction with Yale University researchers, and this collection was made available electronically in January 2012 through a new website, accessed November 23, 2012, http://www.unmultimedia.org/oralhistory//about/. Additionally, Columbia University's Center for Oral History's website portal (http://library.columbia.edu/indiv/ccoh/our_work.html) yields 198 results for the search term "United Nations" (when accessed November 23, 2012), including large oral history collections on U.N. Intellectual History, the secretary-generalship of Dag Hammarskjöld, the World Bank, and the League of Nations as well as collections on individuals who played significant and varied roles in the United Nations, including, for example, George D. Woods (World Bank president), Rajeshwar Dayal (U.N. observation group in Lebanon 1958 and peacekeeping group in Congo), Aleksander Witold Rudzinski (Polish delegate to U.N., 1949–50), Waldo Chamberlain (San Francisco Conference, preparatory commission, and early secretariat member), Philip Caryl Jessup (helped establish the U.N. Relief and Rehabilitation Administration and served as U.S. delegate to the United Nations), and Charles A. Hogan (chief of U.N. NGO section).
12. As a starting point, see the *Public Papers of the Secretaries-General of the United Nations* series published by Columbia University Press for the first three secretaries-general and *The Yearbook of the United Nations*, which is searchable by volume or keyword: http://unyearbook.un.org/content/about-yearbook/. There are so many U.N. publications that the reader/researcher should look for references to them related to specific issues and organizations throughout the notes of this book.
13. The most easily accessible are those of the developed First World. The Office of the Historian of the U.S. Department of State regularly publishes (in paper form as well as online) volumes about American diplomacy—the *Foreign Relations of the United States* series (*FRUS* for short)—and there is a similar series (volumes 12–29 cover the period 1946–63) for the Canadians—*Documents on Canadian External Relations*—that is also available in print and electronic formats. See Office of the Historian of the U.S. Department of State, "Historical Documents," accessed July 3, 2015, https://history.state.gov/historicaldocuments, which

can be searched by volume or presidential administration (Truman to Carter); Canadian Department of Foreign Affairs, Trade and Development, *Documents on Canadian External Relations*, accessed July 3, 2015, http://www.international.gc.ca/history-histoire/documents-documents.aspx?lang=eng. See also the searchable website of the Canadian Department of Foreign Affairs, Trade and Development, accessed July 3, 2015, http://dfait-aeci.canadiana.ca/, which returned 8,431 results in response to the query "United Nations."

14. Linda Tashbook, "UPDATE: Researching the United Nations: Finding the Organization's Internal Resource Trails," New York University Hauser Global Law School Program, last modified June/July 2013, http://www.nyulawglobal.org/globalex/United_Nations_Research1.htm. Useful links from the United Nations History Project website (http://unhistoryproject.org/research/research_guides.html) include the official U.N. research guide, the U.N. Dag Hammarskjöld Library, the American Society of International Law's reports on international organizations, the University of Cambridge Centre for History and Economics' guide to U.N. archives, Heidelberg University's bibliography on the League of Nations and international organizations, the Columbia University and Georgetown University law libraries' research guides, and guides to League of Nations, U.N., and Food and Agriculture Organization (FAO) materials at Harvard University. UNESCO, "Guide to Archives of International Organizations," accessed February 25, 2015, http://www.unesco.org/archives/sio/Eng/ listed eighty intergovernmental organizations (IGOs) at the time of writing.

Chapter 2

1. Thomas Davies, *NGOs: A New History of Transnational Civil Society* (Oxford: Oxford University Press, 2014), 45; F. S. L. Lyons, *Internationalism in Europe, 1815–1914* (Leyden, Netherlands: A. W. Sythoff, 1963), 122, 229, 235; Bob Reinalda, *Routledge History of International Organizations: From 1815 to the Present Day* (London: Routledge, 2009), 97–102; Frank Ninkovich, *Global Dawn: The Cultural Foundation of American Internationalism, 1865–1890* (Cambridge, MA: Harvard University Press, 2009); Young S. Kim, "Constructing a Global Identity: The Role of Esperanto," in *Constructing World Culture: International Nongovernmental Organizations since 1875*, ed. John Boli and George M. Thomas (Stanford, CA: Stanford University Press, 1999), 127–48.
2. Norman Howard-Jones, *The Scientific Background of the International Sanitary Conferences, 1851–1938* (Geneva: World Health Organization, 1975); Morley K. Thomas and W. J. Maunder, *Sixty-Five Years of International Climatology: The History of the WMO Commission for Climatology, 1929–1993* (Downsview, Canada: Environment Canada, 1993); Universal Postal Union, *The Universal Postal Union: Its Foundation and Development* (Berne, Switzerland: UPU, 1955); International Telecommunication Union, *International Telecommunication Union: Celebrating 130 Years, 1865–1995* (London: International Systems and Communications, 1998); Howard Daniel, *One Hundred Years of International Co-operation in Meteorology, 1873–1973: A Historical Review* (Geneva: IMO, 1973).
3. Lyons, *Internationalism in Europe*, 225; Thomas Neville Bonner, *Becoming a Physician: Medical Education in Britain, France, Germany, and the United States, 1750–1945* (New York: Oxford University Press, 1995).
4. Elisabeth Crawford, *Nationalism and Internationalism in Science, 1880–1939* (Cambridge: Cambridge University Press, 1992), esp. 1–48, 148–49. See also Davies, *NGOs*, 47–50.

5. Lyons, *Internationalism in Europe*, 223–45; Davies, *NGOs*, 1–64; Leila J. Rupp, *Worlds of Women: The Making of an International Women's Movement* (Princeton, NJ: Princeton University Press, 1997).

6. Peter M. Haas, "Introduction: Epistemic Communities and International Policy Coordination," *International Organization* 46, no. 1 (Winter 1992): 2.

7. A brief cross-section of this immense literature on the development of nutrition, science, and agriculture includes Jonathan Harwood, *Technology's Dilemma: Agricultural Colleges between Science and Practice in Germany, 1860–1934* (Oxford: Peter Lang, 2005); J. F. M. Clark, "Bugs in the System: Insects, Agricultural Science, and Professional Aspirations in Britain, 1890–1920," *Agricultural History* 75 (Winter 2001): 83–114; H. C. Knoblauch, E. M. Law, and W. P. Meyer, *State Agricultural Experiment Stations: A History of Research Policy and Procedure* (Washington, DC: U.S. Department of Agriculture, May 1962); David Smith, "The Agricultural Research Association, the Development Fund, and the Origins of the Rowett Research Institute," *Agricultural History Review* 46, no. 1 (1998): 47–63; Einar Jensen, *Danish Agriculture, Its Economic Development: A Description and Economic Analysis Centering on the Free Trade Epoch, 1870–1930* (Copenhagen: J. H. Schultz Forlag, 1937); Sir E. John Russell, "Rothamsted and Its Experiment Station," *Agricultural History* 16 (October 1942): 161–83; H. A. M. Snelders, "James F. W. Johnston's Influence on Agricultural Chemistry in the Netherlands," *Annals of Science* 38, no. 5 (1951): 571–84.

8. Amy L. S. Staples, *The Birth of Development: How the World Bank, Food and Agriculture Organization, and World Health Organization Changed the World, 1945–1965* (Kent, OH: Kent State University Press, 2006), 64–81; Lord Boyd Orr, *As I Recall* (London: MacGibbon and Kee, 1966); Warren C. Waite and John D. Black, "Nutrition and Agricultural Policy," *Annals of the American Academy of Political and Social Science* 188 (November 1936): 218–29; Maria Leticia Galluzi Bizzo, "Latin America and International Nutrition: Integrative Channels in the Period," in *Beyond Geopolitics: New Histories of Latin America at the League of Nations*, ed. Alan McPherson and Yannick Wehrli (Albuquerque: University of New Mexico Press, 2015), 223–37.

9. Gary B. Ostrower, *The League of Nations, from 1919 to 1929* (Garden City Park, NY: Avery Publishing, 1996), xv, xvi. See, for example, Akira Iriye, *Global Community: The Role of International Organizations in the Making of the Contemporary World* (Berkeley: University of California Press, 2002), esp. chapter 1; Antoine Fleury, "The League of Nations: Towards a New Appreciation," in *The Treaty of Versailles: A Reassessment after 75 Years*, ed. Manfred F. Boemeke, Gerald D. Feldman, and Elisabeth Glaser (New York: Cambridge University Press, 1998), 516; Alan McPherson and Yannick Wehrli, eds., *Beyond Geopolitics: New Histories of Latin America at the League of Nations* (Albuquerque: University of New Mexico Press, 2015).

10. A concise overview of the trends within this field is provided by Reinalda, *Routledge History of International Organizations*, 5–16. For the best introduction to the historiography on the League of Nations, see Susan Pedersen, "Back to the League of Nations," *American Historical Review* 112, no. 4 (October 2007): 1091–117; idem, *The Guardians: The League of Nations and the Crisis of Empire* (Oxford: Oxford University Press, 2015), 425n9, 425–26n13, 426n20, 427n22.

11. Mazower, *Governing the World*, 22; Ninkovich, *Global Dawn*, 3–4.

12. Davies, *NGOs*, 35–37, 43; Clarence Prouty Shedd, *History of the World's Alliance of Young Men's Christian Associations* (London: World's Committee of YMCAs, 1955); Akira Iriye, "The Making of a Transnational World," part five, in *Global Interdependence: The World after 1945*, ed. Akira Iriye (Cambridge, MA: Belknap Press, 2013), 686; Lyons, *Internationalism in*

Europe, 5; Glenda Sluga, *Internationalism in the Age of Nationalism* (Philadelphia: University of Pennsylvania Press, 2013), 4.

13. Mazower, *Governing the World*, 81–93; Davies, *NGOs*, 39, 61, 104; Martin Ceadel, *Semi-Detached Idealists: The British Peace Movement and International Relations, 1854-1945* (Oxford: Oxford University Press, 2000); Sandi E. Cooper, ed., *Internationalism in Nineteenth-Century Europe: The Crisis of Ideas and Purpose* (New York: Garland Publishing, 1976), which provides a useful anthology of primary sources on European pacifism.
14. Mazower, *Governing the World*, 38–48; Michla Pomerance, *The Advisory Function of the International Court in the League and UN Eras* (Baltimore, MD: Johns Hopkins University Press, 1973); Hague Justice Portal, "The 'Manouba' Case," accessed July 4, 2015, http://www.haguejusticeportal.net/index.php?id=6136; idem, "The 'Carthage' Case," accessed July 4, 2015, http://www.haguejusticeportal.net/index.php?id=6137.
15. Mazower, *Governing the World*, 113–15.
16. Davies, *NGOs*, 37–38, 59–62, 68, 85; Sandi Cooper, *Patriotic Pacifism: Waging War on War in Europe, 1815–1914* (New York: Oxford University Press, 1991), 91–98; William G. Martin, ed., *Making Waves: Worldwide Social Movements, 1750–2005* (Boulder, CO: Paradigm Publishers, 2008); Lyons, *Internationalism in Europe*, 201–22, 338–53; Reinalda, *Routledge History of International Organizations*, 35–56; Mazower, *Governing the World*, 31–38, 67–68, 113–15; David P. Forsythe, *The Humanitarians: The International Committee of the Red Cross* (Cambridge: Cambridge University Press, 2005); International Federation of Red Cross and Red Crescent Societies, "History: The Formation of the IFRC," accessed July 5, 2015, http://www.ifrc.org/en/who-we-are/history/.
17. Davies, *NGOs*, 40, 52–53, 69, 195n152; Anthony Howe, "Free Trade and Global Order: The Rise and Fall of a Victorian Vision," in *Victorian Visions of Global Order*, ed. Duncan Bell (Cambridge: Cambridge University Press, 2008), 26–46; International Association of Public Transport (UITP), "History," accessed July 5, 2015, http://www.uitp.org/history; Emily S. Rosenberg, *Spreading the American Dream: American Economic and Cultural Expansion, 1890–1945* (New York: Hill and Wang, 1982); Arpad Bogsch, *The Paris Convention for the Protection of Industrial Property from 1883 to 1983* (Geneva: International Bureau of Intellectual Property, 1983); idem, *The Berne Convention for the Protection of Literary and Artistic Works, from 1886 to 1986* (Geneva: International Bureau of Intellectual Property, 1986); Peter Koch, *125 Years of the International Union of Marine Insurance: From an Alliance of Insurance Companies in Continental Europe to a Worldwide Organization of National Associations* (Karlsruhe, Germany: Verlag Versicherungswirtschaft, 1999); Asma A. Hussain and Marc J. Ventresca, "Formal Organizing and Transnational Communities: Evidence from Global Finance Governance Associations, 1879–2006," in *Transnational Communities: Shaping Global Economic Governance*, ed. Marie-Laure Djelic and Sigrid Quack (Cambridge: Cambridge University Press, 2010), 153–73.
18. Lyons, *Internationalism in Europe*, 335–38; Reinalda, *Routledge History of International Organizations*, 72–75; Mazower, *Governing the World*, 82; Davies, *NGOs*, 65, 71, 205n353; Warren F. Kuehl and Lynne K. Dunn, *Keeping the Covenant: American Internationalists and the League of Nations, 1920–1939* (Kent, OH: Kent State University Press, 1997), 145.
19. Ostrower, *League of Nations*, 5–6, 11; Davies, *NGOs*, 80–81; George W. Egerton, *Great Britain and the Creation of the League of Nations: Strategy, Politics and International Organisation, 1914–1919* (Chapel Hill: University of North Carolina Press, 2011); Theodor Marburg, *The Development of the League of Nations Idea*, ed. John H. Latané, 2 vols (New York: Macmillan, 1932); Donald S. Birn, *The League of Nations Union, 1918–1945* (Oxford:

Clarendon Press, 1981); Frederic H. Soward, *Canada and the League of Nations* (Ottawa: League of Nations Society in Canada, 1931).

20. Sluga, *Internationalism*, 5. See the electronic bibliography for some of the many published English-language primary sources by participants in the Paris Peace Conference.

21. Avalon Project, "President Woodrow Wilson's Fourteen Points," Lillian Goldman Law Library at Yale Law School, last modified 2008, http://avalon.law.yale.edu/20th_century/wilson14.asp; Ostrower, *League of Nations*, 3. See also Ostrower, *League of Nations*, 7; Ruth Henig, *The League of Nations* (London: Haus Publishing, 2010), 41, 58.

22. Ostrower, *League of Nations*, 5–6, 8, 11, 14; Jan Christiaan Smuts, *The League of Nations: A Practical Suggestion* (London: Hodder and Stoughton, 1918); McPherson and Wehrli, eds., *Beyond Geopolitics*; Henig, *League of Nations*, 26–28, 72.

23. Erez Manela, *The Wilsonian Moment: Self-Determination and the International Origins of Anticolonial Nationalism, 1917-1920* (New York: Oxford University Press, 2007); Indian Council of World Affairs, *India and the United Nations* (New York: Manhattan Publishing Company for the Carnegie Endowment for International Peace, 1957), 3–12; Fredrik Petersson, "Hub of the Anti-imperialist Movement: The League against Imperialism and Berlin, 1927–1933," *Interventions: International Journal of Postcolonial Studies* 16, no. 1 (2014): 49–71; Alan McPherson, "Anti-imperialism and the Failure of the League of Nations," in *Beyond Geopolitics*, 21–32.

24. Davies, *NGOs*, 81, 83–84; David Hunter Miller, *The Drafting of the Covenant* (New York: G. P. Putnam's Sons, 1928), 1: iii, 273, 2: 361–62, 725, 739; Rupp, *Worlds of Women*, 29–30, 207–22; Théodore Ruyssen, *The League of Nations Societies and Their International Federation: Raison d'être, Activities, Results* (Brussels: International Federation of League of Nations Societies, 1930); Birn, *League of Nations Union*; Thomas Richard Davies, "Internationalism in a Divided World: The Experience of the International Federation of League of Nations Societies, 1919–1939," *Peace & Change* 37, no. 2 (April 2012): 227–52.

25. London housed the League Secretariat (its permanent office and staff) until it moved permanently to Geneva, Switzerland, ten months later. Thanks to Swiss lobbying and the sense that Geneva was less tied to memories of the Great War, the Secretariat occupied a couple of temporary locations before moving into its new, permanent League building in 1936 with the help of a $5 million gift from John D. Rockefeller.

26. Ostrower, *League of Nations*, 15–16; F. P. Walters, *A History of the League of Nations*, 2 vols (Oxford: Oxford University Press, 1952), 170–75; Reinalda, *Routledge History of International Organizations*, 200–202; S. Rosenne, *The World Court: What It Is and How It Works*, 4th rev. ed. (Dodrecht, Netherlands: Martinus Nijhoff, 1989).

27. Ostrower, *League of Nations*, xv–xvi; William O. Walker III, *Opium and Foreign Policy: The Anglo-American Search for Order in Asia, 1912–1954* (Chapel Hill: University of North Carolina Press, 1991), 21, 26, 28–29, 21–40; Paul Weindling, ed., *International Health Organisations and Movements, 1918–1939* (Cambridge: Cambridge University Press, 1995); Norman Howard-Jones, *International Public Health between the Two Worlds Wars: The Organizational Problems* (Geneva: World Health Organization, 1978). There is very little discussion about who was responsible for integrating these tasks into the covenant or why. The aspiring researcher might well investigate the role of domestic and international organizations as well as the relative role of the Great Powers and the smaller powers at the Paris Peace Conference on matters outside of what the leaders of the Entente considered to be the most important parts of the treaty.

28. Pedersen, *The Guardians*, 1, 2. See also Quincy Wright, *Mandates under the League of Nations* (Chicago: University of Chicago Press, 1930), 26–34; Ralph Wilde, "Trusteeship Council," in *The Oxford Handbook on the United Nations*, ed. Thomas G. Weiss and Sam

Daws (Oxford: Oxford University Press, 2007), 150, 152–53; League Covenant Article 22, para. 4–6.

29. The first generation of historians writing about the ILO primarily put it within the realm of international relations and focused on its anticommunist origins. Oddly enough, this historiography did not influence the well-established diplomatic history literature that casts the Paris Peace Conference as an ideological battle embodied in the very present Wilson and the absent-but-looming Vladimir Lenin, leader of the new Soviet Union. Not surprisingly, other historians more versed in the history of labor organization have identified a variety of ILO antecedents and have sought to expand the historical context of the new international organization, looking at early efforts to provide international protection for labor, the development of international trade unionism, the work of the First and Second Workers' Internationals, and the development of the International Co-operative Alliance (which sought to put the means of production into the hands of the workers within an overarching framework of democratic government). See John W. Follows, *Antecedents of the International Labour Organization* (Oxford: Clarendon Press, 1951); James T. Shotwell, ed., *The Origins of the International Labor Organization*, vol. 1: *History* (New York: Columbia University Press for the Carnegie Endowment for International Peace, 1934), xx; Jasmien Van Daele, "Writing ILO Histories: A State of the Art," in *ILO Histories: Essays on the International Labour Organization and Its Impact on the World during the Twentieth Century*, ed. Jasmien Van Daele, Magaly Rodriguez García, Geert Van Goethem, and Marcel van der Linden (Bern: Peter Lang, 2010), 13–39, which provide us with a historiography for the ILO.

30. Elizabeth McKillen, *Making the World Safe for Workers: Labor, the Left, and Wilsonian Internationalism* (Urbana: University of Illinois Press, 2013), esp. 181–240; Antony Alcock, *History of the International Labor Organization* (New York: Octagon Books, 1971), esp. 1–46; Walters, *History of the League*, 194–97; Shotwell, *Origins of the ILO*, 1: xxi.

31. Alcock, *History of the ILO*; E. A. Landy, *The Effectiveness of International Supervision: Thirty Years of I.L.O. Experience* (London: Stevens & Sons, 1966); Victor Yves Ghebali, *The International Labour Organisation: A Case Study on the Evolution of U.N. Specialised Agencies* (Dordrecht, Netherlands: Martinus Nijhoff, 1989).

32. As quoted in Lyman Cromwell White, *International Non-governmental Organizations: Their Purposes, Methods, and Accomplishment* (New Brunswick, NJ: Rutgers University Press, 1951), 36. See also Davies, *NGOs*, 85; Jean-Jacques Oechalin, *The International Organisation of Employers: Three-Quarters of a Century in the Service of the Enterprise, 1920–1998* (Geneva: IOE, 2001).

33. Susan Pedersen's recent history of the League of Nations' Mandates Commission reminds us that "the League cannot be treated as if it were a state, possessed of a clear decision-making structure and coercive power," and then suggests that "it is better understood as a force field [made up of the Assembly, the Council, and the Secretariat], one made up of shifting alliances, networks, and institutions, which a host of actors entered and sought to exploit" (*The Guardians*, 5).

34. Pedersen, *The Guardians*, 5–6; Walters, *History of the League*, 297. See also Isabella Löhr and Roland Wenzlhuemer, *The Nation State and Beyond: Governing Globalization Processes in the Nineteenth and Early Twentieth Centuries* (Heidelberg, Germany: Springer, 2013).

35. Pedersen, *The Guardians*, 6–7. See also William E. Rappard, *The Geneva Experiment* (London: Oxford University Press, 1931).

36. Pedersen, *The Guardians*, 7–8. See also Egon F. Ranshofen-Wertheimer, *The International Secretariat: A Great Experiment in International Administration* (Washington, DC: Carnegie Endowment for International Peace, 1945); Walters, *History of the League*, 75–80, 556; Kuehl and Dunn, *Keeping the Covenant*.

37. Donald Page, "The Institute's 'Popular Arm': The League of Nations Society in Canada," *International Journal* 33, no. 1 (Winter 1977/1978): 29. See also ibid., 28–65; Pedersen, *The Guardians*, 8; Walters, *History of the League*, 199–202; Davies, "Internationalism in a Divided World"; Helen McCarthy, *The British People and the League of Nations: Democracy, Citizenship and Internationalism, c. 1918–45* (Manchester, UK: Manchester University Press, 2011).

38. For the League's spectacular diplomatic failures, see, for example, Walters, *History of the League*, 201, 440–45, 500–16, 623–91, 777–800; Henig, *League of Nations*, 105–27, 134–73; Thomas Richard Davies, *The Possibilities of Transnational Activism: The Campaign for Disarmament between the Two World Wars* (Leiden, Netherlands: Martinus Nijhoff Publishers, 2007), 73–148; Christopher Thorne, *The Limits of Foreign Policy: The League, the West and the Far Eastern Crisis of 1931–33* (London: Hamish Hamilton, 1972); George W. Baer, *Test Case: Italy, Ethiopia and the League of Nations* (Stanford, CA: Hoover Institution Press, 1976). For some of its relatively minor diplomatic successes, see Henig, *League of Nations*, 69, 70, 72, 86–94; Walters, *History of the League*, 86–112, 152–61, 171–73, 239–55, 311–15, 792–97; J. Barros, *The Åland Islands Question: Its Settlement by the League of Nations* (New Haven, CT: Yale University Press, 1968); idem, *The Corfu Incident of 1923: Mussolini and the League of Nations* (Princeton, NJ: Princeton University Press, 1965); idem, *The League of Nations and the Great Powers: The Greek–Bulgarian Incident, 1925* (Oxford: Oxford University Press, 1970); Claudena M. Skran, *Refugees in Inter-War Europe: The Emergence of a Regime* (Oxford: Clarendon Press, 1995); Pedersen, *The Guardians*, 2–4, 9–11, 195–203, 427–28n24; Carole Fink, *Defending the Rights of Others: The Great Powers, the Jews, and International Minority Protection, 1878–1938* (Cambridge: Cambridge University Press, 2004).

39. Walters, *History of the League*, 177–78, 205–10; Patricia Clavin, *Securing the World Economy: The Reinvention of the League of Nations, 1920–1946* (Oxford: Oxford University Press, 2013); Christopher Peacock, "The Postal History of ICAO: The 1919 Paris Convention: The Starting Point for the Regulation of Air Navigation," ICAO, last modified January 22, 2015, http://www.icao.int/secretariat/PostalHistory/1919_the_paris_convention.htm; UNESCO, "Guide to Archives of International Organizations: ICAO: International Civil Aviation Organization: History: Origins and Process of Creation," accessed February 25, 2015, http://www.unesco.org/archives/sio/Eng/presentation_short.php?idOrg=1015.

40. Warren C. Waite and John D. Black, "Nutrition and Agricultural Policy," *Annals of the American Academy of Political and Social Science* 188 (November 1936): 220; Staples, *Birth of Development*, 72–74, 129–32; Walters, *History of the League*, 180–83, 186–87, 749–50, 756–58; Amelia M. Kiddle, "Separating the Political from the Technical: The 1938 League of Nations Mission to Latin America," in *Beyond Geopolitics: New Histories of Latin America at the League of Nations*, ed. Alan McPherson and Yannick Wehrli (Albuquerque: University of New Mexico Press, 2015), 239–57; League of Nations, *Ten Years of World Co-operation* (London: Hazell, Watson and Viney for League Secretariat, 1930), 236–41, 245–60; David Dubin, "The League of Nations Health Organisation," and Lenore Manderson, "Wireless Wars in the Eastern Arena: Epidemiological Surveillance, Disease Prevention and the Work of the Eastern Bureau of the League of Nations Health Organisation, 1925–1942," both in *International Health Organisations and Movements, 1918–1939*, ed. Paul Weindling (Cambridge: Cambridge University Press, 1995), 59–60, 63–69, 72–73, 109–33; Michael Worboys, "The Discovery of Colonial Malnutrition between the Wars," in *Imperial Medicine and Indigenous Societies*, ed. David Arnold (Manchester: Manchester University Press, 1988), 208–23; Barbara H. M. Metzger, "Towards an International Human Rights Regime during the Inter-War Years: The League of Nations' Combat of Traffic in Women and Children," and Kevin Grant, "Human Rights and Sovereign Abolitions of

Slavery, c. 1885–1950," both in *Beyond Sovereignty: Britain, Empire and Transnationalism, c. 1880–1950*, ed. Kevin Grant, Philippa Levine, and Frank Trentmann (London: Palgrave Macmillan, 2007), 54–79, 80–102.

41. Walters, *History of the League*, 753–55, 758–62; Martin David Dubin, "Toward the Bruce Report: The Economic and Social Programmes of the League of Nations in the Avenol Era," in *The League of Nations in Retrospect* (Berlin: W. De Gruyter, 1983), 42–72.
42. David L. Bosco, *Five to Rule Them All: The UN Security Council and the Making of the Modern World* (New York: Oxford University Press, 2009), 12; Walters, *History of the League*, 809–10; Gerard Keown, "Seán Lester: Journalist, Revolutionary, Diplomat, Statesman," *Irish Studies in International Affairs* 23 (2012): 143–54; Clavin, *Securing the World Economy*.
43. As quoted in Bosco, *Five to Rule Them All*, 13. See also ibid., 13–21; Staples, *Birth of Development*, 12–17, 76–81, 132–36; *Agreement between the United Nations and the Universal Postal Union* (Lake Success, NY: United Nations, 1949); Szeming Sze, *The Origins of the World Health Organization: A Personal Memoir, 1945–1948* (Boca Raton, FL: LISZ, 1982), 1–9, 27; Walter R. Sharp, *The United Nations Economic and Social Council* (New York: Columbia University Press, 1969).
44. Charlene Mires, *Capital of the World: The Race to Host the United Nations* (New York: New York University Press, 2013), 1, 5. See also Bosco, *Five to Rule Them All*, 39.

Chapter 3

1. Manela, *Wilsonian Moment*; Frank Moraes, *Jawaharlal Nehru* (Mumbai, India: Jaico Publishing House, 2008), 234–38, 266; Manu Bhagavan, *The Peacemakers: India and the Quest for One World* (Noida: HaperCollins Publishers India, 2012).
2. Gaiduk, *Divided Together*, 21–23, 26, 28–30, 35, 43–47, 49–50; Bosco, *Five to Rule Them All*, 13–38; Robert C. Hilderbrand, *Dumbarton Oaks: The Origins of the United Nations and the Search for Postwar Security* (Chapel Hill: University of North Carolina Press, 1990), 135; Schlesinger, *Act of Creation*, 202; United Nations, "Dumbarton Oaks and Yalta," accessed June 30, 2015, http://www.un.org/en/aboutun/history/dumbarton_yalta.shtml; United Nations, "San Francisco Conference," accessed June 30, 2015, http://www.un.org/en/aboutun/history/sanfrancisco_conference.shtml.
3. Bosco, *Five to Rule Them All*, 2, 5–7. See also E. R. Appathurai, "Permanent Missions in New York," in *Diplomacy at the UN*, ed. G. R. Berridge and A. Jennings (New York: St. Martin's Press, 1985), 94–108; Mazower, *Governing the World*, 3–12; Gaiduk, *Divided Together*.
4. The work of the General Assembly is currently divided into six committees: First Committee—Disarmament and International Security; Second Committee—Economic and Financial (focus on economic development); Third Committee—Social, Humanitarian, and Cultural; Fourth Committee—Special Political and Decolonization; Fifth Committee—Administrative and Budgetary (organizational concerns); and Sixth Committee—Legal (development of international law). General Assembly of the United Nations, "Main Committees," accessed July 2, 2015, http://www.un.org/en/ga/maincommittees/index.shtml. See also M. J. Peterson, "General Assembly," in *The Oxford Handbook on the United Nations*, ed. Thomas G. Weiss and Sam Daws (Oxford: Oxford University Press, 2007), 97–100; Anderson, *Eyes off the Prize*; idem, *Bourgeois Radicals*.
5. Peterson, "General Assembly," 97–98. Works documenting the hard work of shaping the decolonization agenda in the General Assembly include Anderson, *Bourgeois Radicals*; Chamberlain, *The Global Offensive*; Connelly, *Diplomatic Revolution*.

6. Of the 14,000+ total U.N. Secretariat staff members in mid-2005, just 3,000 held professional posts, with the rest constituting general service staff and project personnel. By way of comparison, the U.S. State Department website states that the American Foreign Service has 13,000 U.S. employees, who are supplemented by the work of 45,000 locally employed personnel in its overseas posts (U.S. Department of State, "Careers Representing America: Mission," accessed July 9, 2015, http://careers.state.gov/learn/what-we-do/mission).

   A concise summary of each secretary-general is available at United Nations, "Former Secretaries-General," accessed June 20, 2015, http://www.un.org/sg/formersgs.shtml. For the U.N. Secretariat in general, see James O. C. Jonah, "Secretariat: Independence and Reform," in *Oxford Handbook on the U.N.*, 160–74; Earl Sullivan, "Introduction: The Role of International Secretariats," John Mathiason, "International Secretariats: Diplomats or Civil Servants?" Ramesh Thakur, "Multilateral Diplomacy and the United Nations: Global Governance Venue or Actor?" all in *The New Dynamics of Multilateralism: Diplomacy, International Organizations, and Global Governance*, ed. James P. Muldoon Jr., JoAnn Fagot Aviel, Richard Reitano, and Earl Sullivan (Boulder, CO: Westview Press, 2011), 227–36, 237–48, 249–66. See also Brian Urquhart, *Dag Hammarskjöld* (New York: Alfred A. Knopf, 1972), 59–64, 72, 76; Dag Hammarskjöld Library, "Research Guide: Dag Hammarskjöld," last modified January 21, 2016, http://research.un.org/en/hammarskjold.

7. Schlesinger, *Act of Creation*, 13, 50–51, 60–61, 233; Peterson, "General Assembly," 104–105; W. Averell Harriman and Elie Abel, *Special Envoy to Churchill and Stalin, 1941–1946* (New York: Random House, 1975), 440–42.

8. As quoted in Schlesinger, *Act of Creation*, 98. See also ibid., 98–100.

9. Ibid., 79–80, 99–100, 166–67, 232–35; Thomas Campbell and George Herring, eds., *The Diaries of Edward R. Stettinius, Jr., 1943–1946* (New York: F. Watts, 1974), 319–21; Brian Urquhart, *Ralph Bunche: An American Life* (New York: W. W. Norton, 1993), 116–18, 122; Ralph Wilde, "Trusteeship Council," *Oxford Handbook on the U.N.*, 149, 153, 156–57; Anderson, *Eyes off the Prize*; Evan Luard, *A History of the United Nations, vol. 1: The Years of Western Domination, 1945–1955* (New York: St. Martin's, 1982), 59–62; United Nations, "Namibia—UNTAG: Background," accessed July 18, 2015, http://www.un.org/en/peacekeeping/missions/past/untagS.htm.

   The U.N. Trust Territories: (1) the former British mandate of Togoland united with the British colony of Gold Coast in 1957 to become the independent nation of Ghana; (2) the former French mandate of Togoland became the independent nation of Togo in 1960; (3) the former Italian colony of Somaliland united with the British protectorate of Somaliland in 1960 to become the independent nation of Somalia; (4) the mandate of the French Cameroons became the independent nation of Cameroon in 1960; (5) in 1961, the northern section of the mandate of the British Cameroons joined Nigeria, and the southern section joined Cameroon; (6) in 1961, the British mandate of Tanganyika received its independence, and then in 1964 it united with the former British protectorate of Zanzibar to form the United Republic of Tanzania; (7) the Belgian mandate of Ruanda-Urundi was divided into the independent countries of Rwanda and Burundi in 1962; (8) New Zealand's mandate of Western Samoa gained its independence as Samoa in 1962; (9) the Australian mandate of Nauru gained its independence in 1968; (10) the Australian mandate of New Guinea united with the colony of Paua in 1975 to form the independent state of Papua New Guinea; (11) the former Japanese mandates that became the U.S. Strategic Trust Territory of the Pacific Islands evolved into the Federated States of Micronesia in 1990, the Republic of the Marshall Islands in 1990, the U.S. commonwealth of the Northern Mariana Islands in 1990, and Palau in 1994.

10. United Nations, "Resolutions Adopted on the Reports of the First Committee: Establishment of a Commission to Deal with the Problems Raised by the Discovery of Atomic Energy," accessed June 30, 2015, http://daccess-dds-ny.un.org/doc/RESOLUTION/GEN/

NR0/032/52/IMG/NR003252.pdf?OpenElement. Despite the U.N. General Assembly resolution, the question quickly stalemated given the rising distrust between the Soviets and Americans—see Gaiduk, *Divided Together*, 95; David Holloway, *Stalin and the Bomb: The Soviet Union and Atomic Energy, 1939–1956* (New Haven, CT: Yale University Press, 1994); Campbell Craig and Sergey Radchenko, *The Atomic Bomb and the Origins of the Cold War* (New Haven, CT: Yale University Press, 2008). The International Atomic Energy Agency (IAEA) came into being only in 1957, born of Eisenhower's "Atoms for Peace" address to the General Assembly on December 8, 1953, and the IAEA statute approved in October 1956. Under the terms of that agreement, the IAEA conducts its activities in accordance with the U.N. Charter's goals of promoting peace and international cooperation, and the IAEA director-general is a member of the U.N. Chief Executive Board, regularly participating in these meetings, which are chaired by the secretary-general. See also Gaiduk, *Divided Together*, 50–56, 100–101; Bosco, *Five to Rule Them All*, 40–41; United Nations, "History of the United Nations, 1941–1950," accessed June 30, 2015, http://www.un.org/en/aboutun/history/1941-1950.shtml.

11. Gaiduk, *Divided Together*.
12. As quoted in ibid., 86. See also ibid., 56–71; Bosco, *Five to Rule Them All*, 43–45; Louise L'Estrange Fawcett, *Iran and the Cold War: The Azerbaijan Crisis of 1946* (New York: Cambridge University Press, 1992); Bruce Kuniholm, *The Origins of the Cold War in the Near East: Great Power Conflict and Diplomacy in Iran, Turkey, and Greece* (Princeton, NJ: Princeton University Press, 1980); Vladimir Pechatnov, *The Allies Are Pressing on You to Break Your Will: Foreign Policy Correspondence between Stalin and Molotov and Other Members of the Politburo, September 1945–December 1946* (Washington, DC: Woodrow Wilson International Center for Scholars, 1999), http://www.wilsoncenter.org/sites/default/files/ACFB29.PDF.
13. As quoted in Ross N. Berkes and Mohinder S. Bedi, *The Diplomacy of India: Indian Foreign Policy in the United Nations* (Stanford, CA: Stanford University Press, 1958), 2. See also Gaiduk, *Divided Together*, 101–108, 111–17; Thanasis D. Sfikas, "Britain, the United States and the Soviet Union in the United Nations Commission of Investigation in Greece, January–May 1947," *Contemporary European History* 2, no. 3 (November 1993): 243–63; Edward Johnson, "Early Indications of Freeze: Greece, Spain and the United Nations, 1946–47," *Cold War History* 6, no. 1 (February 2006): 49; Dean Acheson, *Present at the Creation* (New York: W. W. Norton, 1969), 247; Peterson, "General Assembly," 103; George T. Mazuzan, *Warren R. Austin at the UN, 1946–1953* (Kent, OH: Kent State University Press, 1977), 137–39; United Nations, *Yearbook of the United Nations, 1947–48* (New York: U.N. Department of Public Information, 1949), 75, 89; *Yearbook of the United Nations, 1948–49* (New York: U.N. Department of Public Information, 1950), 336–37, 343–44—all U.N. yearbooks are available online at http://unyearbook.un.org/.
14. Peterson, "General Assembly," 99; Berkes and Bedi, *Diplomacy of India*, 21, 25, 29; South African History Online (SAHO), "United Nations and Apartheid Timeline, 1946–1994," accessed June 6, 2015, http://www.sahistory.org.za/topic/united-nations-and-apartheid-timeline-1946-1994.
15. As quoted in Anderson, *Bourgeois Radicals*, 216, 219. See also ibid., 204–25; Anne L. Foster, "Avoiding the 'Rank of Denmark': Dutch Fears about Loss of Empire in Southeast Asia," in *Connecting Histories: Decolonization and the Cold War in Southeast Asia, 1945–1962* (Washington, DC: Woodrow Wilson Center Press, 2009), 75; Robert J. McMahon, *Colonialism and Cold War: The United States and the Struggle for Indonesian Independence, 1945–49* (Ithaca, NY: Cornell University Press, 1981), 133–36; Philip C. Jessup, *The Birth of Nations* (New York: Columbia University Press, 1974), 44.

16. As quoted in McMahon, *Colonialism and Cold War*, 172; as quoted in Anderson, *Bourgeois Radicals*, 226. See also Anderson, *Bourgeois Radicals*, 225–39; McMahon, *Colonialism and Cold War*, 168–205. The Good Offices Committee members represented Australia, Belgium, and the United States.

17. McMahon, *Colonialism and Cold War*, 251–303; Anderson, *Bourgeois Radicals*, 239–67; Jessup, *Birth of Nations*, 69, 86.

18. Jawaharlal Nehru, "Text of Address by Pandit Jawaharlal Nehru, Prime Minister of India, at Convocation held in his honor in Low Memorial Library, Columbia University, Monday evening, October 17, [1949] at 9:00 P.M.," Columbia University, accessed June 21, 2015, http://globalcenters.columbia.edu/mumbai/mumbai/files/globalcenters_mumbai/Nehru-1.pdf. See also Gaiduk, *Divided Together*, 108–10; *Yearbook of the United Nations, 1947–48*, 31; Berkes and Bedi, *Diplomacy of India*, 2, 26.

19. Berkes and Bedi, *Diplomacy of India*, 11. See also ibid., 2–20, 29–33, 80–81, 88, 91, 97, 100; Stanley A. Kochanek, "India's Changing Role in the United Nations," *Pacific Affairs* 53, no. 1 (Spring 1980): 48–51, 65–66; T. J. S. George, *Krishna Menon* (Bombay: Jaico Publishing House, 1966), 220–23; Michael Brecher, *Nehru* (London: Oxford University Press, 1959), 572–75. While I have emphasized the views and actions of India in the United Nations in this section, I think there is much fruitful work to be done in looking at a broad variety of countries' motives and goals in the international organization. An intriguing example of this type of work is Tommy T. B. Koh and Li Lin Chang, eds., *50 Years of Singapore and the United Nations* (Singapore: World Scientific, 2015). This collection of essays covers Singapore's interactions with most parts of the United Nations and how it and its citizens have interfaced with the organization as a whole. It provides fascinating insights and would be an interesting type of project that could be done in many different countries to enrich and deepen our understanding especially of how the United Nations works and is perceived in states that generally are not in the spotlight.

20. Gaiduk, *Divided Together*, 150. See also ibid., 126–32; Campbell and Herring, eds., *Diaries of Edward R. Stettinius*, 415; United Nations, *Permanent Missions to the United Nations* (New York: United Nations, 2011).

21. Bosco, *Five to Rule Them All*, 51–53; Acheson, *Present at the Creation*, 261–70; Philip C. Jessup, "Park Avenue Diplomacy—Ending the Berlin Blockade," *Political Science Quarterly* 87, no. 3 (September 1972): 377–400.

22. Gaiduk, *Divided Together*, 150–64; Bosco, *Five to Rule Them All*, 54; Victor S. Kaufman, "Chirep: The Anglo-American Dispute over Chinese Representation in the United Nations, 1950–1971," *English Historical Review* 115, no. 461 (April 2000): 354–77; Nancy Bernkopf Tucker, *Patterns in the Dust: Chinese-American Relations and the Recognition Controversy, 1949-1950* (New York: Columbia University Press, 1983); United Nations, *Yearbook of the United Nations,1950* (New York: Columbia University Press, 1951), 52, 422–23; Trygve Lie, *In the Cause of Peace: Seven Years with the United Nations* (New York: Macmillan, 1954), 251–53, 265–66; Wilson Center Digital Archive, "China at the United Nations," accessed July 8, 2015, http://digitalarchive.wilsoncenter.org/collection/178/china-at-the-united-nations.

23. William Stueck, *The Korean War: An International History* (Princeton, NJ: Princeton University Press, 1997), 59. See also Gaiduk, *Divided Together*, 164–72, 188n76; Bosco, *Five to Rule Them All*, 55, 58; Andrei Gromyko, *Memoirs*, trans. Harold Schukman (New York: Doubleday, 1989), 102; Sergei Goncharov, John W. Lewis, and Xue Litai, *Uncertain Partners: Stalin, Mao, and the Korean War* (Stanford, CA: Stanford University Press, 1993); Wilson Center Digital Archive, "China and the Korean War," http://digitalarchive.wilsoncenter.org/collection/188/china-and-the-korean-war; "Korean War Origins, 1945–1950," http://digitalarchive.wilsoncenter.org/collection/134/korean-war-origins-1945-1950; "Making of the Sino-Soviet Alliance,

1945–1950," http://digitalarchive.wilsoncenter.org/collection/181/making-of-the-sino-soviet-alliance-1945-1950; "Korea at the United Nations," http://digitalarchive.wilsoncenter.org/collection/130/korea-at-the-united-nations, all accessed June 30, 2015.

24. Gaiduk, *Divided Together*, 168. See also ibid., 168–69, 172–77, 180–85, 195–202; Dean Acheson, *The Korean War* (New York: Norton, 1971), 52; Richard Mason, "Containment and the Challenge of Non-Alignment: The Cold War and U.S. Policy toward Indonesia, 1950–1952," in *Connecting Histories: Decolonization and the Cold War in Southeast Asia, 1945–1962*, ed. Christopher E. Goscha and Christian F. Ostermann (Washington, DC: Woodrow Wilson Center Press, 2009), 48–51, 54–55; Bosco, *Five to Rule Them All*, 57–63; M. L. Dockrill, "The Foreign Office, Anglo-American Relations and the Korean War, June 1950–June 1951," *International Affairs* 62, no. 3 (Summer 1986): 459–76; Vladislav Zubok and Constantine Pleshakov, *Inside the Kremlin's Cold War: From Stalin to Khrushchev* (Cambridge, MA: Harvard University Press, 1997), 64; Gladwyn Jeff, *The Memoirs of Lord Gladwyn* (New York: Weybright and Talley, 1972), 234; William Stueck, *The Korean War: An International History* (Princeton, NJ: Princeton University Press, 1997), 47, 119, 139, 149, 152, 164, 169, 204–05; Kochanek, "India's Changing Role," 49, 51–52; Swadesh Rana, "The Changing Indian Diplomacy at the United Nations," *International Organization* 24, no. 1 (1970): 48–73.

25. Mires, *Capital of the World*, 210–18; Bosco, *Five to Rule Them All*, 63, 67–70; Gaiduk, *Divided Together*, 177–80, 196–97, 203–207, 238–40; James Barros, *Trygve Lie and the Cold War: The UN Secretary-General Pursues Peace, 1946-1953* (DeKalb: Northern Illinois University Press, 1989), 271–72.

26. As quoted in Connelly, *Diplomatic Revolution*, 55. See also ibid., 23, 55–56, 59–60; Marie-Claude Smouts, *La France à L'ONU: Premiers rôles et second rang* (France at the United Nations: First-tier and second-tier roles) (Paris: Presses de la Fondation nationale des sciences politiques, 1979), 146–55; Acheson, *Present at the Creation*, 638–39.

27. Non-Aligned Movement, "Background: The Non-Aligned Movement: Description and History," Republic of South African Government Communication and Information System, accessed June 30, 2015, http://www.nam.gov.za/background/history.htm; U.S. Department of State, Office of the Historian, "Bandung Conference (Asian-African Conference), 1955," accessed June 30, 2015, https://history.state.gov/milestones/1953-1960/bandung-conf; Mason, "Containment and the Challenge of Non-Alignment." For primary sources, see Wilson Center Digital Archive, "Bandung Conference, 1955," accessed June 30, 2015, http://digitalarchive.wilsoncenter.org/collection/16/bandung-conference-1955.

28. Robert Bothwell, "Foreword: Pearson's Ambiguous Legacy," in *Pearson's Peacekeepers: Canada and the United Nations Emergency Force, 1956–67*, ed. Michael K. Carroll (Vancouver, Canada: University of British Columbia Press, 2009), x; Gaiduk, *Divided Together*, 87–94, 208–15; United Nations, "Member States," accessed July 11, 2015, http://www.un.org/en/members/growth.shtml.

29. Bosco, *Five to Rule Them All*, 80–81, 83, 86–87, 101; Gaiduk, *Divided Together*, 215–21; Peterson, "General Assembly," 104; *Khrushchev in New York: A Documentary Record of Nikita S. Khrushchev's Trip to New York, September 19th to October 13th, 1960, including All His Speeches and Proposals and News Conferences* (New York: Crosscurrents Press, 1960).

30. Connelly, *Diplomatic Revolution*, 89, 92–96, 101, 110, 113–16, 119–21, 125–30; United Nations, "Member States," accessed July 11, 2015, http://www.un.org/en/members/growth.shtml; Stephan Bernard, *The Franco-Moroccan Conflict, 1943–1956* (New Haven, CT: Yale University Press, 1968), 317–18; Mohamed Alwan, *Algeria before the United Nations* (New York: Robert Speller, 1959), 27–28; "France Retracts on Atrocity Film," *New York Times*, December 31, 1955.

31. Connelly, *Diplomatic Revolution*, 212, 279. See also ibid., 184, 198–99, 205, 208, 229–34, 278–80; Wilson Center Digital Archive, "The Algerian Revolution and the Communist Bloc," accessed June 30, 2015, http://digitalarchive.wilsoncenter.org/collection/229/the-algerian-revolution-and-the-communist-bloc.

32. Yassin el-Ayouty, *The United Nations and Decolonization: The Role of Afro-Asia* (Hague: Martinus Nijhoff, 1971), 141; U.N., "The United Nations and Decolonization: Main Documents: Declaration on the Granting of Independence to Colonial Countries and Peoples Adopted by General Assembly Resolution 1514 (XV) of 14 December 1960," accessed July 10, 2015, http://www.un.org/en/decolonization/declaration.shtml.

33. U.N., "General Assembly Resolution 1654 (XVI): The Situation with Regard to the Implementation of the Declaration on the Granting of Independence to Colonial Countries and Peoples," accessed July 10, 2015, http://www.un.org/en/ga/search/view_doc.asp?symbol=A/RES/1654(XVI); U.N., "General Assembly Resolution 1541 (XV): Principles Which Should Guide Members in Determining whether or Not an Obligation Exists to Transmit the Information Called for under Article 73 e of the Charter," accessed July 10, 2015, http://www.un.org/en/ga/search/view_doc.asp?symbol=A/RES/1541(XV). See also Hollis W. Barber, "Decolonization: The Committee of Twenty-Four," *World Affairs* 138, no. 2 (Fall 1975): 138; Permanent Mission of India to the UN, "Introduction," accessed July 13, 2015, https://www.pminewyork.org/pages.php?id=1981; Peterson, "General Assembly," 105; el-Ayouty, *United Nations and Decolonization*. For the Committee of 24 and its intersection with international law specifically, see Barber, "Decolonization," 128–51.

34. Yassin el-Ayouty, "The United Nations and Decolonisation, 1960–1970," *Journal of Modern African Studies* 8, no. 3 (October 1970): 463–64, 466.

35. Bosco, *Five to Rule Them All*, 89–92; Michael Beschloss, *Mayday: Eisenhower, Khrushchev, and the U-2 Affair* (New York: Harper & Row, 1986); Kenneth Osgood, *Total Cold War: Eisenhower's Secret Propaganda Battle at Home and Abroad* (Lawrence: University Press of Kansas, 2006); Laura A. Belmonte, *Selling the American Way: U.S. Propaganda and the Cold War* (Philadelphia: University of Pennsylvania Press, 2008); Kathryn C. Statler and Andrew L. Johns, eds., *The Eisenhower Administration, the Third World, and the Globalization of the Cold War* (Lanham, MD: Rowman & Littlefield, 2006); Walter Johnson, Carol Evans, and C. Eric Sears, eds., *The Papers of Adlai Stevenson*, vol. VIII: *Ambassador to the United Nations, 1961–1965* (Boston: Little, Brown, 1979).

36. Dean Rusk, *As I Saw It* (New York: Penguin, 1991), 236. See also Bosco, *Five to Rule Them All*, 92–98; Michael Dobbs, *One Minute to Midnight: Kennedy, Khrushchev, and Castro on the Brink of Nuclear War* (New York: Knopf, 2008), 131. Primary sources include Wilson Center Digital Archive, "Cuban Missile Crisis," accessed June 30, 2015, http://digitalarchive.wilsoncenter.org/collection/31/cuban-missile-crisis; Dino A. Brugioni, *Eyeball to Eyeball: The Inside Story of the Cuban Missile Crisis*, ed. Robert F. McCort (New York: Random House, 1991), 318, 393–95, 426–27; Ernest May and Philip Zelikow, *The Kennedy Tapes: Inside the White House during the Cuban Missile Crisis* (New York: Norton, 2002), 403–404.

37. Bosco, *Five to Rule Them All*, 103–104; William J. Durch, ed., *The Evolution of UN Peacekeeping: Case Studies and Comparative Analysis* (London: Palgrave Macmillan, 1993), 206–36; Linda Fasulo, *Representing America: Experiences of U.S. Diplomats at the UN* (New York: Praeger, 1984), 101; Rana, "Changing Indian Diplomacy," 65–73; Kochanek, "India's Changing Role," 48, 52–54, 57–58; T. Ramakrishna Reddy, *India's Policy in the United Nations* (Madison, NJ: Fairleigh Dickinson University Press, 1968), 35–38; Lawrence A. Veit, *India's Second Revolution* (New York: McGraw-Hill, 1976), 121.

38. Bosco, *Five to Rule Them All*, 98; Piero Gleijeses, *The Dominican Crisis: The 1965 Constitutionalist Revolt and American Intervention* (Baltimore, MD: Johns Hopkins University

Press, 1978); Michael Grow, *U.S. Presidents and Latin American Interventions: Pursuing Regime Change in the Cold War* (Lawrence: University Press of Kansas, 2008); U Thant, *View from the UN* (Garden City, NY: Doubleday, 1978), 374; London School of Economics, "Chronology: Rhodesia UDI: Road to Settlement," accessed June 30, 2015, http://www.lse.ac.uk/IDEAS/programmes/africaProgramme/pdfs/rhodesiaUDIChronology.pdf; Carl Peter Watts, *Rhodesia's Unilateral Declaration of Independence: An International History* (London: Palgrave Macmillan, 2012); Nancy Mitchell, "Terrorists or Freedom Fighters? Jimmy Carter and Rhodesia," in *Cold War in Southern Africa: White Power, Black Liberation*, ed. Sue Onslow (New York: Routledge, 2009), 177–200; Andrew DeRoche, *Black, White, and Chrome: The United States and Zimbabwe, 1953 to 1998* (Trenton, NJ: Africa World Press, 2001).

39. Bosco, *Five to Rule Them All*, 99–103.

40. El-Ayouty, *United Nations and Decolonisation*, 464; African Union, "AU in a Nutshell," accessed July 18, 2015, http://www.au.int/en/about/nutshell; Rupert Emerson, *Self-Determination Revisited in the Era of Decolonization* (Cambridge, MA: Harvard Center for International Affairs, 1964), 4–5, 25–36.

41. Barber, "Decolonization," 128–34; el-Ayouty, *United Nations and Decolonisation*, 464–65; U.N. General Assembly Resolution 2621 (XXV), "Programme of Action for the Full Implementation of the Declaration on the Granting of Independence to Colonial Countries and Peoples," accessed July 10, 2015, http://daccess-dds-ny.un.org/doc/RESOLUTION/GEN/NR0/348/86/IMG/NR034886.pdf?OpenElement; General Assembly Resolution 2918 (XXVII), November 14, 1972; John P. Cann, *Counterinsurgency in Africa: The Portuguese Way of War, 1961–1974* (New York: Praeger, 1997); Jamie Miller, "Things Fall Apart: South Africa and the Collapse of the Portuguese Empire, 1973–74," *Cold War History* 12, no. 2 (May 2012): 183–204; Douglas L. Wheeler, "'May God Help Us': Angola's First Declaration of Independence: The 1951 Petition/Message to the United Nations and U.S.A.," *Portuguese Studies Review* 19, no. 1/2 (2001): 271–91.

42. Bosco, *Five to Rule Them All*, 139–40, 154; General Assembly Resolution 3111 (XXVIII), December 12, 1973; Barber, "Decolonization," 133–34; General Assembly Resolution 3112 (XXVIII), December 12, 1973; Richard Dale, *The Namibian War of Independence, 1966–1989: Diplomatic, Economic and Military Campaigns* (Jefferson, NC: McFarland, 2014); Piero Gleijeses, *Visions of Freedom: Havana, Washington, Pretoria, and the Struggle for Southern Africa, 1976–1991* (Chapel Hill: University of North Carolina Press, 2013); John Dugard, ed., *The South West Africa/Namibia Dispute: Documents and Scholarly Writings on the Controversy between South Africa and the United Nations* (Berkeley: University of California Press, 1973); el-Ayouty, *United Nations and Decolonisation*, 463, 466–67; Cedric Thornberry, *A Nation Is Born: The Inside Story of Namibia's Independence* (Windhoek, Namibia: Gamsberg Macmillan Publishers, 2004); United Nations, "Namibia—UNTAG: Background"; Wilson Center Digital Archive, "Cuba and Southern Africa," accessed June 30, 2015, http://digitalarchive.wilsoncenter.org/collection/173/cuba-and-southern-africa; Dag Hammarskjöld Library, "The United Nations Security Council and Namibia," last modified 2002, http://www.un.org/Depts/dhl/namibia/, which includes a selection of 315 U.N. documents covering the period from 1968 to 1990.

43. Bosco, *Five to Rule Them All*, 118–19; Barber, "Decolonization," 135–37; Diane Polan, *Irony in Chrome: The Byrd Amendment Two Years Later* (New York: Carnegie Endowment for International Peace, 1973); Stephen Park and Anthony Lake, *Business as Usual: Transactions Violating Rhodesian Sanctions* (New York: Carnegie Endowment for International Peace, 1973); el-Ayouty, *United Nations and Decolonisation*, 466–67.

44. As quoted in Bosco, *Five to Rule Them All*, 117. See also ibid., 99–100; el-Ayouty, *United Nations and Decolonisation*, 464; Barber, "Decolonization," 130; Andrew Boyd, *Fifteen Men*

on a Powder Keg: A History of the UN Security Council (London: Methuen, 1971), 136; Anatoly Dobrynin, *In Confidence* (New York: Times Books, 1995), 135–36.

45. Bosco, *Five to Rule Them All*, 114. See also ibid., 112–13; Peterson, "General Assembly," 97; Abdulrahmin Abby Farah, "The Council Meets in Africa," in *Paths to Peace: The UN Security Council and Its Presidency*, ed. Davidson Nicol (New York: Pergamon Press, 2015), 98–116; Dag Hammarskjöld Library, United Nations Research Guides and Resources, "6th Special Session—1974: New International Economic Order, Convened by A/9541," "7th Special Session—1975: Development and International Economic Cooperation, Convened by A/RES/3172 (XXVIII)," "10th Special Session—1978: New International Economic Order, Convened by A/RES/31/189 B," and "11th Special Session—1980: New International Economic Order, Convened by A/RES/32/174," all accessed July 18, 2015, http://www.un.org/depts/dhl/resguide/rspec_en.shtml.
46. Bosco, *Five to Rule Them All*, 120–24, 131–32, 136–37; Gaiduk, *Divided Together*, 241–44; Wilson Center Digital Archive, "Chinese Nuclear History," accessed June 30, 2015, http://digitalarchive.wilsoncenter.org/collection/105/chinese-nuclear-history.
47. Bosco, *Five to Rule Them All*, 124–25, 139; Henry Tanner, "Bhutto Denounces Council and Walks out in Tears," *New York Times*, December 16, 1971, A1.
48. Kochanek, "India's Changing Role," 48, 54–58, 60–61, 66–67; Rajan Menon, "India and the Soviet Union: A New Stage of Relations," *Asian Survey* 18, no. 7 (July 1978): 733–34; Robert S. Anderson, *Nucleus and Nation: Scientists, International Networks, and Power in India* (Chicago: University of Chicago Press, 2010); Rikhi Jaipal, "The South African Arms Embargo Debate, 1977," in *Paths to Peace*, 154–60.
49. Bosco, *Five to Rule Them All*, 140, 142–45; Seymour Maxwell Finger, "The Reagan–Kirkpatrick Policies and the United Nations," *Foreign Affairs* 62, no. 2 (Winter 1983–84): 441.
50. Bosco, *Five to Rule Them All*, 146–47; Michael J. Allen, "UNESCO and the ILO: A Tale of Two UN Agencies," *Notre Dame Journal of Law, Ethics and Public Policy* 1 (Winter 1985): 391–419; Ghebali, *International Labour Organisation*, 113–16; R. S. Jordan, "Boycott Diplomacy: The U.S., the UN, and UNESCO," *Public Administration Review* 44 (July/August 1984): 283–91.
51. Bosco, *Five to Rule Them All*, 149–52.
52. Ibid., 153–54; U.N. Security Council Resolution 644 (November 7, 1989).
53. U.N., "General Assembly Resolution 53/68: Implementation of the Declaration on the Granting of Independence to Colonial Countries and Peoples," accessed July 10, 2015, http://www.un.org/en/ga/search/view_doc.asp?symbol=A/RES/53/68; U.N. Secretary-General, "International Decade for the Eradication of Colonialism: Report of the Secretary General," A/46/634/Rev.1, December 13, 1991, http://www.un.org/en/ga/search/view_doc.asp?symbol=A/46/634/Rev.1; Oliver Turner, "'Finishing the Job': The UN Special Committee on Decolonization and the Politics of Self-Governance," *Third World Quarterly* 34, no. 7 (2013): 1193–208.
54. Bosco, *Five to Rule Them All*, 166–71, 202–06, 247.
55. Ibid., 171–72, 176–81, 185, 193–94; U.N. Department of Public Information, "United Nations Peace-Keeping: Former Yugoslavia, UNPROFOR," last modified September 1996, http://www.un.org/en/peacekeeping/missions/past/unprof_b.htm.
56. Bosco, *Five to Rule Them All*, 172–76, 181–82, 184–85; Paul Lewis, "Reined in by U.S., U.N. Limits Mission to Somalia," *New York Times*, April 26, 1992, 15; Boutros Boutros-Ghali, *Unvanquished: A U.S.-U.N. Saga* (New York: Random House, 1999), 43–44.

57. Bosco, *Five to Rule Them All*, 186–93, 196–97.
58. Ibid., 198–200, 206–15, 243; David Malone, *The International Struggle over Iraq: Politics in the UN Security Council, 1980–2005* (New York: Oxford University Press, 2006); Hans Blix, *Disarming Iraq* (New York: Pantheon, 2004).
59. Bosco, *Five to Rule Them All*, 216–20.
60. Ibid., 223–45; Bob Woodward, *Plan of Attack* (New York: Simon & Schuster, 2005), 183–84, 291; U.N. Security Council Resolution 1441 (November 9, 2002); Blix, *Disarming Iraq*; George Tenet, *At the Center of the Storm: My Years at the CIA* (New York: HarperCollins, 2007), 361, 375; Peter Stothard, *Thirty Days: Tony Blair and the Test of History* (New York: HarperCollins, 2003), 41; Heraldo Munoz, *A Solitary War: A Diplomat's Chronicle of the Iraq War* (Golden, CO: Fulcrum, 2008).
61. John Bolton, *Surrender Is Not an Option: Defending America at the United Nations and Abroad* (New York: Threshold, 2007), 309. See also Bosco, *Five to Rule Them All*, 245–48; U.N. Security Council Resolution 1718 (October 14, 2006); Arms Control Association, "Timeline of Nuclear Diplomacy with Iran: Fact Sheets & Briefs," July 2015, https://www.armscontrol.org/factsheet/Timeline-of-Nuclear-Diplomacy-With-Iran.

Chapter 4

1. Sluga, *Internationalism*, 8.
2. ECOSOC originally consisted of eighteen national members elected on a geographic basis by the General Assembly to staggered three-year terms. It expanded to twenty-seven members in 1965 and has stood at fifty-four since 1973. In the current configuration, the geographical distribution is fourteen members from Africa, eleven from Asia, six from Eastern Europe, ten from Latin America and the Caribbean, and thirteen from Western Europe and other areas.
3. Gert Rosenthal, "Economic and Social Council," in *Oxford Handbook on the U.N.*, 136–48.
4. Ibid., 143. See also ECOSOC, "About ECOSOC," accessed April 3, 2014, http://www.un.org/en/ecosoc/about/index.shtml; Peterson, "General Assembly," 105; Rosenthal, "Economic and Social Council," 141–46; Sharp, *U.N. Economic and Social Council*; Hernán Santa Cruz, *Cooperar o Perecer: El dilema de la comunidad mundial* (To cooperate or to perish: The dilemma of the world community) (Buenos Aires: Grupo Editor Latinoamericano, 1984), vol. I, esp. 95–96 and 118–28.
5. U.N., "Information and Communication and Technologies Task Force: Note by the Secretary-General," E/200/635, May 2006, http://www.un.org/en/ecosoc/docs/report.asp?id=1132; U.N., "World Summit on the Information Society: Geneva 2003—Tunis 2005," last modified 2015, https://www.itu.int/wsis/basic/faqs_answer.asp?lang=en&faq_id=88; World Economic Forum, "Annual Report of the Global Digital Divide Initiative, 2001/2002," accessed February 13, 2015, http://www.weforum.org/pdf/Initiatives/Digital_Divide_Report_2001_2002.pdf; Cheryl L. Brown, "G-8 Collaborative Initiatives and the Digital Divide: Readiness for e-Government," Proceedings of the 35th Hawaii International Conference on System Sciences, last modified 2002, http://www.hicss.hawaii.edu/HICSS_35/HICSSpapers/PDFdocuments/ETEPO06.pdf; ITU, "What Was the UN ICT Task Force?" accessed February 13, 2015, https://www.itu.int/wsis/basic/faqs_answer.asp?lang=en&faq_id=88.
6. Avalon Project, "Constitution of the International Refugee Organization, December 15, 1946," last modified 2008, http://avalon.law.yale.edu/20th_century/decad053.asp. See also

George Woodbridge, *UNRRA: The History of the United Nations Relief and Rehabilitation Administration*, 3 vols. (New York: Columbia University Press, 1950); Louise W. Holborn, *The International Refugee Organization: A Specialized Agency of the United Nations, Its History and Work, 1946–1952* (London: Oxford University Press, 1956); Amanda Bundy, "Politically in Play: UNRRA in Poland and Yugoslavia," paper presented at the annual meeting of the Society for Historians of American Foreign Relations, June 27, 2015, cited with permission; this is part of her larger dissertation project at Ohio State University tentatively titled, "There Was a Man of UNRRA: Humanitarianism, Leadership and the Cold War, 1943–1947." UNRRA established offices to coordinate operations in the Balkans, China, the Middle East, and the Southwest Pacific; procurement offices in Hawaii and Latin America; and country missions to Austria, the Balkans, Belgium, Byelorussia, Czechoslovakia, Denmark, the Dodecanese Islands, Ethiopia, Finland, France, Germany, Greece, Hungary, India, Italy, Korea, Luxembourg, Norway, the Philippines, Poland, Sweden, Switzerland, Turkey, Ukraine, and Yugoslavia. UNRRA's first director-general, Herbert Lehman, ran the organization from January 1, 1944 until March 31, 1946, followed by a short, nine-month tenure by former New York City Mayor Fiorello H. LaGuardia before Major-General Lowell P. Rooks oversaw its consolidation and demise (January 1, 1947 until September 30, 1948). See U.N. Archives and Records Management Section, "Archival Finding Aids of UN Predecessor Organizations: United Nations Relief and Rehabilitation Administration—UNRRA (1943–1948)," accessed February 20, 2015, https://archives.un.org/content/predecessor-organizations.

7. Ryan McMahon, "The Many Affiliations of the United Nations Korean Reconstruction Agency, 1951–1958," PhD diss., Ohio State University, forthcoming; Greg Donaghy, "Diplomacy of Constraint Revisited: Canada and the UN Korean Reconstruction Agency, 1950–55," *Journal of the Canadian Historical Association* 25, no. 2 (2014): 159–85.
8. Roger Normand and Sarah Zaidi, *Human Rights at the UN: The Political History of Universal Justice* (Bloomington: Indiana University Press, 2008), 282–84; Staples, *Birth of Development*, 101, 140, 153–54, 164, 170–72; Maggie Black, *Children First: The Story of UNICEF Past and Present* (New York: Oxford University Press, 1996); idem, *The Children and the Nations* (New York: UNICEF, 1986); Richard Jolly, *UNICEF (United Nations Children's Fund): Global Governance That Works* (London: Routledge, 2010).

Maggie Black, review of *UNICEF (United Nations Children's Fund): Global Governance That Works* by Richard Jolly, *E-International Relations*, last modified June 22, 2014, http://www.e-ir.info/2014/06/22/review-unicef-united-nations-childrens-fund-global-governance-that-works/, demonstrates a key historiographical divide between Jolly's focus on the organization's executives, directors, and planners and the "big ideas" that drove them and Black's focus on the staff and bureaucracy's fieldwork, focusing, for example, on the thirty-year service of E. J. R. "Dick" Heyward (eventually co-deputy executive director) rather than on Executive Director James P. Grant. She contends, "It is because of the UNICEF network on the ground that Grant managed to realise the profile of children on the international agenda and start the process that led to the adoption of the Millennium Development Goals [MDGs]. Jolly is correct in attributing to Grant the seed and germination of the MDGs. There would have been no 'global' crusade against poverty post-2000 if Grant had not earlier deployed UNICEF's country programme machinery to support childhood immunization and other components of a pro-health, anti-poverty agenda." She concludes by dismissing Jolly's argument about UNICEF's contribution to "global governance," which she sees as an elitist academic discourse that seeks to reprise "the idealism that was once attached to international effort as a morally superior alternative to nationalist enterprise and confrontation. But whatever 'global governance' is, . . . this is not what UNICEF is about. . . . For UNICEF, the primary consideration is what happens for children and families actually, where they are, in Africa, Asia, and elsewhere."

9. Staples, *Birth of Development*, 75–121; Sergio Marchisio and Antonietta di Blase, *Food and Agriculture Organization (FAO)* (Dordrecht, Netherlands: M. Nijhoff, 1991); P. Lamartine Yates, *So Bold an Aim: Ten Years of International Co-operation toward Freedom from Want* (Rome: FAO, 1955); B. R. Sen, *Towards a Newer World* (Dublin: Tycooly, 1982).

10. Office of the High Commissioner for Human Rights, "Universal Declaration on the Eradication of Hunger and Malnutrition," November 16, 1974, http://www.ohchr.org/EN/ProfessionalInterest/Pages/EradicationOfHungerAndMalnutrition.aspx; IFAD, "IFAD at a Glance," p. 2, accessed February 1, 2015, http://www.ifad.org/pub/brochure/ifadglance.pdf. See also John Andrews King, "The International Fund for Agricultural Development: The First Six Years," *Development Policy* 3 (May 1985): 3–20; FAO, "The International Conference on Nutrition," FAO Corporate Document Repository, accessed July 20, 2015, http://www.fao.org/docrep/v7700t/v7700t02.htm; FAO, "World Food Summit, 13–17 November 1996, Rome, Italy," archived copy of website, http://www.fao.org/wfs/.

11. Walters, *History of the League*, 190–94.

12. UNESCO Legal Instruments, "UNESCO Constitution," November 16, 1945, http://portal.unesco.org/en/ev.phpURL_ID=15244&URL_DO=DO_TOPIC&URL_SECTION=201.html. See also Julian Huxley, *UNESCO: Its Purpose and Philosophy* (Washington, DC: Public Affairs Press, 1947); *Many Voices, One World: Towards a New, More Just and More Efficient World Information and Communication Order* (Paris: UNESCO, 1980); Walter A. C. Haves and Charles A. Thomason, *UNESCO: Purpose, Progress, Prospects* (Bloomington: Indiana University Press, 1957); T. V. Sathyamurthy, *The Politics of International Cooperation: Contrasting Conceptions of UNESCO* (Geneva: Droz, 1966); James P. Sewell, *UNESCO and World Politics: Engaging in International Relations* (Princeton, NJ: Princeton University Press, 1975); Alcira Argumedo, "The New World Information Order and International Power," *Journal of International Affairs* 35, no. 2 (Fall/Winter 1981/1982): 179–88; UNESCO, "Milestones," accessed July 12, 2015, http://www.unesco.org/new/en/unesco/about-us/who-we-are/history/milestones/; UNESCO, "World Education Forum," accessed July 20, 2015, http://www.unesco.org/education/efa/wef_2000/. The UNESCO archives website (http://www.unesco.org/archives/new2010/index.html) provides information on the archive's holdings, suggests research strategies, and gives tips on visiting the archives in Paris.

13. ICAO member states act through the Assembly of all member states that meets every three years and the Council, currently thirty-six elected state representatives who meet between assemblies and who are elected to represent the states "of chief importance in air transport" and to provide broad geographic representation. The ICAO regional offices are in Bangkok (Asia and Pacific office), Nairobi (Eastern and Southern Africa office), Paris (European and North Atlantic office), Cairo (Middle East office), Mexico City (North American, Central American and Caribbean office), Lima (South American office), and Dakar (Western and Central African office). See International Civil Aviation Organization, "About ICAO," accessed February 25, 2015, http://www.icao.int/about-icao/Pages/default.aspx; David MacKenzie, *ICAO: A History of the International Civil Aviation Organization* (Toronto: University of Toronto Press, 2010); Eugene Sochor, *The Politics of International Aviation* (Ames: Iowa State University Press, 1991); Asaad Kotaite, *My Memoirs: 50 Years of International Diplomacy and Conciliation in Aviation* (Montreal: ICAO, 2013); ICAO, *100 Years of Civil Aviation* (Montreal, Canada: ICAO, 2003); Ludwig Weber, *International Civil Aviation Organization: An Introduction* (Alphen aan den Rijn, Netherlands: Kluwer Law International, 2007); J. Vivian, "ICAO Assistance to Civil Aviation in the Developing World," *Impact of Science on Society* 31 (July/September 1981): 305–12; Christopher Peacock, "The Postal History of ICAO: PICAO Bulletin-ICAO Bulletin," ICAO, last modified June 6, 2014, http://www.icao.int/secretariat/PostalHistory/picao_bulletin_icao_bulletin_and_journal.htm.

14. The League's Secretariat convened the First General Conference on Communications and Transit in Barcelona from March 10 until April 20, 1921. The forty-four states attending drew up two treaties—the Convention on Freedom of Transit and the Convention on the Regime of International Waterways (which remained in force until 1939)—and established a permanent organization to oversee the implementation of the terms of these and future conventions dealing with communication and transit. The resulting Communications and Transit Organization of the League of Nations was directed by Frenchman Robert Haas, but it also had provisions for the membership of non-League members (Germany was a member before its admission to the League and Brazil after it left the League). Its working committees dealt with rail transport, inland navigation, ports and maritime navigation, road traffic, and power transmission. Its 1923 Geneva Conference drafted the International Regime of Maritime Ports (as well as the International Regime of Railways) that, for example, established a common standard for the lights guiding ships into the ports. See Walters, *History of the League*, 143, 175, 178–80; Jacob Darwin Hamblin, "Visions of International Scientific Cooperation: The Case of Oceanic Science, 1920–1955," *Minerva* 38, no. 4 (2000): 393–423.
15. The IMCO grew out of the 1948 Geneva Maritime Conference, whose convention entered into force on March 17, 1959. See IMO, *1948–1998: A Process of Change* (London: IMO, 1998); Jacob Darwin Hamblin, "Gods and Devils in the Details: Marine Pollution, Radioactive Waste, and an Environmental Regime circa 1972," *Diplomatic History* 32, no. 4 (September 2008): 539–60; idem, "Environmental Diplomacy in the Cold War: The Disposal of Radioactive Waste at Sea during the 1960s," *International History Review* 24, no. 2 (June 2002): 348–75; Peter Seidel, "IMO: International Maritime Organization," in *United Nations: Law, Policies and Practice*, ed. Rüdiger Wolfrum and Christiane Philipp, vol. 1 (Dodrecht, Netherlands: Martinus Nijhoff, 1995), 734–42; Samir Mankabady, *The International Maritime Organisation* (London: Croom Helm, 1984).
16. Yves Beigbeder, *The World Health Organization* (Hague, Netherlands: Martinus Nijhoff, 1999); Staples, *Birth of Development*, 122–36; John Farley, *Brock Chisholm, the World Health Organization, and the Cold War* (Vancouver: University of British Columbia Press, 2008); Brock Chisholm, *Prescription for Survival* (New York: Columbia University Press, 1957); Sunil S. Amrith, *Decolonizing International Health: India and Southeast Asia, 1930–1965* (Basingstoke, UK: Palgrave Macmillan, 2006); Alice C. Andrews, "Worldwide Disease Eradication: Malaria and Smallpox," *Virginia Social Science Journal* 17 (April 1982): 42–51; Randall M. Packard and Peter J. Brown, "Rethinking Health, Development, and Malaria: Historicizing a Cultural Model in International Health," *Medical Anthropology* 17 (1997): 181–94; Bob H. Reinhardt, *The End of a Global Pox: America and the Eradication of Smallpox in the Cold War Era* (Chapel Hill: University of North Carolina Press, 2015); World Health Organization, "Ebola Virus Disease Outbreak," accessed April 2, 2016, http://apps.who.int/csr/disease/ebola/en/index.html.
17. J. Keith Horsefield and Margaret G. De Vries, *The International Monetary Fund, 1945–1965: Twenty Years of International Monetary Cooperation*, 3 vols (Washington, DC: IMF, 1969); Margaret G. DeVries, *The IMF, 1966–1971: The System Under Stress* (Washington, DC: IMF, 1977); International Monetary Fund, "About the IMF: Archives of the International Monetary Fund," last modified January 5, 2015, http://www.imf.org/external/np/arc/eng/archive.htm. Since its archives remained closed to scholars until 2010, there are fewer, external scholarly histories of the organization: Alfred E. Eckes Jr., *A Search for Solvency: Bretton Woods and the International Monetary System, 1941–1971* (Austin: University of Texas Press, 1975); Richard Gardner, *Sterling-Dollar Diplomacy: The Origins and Prospects of Our International Economic Order* (New York: McGraw-Hill, 1969); Richard Swedberg, "The Doctrine of Economic Neutrality of the IMF and the World Bank," *Journal of Peace*

Research 23, no. 4 (December 1986): 377–90. Works that focus on IMF-Third World relations (esp. structural adjustment programs) include Tyrone Ferguson, *The Third World and Decision Making in the International Monetary Fund: The Quest for Full and Effective Participation* (Albuquerque, NM: Pinter Publishers, 1988); Graham Bird, “The International Monetary Fund and Developing Countries: Retrospect and Prospect,” *Economist* 131, no. 2 (May 1983): 161–95; Manuel Pastor Jr., “Latin America, the Debt Crisis, and the International Monetary Fund,” *Latin American Perspectives* 16, no. 1 (Winter 1989): 79–109; Tony Killick, ed., *The IMF and Stabilization: Developing Country Experiences* (New York: St. Martin's Press, 1984); Andrew I. Schoenholtz, “The IMF in Africa: Unnecessary and Undesirable Western Restraints on Development,” *Journal of Modern African Studies* 25, no. 3 (September 1987): 403–33.

18. Traditional Bank development loans carried an interest rate of 6 percent over a fifteen- to twenty-year term. See Edward S. Mason and Robert E. Asher, *The World Bank Since Bretton Woods* (Washington, DC: Brookings Institution, 1973); International Centre for Settlement of Investment Disputes, “ICSID Convention, Regulations and Rules (as Amended and Effective April 10, 2006): Introduction,” p. 1, https://icsid.worldbank.org/ICSID/StaticFiles/basicdoc/basic-en.htm; B. E. Matecki, *Establishment of the International Finance Corporation and United States Policy* (New York: Praeger, 1957); James H. Weaver, *The International Development Association: A New Approach to Foreign Aid* (New York: Praeger, 1965); MIGA, “Who We Are: History,” accessed February 19, 2015, http://www.miga.org/whoweare/index.cfm?stid=1787; Staples, *Birth of Development*, 22–63; Gardner, *Sterling-Dollar Diplomacy*; N. D. Gulhati, *Indus Waters Treaty: A Successful Exercise in International Mediation* (New Delhi: Allied Publishers, 1972); B. K. Nehru, “The Way We Looked for Money Abroad,” in *Two Decades of Indo-U.S. Relations*, ed. Vadilal Dagli (Bombay: Vora and Company, 1969); Henri Bonnet, *Les Institutions Financières Internationales* (International Financial Institutions) (Paris: Presses Universitaires de France, 1968); A. Carlin, “Project versus Program Aid: From the Donor's Viewpoint,” *Economic Journal* 77 (March 1967): 48–58, available at http://www.rand.org/content/dam/rand/pubs/papers/2008/P3283.pdf; Frederick T. Moore, “The World Bank and Its Economic Missions,” *Review of Economics and Statistics* 42 (February 1960): 81–93; James Patrick Sewell, *Functionalism and World Politics: A Study Based on United Nations Programs for Financing Economic Development* (Princeton, NJ: Princeton University Press, 1966); Michel Chossudovsky, *The Globalisation of Poverty: Impacts of IMF and World Bank Reforms* (London: Zed Books, 1997).

19. For the IMO's early history, see Daniel, *One Hundred Years*; I. R. Tannehill, “The History and Status of the International Meteorological Organization (I.M.O.),” *Bulletin of the American Meteorological Society* 28, no. 5 (May 1947): 207–19; Frances Leigh Williams, *Matthew Fontaine Maury: Scientist of the Sea* (New Brunswick, NJ: Rutgers University Press, 1963).

20. Avalon Project, “Convention of the World Meteorological Organization, October 11, 1947,” Yale Law School Library, last modified 2008, http://avalon.law.yale.edu/20th_century/decad055.asp. A sampling of the large literature on the WMO includes Daniel, *One Hundred Years*; W. Baier, I. G. Gringof, and N. D. Strommen, *History of the Commission for Agricultural Meteorology of the World Meteorological Organization* (Geneva: WMO, 1991); WMO Commission for Climatology, *Commission for Climatology: Over Eighty Years of Service* (Geneva: WMO, 2011); Paul N. Edwards, “Meteorology as Infrastructural Globalism,” *Osiris* 21, no. 1 (2006): 229–50; Eugene W. Bierly, “The World Climate Program: Collaboration and Communication on a Global Scale,” *Annals of the American Academy of Political and Social Science* 495 (January 1988): 106–16; Dag Hammarskjöld Library, “Research Guide: Climate Change—A Global Issue,” last modified December 15, 2015, http://research.un.org/en/climate-change.

21. The ICSU, established in 1931, grew out of the earlier International Association of Academies (1899–1914) and the International Research Council (1919–31). It rebranded itself as the International Council for Science in 1998 but kept its historical acronym of ICSU. In 2015, its website noted the membership of 121 national scientific bodies and thirty-two international scientific unions. See ICSU: International Council for Science, "About ICSU," http://www.icsu.org/about-icsu/about-us, and "A Brief History of ICSU," both accessed February 17, 2015, http://www.icsu.org/about-icsu/about-us/a-brief-history; Frank Greenaway, *Science International: A History of the International Council of Scientific Unions* (Cambridge: Cambridge University Press, 1996).

22. Alan T. Waterman, "The International Geophysical Year," *American Scientist* 44, no. 2 (April 1956): 130. See also Dian Olson Belanger, *Deep Freeze: The United States, the International Geophysical Year, and the Origins of Antarctica's Age of Science* (Boulder: University Press of Colorado, 2006); Ronald E. Doel, "The Earth Sciences and Geophysics," in *Science in the Twentieth Century*, ed. John Krige and Dominique Pestre (Amsterdam: Harwood Academic Publishers, 1997), 391–416; Harold Bullis, *The Political Legacy of the International Geophysical Year* (Washington, DC: Government Printing Office, 1973); Sydney Chapman, *IGY: Year of Discovery: The Story of the International Geophysical Year* (Ann Arbor: University of Michigan Press, 1959).

23. I. Allison, M. Béland, D. Carlson, D. Qin, E. Sarukhanian, and C. Smith, "International Polar Year, 2007–2008," *WMO Bulletin* 56, no. 4 (October 2007): 244, http://public.wmo.int/en/bulletin/international-polar-year-2007-2008. See also ibid., 244–49; Igor Krupnik, Michael A. Lang, and Scott E. Miller, *Smithsonian at the Poles: Contributions to International Polar Year Science* (Washington, DC: Smithsonian Institution Scholarly Press, 2009); I. Allison et al., *The Scope of Science for the International Polar Year, 2007–2008*, WMO/TD-No.1364 (Geneva: WMO, 2007); International Council for Science International Polar Year Planning Group, *A Framework for the International Polar Year, 2007–2008* (n.p.: ICSU, 2004), http://www.icsu.org/publications/reports-and-reviews/a-framework-for-the-international-polar-ye ar-2007-2008/IPY-framework.pdf. The IPY actually stretched from March 1, 2007, until March 1, 2009, to include a complete annual cycle of observations for both poles.

24. WMO, *World Weather Watch: The Plan and Implementation Programme, 1976–1979* (New York: WMO, 1975); WMO, "World Weather Watch (WWW)," accessed February 17, 2015, http://www.wmo.int/pages/prog/www/; Hurricanes: Science and Society, "1970: The Great Bhola Cyclone," University of Rhode Island Graduate School of Oceanography, accessed February 17, 2015, http://www.hurricanescience.org/history/storms/1970s/greatbhola/; Kerry A. Emanuel, *Divine Wind: The History and Science of Hurricanes* (New York: Oxford University Press, 2005), 221–25; WMO, "Historical Background of the Tropical Cyclone Programme," accessed February 17, 2015, http://www.wmo.int/pages/prog/www/tcp/history.html; GATE (GARP Atlantic Tropical Experiment), "History of the GARP [Global Atmospheric Research Programme] Atlantic Tropical Experiment," American Meteorological Society, last modified 1998, http://www.ametsoc.org/sloan/gate/; ICSU, "ICSU and Climate Science: 1962–2006 and Beyond: From GARP to IPCC" (n.p: ICSU, June 2006), 2, accessed February 17, 2015, http://www.icsu.org/publications/about-icsu/icsu-climate-science-2006/2650_DD_FILE_ICSU_a nd_Climate_Change.pdf; Jacob Darwin Hamblin, *Oceanographers and the Cold War: Disciples of Marine Science* (Seattle: University of Washington Press, 2005).

25. Stephen O. Anderson and K. Madhava Sarma, *Protecting the Ozone Layer: The United Nations History* (London: Earthscan for UNEP, 2002); *WMO and the Ozone Issue* (Geneva: WMO, 1992); *The Changing Atmosphere: Implications for Global Security: World Conference, Toronto, Canada, June 27–30, 1988* (Geneva: WMO, 1988).

26. UN and Climate Change, "Climate Change Threatens Irreversible and Dangerous Impacts, but Options Exist to Limit its Effects," IPCC press release, November 2, 2014, http://www.un.org/climatechange/blog/2014/11/climate-change-threatens-irreversible-dangerous-impacts-options-exist-limit-effects/. See also *Proceedings of the World Climate Conference: A Conference of Experts on Climate and Mankind, Geneva, 12–23 February 1979* (Geneva: Secretariat of the WMO, 1979); ICSU, "ICSU and Climate Science"; WMO, *The Global Climate System Review* (its periodical published since 1984); W. J. McG. Tegart and Gordon Sheldon, *Climate Change: The IPCC Impacts Assessment* (Canberra: Australian Government Publication Service, 1990); J. T. Houghton and G. J. Jenkins, *Climate Change: The IPCC Scientific Assessment* (Cambridge: Cambridge University Press, 1993).

27. United Nations, "United Nations Observances, 1967," link to U.N. General Assembly, 21st Session, A/RES/2148 (XXI), on p. 24, accessed February 17, 2015, http://www.un.org/en/ga/search/view_doc.asp?symbol=A/RES/2148 (XXI). See also World Tourism Organization UNWTO, "History," accessed February 10, 2015, http://www2.unwto.org/content/history-0; Arjun Kumar Bhatia, *International Tourism Management*, rev. ed. (New Delhi: Sterling Publishers, 2001).

28. World Tourism Organization UNWTO, "Who We Are," accessed April 16, 2016, http://www2.unwto.org/content/who-we-are-0. See also Ernst Steinicke and Martina Neuburger, "The Impact of Community-Based Afro-Alpine Tourism on Regional Development: A Case Study in the Mt. Kenya Region," *Mountain Research and Development* 32, no. 4 (November 2012): 420–30; Stuart Cottrell, Philip Pearce, and Jaap Arntzen, "Tourism as an Income Earner," *Botswana Notes and Records* 39 (2008): 13–22; Frances Brown and Derek Hall, "Tourism and Development in the Global South: The Issues," *Third World Quarterly* 29, no. 5 (2008): 839–49; UNWTO, "History"; Patrick Vrancken and Kasturi Chetty, "International Child Sex Tourism: A South African Perspective," *Journal of African Law* 53, no. 1 (2009): 111–41; Eduardo Fayos-Solà, "Globalization, Tourism Policy and Tourism Education," *Acta Turistica* 14, no. 1 (July 2002): 5–12.

29. UNWTO, "History" and "Who We Are"; UNWTO, "World Tourism Organization UNWTO," last modified July 2013, http://dtxtq4w60xqpw.cloudfront.net/sites/all/files/docpdf/fichaaboutunwtoennomarc.pdf; Esther Blanco, "A Social-Ecological Approach to Voluntary Environmental Initiatives: The Case of Nature-Based Tourism," *Policy Sciences* 44, no. 1 (March 2011): 35–52; Paul Lansing and Paul De Vries, "Sustainable Tourism: Ethical Alternative or Marketing Ploy?" *Journal of Business Ethics* 72, no. 1 (April 2007): 77–85.

30. See, for example, Christopher Endy, *Cold War Holidays: American Tourism in France* (Chapel Hill: University of North Carolina Press, 2004); John Towner, "Approaches to Tourism History," *Annals of Tourism Research* 15, no. 1 (1988): 47–62; Piers Brendon, *Thomas Cook: 150 Years of Popular Tourism* (London: Martin Secker & Warburg, 1991).

31. Intellectual property in the WIPO Convention is defined as "the rights relating to: literary, artistic and scientific works; performances of performing artists, phonograms, and broadcasts; inventions in all fields of human endeavor; scientific discoveries; industrial designs; trademarks, service marks, and commercial names and designations; and protection against unfair competition." Article 2: Definitions, in WIPO, "Convention Establishing the World Intellectual Property Organization (Signed at Stockholm on July 14, 1967 and as Amended on September 28, 1979)," http://www.wipo.int/treaties/en/text.jsp?file_id=283854. See also WIPO, "WIPO: A Brief History," accessed February 17, 2015, http://www.wipo.int/about-wipo/en/history.html; WIPO, *The First Twenty-Five Years of the World Intellectual Property Organization, from 1967 to 1992* (Geneva: WIPO, 1992); Kamil Idris, *Intellectual Property: A Power Tool for Economic Growth* (Hague: WIPO, 2003); Christopher May, *The World Intellectual Property Organization: Resurgence and the Development Agenda* (London: Routledge, 2007); Michael K. Kirk, "WIPO's Involvement in International Developments,"

and Arpad Bogsch, "The World Intellectual Property Organization: Its Recent Past and its Future Plans," both in *Peace by Pieces: United Nations Agencies and Their Roles: A Reader and Selective Bibliography*, ed. Robert N. Wells Jr. (Metuchen, NJ: Scarecrow Press, 1991), 372–92; Peggy Chaudhry and Alan S. Zimmerman, *The Economics of Counterfeit Trade: Governments, Consumers, Pirates, and Intellectual Property Rights* (Berlin: Springer, 2009); Neil Netanel, *The Development Agenda: Global Intellectual Property and Developing Countries* (Oxford: Oxford University Press, 2009).

32. U.N. ECOSOC, *Rules of Procedure of the Functional Commissions of the Economic and Social Council* (New York: UN, 1983).

33. U.N. Department of Economic and Social Affairs (DESA), "Social Policy and Development Division: Commission for Social Development (CsocD)," accessed February 18, 2015, http://undesadspd.org/commissionforsocialdevelopment.aspx; "International Organizations: Summary of Activities," *International Organization* 21, no. 3 (Summer 1967): 634–38.

34. "Preliminary Report of the World Summit for Social Development, Copenhagen, Denmark, 6–12 March 1995," A/CONF.166.9, April 19, 1995, http://www.un.org/documents/ga/conf166/aconf166-9.htm. See also U.N. Social Policy and Development Division, "Results of Social Summit +5," accessed July 25, 2015, http://undesadspd.org/Home/Geneva2000/ResultsoftheSocialSummit5.aspx.

35. Devaki Jain, *Women, Development, and the UN: A Sixty-Year Quest for Equality and Justice* (Bloomington: Indiana University Press, 2005), 7, 12; Hilkka Pietilä, *Engendering the Global Agenda: The Story of Women and the United Nations* (Geneva: U.N. Non-Governmental Liaison Services, 2002), 9; Megan Threlkeld, *Pan American Women: U.S. Internationalists and Revolutionary Mexico* (Philadelphia: University of Pennsylvania Press, 2014); Ann Towns, "The Inter-American Commission of Women and Women's Suffrage, 1920–1945," *Journal of Latin American Studies* 42, no. 4 (November 2010): 779–807; Katherine M. Marino, "Marta Vergara, Popular-Front Pan-American Feminism and the Transnational Struggle for Working Women's Rights in the 1930s," *Gender & History* 26, no. 3 (November 2014): 642–60. A great website for primary sources related to this topic is Alexander Street, "Women and Social Movements, International, 1840 to Present," http://wasi.alexanderstreet.com/, last modified September 2013, which includes 4,660 sources as well as 124 links to other online resources and twenty-five scholarly essays to ground the user in the context for these primary sources.

36. Jain, *Women, Development, and the UN*, 6, 13–14, 17–19, 21–23,170n12; "Economic and Social Council (ECOSOC) Resolution Establishing the Commission on Human Rights and the Subcommission on the Status of Women, E/RES/5(1), 16 February 1946," in *The United Nations and the Advancement of Women, 1945–1996* (New York: U.N. Department of Public Information, 1996), 8, 109–10, 112, 124; Margaret E. Galey, "Women Find a Place," in *Women, Politics, and the United Nations*, ed. Anne Winslow (Westport, CT: Greenwood Press, 1995), 14; Mary Ann Glendon, *A World Made New: Eleanor Roosevelt and the Universal Declaration of Human Rights* (New York: Random House, 2002), 111–12.

37. Jain, *Women, Development, and the UN*, 6; Paul E. Bangasser, *The ILO and the Informal Sector: An Institutional History* (Geneva: International Labour Organization, 2000), http://www.ilo.int/wcmsp5/groups/public/---ed_emp/documents/publication/wcms_142295 .pdf.

38. U.N. Department of Public Information, "The Four Global Women's Conferences, 1975–1995: Historical Perspective," UN Women, May 2000, http://www.un.org/womenwatch/daw/followup/session/presskit/hist.htm.

39. Ibid. In May 2000, 165 U.N. member states were signatories to the Convention, which obligates them to report every four years "on the steps they have taken to remove obstacles they face in implementing the Convention."

40. U.N. Department of Public Information, “The Four Global Women’s Conferences, 1975–1995: Historical Perspective.”
41. Ibid.; Jain, *Women, Development, and the UN*, 9. The twelve areas laid out in the Beijing Declaration and Platform for Action that attempted to draw concrete action from governments and civil society were the feminization of poverty, education and training of women, women’s health issues, violence against women, women and armed conflict, women’s roles in the economy, women’s roles in decision-making, institutional mechanisms for the advancement of women, human rights of women, women and the media, women and the environment, and the girl child.
42. Jain, *Women, Development, and the UN*, 8.
43. Frank W. Swacker, “The Control of Narcotic Drugs and United Nations Technical Assistance,” *American Bar Association Journal* 46, no. 2 (February 1960): 182. See also ibid., 182–83; “United Nations Commission on Narcotic Drugs,” *Journal of Criminal Law and Criminology* 39, no. 3 (September–October 1948): 366–67; ECOSOC Resolution 548E (XVIII), July 12, 1954; United Nations, “Final Act of the United Nations Conference for the Adoption of the Convention against Illicit Traffic in Narcotic Drugs and Psychotropic Substances,” 1988, https://www.unodc.org/pdf/convention_1988_en.pdf. International histories of narcotic-control efforts include William O. Walker III, *Drug Control in the Americas* (Albuquerque: University of New Mexico Press, 1981); Daniel Weimer, *Seeing Drugs: Modernization, Counterinsurgency, and U.S. Narcotics Control in the Third World, 1969–1976* (Kent, OH: Kent State University Press, 2011).
44. The International Penal Commission was founded in 1872, following the First International Congress on the Prevention and Repression of Crime (London, 1872), with the mandate to collect penitentiary statistics, encourage penal reform, and host future international conferences so as to advise the participating governments on the reform of criminals, the prevention of crime, and the reform of prisons; it established a permanent office in Berne, Switzerland, in 1926 to further this work and renamed itself the International Penal and Penitentiary Commission (IPPC) in 1929. It hosted joint conferences with the League of Nations in 1925 (in Berlin), 1930 (London), and 1935 (Paris). It was dormant during the Second World War and thereafter devoted itself primarily to organizing a conference every five years. ECOSOC therefore recommended (and the U.N. General Assembly agreed on December 14, 1950) that the IPCC functions (and archives) be transferred to the United Nations, a process that was completed in 1955. The subsequent conferences were called U.N. Congresses on the Prevention of Crime and the Treatment of Offenders. A guide to their archival records (1893–1958) is available at U.N. Archives and Records Management Section, “Archival Finding Aids of UN Predecessor Organizations: International Penal and Penitentiary Commission (1893–1958),” accessed February 20, 2015, https://archives.un.org/sites/archives.un.org/files/files/Finding%20Aids/Predecessors/AG-010_IP CC.pdf.
45. The regional organizations of the U.N. Crime Prevention and Criminal Justice Network—the U.N. Asia and Far East Institute (UNAFEI, est. 1961), the U.N. Latin American Institute for the Prevention of Crime and the Treatment of Offenders (ILANUD, est. 1975), the European Institute for Crime Prevention and Control (HEUNI, est. 1982), Naif Arab Academy for Security Sciences (NAASS, est. 1982), and the U.N. African Institute for the Prevention of Crime and the Treatment of Offenders (UNAFRI, est. 1989)—were coordinated first by the U.N. Social Defense Research Institute (UNSDRI, est. 1969) and now by the U.N. Interregional Crime and Justice Research Institute (UNICRI, est. 1989). See also INTERPOL, “History,” last modified 2015, http://www.interpol.int/About-INTERPOL/History; Manuel Lopez-Rey, *A Guide to United Nations Criminal Policy* (Cambridge: Gower Publishing, 1985); Leonard P. Shaidi, “The Role of UNAFRI in the Ninth United Nations

Congress on the Prevention of Crime and the Treatment of Offenders: An Overview," *Journal of African Law* 39, no. 2 (1995): 183–87.

46. Roger S. Clark, *The United Nations Crime Prevention and Criminal Justice Program: Formulation of Standards and Efforts and Their Implementation* (Philadelphia: University of Pennsylvania Press, 1994); "United Nations General Assembly: Convention against Transnational Organized Crime; Protocol to Prevent, Suppress and Punish Trafficking in Persons, Especially Women and Children; and Protocol against the Smuggling of Migrants by Land, Sea and Air," *International Legal Materials* 40, no. 2 (March 2001), 335–53; Anne L. Clunan, "The Fight against Terrorist Financing," *Political Science Quarterly* 121, no. 4 (Winter 2006/2007): 569.

47. Michael Ward, *Quantifying the World: UN Ideas and Statistics* (Bloomington: Indiana University Press, 2004); "Counting Heads in Two Hundred Lands," *United Nations Review* 6 (May 1960): 6; Jain, *Women, Development, and the UN*, 4, 30–33, 35–40, 51–58, 73–101; *United Nations Statistical Commission: Sixty Years of Leadership and Professionalism in Building the Global Statistical System, 1947–2007* (New York: United Nations, 2007); *Statistical Journal of the United Nations Economic Commission for Europe* (published quarterly, 1982–2006; ended with vol. 23, no. 4); "Statistical Commission: Its Fifteenth Anniversary," *United Nations Review* 9 (July 1962): 34–37; Stuart A. Rice, "The United Nations Statistical Commission," *Econometrica* 14, no. 3 (July 1946): 242–50.

48. Yves Berthelot, ed., *Unity and Diversity in Development Ideas: Perspectives from the UN Regional Commissions* (Bloomington: Indiana University Press, 2004); W. R. Malinowski, "Centralization and Decentralization in the United Nations Economic and Social Activities," *International Organization* 16, no. 3 (Summer 1962): 522–24.

49. Yves Berthelot and Paul Rayment, "The ESE: A Bridge between East and West," in *Unity and Diversity in Development Ideas*, 1–50; United Nations, *Survey of the Economic Situation and Prospects of Europe* (Geneva: U.N., 1948); UNECE, "History," accessed July 25, 2015, http://www.unece.org/oes/history/history.html.

50. Leelananda de Silva, "From ECAFE to ESCAP: Pioneering a Regional Perspective," in *Unity and Diversity in Development Ideas*, 51–131; Robert W. Gregg, "The UN Regional Economic Commissions and Integration in the Underdeveloped Regions," *International Organization* 20, no. 2 (Spring 1966): 213, 220–23; ESCAP, "About ESCAP: History," accessed July 25, 2015, http://www.unescap.org/about.

51. James F. Siekmeier, *Latin American Nationalisms*, New Approaches to International History series (London: Bloomsbury Academic, 2016); Gert Rosenthal, "ECLAC: A Commitment to a Latin American Way toward Development," in *Unity and Diversity in Development Ideas*, 168–232; Gregg, "UN Regional Economic Commissions," 215–18; Towards a Dynamic Development Policy for Latin America, U.N. Document E/CN.12/680/Rev. December 1, 1963.

52. B. T. G. Chidzero, "The United Nations Economic Commission for Africa," *African Studies Bulletin* 6, no. 2 (May 1963): 5. See also ibid., 1, 3–4; Adebayo Adedeji, "The ECA: Forging a Future for Africa," in *Unity and Diversity in Development Ideas*, 233–306; Gregg, "UN Regional Economic Commissions," 224–26, 228; U.N. Economic Commission for Africa, "Overview," accessed July 25, 2015, http://www.uneca.org/pages/overview. The five regional offices are currently as follows: North African office in Rabat, Morocco; West African office in Niamey, Niger; Central African office in Yaounde, Cameroon; East African office in Kigali, Rwanda; and South African office in Lusaka, Zambia.

53. "Planning for Economic Development" and "Decentralization of the Economic and Social Activities of the United Nations and Strengthening of the Regional Economic Commissions," U.N. General Assembly Resolutions 1708 (XVI) and 1709 (XVI), both

December 19, 1961; Malinowski, "Centralization and Decentralization," 521, 524–25; Walter R. Sharp, "The Administration of United Nations Operational Programs," *International Organization* 19, no. 3 (Summer 1965): 591; Gregg, "UN Regional Economic Commissions," 208–209.

54. U.N., "Outcomes on Population," accessed April 13, 2016, http://www.un.org/en/development/devagenda/population.shtml. See also U.N. Department of Economic and Social Affairs Population Division, "About United Nations Population Division: Overview," accessed July 25, 2015, http://www.un.org/en/development/desa/population/about/index.shtml.

55. Staples, *Birth of Development*, 161–79; Thomas Zimmer, "In the Name of World Health and Development: The World Health Organization and Malaria Eradication in India, 1949–1970," in *International Organizations and Development, 1945–1990*, ed. Marc Frey, Sönke Kunkel, and Corinna R. Unger (London: Palgrave Macmillan, 2014), 126–49; Olav Stokke, *The UN and Development: From Aid to Cooperation* (Bloomington: Indiana University Press, 2009), 149; "World Population Conference, Belgrade, 1965," *Journal of the Institute of Actuaries* 92, no. 1 (June 1966): 91–96; Thomas Robertson, *The Malthusian Moment: Global Population Growth and the Birth of American Environmentalism* (New Brunswick, NJ: Rutgers University Press, 2012), 13–60, 70–72, 170–71; U.N. Population Commission, *Report of the 5th-28th Session*, periodical published 1950–94.

56. United Nations Population Fund, "About Us," accessed July 25, 2015, http://www.unfpa.org/about-us; Connelly, *Fatal Misconception*, 232, 242, 278–79, 286–93, 298–99, 302–04, 307, 311, 314–15, 334–35, 351–54, 375–76, 378.

57. Asha Nadkarni, *Eugenic Feminism: Reproductive Nationalism in the United States and India* (Minneapolis: University of Minnesota Press, 2014); Nick Cullather, "LBJ's Third War: The War on Hunger," in *Beyond the Cold War: Lyndon Johnson and the New Global Challenges of the 1960s*, ed. Francis J. Gavin and Mark Atwood Lawrence (New York: Oxford University Press, 2014), 118–40; Kristin L. Ahlberg, *Transplanting the Great Society: Lyndon Johnson and Food for Peace* (Columbia: University of Missouri Press, 2008); 106–46; P. N. Dhar, *Indira Gandhi, the "Emergency," and Indian Democracy* (New Delhi: Oxford University Press, 2000).

58. Connelly, *Fatal Misconception*, 155–327.

59. Ibid.

60. Robertson, *Malthusian Moment*.

61. United Nations Population Fund, "International Conference on Population and Development: Overview," accessed February 18, 2015, http://www.unfpa.org/icpd.

62. Laura Belmonte, *The International LGBT Rights Movement*, New Approaches to International History series (London: Bloomsbury, forthcoming). See also Patrick Kenis, "Why Do Community-Based AIDS Organizations Co-ordinate at the Global Level?" in *Private Organisations in Global Politics*, ed. Karsten Ronit and Volker Schneider (London: Routledge, 2000), 124–45; Godfrey Linge and Doug Porter, eds., *No Place for Borders: The HIV/AIDS Epidemic and Development in Asia and the Pacific* (New York: St. Martin's Press, 1997); Douglas Sanders, "Getting Lesbian and Gay Issues on the International Human Rights Agenda," *Human Rights Quarterly* 18, no. 1 (February 1996): 67–106.

Chapter 5

1. Martin Dubin, "Toward the Bruce Report," 42–72; Staples, *Birth of Development*, 72–74, 129–32; Pedersen, *The Guardians*; Pedersen, "Back to the League of Nations"; Clavin, *Securing the World Economy*.
2. Joseph Morgan Hodge, *Triumph of the Expert: Agrarian Doctrines of Development and the Legacies of British Colonialism* (Athens: Ohio University Press, 2007), 2. See also ibid., 2–3, 7–8, 13–18; Frederick Cooper and Randall Packard, "Introduction," in *International Development and the Social Sciences: Essays on the History and Politics of Knowledge*, ed. Frederick Cooper and Randall Packard (Berkeley: University of California Press, 1997), 1–41; Richard Drayton, *Nature's Government: Science, Imperial Britain, and the "Improvement" of the World* (New Haven, CT: Yale University Press, 2000), 221–68; Suzanne Moon, *Technology and Ethical Idealism: A History of Development in the Netherlands East Indies* (Leiden, Netherlands: Leiden University Press, 2013). For resistance, see Monica van Beusekom and Dorothy Hodgson, "Lessons Learned? Development Experiences in the Late Colonial Period," *Journal of African History* 41, no. 1 (2000): 29–33; Joanna Lewis, *Empire State-Building: War and Welfare in Kenya, 1925–52* (Oxford: James Currey, 2000); Monica M. van Beusekom, *Negotiating Development: African Farmers and Colonial Experts at the Office du Niger, 1920–1960* (Oxford: James Currey, 2002).
3. Hodge, *Triumph of the Expert*, 4–5, 8–13, 19–20. In 1964, Great Britain combined the Department of Technical Cooperation and the foreign aid functions of primarily the Colonial, Foreign, and Commonwealth Relations offices to establish the Ministry of Overseas Development. In October 1970, this office was incorporated into the Foreign Office and renamed the ODA.
4. Hodge, *Triumph of the Expert*, 20. See also ibid., 5–7, 12, 14–15; Frederick Cooper, "Conflict and Connection: Rethinking Colonial African History," *American Historical Review* 99, no. 5 (1994): 1516–45; Nicholas Thomas, *Colonialism's Culture: Anthropology, Travel and Government* (Princeton, NJ: Princeton University Press, 1994); Frederick Cooper and Ann Laura Stoler, eds., *Tensions of Empire: Colonial Cultures in a Bourgeois World* (Berkeley: University of California Press, 1997); Cosmos Parkinson, *The Colonial Office from Within, 1909–1945* (London: Faber and Faber, 1945), 55–56; M. P. Cowen and R. W. Shenton, *Doctrines of Development* (New York: Routledge, 1996), 56–57; Alice Conklin, *A Mission to Civilize: The Republican Idea of Empire in France and West Africa, 1895–1930* (Berkeley: University of California Press, 1997).
5. Nick Cullather, *The Hungry World: America's Cold War Battle against Poverty in Asia* (Cambridge, MA: Harvard University Press, 2010), ix, 3. See also ibid., ix–x, 1–5; Hodge, *Triumph of the Expert*, 8–11, 19.
6. Hodge, *Triumph of the Expert*, 19; Cullather, *Hungry World*, 6. See also James Ferguson, *The Anti-Politics Machine: Development, Depoliticization, and Bureaucratic Power in Lesotho* (Minneapolis: University of Minnesota Press, 1994); Daniel Speich Chassé, "Technical Internationalism and Economic Development at the Founding Moment of the UN System," in *International Organizations and Development*, 23–45.
7. Jain, *Women, Development, and the UN*, 5.
8. Ibid.; Rosenthal, "ECLAC," 168–232; Khadija Haq and Richard Ponsio, eds., *Pioneering the Human Development Revolution: An Intellectual Biography of Mahbub ul Haq* (New Delhi: Oxford University Press, 2008); Mahbub ul Haq, *The Poverty Curtain: Choices for the Third World* (New York: Columbia University Press, 1976).

9. Colombo Plan for Cooperative Economic and Social Development in Asia and the Pacific, "History," last modified 2011, http://www.colombo-plan.org/index.php/about-cps/history/; Helge Ø. Pharo and Monika Pohle Fraser, eds., *The Aid Rush: Aid Regimes in Northern Europe during the Cold War*, vol. 1 (Oslo: Oslo Academic Press, 2008); William Erath and Dirk Kruijt, "The Netherlands Development Cooperation Agency: Policies, Organization, and Implementation," and Réal P. Lavergne, "The Management of Canadian Foreign Aid: Structure, Objectives, and Constraints," both in *The Hidden Crisis in Development: Development Bureaucracies*, ed. Philip Quarles van Ufford, Dirk Kruijt, and Theodore Downing (Tokyo: United Nations University; and Amsterdam: Free University Press, 1988), 39–40, 43, 57, 62–64, 66.
10. The best historiographical article on the early historical literature on development is Nick Cullather, "Development? It's History," *Diplomatic History* 24, no. 4 (Fall 2000): 641–53. The quotation in the text is from Marc Frey, Sönke Kunkel, and Corinna R. Unger, "Introduction: International Organizations, Global Development, and the Making of the Contemporary World," in *International Organizations and Development*, 2; however they fail to cite any works that specifically fall into either the optimistic or the pessimistic "school." Elsewhere, however, they do cite William Easterly, *The White Man's Burden: Why the West's Efforts to Aid the Rest Have Done So Much Ill and So Little Good* (New York: Penguin, 2006); Dambisa Moyo, *Dead Aid: Why Aid Is Not Working and How There Is Another Way for Africa* (New York: Farrar, Straus and Giroux, 2009); Volker Seitz, *Afrika wird armregiert oder Wie man Afrika wirklich helfen kann* (Governments impoverish Africa, or how to really help Africa) (Munich, Germany: DTV, 2009) as studies that are critical of aspects of the development enterprise, especially its focus on comprehensive planning and its tendency to disregard local circumstances.
11. Some of the recent scholarship that takes a more historical view of the U.N. development enterprise includes Daniel Maul, *Human Rights, Development and Decolonization: The International Labour Organization, 1940–70* (Basingstoke, UK: Palgrave Macmillan, 2012); Sunil Amrith and Glenda Sluga, "New Histories of the UN," *Journal of World History* 19, no. 3 (2008): 251–74.
12. Canadian economist Michael Hart's *Also Present at the Creation: Dana Wilgress and the United Nations Conference on Trade and Employment at Havana* (Ottawa: Centre for Trade Policy and Law, 1995), esp. 44–45, 53–57, takes the perspective that the preparatory work on the ITO by the key Western powers was unnecessarily bogged down at the Havana Conference by demands to include commodities and other areas of key interest by the Latin American countries who had been largely closed out of the preparatory work. A very engaging counterpoint discussion emerges in Rubens Ricupero, "Preface: Nine Years at UNCTAD: A Personal Testimony," in *Beyond Conventional Wisdom in Development Policy: An Intellectual History of UNCTAD, 1964–2004*, ed. Shigehisa Kasahara, Charles Gore, and Rubens Ricupero (New York and Geneva: United Nations, 2004), xxvi–xxxiv, which argues that rather than being extraneous, these issues were central to the development of any fair and truly international trade policy and shows the existence of different economic interests before the full emergence of the Cold War and the resulting "North-South" split. Works dealing with the early history and work of GATT (which resulted from the abortive ITO) include Thomas W. Zeiler, "Opening Doors in the World Economy," in *Global Interdependence: The World after 1945*, ed. Akira Iriye (Cambridge, MA: Belknap, 2014), 212–16; Richard Toye, "Developing Multilateralism: The Havana Charter and the Fight for the International Trade Organisation, 1947–1948," *International History Review* 25, no. 2 (2003): 282–305.

13. OECD, "Convention on the Organisation for Economic Co-operation and Development," accessed March 26, 2015, http://www.oecd.org/general/conventionontheorganisationforecon omicco-operationanddevelopm ent.htm. Even before the creation of the OECD, the European members of the group created the European Development Fund through Articles 131 and 136 of the 1957 Treaty of Rome (that furthered the development of the European Union) with the goal of providing technical and financial assistance to Europe's remaining African colonies as well as some other countries with which it had historical links. The first funding cycle began in 1959, before the addition of the North American countries (Europa: Summaries of EU Legislation, "European Development Fund (EDF)," last modified June 14, 2007, http://europa.eu/legislation_summaries/development/overseas_countries_territories/r12102_en.htm).

14. Staples, *Birth of Development*, 30–37, 96–103, 140–41; Richard Jolly, Louis Emmerij, Dharam Ghai, and Frédéric Lapeyre, *UN Contributions to Development Thinking and Practice* (Bloomington: Indiana University Press, 2004), 49; Craig N. Murphy, *The United Nations Development Programme: A Better Way?* (Cambridge: Cambridge University Press, 2006), 5.

15. Colombo Plan for Cooperative Economic and Social Development in Asia and the Pacific, "History"; Sir Percy Spender, *Exercises in Diplomacy: The ANZUS Treaty and the Colombo Plan* (Sydney: Sydney University Press, 1969).

16. Murphy, *United Nations Development Programme*, 13. See also ibid., 8, 18–19; Staples, *Birth of Development*, 37–40, 84–102; Ronald A. Manzer, "The United Nations Special Fund," *International Organization* 18, no. 4 (Autumn 1964): 766–89.

17. In 1984, the ECLA changed its name to the Economic Commission for Latin America and the Caribbean (ECLAC). Rosenthal, "ECLAC," 168–94; Raúl Prebisch, *El desarrollo económico de la América Latina y algunos de sus principales problemas* (The economic development of Latin America and some of its principal problems) (Santiago: ECLA, 1949); ECLA, *Economic Survey of Latin America, 1949* (New York: United Nations Department of Economic Affairs, 1951); Enrique V. Iglesias, ed., *The Legacy of Raúl Prebisch* (Washington, DC: Inter-American Development Bank, 1993); Raúl Prebisch, "Five Stages in My Thinking on Development," in *Pioneers in Development*, ed. G. M. Meier and D. Seers (Oxford: Oxford University Press, 1984), 173–91; Octavio Rodríguez, *La teoría del subdesarrollo de la CEPAL* (ECLAC's theory of underdevelopment) (Mexico: Siglo XXI, 1981). The Central American economic integration efforts were formalized in the Central American Regime of Integration Industries, which resulted concretely in a tire plant in Guatemala and a caustic soda and insecticide plant in Nicaragua overseen by the Committee of Economic Cooperation of the Central American Isthmus (with the ECLA office staff in Mexico City serving as its secretariat). A formal multilateral trade agreement was signed in 1958, followed by a general treaty in 1960 (signed by five Central American countries) that complied with GATT requirements. For this specific effort, see Rosenthal, "ECLAC," 184–87; Isaac Cohen Orantes, *Regional Integration in Central America* (Lexington, MA: Heath, 1972), 13–35; ECLA, *Evaluación de la integración económica en Centroamérica* (Evaluation of Central American economic integration) (Santiago: ECLA, 1966).

18. However, the Non-Aligned Movement formally established itself at Belgrade in 1961. Mason, "Containment and the Challenge of Non-Alignment," in *Connecting Histories*, 39–67. Countries participating at Bandung included Afghanistan, Cambodia, Egypt, Ethiopia, Gold Coast (still a colony and soon to be Ghana), Iran, Iraq, Japan, Jordan, Laos, Lebanon, Liberia, Libya, Nepal, Pakistan, the People's Republic of China, the Philippines, Saudi Arabia, Siam, Sudan (still a colony at this time), Turkey, both Vietnams, and Yemen—see Nicholas Tarling, *Regionalism in Southeast Asia: To Foster the Political Will* (London: Routledge, 2006), 69–92; Cary Fraser, "An American Dilemma: Race and Realpolitik in the American Response to the

Bandung Conference, 1955," in *Window on Freedom: Race, Civil Rights, and Foreign Affairs, 1945–1988*, ed. Brenda Gayle Plummer (Chapel Hill: University of North Carolina Press, 2003), 115–40; Christopher J. Lee, ed., *Making a World after Empire: The Bandung Moment and Its Political Afterlives* (Athens: Ohio University Press, 2010). First-person accounts of Bandung include Richard Wright, *The Color Curtain: A Report on the Bandung Conference* (Cleveland, OH: World Publishing, 1956); Carlos P. Romulo, *The Meaning of Bandung* (Chapel Hill: University of North Carolina Press, 1956); A. Appadorai, *The Bandung Conference* (New Delhi: Indian Council of World Affairs; New York: Institute of Pacific Relations, 1955).

19. Murphy, *United Nations Development Programme*, 15.
20. John F. Kennedy, "387—Address in New York City before the General Assembly of the United Nations, September 25, 1961," American Presidency Project, http://www.presidency.ucsb.edu/ws/index.php?pid=8352&st=&st1=.
21. "United Nations Development Decade: A Programme for International Economic Co-operation (I)," A/RES/1710(XVI), http://www.un.org/en/ga/search/view_doc.asp?symbol=A/RES/1710(XVI). The 5 percent figure came from the U.N. Secretariat and was meant to prevent an increase in the relative gap between developed and developing countries. The U.N. Special Fund established its economic development and planning institutes in Latin America (1962), Africa (1963), and Asia (1964). See Jolly et al., *UN Contributions to Development*, 86, 92–93; Stokke, *UN and Development*, 137–56; U.N., *The United Nations Development Decade: Proposals for Action* (New York: UN, 1962).
22. The Development Assistance Group (est. January 13, 1960) was renamed the Development Assistance Committee (DAC) on July 23, 1961. By 2015, the OECD had twenty-nine member states; the World Bank, IMF, and UNDP as advisers; and nonmember countries or "emerging donors" (most recently China) participating in DAC's development mandate. See OECD, "Development Assistance Committee (DAC)," accessed May 22, 2015, http://www.oecd.org/dac/developmentassistancecommitteedac.htm; OECD, *DAC in Dates: The History of OECD's Development Assistance Committee*, 2006 edition, http://www.oecd.org/dac/1896808.pdf.
23. OECD, *DAC in Dates*, 3, 8–12; Matthias Schmelzer, "A Club of the Rich to Help the Poor? The OECD, 'Development,' and the Hegemony of Donor Countries," in *International Organizations and Development*, 171–95. Schmelzer argues that the OECD is understudied, especially given its importance in "making development aid a normal function of a modern state," "coordinating aid flows of the capital-exporting countries," and establishing the key "norms, standards, and benchmarks in the development field, most importantly . . . how much aid a modern industrialized country is supposed to give." He argues that political scientists, in particular, have overlooked the organization until the recent constructivist turn, because it did not fit well with realist analyses focused on international organizations with clear power to mandate governmental action (p. 172). He points to some books written by former OECD decision-makers, including Seymour J. Rubin, *The Conscience of the Rich Nations: The Development Assistance Committee and the Common Aid Effort* (New York: Harper & Row, 1966) and Helmuth Führer, *The Story of Official Development Assistance: A History of the Development Assistance Committee and the Development Co-operation Directorate in Dates, Names and Figures* (Paris: OECD, 1996). See also Peter Carrol and Aynsley Kellow, eds., *The OECD: A Study of Organisational Adaptation* (Cheltenham, UK: Edward Elgar, 2011); Richard Woodward, *The Organisation for Economic Co-operation and Development* (OECD) (New York: Routledge, 2009); Keith Spicer, *A Samaritan State? External Aid in Canada's Foreign Policy* (Toronto, Canada: University of Toronto Press, 1966); Stephen Brown, ed., *Struggling for Effectiveness: CIDA and Canadian Foreign Aid* (Montreal: McGill-Queen's University

Press, 2012); CIDA, *Taking Stock: A Review of CIDA Activities, 1970–1974* (Ottawa: Information Division of the CIDA Communications Branch, 1974).

24. For the Kennedy administration's foreign aid policies, see, for example, Randall B. Woods, "Beyond Vietnam: The Foreign Policies of the Kennedy–Johnson Administrations," in *A Companion to American Foreign Relations*, ed. Robert Schulzinger (Malden, MA: Blackwell, 2003), 330–74; Michael E. Latham, *Modernization as Ideology: American Social Science and "Nation-Building" in the Kennedy Era* (Chapel Hill: University of North Carolina Press, 2000).

25. U.N., *U.N. Development Decade; U.N., Studies in Long-Term Economic Projections for the World Economy: Aggregate Models* (New York: U.N., 1963); Berthelot, ed., *Unity and Diversity*; Jolly et al., *UN Contributions to Development*, 88–89, 91–93; U.N. Center for Development Planning, Projections, and Policies, *Some Problems of Implementation in the Private Sector of the Economy*, ECOSOC document E/AC.54/L.10, 1967; idem, *Some General Conditions for the Effective Implementation of Plans*, ECOSOC document E/AC.54/L.8, 1967.

26. Stokke, *UN and Development*, 191–92.

27. As quoted in World Food Programme, "About: History," accessed April 3, 2015, http://www.wfp.org/about/corporate-information/history. See also Stokke, *UN and Development*, 138, 251–300, 419–41; U.N., *U.N. Development Decade*; Jolly et al., *UN Contributions to Development*, 97–99; Staples, *Birth of Development*, 105–21.

28. Stokke, *UN and Development*, 138–39; Francine McKenzie, "Free Trade and Freedom to Trade: The Development Challenge to GATT, 1947-1968," in *International Organizations and Development, 1945-1990*, ed. Marc Frey, Sönke Kunkel, and Corinna R. Unger (London: Palgrave Macmillan, 2014), 156–62; Kasahara et al., *Beyond Conventional Wisdom*, xi, xxiv–xxxvii, xxxix–xl; Sönke Kunkel, "Contesting Globalization: The United Nations Conference on Trade and Development and the Transnationalization of Sovereignty," in *International Organizations and Development*, 246–49; UNCTAD, *The History of UNCTAD, 1964–1984* (New York: United Nations, 1985).

29. UNCTAD, "UNCTAD Conferences," accessed May 27, 2015, http://unctad.org/en/Pages/Meetings/UNCTAD-Conferences.aspx.

30. Ricupero, "Preface," in *Beyond Conventional Wisdom*, xii–xiii; Kunkel, "Contesting Globalization," 248–49; John Toye and Richard Toye, *The UN and Global Political Economy: Trade, Finance, and Development* (Bloomington: Indiana University Press, 2004), 219.

31. Constitution of the United Nations Industrial Development Organization, accessed February 20, 2015, http://www.unido.org/fileadmin/user_media/UNIDO_Header_Site/About/UNIDO_Constitution. pdf. See also Youry Lambert, *The United Nations Industrial Development Organization: UNIDO and Problems of International Economic Cooperation* (New York: Praeger, 1993); UNIDO, "A Brief History," accessed May 25, 2015, http://www.unido.org/en/who-we-are/history.html.

32. Murphy, *U.N. Development Programme*, 2. See also ibid., 6n7, 21; Stokke, *UN and Development*, 189–91.

33. This title—administrator—came from Hoffman's title while working on the Marshall Plan and stuck. The American appointment practice changed in 1999. See Stokke, *UN and Development*, 188, 190, 192–94, 196–97; ECOSOC Resolutions 1444 (XLVII), July 31, 1969, and 1539 (XLIX), July 28, 1970; U.N. General Assembly Resolution 2659 (XXV), December 7, 1970. Materials on the U.N. Volunteers (UNV) generally are published by the U.N., the program, or participants, but see also David Horton Smith and Frederick Elkin, *Volunteers, Voluntary Associations, and Development* (Leiden, Netherlands: Brill, 1981).

34. U Thant, *The United Nations Development Decade at Mid-Point: An Appraisal by the Secretary General* (New York: U.N., 1965), as quoted in Stokke, *UN and Development*, 141.

See also Stokke, *UN and Development*, 139, 141–43, 155–56, 191; U.N., *U.N. Development Decade*; Jolly et al., *UN Contributions to Development*, 89–97; Ibrahim H. Abdel-Rahman, "A Framework for Evaluation," and Paul Bairoch, "Trends in 1960–67 and Short-Term Perspectives on Third World Economy," both in *The First U.N. Development Decade and Its Lessons for the 1970's*, ed. Colin Legum (New York: Praeger Publishers, 1970), 4, 7–36.

35. *Proceedings of the United Nations Conference on Trade and Development: Second Session, New Delhi, 1 February–29 March 1968*, vol. I: *Report and Annexes* (New York: United Nations, 1968), http://unctad.org/en/Docs/td97vol1_en.pdf, with quotations on pp. 17, 18, 20, 23; Group of 77 at the United Nations, "First Ministerial Meeting of the Group of 77: Charter of Algiers, Algiers, 10–25 October 1967," http://www.g77.org/doc/algier~1.htm.

36. *Proceedings of the UNCTAD: Second Session*, 20, 21, 23; Kunkel, "Contesting Globalization," 248.

37. Jolly et al., *UN Contributions to Development*, 111–12; Gunnar Myrdal, *The Challenge of World Poverty* (London: Penguin Press, 1970); Bagich S. Minhas, *Planning and the Poor* (New Delhi: S. Chand, 1971); ILO, *World Employment Programme: Report of the Director-General* (Geneva: ILO, 1969); "International Development Strategy for the Second Development Decade," U.N. General Assembly Resolution 2626 (XXV), 24 October 1970, para. B.

38. R. G. A. Jackson, *A Study of the Capacity of the United Nations Development System*, 2 vols (Geneva: United Nations, 1969), 1:13. See also ibid., 1:12, 1:44, 2:423–30; Stokke, *UN and Development*, 198–203; Murphy, *U.N. Development Programme*, 1, 10, 16–17.

39. Gilbert Rist, *The History of Development: From Western Origins to Global Faith*, 4th ed., trans. Patrick Camiller (London: Zed Books, 2014), 140–42; Jolly et al., *UN Contributions to Development*, 121, 123.

40. United Nations, "Development: Outcomes on Least Development Countries," accessed March 3, 2015, http://www.un.org/en/development/devagenda/ldc.shtml; Dag Hammarskjöld Library, "Research Guide: Small Island Developing States: Quick Guide," last modified December 8, 2015, http://research.un.org/en/island. In the early 1970s, ECOSOC's Planning and Development Committee defined the LDCs as those nations with a per capita gross domestic product of less than $100 (based on the 1968 value), a literacy among those aged fifteen and below of less than 15 percent, and an industrial sector that accounted for less than 10 percent of the nation's gross income (Rist, *History of Development*, 153).

41. Khalil A. Hamdani and Lorraine Turner Ruffing, *United Nations Centre on Transnational Corporations: Corporate Conduct and the Public Interest* (London: Routledge, 2015), esp. 9–11; Karl P. Sauvant, "The Negotiations of the United Nations Code of Conduct on Transnational Corporations," *Journal of World Investment and Trade* 16 (2015): 11–87.

42. For the earlier approach, see Hollis Chenery, Montek S. Ahluwalia, C. L. G. Bell, John H. Duloy, and Richard Jolly, *Redistribution with Growth: Policies to Improve Income Distribution in Developing Countries in the Context of Economic Growth* (London: Oxford University Press, 1974); ILO, *Employment, Incomes and Equality: A Strategy for Increasing Productive Employment in Kenya* (Geneva: ILO, 1972); Jolly et al., *UN Contributions to Development*, 113, 116, 199. For the basic human needs approach, see Dag Hammarskjöld Foundation, *What Now? Another Development* (Uppsala, Sweden: Dag Hammarskjöld Foundation, 1975); Amílcar O. Herrera, Hugo D. Scolnick, Gabriel Chichilnisky, Gilberto C. Gallopin, Jorge E. Hardoy, Diana Mosovich, Enrique Oteiza, Gilda L. de Romero Brest, Carlos E. Suárez, and Luis Talavera, *¿Catastrofe o Nueva Sociedad? Modelo Mundial Latinoamericano: 30 años después* (Catastrophe or new society? The Latin American global model: Thirty years later), 2nd ed. (Ottawa: Centro Internacional de Investigaciones para el Desarrollo, 2004), which contains the first edition from 1977 as well as the 2004 analysis of the original ideas.

43. U.N., *Problems of the Human Environment: Report of the Secretary-General* (New York: U.N., 1969), 4, as quoted in Jolly et al., *UN Contributions to Development*, 125. For the

Stockholm Conference, see also, ibid., 125–26; *Stockholm Thirty Years On: Progress Achieved and Challenges Ahead in International Environmental Co-operation: Proceedings from an International Conference, 17–18 June 2002* (Stockholm: Swedish Ministry of the Environment, 2002); *Sweden and the United Nations* (New York: Manhattan Publishing Company for the Carnegie Endowment for International Peace, 1956); Bengt Sundelius, ed., *The Committed Neutral: Sweden's Foreign Policy* (Boulder, CO: Westview Press, 1989). Maurice Strong, *Where on Earth Are We Going?* (Abingdon, MD: Texere Publishing, 2001) provides a first-person account of the global environmental movement. The Canadian served as secretary-general of both the 1972 Stockholm Conference and 1992 Rio Earth Summit and as the first executive director of the U.N. Environment Programme.

44. Indira Gandhi, "Address by the Prime Minister of India," in *Evolving Environmental Perceptions: From Stockholm to Nairobi*, ed. Mostafa Kamal Tolba (London: Butterworths for the U.N. Environmental Programme, 1988), 97, 99. See also Jolly et al., *UN Contributions to Development*, 125–26; "Environment and Development: The Founex Report on Development and Environment, with commentaries by Miguel Ozorio de Almedia, Wilfred Beckerman, Ignacy Sachs, and Gamani Corea," *International Conciliation* 586 (January 1972); U.N., *Development and Environment: Report of a Panel of Experts* (Founex, 1971); United Nations, *Proceedings of the United Nations Conference on the Human Environment: Development and Environment* (New York: UN, 1972); MauriceStrong.net, "Short Biography," Manitou Foundation, last modified 2012, http://www.mauricestrong.net/index.php/short-biography-mainmenu-6; Strong, *Where on Earth?*; Karl Mathiesen, "Climate Change and Poverty: Why Indira Gandhi's Speech Matters," *Guardian*, May 6, 2014, http://www.theguardian.com/global-development-professionals-network/2014/may/06/indira-gan dhi-india-climate-change.

45. UNEP, "Declaration of the United Nations Conference on the Human Environment," accessed June 12, 2015, http://www.unep.org/Documents.Multilingual/Default.asp?documentid=97&articleid=1503. See also United Nations Environment Programme, "About UNEP," accessed March 28, 2016, http://www.unep.org/About/.

46. William G. Martin, "Conclusion: World Movement Waves and World Transformations," in *Making Waves*, 157. In the wake of Stockholm, there was a new awareness of the need to consider the environment in determining developmental goals and projects, but no real experience in doing so. As a result, even those developmental organizations that embraced the ideas of environmentalism, such as the Canadian International Development Agency, took some time to develop concrete environmental procedures and either to bring on new staff or to train existing staff. But creating an office that specialized in environmental issues, like the World Bank and USAID did early on, presented the challenge of how to weave environmental concerns into the entire organization's culture. It similarly took time and effort for recipient countries to integrate environmental ideas into their national development plans and ways of thinking (Roger B. Ehrhardt, *Canadian Aid and the Environment: The Politics and Performance of the Canadian International Development Agency* (Ottawa: North-South Institute and Halifax: Institute for Resource and Environmental Studies of Dalhousie University, 1981)).

47. S. K. Chatterjee, "The Charter of Economic Rights and Duties of States: An Evaluation after 15 Years," *International and Comparative Law Quarterly* 40, no. 3 (July 1991): 669–84, identifies sixteen different U.N. resolutions, draft conventions, and declarations as the immediate (1969–74) precedents for the Charter that ranged across issues related to monetary reform, the law of the sea, peaceful international relations, the environment, apartheid, and multinational corporations. See also Rist, *History of Development*, 150, who disdains the NIEO's goal as realizing "a long-standing dream of world capitalism: that is, to ensure continuing growth of the system as a whole by better integrating the peripheral

countries," and Craig N. Murphy, *Global Institutions, Marginalization, and Development* (London: Routledge, 2005), 103, who calls NIEO thinking "relatively conventional" and says "it responded to real problems."

48. As quoted in Kunkel, "Contesting Globalization," 246. See also 240–46, 252; M. Shamim, "The Colombo Nonaligned Summit: An Appraisal," *Indian and Foreign Review* 13 (September 1976): 15–18; "The Arusha Declaration," January 29, 1967, in Julius Nyerere, *Freedom and Socialism, Uhuru na Ujamaa: A Selection from Writings and Speeches, 1965–1967* (Dar es Salaam: Oxford University Press, 1968), 231–50; Annar Cassam and Chambi Chachage, *Africa's Liberation: The Legacy of Nyerere* (Nairobi: Pambazuka Press, 2010).
49. As quoted in Emilio O. Rabasa, "The Charter of Economic Rights and Duties of States," *Proceedings of the Annual Meeting of the American Society of International Law* 68 (April 1974): 302. See also ibid., 302–305; Kunkel, "Contesting Globalization," 250–52; Zeiler, "Opening Doors," 296–305; Chatterjee, "Charter of Economic Rights," 669–84.
50. Jolly et al., *UN Contributions to Development*, 122–23; Rist, *History of Development*, 143–44.
51. Henry Kissinger, *Years of Renewal* (New York: Simon & Schuster, 1999), 953. See also Kasahara et al., *Beyond Conventional Wisdom*, xii, xxxvii; Kunkel, "Contesting Globalization," 240; Rist, *History of Development*, 153.
52. Kunkel, "Contesting Globalization," 252–54; Jolly et al., *UN Contributions to Development*, 122–23; Colette Chabbott, "Development INGOs," in *Constructing World Culture: International Nongovernmental Organizations since 1875*, ed. John Boli and George M. Thomas (Stanford, CA: Stanford University Press, 1999), 222–48; Maggie Black, *A Cause for Our Times: OXFAM, the First 50 Years* (Oxford: Oxford University Press, 1992).
53. Jain, *Women, Development, and the UN*, 35, 45, 51.
54. Ibid., 49. See also ibid., 48–49, 55, 65–66; Galey, "Women Find a Place," 20; "Resolution IX Adopted by the International Conference on Human Rights in Teheran on Measures to Promote Women's Rights in the Modern World and Endorsing the Secretary-General's Proposal for a Unified Long-Term United Nations Program for the Advancement of Women," General Assembly document A/CONF.32/41, May 12, 1968, in *U.N. and the Advancement of Women*, 177–79; Margaret Snyder and Mary Tadesse, *African Women and Development: A History* (Atlantic Highlands, NJ: Zed Books, 1995), 28, 32.
55. "International Development Strategy for the Second United Nations Decade," U.N. General Assembly Resolution 2626 (XXV), October 24, 1970. See also Jain, *Women, Development, and the UN*, 24–25, 43–44, 49–53; U.N. Department of Public Information, "The Four Global Women's Conferences, 1975–1995"; Ester Boserup, *Woman's Role in Economic Development* (London: George Allen & Unwin, 1970); idem, *My Professional Life and Publications, 1929–1998* (Copenhagen: Museum Tusculanum Press, 1999); Shahra Razavi and Carol Miller, "From WID to GAD: Conceptual Shifts in the Women and Development Discourse," Occasional Paper 1, U.N. Research Institute for Social Development and UNDP, February 1995, http://www.eldis.org/static/DOC1651.htm; "Resolution IX Adopted by the International Conference on Human Rights," in *U.N. and the Advancement of Women*, 177–79.
56. Jain, *Women, Development, and the UN*, 53, 55–56, 65; Snyder, "Politics of Women and Development," 97; Boutros-Ghali, "Introduction," in *U.N. and the Advancement of Women*, 32; Snyder and Tadesse, *African Women and Development*, 28, 32; Thomas G. Weiss and Robert S. Jordan, *The World Food Conference and Global Problem-Solving* (New York: Praeger, 1976). Swedish legislation passed in 1974 that required that some development funds be earmarked for women's programs; the International Labour Organization's integration of women into all aspects of its new human resource development convention

(No. 142) of 1975; and that same year the OECD started convening expert groups on the role of women in development that prompted other donors to include among its lending criteria that women be involved in the planning of economic development programs (Jain, *Women, Development, and the UN*, 50, 56–57; ILO, "Convention (No. 142) Concerning Vocational Guidance and Vocational Training in the Development of Human Resources," http://www.austlii.edu.au/au/other/dfat/treaties/1986/2.html). Nonetheless, the reader should not assume that these early initiatives did not suffer from a continuation of gendered thinking. In fact, many of the early "women in development" projects still came from bureaucracies that male decision-makers dominated, and the resulting projects were often simply tacked on to existing programs (Jain, *Women, Development, and the UN*, 58; Nüket Kardam, *Bringing Women In: Women's Issues in International Development Programs* [Boulder, CO: Lynn Rienner, 1991], 24–25).

57. As quoted in Jain, *Women, Development, and the UN*, 8. See also ibid., 24–25, 67, 70; U.N. Department of Public Information, "The Four Global Women's Conferences, 1975–1995"; Marta Lamas, Alicia Martínez, María Tarrés, and Esperanza Tuñon, "Building Bridges: The Growth of Popular Feminism in Mexico," in *The Challenge of Local Feminisms: Women's Movements in Global Perspective*, ed. Amrita Basu (Boulder, CO: Westview Press, 1995), 324–50.

58. "Report of the World Conference of the International Women's Year," in *U.N. and the Advancement of Women*, 210. See also Jain, *Women, Development, and the UN*, 4, 24–25, 69, 74–79; U.N. Department of Public Information, "The Four Global Women's Conferences, 1975–1995."

59. As quoted in Jain, *Women, Development, and the UN*, 8.

60. Jennifer Kingson Bloom, "Bradford Morse Is Dead at 73: Held High-Ranking U.N. Posts," *New York Times*, December 19, 1994, http://www.nytimes.com/1994/12/19/world/bradford-morse-is-dead-at-73-held-high-ranking-un-posts.html.

61. Murphy, *U.N. Development Programme*, 15, 170–72. For the theory about socialization to international norms, see G. John Ikenberry and Charles A. Kupchan, "Socialization and Hegemonic Power," *International Organization* 44, no. 3 (Summer 1990): 283–315.

62. Murphy, *U.N. Development Programme*, 173–75; Pethu Serote, "Solomon Mahlangu Freedom College: A Unique South African Educational Experience in Tanzania," *Transformation* 20 (1992): 47–60.

63. Murphy, *United Nations Development Programme*, 177–80.

64. Zeiler, "Opening Doors," 339–40; "International Development Strategy for the Third United Nations Development Decade," U.N. General Assembly Resolution 35/56, December 5, 1980, annex I, preamble, para. 8; Jolly et al., *UN Contributions to Development*, 116.

65. British economist John Williamson coined this term in 1989 to refer to the package of ten specific economic policy prescriptions included in the reform packages prescribed by the IMF, World Bank, and U.S. Treasury Department, all of which are based in Washington, DC. Since that time it has lost much of that specificity and has simply become short-hand for the general, neoliberal, structural adjustment programs of the time.

66. Kasahara et al., *Beyond Conventional Wisdom*, xiv–xv; Jolly et al., *UN Contributions to Development*, 119, 124.

67. Zeiler, "Opening Doors," 349–50.

68. Ibid., 329–34; Alfred E. Eckes Jr., "Europe and Economic Globalization," in *A Companion to Europe since 1945*, ed. Klaus Larres (Malden, MA: Wiley-Blackwell, 2009), 257–65; Frans A. M. Alting von Geusau and J. C. Anyiwo, *The Lomé Convention and a New International*

Economic Order (Leyden, Netherlands: Sijthoff, 1977); Olufemi A. Babarinde, *The Lomé Conventions and Development: An Empirical Assessment* (Aldershot, UK: Avebury, 1994); Adrian Flint, *Trade, Poverty and the Environment: The EU, Cotonou and the African-Caribbean-Pacific Bloc* (Basingstoke, UK: Palgrave Macmillan, 2008).

69. Zeiler, "Opening Doors," 331–33, 349; Ricupero, "Preface," and Shigehisa Kasahara and Charles Gore, "Editors' Introduction," both in *Beyond Conventional Wisdom*, xiii–xiv, xviii–xix, xl; Aldo Musacchio, "Mexico's Financial Crisis of 1994–1995," Harvard Business School Working Paper no. 12-101 (May 2012), available through Digital Access to Scholarship at Harvard (DASH), http://nrs.harvard.edu/urn-3:HUL.InstRepos:9056792 (March 26, 2015).

70. Zeiler, "Opening Doors," 334, 340–41; Ricupero, "Preface," ix–x, xiv–xvi, xviii, xx–xxi, xxiv–xxv; William Greider, *One World, Ready or Not: The Manic Logic of Global Capitalism* (New York: Simon & Schuster, 1997), 13–19.

71. Ricupero, "Preface," xix; Murphy, *United Nations Development Programme*, 6. The members of the U.N. Development Group are the U.N. Development Programme, UNICEF, the U.N. Population Fund, the World Food Programme, the office of the High Commissioner for Human Rights, U.N. Women, the U.N. Office for Project Services, the Joint U.N. Programme on HIV/AIDS, the U.N. Human Settlements Programme, the U.N. Office on Drugs and Crime, the World Health Organization, the U.N. Department of Economic and Social Affairs, the International Fund for Agricultural Development, UNESCO, the Food and Agriculture Organization, the U.N. Industrial Development Organization, the International Labour Organization, the U.N. Department of Public Information, the Special Representative of the Secretary-General for Children and Armed Conflict, the U.N. Environment Programme, the U.N. High Commissioner for Refugees, the Special Adviser on Africa in the Office of the Under-Secretary General, the U.N. World Tourism Organization, the World Meteorological Organization, the International Telecommunications Union, and the U.N. Office of the High Representative for the Least Developed Countries, Landlocked Developing Countries, and Small Island Developing States. There are also observers from the World Bank Group, the U.N. Fund for International Partnerships, the Office for the Coordination of Humanitarian Affairs, the U.N. Office for Disaster Risk Reduction, and offices of the Secretary-General's office.

72. Zeiler, "Opening Doors," 350–52; Gerald Tan, *ASEAN: Economic Development and Cooperation* (Singapore: Times Academic, 2003), 200–33; Alfred E. Eckes Jr. and Thomas W. Zeiler, *Globalization and the American Century* (Cambridge: Cambridge University Press, 2003), 249–51.

73. Murphy, *United Nations Development Programme*, 7; U.N. Department of Public Information, "The Four Global Women's Conferences, 1975–1995."

74. Giovanni Andrea Cornia, Richard Jolly, and Frances Stewart, eds., *Adjustment with a Human Face*, vol. 1: *Protecting the Vulnerable and Promoting Growth* (Oxford: Oxford University Press, 1987); UNICEF, "James P. Grant Biography," last updated April 7, 2003, http://www.unicef.org/about/who/index_bio_grant.html.

75. Ricupero, "Preface," xiii–xv, xx; Murphy, *United Nations Development Programme*, 15.

76. Ricupero, "Preface," xxxii. See also ibid., xvii, xxi–xxii, xxv, xxxiii–xxxiv; Zeiler, "Opening Doors," 335–37, 343, 346–47; Eckes and Zeiler, *Globalization*; World Trade Organization, "The Third WTO Ministerial Conference," accessed May 27, 2015, https://www.wto.org/english/thewto_e/minist_e/min99_e/min99_e.htm; World Trade Organization, "The Fifth WTO Ministerial Conference," accessed May 27, 2015, https://www.wto.org/english/thewto_e/minist_e/min03_e/min03_e.htm. The WTO History Project (a project of the University of Washington and its libraries, the Harry Bridges

Center for Labor Studies, and the Center for Communication and Civic Engagement) offers information, interviews, and resources related to the protests at http://depts.washington.edu/wtohist/.

77. Stokke, *UN and Development*, 344–47; Haq and Ponsio, eds., *Pioneering the Human Development Revolution*; Murphy, *United Nations Development Programme*, 8–9, 14–15, 177–81, 188–94; UNDP, *Human Development Report 1990* (New York: Oxford University Press, 1990), 1–7; UNDP, *Human Development Report 1995* (New York: Oxford University Press, 1995).

78. Stokke, *UN and Development*, 343–44, 350–52; Zeiler, "Opening Doors," 344–46; Walter LaFeber, *Michael Jordan and the New Global Capitalism* (New York: W. W. Norton, 1999), 126, 147–51; World Bank, *Poverty Reduction and the World Bank: Progress in Fiscal 1993* (Washington, DC: World Bank, 1994); United Nations, "Development: Outcomes on Least Development Countries: Second United Nations Conference on the Least Developed Countries," accessed March 3, 2015, http://www.un.org/en/development/devagenda/ldc.shtml (links to the final report [A/RES/44/241] and the conference's official website are also connected to this page).

79. Stephen Macekuras, *Of Limits and Growth: Global Environmentalism and the Rise of "Sustainable Development" in the Twentieth Century* (Cambridge: Cambridge University Press, 2015); United Nations Conference on Environment and Development, Rio de Janeiro, Brazil, June 3–14, 1992, *Agenda 21* (New York: United Nations, 1992), https://sustainabledevelopment.un.org/content/documents/Agenda21.pdf. Other, specialized conference documents included the Rio Declaration on Environment and Development, the Statement of Forest Principles, the U.N. Framework Convention on Climate Change, and the U.N. Convention on Biological Diversity. For Rio's impact, see also C. Alison McIntosh and Jason L. Finkle, "The Cairo Conference on Population and Development: A New Paradigm?" *Population and Development Review* 21, no. 2 (June 1995): 223–60; Peter M. Haas, "UN Conferences and Constructivist Governance of the Environment," *Global Governance* 8 (2002): 73–91; Cecile Jackson, "Rescuing Gender from the Poverty Trap," *World Development* 24, no. 3 (March 1996): 489–504.

80. Mark Lynas, "How Do I Know China Wrecked the Copenhagen Deal? I Was in the Room," *Guardian*, December 22, 2009, https://www.theguardian.com/environment/2009/dec/22/copenhagen-climate-change-mark-lynas; Zeiler, "Opening Doors," 347; UNEP and Climate Action, "Sustainable Innovation Forum 2015: Find out More about COP21," last modified 2015, http://www.cop21paris.org/about/cop21; Alister Doyle and Roberta Rampton, "Paris Climate Accord to Take Effect; Obama Hails 'Historic Day,'" *Reuters World News*, last modified October 5, 2016, http://www.reuters.com/article/us-climatechange-paris-idUSKCN12.

81. Stokke, *UN and Development*, 442–45; U.N., *United Nations Millennium Declaration* (New York: U.N. Department of Public Information, 2000); "MDGs: What They Are," last modified 2006, http://www.unmillenniumproject.org/index.htm; Murphy, *United Nations Development Programme*, 4, 6; Zeiler, "Opening Doors," 353–58; "Timeline: Key Events in Financial Crisis," *USA Today*, September 9, 2013, http://www.usatoday.com/story/money/Business/2013/09/08/chronology-2008-financial-crisis-lehman/2779515/. For example, the period 2000–15 witnessed the third and fourth U.N. Conferences on the LDCs (2001 and 2011); the Monterrey International Conference on Financing for Development (2002), which signaled greater cooperation between the Bretton Woods institutions and the rest of the United Nations; the World Summit on Sustainable Development (2002); the World Food Summit +5 (2002); the second World Assembly on Aging (2002); the International Ministerial Conference of Landlocked and Transit-Developing Countries (2003); the World

Summit on Food Security (2009); and follow-up meetings on the Copenhagen and Beijing declarations and programs of action (2005 and 2010), the implementation of the Monterrey Consensus (2008), the Barbados Programme of Action for the Sustainable Development of Small Island Developing States (2010), and Rio's Agenda 21 on Sustainable Development (2012).

82. Cullather, *The Hungry World*, ix. See also ibid., 3–5; Hodge, *Triumph of the Expert*, 8–11, 19, for this chapter's definition of development. For the U.N. response to the failure of the MDGs, see United Nations Population Fund, "International Conference on Population and Development: The ICPD Beyond 2014," accessed February 18, 2015, http://www.unfpa.org/icpd; U.N. Department of Economic and Social Affairs, "Third International Conference on Financing for Development: Addis Ababa Conference," accessed February 18, 2015, http://www.un.org/esa/ffd/; "Population Dynamics in the Post-2015 Development Agenda: Report of the Global Thematic Consultation on Population Dynamics (UNFPA, UNDESA, UN-HABITAT, & IOM, 2013)," accessed February 18, 2015, http://www.unfpa.org/sites/default/files/pub-pdf/Population%20Dynamics%20in%20Post-2015%20FINAL.pdf.

Chapter 6

1. An excellent overview of U.N. peacekeeping operations is the recent and comprehensive Joachim A. Koops, Norrie MacQueen, Thierry Tardy, and Paul D. Williams, eds., *The Oxford Handbook of United Nations Peacekeeping Operations* (Oxford: Oxford University Press, 2015), which contains an introduction to the volume as a whole, introductions to each chronological period, a theoretical "Part I," and a chapter on each individual peacekeeping operation.
2. Egil Aarvik, "The Nobel Peace Prize 1988: Presentation Speech," Oslo, Norway, December 10, 1988, accessed June 15, 2015, http://www.nobelprize.org/nobel_prizes/peace/laureates/1988/presentation-speech.html; Boutros Boutros-Ghali, "Empowering the United Nations," *Foreign Affairs* 71, no. 5 (Winter 1992): 89. See also United Nations Peacekeeping, "Department of Peacekeeping Operations," accessed June 23, 2014, http://www.un.org/en/peacekeeping/about/dpko/; Joachim A. Koops, Norrie MacQueen, Thierry Tardy, and Paul D. Williams, "Introduction: Post-Cold War Peacekeeping, 1988–1998," in *Oxford Handbook of United Nations Peacekeeping Operations*, 261–68.
3. Gil Loescher, *The UNHCR and World Politics: A Perilous Path* (Oxford: Oxford University Press, 2001), 1; U.N., "Global Issues: Refugees by the Numbers," accessed July 21, 2015, http://www.un.org/en/globalissues/briefingpapers/refugees/index.shtml; UNHCR, "About Us," accessed August 22, 2015, http://www.unhcr.org/pages/49c3646c2.html. From this page, you can also link to a pdf version of General Assembly Resolution 428 (V), December 14, 1950, which established the UNHCR.
4. Loescher, *UNHCR and World Politics*, 4, 19n4; Louise Holborn's *Refugees: A Problem of Our Time: The Work of the United Nations High Commissioner for Refugees*, 2 vols (Metuchen, NJ: Scarecrow Press, 1975), was sponsored by UNHCR.
5. While peacekeeping operations have often received significant attention in the writings of the secretaries-general and their staff members, such operations are but one facet of the work they undertake. And the military leaders and soldiers involved in these conflicts do not seem to have generated a significant body of writing about their experiences. For chapters on peacekeeping in larger, edited works, see Michael W. Doyle and Nicholas Sambanis, "Peacekeeping Operations" and Roland Paris, "Post-Conflict Peacebuilding," both in *Oxford Handbook on the United Nations*, 323–48, 404–26; Ramesh Thakur,

"International Peacekeeping," in *International Conflict Resolution*, ed. Ramesh Thakur (Boulder, CO: Westview Press, 1988), 175–96; Jan Erik Schultz, "From the Protection of Sovereignty to Humanitarian Intervention? Traditions and Developments of United Nations Peacekeeping in the Twentieth Century," in *The Emergence of Humanitarian Intervention: Ideas and Practice from the Nineteenth Century to the Present*, ed. Fabian Klose (Cambridge: Cambridge University Press, 2015), 253–79. United Nations Peacekeeping, "Peacekeeping Operations," http://www.un.org/en/peacekeeping/, and "Past Peacekeeping Operations," http://www.un.org/en/peacekeeping/operations/past.shtml, both accessed March 19, 2016.

For edited volumes on peacekeeping, see Chiyuki Aoi, Cedric de Coning, and Ramesh Thakur, eds., *Unintended Consequences of Peacekeeping Operations* (Tokyo: United Nations University Press, 2007); Koops, MacQueen, Tardy, and Williams, eds., *The Oxford Handbook of United Nations Peacekeeping Operations*; William J. Durch, ed., *The Evolution of UN Peacekeeping: Case Studies and Comparative Analysis* (London: Palgrave Macmillan, 1993). For new works from the political science perspective, see Michael W. Doyle and Nicholas Sambanis, *Making War and Building Peace: United Nations Peace Operations* (Princeton, NJ: Princeton University Press, 2006); Joshua S. Goldstein, *Winning the War on War: The Decline of Armed Conflict Worldwide* (New York: Plume, 2011).

6. Works by and about UNHCR staff include Jeroen Corduwener, *Riemen om de kin!: Biografie van Mr. Dr. Gerrit Jan van Heuven Goedhart* (Amsterdam: Bakker, 2011); Auguste Lindt, *The Refugee* (London: United Nations Association, 1960); Sadako N. Ogata, *The Turbulent Decade: Confronting the Refugee Crises of the 1990s* (New York: W. W. Norton, 2005); Angelina Jolie, *Notes from My Travels: Visits with Refugees in Africa, Cambodia, Pakistan and Ecuador* (New York: Pocket Books, 2014). The words of refugees are captured in John Ajak and Rick Hilscher, *Unspeakable: My Journey as a Lost Boy of Sudan* (Newton, KS: Mennonite Press, 2013); *Refugees: Telling Their Stories, 2004* (Geneva: UNHCR, 2004). For the rise of refugee studies, see the *Journal of Refugee Studies*, the University of Oxford Refugee Studies Centre, "About Us," accessed September 10, 2015, http://www.rsc.ox.ac.uk/about, and its recent publication: Elena Fiddian-Qasmiyeh, Gil Loescher, Katy Long, and Nando Sigona, eds., *The Oxford Handbook of Refugee and Forced Migration Studies* (Oxford: Oxford University Press, 2014). To sample the variety within the field, see a refugee case study in Gaim Kibreab, "Resistance, Displacement, and Identity: The Case of Eritrean Refugees in Sudan," *Canadian Journal of African Studies/Revue Canadienne des Études* 34, no. 2 (2000): 249–96; and a postmodern approach in Lynellyn D. Long, *Ban Vinai, the Refugee Camp* (New York: Columbia University Press, 1993), 9.

7. U.N., "United Nations Relief and Rehabilitation Administration, Summary of Administrative History," p. 1, accessed June 15, 2015, https://archives.un.org/sites/archives.un.org/files/files/Finding%20Aids/2015_Finding_Aids/AG-018.pdf. For pre–Second World War efforts, see Loescher, *UNHCR and World Politics*, 1; Bruno Cabanes, *The Great War and the Origins of Humanitarianism, 1918-1924* (Cambridge: Cambridge University Press, 2014), 133–88; John Hope Simpson, *The Refugee Problem: Report of a Survey* (London: Oxford University Press, 1939), 4; Richard Robbins, "The Refugee Status: Challenge and Response," *Law and Contemporary Problems* 21, no. 2 (Spring 1956): 320, also available at http://scholarship.law.duke.edu/cgi/viewcontent.cgi?article=2677&context=lcp. For UNRRA, see Andrew Harder, "The Politics of Impartiality: The United Nations Relief and Rehabilitation Administration in the Soviet Union, 1946–7," *Journal of Contemporary History* 47, no. 2 (April 2012): 347–69; Grace Fox, "The Origins of UNRRA," *Political Science Quarterly* 65, no. 4 (December 1950): 561–84.

8. U.N., "Constitution of the International Refugee Organization, adopted by the General Assembly on February 12, 1946," http://avalon.law.yale.edu/20th_century/decad053.asp;

U.N., "Constitution of the International Refugee Organization, Annexe 1, Part II: 'Persons who will not be the Concern of the Organization,'" in Guy S. Goodwin-Gill and Jane McAdams, *The Refugee in International Law* Online Resource Centre, accessed July 23, 2015, http://global.oup.com/booksites/content/9780199207633/resources/annexe1.

9. UNHCR, *Convention and Protocol Relating to the Status of Refugees: Text of the 1951 Convention Relating to the Status of Refugees; Text of the 1967 Protocol Relating to the Status of Refugees; Resolution 2198 (XXI) adopted by the United Nations General Assembly, with an Introductory Note by the Office of the United Nations High Commissioner on Refugees*, last modified December 2010, http://www.unhcr.org/3b66c2aa10.html. See also Loescher, *UNHCR and World Politics*, 5–7; U.N. Resolution 319 (IV), December 3, 1949, http://daccess-dds-ny.un.org/doc/RESOLUTION/GEN/NR0/051/38/IMG/NR005138.pdf?OpenElement; UNHCR, "About Us," accessed February 18, 2015, http://www.unhcr.org/pages/49c3646c2.html; Peter Gattrell, *The Making of the Modern Refugee* (Oxford: Oxford University Press, 2013), 86–87, 115.

10. Evelyn Goh and Rosemary Foot, "US Relations with China Since 1949," in *A Companion to American Foreign Relations*, ed. Robert D. Schulzinger (Malden, MA: Blackwell Publishing, 2006), 260. See also Clay Blair, *The Forgotten War: America in Korea* (New York: Crown Books, 1987); Sergei Goncharov, John W. Lewis, and Litai Xue, *Uncertain Partners: Stalin, Mao and the Korean War* (Stanford, CA: Stanford University Press, 1993); Bruce Cumings, *The Korean War: A History* (New York: Modern Library, 2011).

11. Cumings, *Korean War*; William W. Stueck, *The Korean War: An International History* (Princeton, NJ: Princeton University Press, 1995).

12. Bosco, *Five to Rule Them All*, 53–54; Gaiduk, *Divided Together*, 150–94.

13. For orthodox accounts of the Korean conflict include General Matthew B. Ridgway, *The Korean War* (Garden City, NY: Doubleday, 1967), while the revisionist historiography is sketched out in James I. Matray, "The Korean War," in *A Companion to American Foreign Relations*, 275–91.

14. Matray, "Korean War," 280. A sampling of the post–Cold War scholarship includes Goncharov et al., *Uncertain Partners*; Cumings, *Korean War*; Gaiduk, *Divided Together*. For some of the primary sources that supported these new interpretations, see Wilson Center Digital Archive (all accessed June 30, 2015): "Korean War Origins, 1945–1950," http://digitalarchive.wilsoncenter.org/collection/134/korean-war-origins-1945-1950; "Korean War, 1950–1953," http://digitalarchive.wilsoncenter.org/collection/50/korean-war-1950-1953; "Making of the Sino-Soviet Alliance, 1945–1950," http://digitalarchive.wilsoncenter.org/collection/181/making-of-the-sino-soviet-alliance-1945-1950.

15. U.N. Security Council Resolution 82, June 25, 1950, http://www.refworld.org/cgi-bin/texis/vtx/rwmain?docid=3b00f15960; U.N. Security Council Resolution 83, June 27, 1950, http://www.refworld.org/cgi-bin/texis/vtx/rwmain?docid=3b00f20a2c. See also Bosco, *Five to Rule Them All*.

16. Cumings, *Korean War*; Masuda Hajimu, *Cold War Crucible: The Korean Conflict and the Postwar World* (Cambridge, MA: Harvard University Press, 2015), 85–113.

17. "The 'Uniting for Peace' Resolution of the United Nations," *American Journal of International Law* 45, no. 21 (1950): 129–37; Gabriel Kolko, *Century of War: Politics, Conflicts, and Society since 1914* (New York: W. W. Norton, 1994), 395–411.

18. Adam Roberts, *The Crisis in Peacekeeping* (Oslo: Institutt for Forsvarsstudier, 1994); Odd Arne Westad, *The Global Cold War: Third World Interventions and the Making of Our Times* (New York: Cambridge University Press, 2005), 136–40; Jason C. Parker, "Decolonization,

the Cold War, and the Post-Columbian Era," in *The Cold War in the Third World*, ed. Robert J. McMahon (Oxford: Oxford University Press, 2013), 124–38.

19. Ryan McMahon, "Defining UNKRA: The Many Affiliations of the United Nations Korean Reconstruction Agency, 1951–1958," PhD diss., Ohio State University, forthcoming; Steven Hugh Lee, "The United Nations Korean Reconstruction Agency in War and Peace: An Economic and Social History of Korea in the 1950s," in *Korea and the Korean War*, ed. Cha-Jin Lee and Young Ick Lew (Seoul: Yonaei University Press, 2002), 357–96.

20. Loescher, *UNHCR and World Politics*, 7–8; Susan L. Carruthers, "Between Camps: Eastern Bloc 'Escapees' and Cold War Borderlands," *American Quarterly* 57, no. 3 (September 2005): 911–42; George L. Warren, "The Escapee Program," *Journal of International Affairs* 7, no. 1 (1953): 82–85; Robbins, "Refugee Status," 329–30, 333; Edward Marks, "Internationally Assisted Migration: ICEM Rounds out Five Years of Resettlement," *International Organization* 11, no. 3 (Summer 1957): 481–94. In addition to "voting with their feet," some escaped by hijacking airlines, which the United States also countenanced during this period (Mackenzie, *ICAO*, 246–47).

21. Loescher, *UNHCR and World Politics*, 6–8; *A Century of Nobel Peace Prize Laureates, 1901–2005: From Peace Movements to the United Nations* (Geneva: U.N., 2006).

22. UNHCR, "Gerrit Jan van Heuven Goedhart (Netherlands), 1951–56," accessed September 10, 2015, http://www.unhcr.org/pages/49da0b4d6.html, which also includes links to a set of his speeches; Loescher, *UNHCR and World Politics*, 9; UNHCR, "Statement by Dr. Auguste R. Lindt, United Nations High Commissioner for Refugees, to the United Nations Economic and Social Council (ECOSOC), 25 July 1960," http://www.unhcr.org/3ae68fb80.html.

23. Loescher, *UNHCR and World Politics*, 8; Holborn, *Refugees*, 1: 347–54, 358–63; Robbins, "Refugee Status," 333. These four umbrella humanitarian organizations worked with the UNHCR to identify additional funding sources, had worked with the IRO, had worked internationally with all major ethnic and religious groups, and had the staff and skills needed to carry out effective programs in the countries of first asylum. The Ford Foundation also included the Young Men's Christian Association (YMCA) and the American Friends Service Committee (the Quakers) in the grant-funded activities.

24. Loescher, *UNHCR and World Politics*, 8; Peter Gatrell, *Free World? The Campaign to Save the World's Refugees, 1956–1963* (Cambridge: Cambridge University Press, 2011), 50–53; UNHCR, "Auguste R. Lindt (Switzerland), 1956–60," accessed September 10, 2015, http://www.unhcr.org/pages/49da0b296.html; Nándor F. Dreisziger, "The Hungarian Revolution of 1956: The Legacy of the Refugees," *Nationalities Papers* 13, no. 2 (1985): 198–208; Robbins, "Refugee Status," 311–33; U.S. Displaced Persons Commission, *Memo to America: The DP Story* (Washington, DC: USGPO, 1952), 77–83; James Rorty, "Our Broken Promise to the Refugees: Unsmiling Goddess of Liberty," *Commentary* 20 (October 1, 1955), https://www.commentarymagazine.com/articles/our-broken-promise-to-the-refugeesunsmiling-goddess-of-liberty/.

25. Loescher, *UNHCR and World Politics*, 8. See also Gattrell, *Making of the Modern Refugee*, 117.

26. UNHCR, "Auguste R. Lindt (Switzerland), 1956–60"; Loescher, *UNHCR and World Politics*, 9; Connelly, *A Diplomatic Revolution*, 140–41, 160–70; Gatrell, *Free World?*, 66–67, 69; Keith Sutton, "Population Resettlement: Traumatic Upheavals and the Algerian Experience," *Journal of African Studies* 15, no. 2 (1977): 279–300; Cecilia Ruthström-Ruin, *Beyond Europe: The Globalization of Refugee Aid* (Lund, Sweden: Lund University Press, 1993), 84–92; Gatrell, *Free World?*, 67–69; UNHCR, "Statement by Lindt to ECOSOC, 25 July 1960."

27. UNHCR, "World Refugee Year: General Assembly Resolution 1285 (XIII), 5 December 1958," accessed September 11, 2015, http://www.unhcr.org/3ae69ef3a.html; Long, *Ban Vinai*, 26–27; Gattrell, *Free World?*; UNHCR, "Statement by Lindt to ECOSOC, 25 July 1960."

28. Gatrell, *Free World?*, 53; Robbins, "Refugee Status," 319, 322–24, 332; Loescher, *UNHCR and World Politics*, 5. Refugees who fell outside of the UNHCR mandate also included more than half a million Vietnamese Roman Catholics who fled northern Vietnam after the Geneva Accords were signed.

29. For an overview of the historical context of the Congo crisis, see William J. Durch, "The UN Operation in the Congo: 1960–1964," in *The Evolution of UN Peacekeeping: Case Studies and Comparative Analysis*, ed. William J. Durch (New York: St. Martin's Press, 1993), 315; Adam Hochschild, *King Leopold's Ghost: A Story of Greed, Terror, and Heroism in Colonial Africa* (New York: Mariner Books, 1998). Scholars focusing on the conflict's military aspects include Ernst Lefever, *Crisis in the Congo: A UN Force in Action* (Washington, DC: Brookings Institution Press, 1965); Madeleine Kalb, *Congo Cables: The Cold War in Africa from Eisenhower to Kennedy* (New York: Macmillan, 1982); Marco Wyss and Thierry Tardy, *Peacekeeping in Africa: The Evolving Security Architecture* (London: Routledge, 2014). Increasingly, historians and other scholars revisiting Cold War conflicts have focused on the ways in which U.N. efforts reflected issues of racism and colonialism prevalent in its member states at the time and how that racism might have affected peacekeeping strategies: Thomas Borstelmann, *Apartheid's Reluctant Uncle: The United States and Southern Africa in the Early Cold War* (New York: Oxford University Press, 1993); David Gibbs, *The Political Economy of Third World Intervention: Mines, Money, and U.S. Policy in the Congo Crisis* (Chicago: University of Chicago Press, 1991); Westad, *Global Cold War*, 136–43. As former Soviet archives opened, new information concerning the Soviet Union's public and clandestine participation in the Congo crisis sparked new scholarship that indicates that Soviet participation in the Congo was not necessarily as nefarious or intentional as analysts of the 1960s had believed: Sergey Mazov, *A Distant Front in the Cold War: The USSR in West Africa and the Congo, 1956–1964* (Stanford, CA: Stanford University Press, 2010); Mazower, *Governing the World*, 244–72.

30. Parker, "Decolonization, the Cold War, and the Post-Columbian Era," 132. See also Durch, "UN Operation in the Congo," 316–17; U.N., "Republic of the Congo: ONUC Background," last modified 2001, http://www.un.org/depts/DPKO/Missions/onucB.htm; Jane Boulden, "United Nations Operation in the Congo (ONUC)," in *Oxford Handbook of United Nations Peacekeeping Operations*, 160–70; Herbert Nicholas, "An Appraisal: UN Forces and Lessons of Suez and Congo," in *International Military Forces: The Question of Peacekeeping in an Armed and Disarming World*, ed. Lincoln P. Bloomfield (Boston: Little, Brown and Company, 1964), 105–26.

31. As quoted in United Nations, "Republic of the Congo: ONUC Background"; Durch, "UN Operation in the Congo," 346. Lumumba's death remains a hotly contested topic within Cold War history. A number of historians assign blame, directly or indirectly, for his assassination to the Central Intelligence Agency (CIA) of the United States, which saw Lumumba as anti-American: Stephen R. Weissman, "What Really Happened in the Congo: The CIA, the Murder of Lumumba, and the Rise of Mobutu," *Foreign Affairs* 93 (July/August 2014), https://www.foreignaffairs.com/articles/democratic-republic-congo/2014-06-16/what-really-happened-congo; Emmanuel Gerard and Bruce Kuklick, *Death in the Congo: Murdering Patrice Lumumba* (Cambridge, MA: Harvard University Press, 2015).

32. Durch, "UN Operation in the Congo," 345. See also ibid., 330; United Nations, "Republic of the Congo: ONUC Background."

33. Long, *Ban Vinai*, 19, 23–24, 29; Loescher, *UNHCR and World Politics*, 10; Piero Gleijeses, *Conflicting Missions: Havana, Washington, and Africa, 1959–1976* (Chapel Hill: University of North Carolina Press, 2002).

34. "OAU Convention Governing the Specific Aspects of Refugee Problems in Africa," July 20, 1974, UNHCR, http://www.unhcr.org/45dc1a682.html; Loescher, *UNHCR and World Politics*, 5–6, 10; Long, *Ban Vinai*, 23–25.

35. Loescher, *UNHCR and World Politics*, 10–11; Long, *Ban Vinai*, 25–26.

36. Loescher, *UNHCR and World Politics*, 11–12, 20n10; Artistide Zolberg, Astri Suhrke, and Sergio Aguayo, *Escape from Violence: Conflict and the Refugee Crisis in the Developing World* (New York: Oxford University Press, 1989); Stephen John Stedman and Fred Tanner, eds., *Refugee Manipulation: War, Politics and the Abuse of Human Suffering* (Washington, DC: Brookings Institution Press, 2003).

37. Daniel Unger, "Ain't Enough Blanket: International Humanitarian Assistance and Cambodian Political Resistance," in *Refugee Manipulation*, 17–56; Josephine Reynell, *Refugees on the Thai–Kampuchean Border* (Oxford: Oxford University Press, 1989); Frédéric Grare, "The Geopolitics of Afghan Refugees in Pakistan," Howard Adelman, "The Use and Abuse of Refugees in Zaire," and Stephen John Stedman, "Conclusions and Policy Recommendations," all in *Refugee Manipulation*, 57–94, 95–134, 167–90; Fiona Terry, *Condemned to Repeat? The Paradox of Humanitarian Action* (Ithaca, NY: Cornell University Press, 2002), chapters 2 and 3.

38. As quoted in Loescher, *UNHCR and World Politics*, 206.

39. Luise Druke, *Innovations in Refugee Protection: A Compendium of UNHCR's 60 Years, including Case Studies on IT Communities, Vietnamese Boatpeople, Chilean Exile and Namibian Repatriation* (Frankfurt, Germany: Peter Lang, 2013), 26–27, 153–288; W. Courtland Robinson, *Terms of Refuge: The Indochinese Exodus and the International Response* (London: Zed Books, 1998), 192; Sara Ellen Davies, *Legitimizing Rejection: International Refugee Law in Southeast Asia* (Leiden, Netherlands: Martinus Nijhoff, 2008); Milton Osborne, "The Indochinese Refugees: Cause and Effects," *International Affairs* 56, no. 1 (January 1980): 37–53.

40. Loescher, *UNHCR and World Politics*, 207. See also ibid., 203–209; Barry Wain, *The Refused: The Agony of the Indochinese Refugees* (New York: Simon and Schuster, 1981); Valerie Sutter, *The Indochinese Refugee Dilemma* (Baton Rouge: Louisiana State University Press, 1990).

41. Loescher, *UNHCR and World Politics*, 5, 12.

42. As quoted in Alexander Belts, Gil Loescher, and James Milner, *UNHCR: The Politics and Practice of Refugee Protection into the 21st Century* (New York: Routledge, 2008), 38. See also Dag Hammarskjöld Library, "The United Nations Security Council and Namibia," http://www.un.org/Depts/dhl/namibia/; Loescher, *UNHCR and World Politics*, 12–13; Jean-Pierre Hocke, "Beyond Humanitarianism: The Need for Political Will to Resolve Today's Refugee Problem," in *Refugees and International Relations*, ed. Gil Loescher and Laila Monahan (Oxford: Clarendon Press, 1989), 37–48; Druke, *Innovations in Refugee Protection*, 28–29, 289–443.

43. Doyle and Sambanis, *Making War and Building Peace*, 1. See also Stefan Kroll, "The Legal Justification of International Intervention: Theories of Community and Admissability," in *The Emergence of Humanitarian Intervention: Ideas and Practice from the Nineteenth Century to the Present*, ed. Fabian Klose (Cambridge: Cambridge University Press, 2015), 73–89.

44. Quoted in Doyle and Sambanis, *Making War and Building Peace*, 6, 11. See also Boutros Boutros-Ghali, *An Agenda for Peace: Preventive Diplomacy, Peacemaking, and Peace-keeping: Report of the Secretary-General to the United Nations General Assembly and Security Council*, A/47/277-S/24111, June 17, 1992, http://www.un.org/Docs/SG/agpeace.html; Jan Erik Schultz, "From the Protection of Sovereignty to Humanitarian Intervention? Traditions and

Developments of United Nations Peacekeeping in the Twentieth Century," in *Emergence of Humanitarian Intervention*, 253–79.

45. CNN/Time All Politics, "Madeleine Albright," last modified 1997, http://www.cnn.com/ALLPOLITICS/1997/gen/resources/players/albright/. See also Doyle and Sambanis, *Making War and Building Peace*, 7–9, 11; Thomase Franchk, "Interpretation and Change in the Law of Humanitarian Intervention," in *Humanitarian Intervention: Ethical, Legal, and Political Dilemmas*, ed. J. L. Holzgrefe and Robert Keohane (Cambridge: Cambridge University Press, 2003), 227; Manuel Fröhlich, "The Responsibility to Protect: Foundation, Transformation, and Application of an Emerging Norm," in *Emergence of Humanitarian Intervention*, 299–330; Paul D. Williams, "United Nations Operation in Somalia I (UNOSOM I)" and "United Nations Operation in Somalia II (UNOSOM II)," both in *Oxford Handbook of United Nations Peacekeeping Operations*, 408–15, 429–42.

46. United Nations, "Cambodia: UNTAC Background," accessed July 20, 2015, http://www.un.org/en/peacekeeping/missions/past/untacbackgr1.html; United Nations, "Agreements on a Comprehensive Settlement of the Cambodia Conflict: Paris, October 23, 1991," http://www.usip.org/sites/default/files/file/resources/collections/peace_agreements/final_act_10231991.pdf; William J. Durch, "Epilogue: Peacekeeping in Uncharted Territory," in *Evolution of UN Peacekeeping*, 465; Janet E. Heininger, *Peacekeeping in Transition: The United Nations in Cambodia* (New York: Twentieth Century Fund Press, 1994).

47. United Nations, "Cambodia: UNTAC Background." See also Heininger, *Peacekeeping in Transition*, 35.

48. Boutros-Ghali, *Agenda for Peace*; United Nations, "Cambodia—UNTAC—Facts and Figures," accessed July 20, 2015, http://www.un.org/en/peacekeeping/missions/past/untacfacts.html; Simon Chesterman, *You, The People: The United Nations, Transitional Administration, and State-Building* (Oxford: Oxford University Press, 2004), 158; Aoi, de Coning, and Thakur, *Unintended Consequences of Peacekeeping Operations*; Doyle and Sambanis, *Making War and Building Peace*, 2.

49. Doyle and Sambanis, *Making War and Building Peace*, 2–3; Finn Stepputat, "Repatriation and Everyday Forms of State Formation in Guatemala," in *The End of the Refugee Cycle?: Refugee Repatriation and Reconstruction*, ed. Richard Black and Khalid Koser (New York: Berghahn Books, 1999), 210–26; Brian D. Smith and William J. Durch, "UN Observer Group in Central America," in *Evolution of UN Peacekeeping*, 406–35; Joachim A. Koops. "United Nations Observer Group in Central America (ONUCA)" and Thierry Tardy, "United Nations Protection Force (UNPROFOR—Croatia)," both in *The Oxford Handbook of United Nations Peacekeeping Operations*, 306–13, 371–82; Bradley Simpson, "A Not So Humanitarian Intervention," in *Emergence of Humanitarian Intervention*, 281–98.

50. Lawrence Freedman and Efraim Karsh, *The Gulf Conflict, 1990–1991: Diplomacy and War in the New World Order* (Princeton, NJ: Princeton University Press, 1995).

51. United Nations Security Council, "UNIKOM: Mandate," accessed July 29, 2015, http://www.un.org/en/peacekeeping/missions/past/unikom/mandate.html. See also United Nations Security Council, Resolution 660, accessed July 22, 2015, http://daccess-dds-ny.un.org/doc/RESOLUTION/GEN/NR0/575/10/IMG/NR057510.pdf?OpenElement; Freedman and Karsh, *Gulf Conflict*; United Nations Security Council, Resolution 660, accessed July 22, 2015, http://daccess-dds-ny.un.org/doc/RESOLUTION/GEN/NR0/575/10/IMG/NR057510.pdf?OpenElement; United Nations Security Council, "UNIKOM: Background," accessed July 29, 2015, http://www.un.org/en/peacekeeping/missions/past/unikom/background.html; United Nations Security Council, "Report of the Secretary-General on the activities of the United Nations Iraq-Kuwait Observation Mission for the period 16 June–1 October 2003,"

accessed July 29, 2015, http://daccess-dds-ny.un.org/doc/UNDOC/GEN/N03/533/93/PDF/N0353393.pdf?OpenElement.

52. Doyle and Sambanis, *Making War and Building Peace*, 3–4; Hazem Ghobarah, Paul Huth, and Bruce Russett, "Civil Wars Kill and Maim People, Long after the Fighting Stops," *American Political Science Review* 97, no. 2 (2003): 189–202; James C. Murdoch and Todd Sandler, "Economic Growth, Civil Wars, and Spatial Spillovers," *Journal of Conflict Resolution* 46 (February 2002): 91–110; Linda Melvern, "United Nations Observer Mission Uganda-Rwanda (UNOMUR) and United Nations Assistance Mission for Rwanda I (UNAMIR I)" and "United Nations Assistance Mission for Rwanda II (UNAMIR II)," both in *Oxford Handbook of United Nations Peacekeeping Operations*, 462–72, 473–83.

53. Doyle and Sambanis, *Making War and Building Peace*, 4. See also ibid., 4–6; Michael Doyle and Nicholas Sambanis, "International Peacebuilding: A Theoretical and Quantitative Analysis," *American Political Science Review* 94, no. 4 (2000): 779–801.

54. Loescher, *UNHCR and World Politics*, 13; Adam Roberts, "More Refugees, Less Asylum: A Regime in Transformation," *Journal of Refugee Studies* 11 (December 1998): 375–95; Guy Goodwin-Gill, "The Right to Leave, the Right to Return and the Question of a Right to Remain," in *The Problem of Refugees in Light of Contemporary Law Issues*, ed. Vera Gowlland-Debbas (Dordrecht, Netherlands: Martinus Nijhoff, 1995).

55. Loescher, *UNHCR and World Politics*, 14–18; Michael Barnett, "Humanitarianism with a Sovereign Face: UNHCR in the Global Undertow," *International Migration Review* 35, no. 1 (March 2001): 244–77; S. Neil MacFarland and Yuen Foong Khong, *Human Security and the UN: A Critical History* (Bloomington: Indiana University Press, 2006), 219–20; Jacob Stevens, "Prisons of the Stateless: The Derelictions of UNHCR," *New Left Review* 42 (November–December 2006): 53–67.

56. Loescher, *UNHCR and World Politics*, 16. See also ibid., 13–15; "OAU/UNHCR: Commemorative Symposium on Refugees and the Problems of Forced Population Displacements in Africa," special issue of *International Journal of Refugee Law* (July 1995); Rosemary Sales and Brad K. Blitz, "Unwelcome Return," *World Today* 59, no. 4 (April 2003): 21.

57. Loescher, *UNHCR and World Politics*, 18. See also ibid., 16–17; Marita Eastmond and Joakim Öjendal, "Revisiting a 'Repatriation Success': The Case of Cambodia," Peter Marsden, "Repatriation and Reconstruction: The Case of Afghanistan," and Chris Dolan, "Repatriation from South Africa to Mozambique: Undermining Durable Solutions?" all in *The End of the Refugee Cycle: Refugee Repatriation and Reconstruction*, ed. Richard Black and Khalid Koser (New York: Berghahn Books, 1999), 38–55, 56–68, 85–107; Sales and Blitz, "Unwelcome Return," 20.

58. Guiding Principles on Internal Displacement (extract from ECOSOC document E/CN.4/1998/53/Add.2), February 11, 1998, available online at http://www.unhchr.ch/html/menu2/7/b/principles.htm; Internal Displacement Monitoring Centre, "Global Figures," accessed September 14, 2015, http://www.internal-displacement.org/global-figures; MacFarland and Khong, *Human Security and the UN*, 220, 221–22, 317n69; Roberta Cohen and Francis Deng, eds., *The Forsaken People* (Washington, DC: Brookings Institution Press, 1998), 1; Roberta Cohen and Francis M. Deng, *Masses in Flight* (Washington, DC: Brookings Institution, 1992), 275–80.

59. U.N. General Assembly Resolution 58/153, February 24, 2004, https://www.iom.int/jahia/webdav/shared/shared/mainsite/policy_and_research/un/58/A_RES_58_153_en.pdf. See also MacFarland and Khong, *Human Security and the UN*, 222–23; Francis Mading Deng, "The Global Challenge of Internal Displacement," *Washington University Journal of Law*

& Policy 5, no. 1 (January 2001): 149, http://openscholarship. wustl.edu;cgi/viewcontent. cgi?article=1556&context=law_journal_law_policy; George Okoth-Obbo, "Foreword," in *Collection of International Instruments and Legal Texts Concerning Refugees and Others of Concern to UNHCR*, ed. Office of the United Nations High Commissioner on Refugees, vol. 1 (New York: U.N., 2007); Erika Feller, Volker Türk, and Frances Nicholson, eds., *Refugee Protection in International Law: UNHCR's Global Consultations on International Protection* (Cambridge: Cambridge University Press for UNHCR, 2003).

Chapter 7

1. Chamberlain, *Global Offensive*, 10.
2. Bosco, *Five to Rule Them All*, 48–49; Gaiduk, *Divided Together*, 131–32; "United Nations Special Committee on Palestine: Report to the General Assembly, Volume 1," *Official Records of the Second Session of the General Assembly*, Supplement No. 11, A/364, September 3, 1947, https://unispal.un.org/DPA/DPR/unispal.nsf/5ba47a5c6cef541b802563e000493b8c/07175de9fa2e563852568d3006e10f3?OpenDocument (the United Nations Information System on the Question of Palestine (UNISPAL) is an initiative by the U.N. Division for Palestinian Rights); Edward H. Buehrig, *The UN and the Palestinian Refugees: A Study in Nonterritorial Administration* (Bloomington: Indiana University Press, 1971), 3–5, 10.
3. Military forces from Egypt (including a Saudi formation under Egyptian command), Lebanon, Syria, and Iraq invaded Palestine; Transjordan also sent troops, but only into the areas that the United Nations had designated as the potential Arab state around the West Bank and Jerusalem. See U.S. Department of State Office of the Historian, "Milestones, 1945–1952: The Arab-Israeli War of 1948," accessed May 14, 2015, https://history.state.gov/milestones/1945-1952/arab-israeli-war; Gaiduk, *Divided Together*, 133–35; Ruth Gavison, ed., *The Two-State Solution: The UN Partition Resolution of Mandatory Palestine: Analysis and Sources*, trans. from Hebrew by Gadi Weber (New York: Bloomsbury for Metzilah Center for Zionist, Jewish, Liberal and Humanist Thought, 2013) is divided into a part on "Studies on the Partition Resolution" from both Jewish and Arab perspectives and then a section of documents, including the proposals made to the British in the 1930s, the addresses to the Anglo-American Committee of Inquiry in March–April 1946 and its recommendations, and the November 1947 U.N. resolution and its aftermath.
4. For Bernadotte mission, see Buehrig, *UN and the Palestinian Refugees*, 4–5, 10; Joseph Heller, "Bernadotte's Mission to Palestine, 1948," *Middle Eastern Studies* 20, no. 4 (July 1984): 224–32; Mordechai Gazit, "American and British Diplomacy and the Bernadotte Mission," *Historical Journal* 29, no. 3 (1986): 677–96. For aid efforts, see Georgiana G. Stevens, "Arab Refugees, 1948–1952," *Middle East Journal* 6, no. 3 (Summer 1952): 284; Channing B. Richardson, "The United Nations Relief for Palestine Refugees," *International Organization* 4, no. 1 (February 1950): 44–45 (at the time he wrote the article, Richardson was serving with the American Friends Service Committee in the Middle East; he had previously served as liaison officer with the United Nations at Columbia University).
5. As quoted in Buehrig, *UN and the Palestinian Refugees*, 12. See also ibid., 11–13; Richardson, "U.N. Relief," 44–45.
6. Richardson, "U.N. Relief," 45–46.
7. Folke Bernadotte, "Report on Palestine," *Current History* 15 (November 1948): 296–98; Richardson, "U.N. Relief," 45–46; Cary David Stranger, "A Haunting Legacy: The Assassination of Count Bernadotte," *Middle East Journal* 42, no. 2 (1988): 260–72; Peter L.

Hahn, *Crisis and Crossfire: The United States and the Middle East since 1945* (Washington, DC: Potomac Books, 2005), 26; idem, *Caught in the Middle East: U.S. Policy toward the Arab-Israeli Conflict, 1945–61* (Chapel Hill: University of North Carolina Press, 2004), 51–53; Itmar Rabinovich, *The Road Not Taken: Early Arab-Israeli Negotiations* (New York: Oxford University Press, 1991), 47–54; Avi Shlaim, *The Iron Wall: Israel and the Arab World* (New York: W. W. Norton, 2001), 41–47.

8. Richardson, "U.N. Relief," 54.
9. As quoted in Buehrig, *UN and the Palestinian Refugees*, 13–14. See also ibid., 5; Stevens, "Arab Refugees," 285; Hahn, *Crisis and Crossfire*, 26; Rabinovich, *Road Not Taken*, 47–54; Shlaim, *Iron Wall*, 41–47; "International Refugee Organization," 351.
10. Buehrig, *UN and the Palestinian Refugees*, 16–17; Don Peretz, *Israel and the Palestine Arabs* (Washington, DC: Middle East Institute, 1958), 44–50; Hahn, *Crisis and Crossfire*, 26; Rabinovich, *Road Not Taken*, 47–54.
11. Benjamin N. Schiff, *Refugees unto the Third Generation: UN Aid to Palestinians* (Syracuse, NY: Syracuse University Press, 1995), 4–5. See also ibid., 7; Buehrig, *UN and the Palestinian Refugees*, 6, 8, 14, 126–66; Richardson, "U.N. Relief," 53–54.
12. UNTSO, "Helping to Bring Stability in the Middle East," accessed May 15, 2015, http://www.un.org/en/peacekeeping/missions/untso/; Mona Ghali, "United Nations Truce Supervision Organization," in *Evolution of UN Peacekeeping*, 84–103; Andrew Theobald, "The United Nations Truce Supervision Organization (UNTSO)," in *The Oxford Handbook of United Nations Peacekeeping Operations*, 121–32.
13. As quoted in Study Group of the Hebrew University of Jerusalem, *Israel and the United Nations* (New York: Manhattan Publishing Company for the Carnegie Endowment for International Peace, 1956), 50. See also ibid., 49–51, 58–60; United Nations. "Application of Israel for Admission to Membership in the United Nations: Report of the Ad Hoc Political Committee (A/855)," in *General Assembly Official Record*, 3rd sess., 2nd part. 306–36, http://www.un.org/en/ga/search/view_doc.asp?symbol=A/PV.207.
14. Study Group, *Israel and the U.N.*, 51; Staples, *Birth of Development*, 148.
15. As quoted in Mackenzie, *ICAO*, 199. See also ibid., 155, 231, 281.
16. Study Group, *Israel and the U.N.*, 291. See also ibid., 290–92; Murphy, *United Nations Development Programme*, 182.
17. Buehrig, *UN and the Palestinian Refugees*, 18, 22–23, 25; Peretz, *Israel and the Palestine Arabs*, 143–44, 196–98, 222–23.
18. Buehrig, *UN and the Palestinian Refugees*, 15, 21, 24; Peretz, *Israel and the Palestine Arabs*, 50–56, 222–23; Terry Rempel, "Housing and Property Restitution: The Palestinian Refugee Case," in *Returning Home: Housing and Property Restitution Rights of Refugees and Displaced Persons*, ed. Scott Leckie (Ardsley, NY: Transnational Publishers, 2003), 275–315.
19. "A person normally resident in Palestine who has lost his home and his livelihood as a result of the hostilities, and who is in need" (as quoted in Stevens, "Arab Refugees," 289).
20. Stevens, "Arab Refugees," 288. See also ibid., 289–90; Robert Bowker, *Palestinian Refugees: Mythology, Identity, and the Search for Peace* (Boulder, CO: Lynne Rienner Publishers, 2003), 124; Schiff, *Refugees unto the Third Generation*, 8; Milton Viorst, *Reaching for the Olive Branch: UNRWA and Peace in the Middle East* (Washington, DC: Middle East Institute, 1989), 36–39.
21. Staples, *Birth of Development*, 56–62; idem, "Seeing Diplomacy through Bankers' Eyes: The World Bank's Diplomacy toward the Anglo-Iranian Oil Crisis and the Aswan High Dam," *Diplomatic History* 26 (Summer 2002): 397–418; United Nations, "Middle East—UNEF

I: Background (Full Text)," accessed May 6, 2015, http://www.un.org/en/peacekeeping/missions/past/unef1backgr2.html#one; Paul F. Diehl, "First United Nations Emergency Force (UNEF I)," in *Oxford Handbook of United Nations Peacekeeping Operations*, 144–52; Bosco, *Five to Rule Them All*, 73–77; Urquhart, *Hammarskjöld*, 166–68; Hahn, *United States, Great Britain, and Egypt*, 211–39; Keith Kyle, *Suez* (New York: St. Martin's Press, 1991), 135–290.

22. Bosco, *Five to Rule Them All*, 76–78; Robert Bothwell, "Foreword: Pearson's Ambiguous Legacy," in *Pearson's Peacekeepers: Canada and the United Nations Emergency Force, 1956–67*, ed. Michael K. Carroll (Vancouver, Canada: University of British Columbia Press, 2009), xi.

23. Hahn, *Crisis and Crossfire*, 31–32; Hahn, *Caught in the Middle East*, 195–98, 200–07.

24. U.N., "Middle East—UNEF I."

25. UNEF reached its desired strength of 6,000 in February 1957. As the area remained quiet and funding the force became more difficult, the size of the force declined to 5,341 soldiers in 1960; 5,102 in 1963; 4,581 in 1965; 3,959 in 1966; and 3,378 prior to the beginning of UNEF's withdrawal in May 1967. As national UNEF contingents appointed their staff officers, the UNTSO military observers returned to Jerusalem. With the exception of Indonesia (September 1957), Finland (December 1957), and Colombia (December 1958), these contingents remained with UNEF until its withdrawal in 1967. See U.N., "Middle East—UNEF I"; Ghali, "United Nations Emergency Force I."

26. Staples, *Birth of Development*, 61–62.

27. U.N., "Middle East—UNEF I"; Hahn, *Crisis and Crossfire*, 31–32; Hahn, *Caught in the Middle East*, 200–07.

28. Staples, *Birth of Development*, 61–62.

29. U.N., "Middle East—UNEF I"; Carroll, *Pearson's Peacekeepers*; Norman J. Padelford, "Financing Peacekeeping: Politics and Crisis," *International Organization* 19, no. 3 (Summer 1965): 444–62; Sean M. Maloney, *Canada and UN Peacekeeping: Cold War by Other Means, 1945–1970* (St. Catharines, Canada: Vanwell Publishing, 2002), 20–23, 61–78.

30. United Nations, "Lebanon—UNOGIL: Background," accessed April 25, 2015, http://www.un.org/en/peacekeeping/missions/past/unogilbackgr.html; Mona Ghali, "United Nations Observation Group in Lebanon," in *Evolution of UN Peacekeeping*, 163–80; Ana Guedes Mesquita and Nigel D. White, "United Nations Observation Group in Lebanon (UNOGIL)," in *Oxford Handbook of United Nations Peacekeeping Operations*, 153–59; Bosco, *Five to Rule Them All*, 82; U.S. Department of State Office of the Historian, "The Eisenhower Doctrine, 1957," accessed July 23, 2015, https://history.state.gov/milestones/1953-1960/eisenhower-doctrine; Salim Yaqub, *Containing Arab Nationalism: The Eisenhower Doctrine and the Middle East* (Chapel Hill: University of North Carolina Press, 2004); President Fouad Chehab Official Website, "Presidency: The 1958 Crisis," accessed April 25, 2015, http://www.fouadchehab.com/en/; Uriel Dann, *King Hussein and the Challenge of Arab Radicalism* (Oxford: Oxford University Press, 1989), 86–96.

31. United Nations, "Yemen—UNYOM: Background," last modified 2001, http://www.un.org/en/peacekeeping/missions/past/unyombackgr.html; Karl Th. Birgisson, "United Nations Yemen Observation Mission," in *Evolution of UN Peacekeeping*, 206–18; Norrie MacQueen, "United Nations Yemen Observation Mission (UNYOM)," in *Oxford Handbook of United Nations Peacekeeping Operations*, 179–87; Paul Dresch, *A History of Modern Yemen* (Cambridge: Cambridge University Press, 2000), 28–88.

32. Hahn, *Crisis and Crossfire*, 50; Shlaim, *Iron Wall*, 228–36.

33. As quoted in U.N., "Middle East—UNEF I." See also Hahn, *Crisis and Crossfire*, 50–54; Bosco, *Five to Rule Them All*, 104–108; Abba Eban, *An Autobiography* (New York: Random House, 1977); Michael B. Oren, *Six Days of War: June 1957 and the Making of the Modern Middle East* (Oxford: Oxford University Press, 2002), 296–97; "Letter dated 13 June 1967 from the Minister for Foreign Affairs of the Union of Soviet Socialist Republics," U.N. General Assembly Fifth Emergency Special Session, June 19, 1967, http://unispal.un.org/UNISPAL.NSF/0/729809A9BA3345EB852573400054118A.

34. U.N. General Assembly Fifth Emergency Special Session, "U.N. General Assembly Resolution on Humanitarian Assistance in Middle East Conflict," A/RES/2252 (ES-V), July 1, 1967, 2, in *International Legal Materials* 6, no. 4 (July 1967): 834; Paul Cossali and Clive Robson, *Stateless in Gaza* (London: Zed Books, 1986), 90–91, 120–21.

35. Hahn, *Crisis and Crossfire*, 54–55; Bosco, *Five to Rule Them All*, 109; Sydney D. Bailey, *The Making of Resolution 242* (Dordrecht, Netherlands: Martinus Nijhoff, 1985); Boyd, *Fifteen Men on a Powder Keg*, 37; Eban, *Autobiography*, 451–52; Richard Bordeaux Parker, *The Politics of Miscalculation in the Middle East* (Bloomington: Indiana University Press, 1993), 127–29, 133–36.

36. Hahn, *Crisis and Crossfire*, 55–56; Yaacov Bar-Siman-Tov, *The Israeli–Egyptian War of Attrition, 1967–1970: A Case Study in Limited Local War* (New York: Columbia University Press, 1980), 175–208; David A. Korn, *Stalemate: The War of Attrition and Great Power Diplomacy in the Middle East, 1967–1970* (Boulder, CO: Westview Press, 1992), 143–88; Parker, *Politics of Miscalculation*, 133–47.

37. Chamberlain, *Global Offensive*, 3, 7. He divides the scholarly literature on the PLO into three main groupings: (1) works by Middle East specialists that generally take a Palestine-centric approach that has resulted in excellent studies on Palestinian politics and society—see, for example, Nadine Picaudou, *Le Mouvement national palestinien: Genèse et structures* (The Palestinian National Movement: Genesis and structures) (Paris: Harmattan, 1989); Rashid Khalidi, *The Iron Cage: The Story of the Palestinian Struggle for Statehood* (Boston: Beacon, 2006); (2) works by scholars of the Arab-Israeli conflict specifically or U.S. foreign relations generally that tend to take the perspective of the United States and/or Israel due to their reliance on archives in those countries—for example, Hahn, *Caught in the Middle East*; Benny Morris, *Righteous Victims: A History of the Zionist-Arab Conflict, 1881–1999* (London: John Murray, 2000); and (3) those works that focus on "international terrorism," with a tight focus on tactics, such as Bruce Hoffman, *Inside Terrorism* (New York: Columbia University Press, 2006). He concludes by stating that his study "moves beyond the regional framework of the Arab-Israeli conflict to focus on the international dimensions of the Palestinian armed struggle and place the PLO in the global context of revolutionary change during the Cold War era" (Chamberlain, *Global Offensive*, 9. See also ibid., 270n13, 270n14).

38. Chamberlain, *Global Offensive*, 6. See also ibid., 3, 5–7; William Quandt, *Peace Process* (Washington, DC: Brookings Institution Press, 2005), 94–111.

39. Mackenzie, *ICAO*, 246–57, 259–75; Robert G. Bell, "The U.S. Response to Terrorism against International Civil Aviation," *Orbis* 19, no. 4 (Winter 1976): 1326–43.

40. All of the quotes are included in U.N. General Assembly Resolution 3379 (XXX), "Elimination of All Forms of Racial Discrimination," November 10, 1975, http://unispal.un.org/UNISPAL.NSF/0/761C1063530766A7052566A2005B74D1. See also Barber, "Decolonization," 134; Bosco, *Five to Rule Them All*, 132, 134, 136–37.

41. Schiff, *Refugees unto the Third Generation*, 8, 70.

42. Hahn, *Crisis and Crossfire*, 57–58; Quandt, *Peace Process*, 116–33, 136–47.

43. Hahn, *Crisis and Crossfire*, 58–60; Walter Isaacson, *Kissinger: A Biography* (New York: Simon & Schuster 1992), 512–24; Kenneth W. Stein, *Heroic Diplomacy: Sadat, Kissinger, Carter, Begin, and the Quest for Arab-Israeli Peace* (New York: Routledge, 1999), 80–96; Bosco, *Five to Rule Them All*, 126–31.

44. Hahn, *Crisis and Crossfire*, 60–61; Isaacson, *Kissinger*, 537–38, 550–72; Stein, *Heroic Diplomacy*, 97–162, 175–81; Quandt, *Peace Process*, 229–46.

45. Shlaim, *Iron Wall*, 384–400; United Nations, "UNDOF: United Nations Disengagement Observer Force," accessed April 26, 2015, http://www.un.org/en/peacekeeping/missions/undof/; U.N. Security Council Resolution 350 (1974), accessed April 26, 2015, http://www.un.org/en/ga/search/view_doc.asp?symbol=S/RES/350(1974); Peter Rudloff and Paul F. Diehl, "United Nations Disengagement Observer Force (UNDOF)," in *Oxford Handbook of United Nations Peacekeeping Operations*, 238–47.

46. United Nations, "UNIFIL—United Nations Interim Force in Lebanon: Background," accessed April 26, 2015, http://www.un.org/en/peacekeeping/missions/unifil/background.shtml; Edgar O'Ballance, *Civil War in Lebanon, 1975–92* (Houndsmills, UK: Macmillan, 1998), 61–78; Mona Ghali, "United Nations Interim Force in Lebanon," in *Evolution of UN Peacekeeping*, 181–205; Alexandra Novosseloff, "United Nations Interim Force in Lebanon (UNIFIL I)," in *Oxford Handbook of United Nations Peacekeeping Operations*, 248–59.

47. Hahn, *Crisis and Crossfire*, 64–65; John Boykin, *Cursed Is the Peacemaker: The American Diplomat versus the Israeli General, Beirut 1982* (Belmont, CA: Applegate Press, 2002); O'Ballance, *Civil War in Lebanon*, 98–116.

48. Hahn, *Crisis and Crossfire*, 65–66; Ronald Reagan, *An American Life: The Autobiography* (New York: Simon & Schuster, 1990), 430–42; Shlaim, *Iron Wall*, 407–12; Schiff, *Refugees unto the Third Generation*, 71; Bosco, *Five to Rule Them All*, 136.

49. Hahn, *Crisis and Crossfire*, 66–67; Itamar Rabinovich, *The War for Lebanon, 1970–1985*, rev. ed. (Ithaca, NY: Cornell University Press, 1985), 143–45; Michael Johnson, *All Honourable Men: The Social Origins of War in Lebanon* (London: I. B. Tauris for the Centre for Lebanese Studies, 2001); O'Ballance, *Civil War in Lebanon*, 117–35.

50. U.N., "UNIFIL—United Nations Interim Force in Lebanon"; Schiff, *Refugees unto the Third Generation*, 71–72, 74, 112; Ghada Hashem Talhami, *Palestinian Refugees: Pawns to Political Actors* (New York: Nova Science Publishers, 2003), 136, 140, 144; Viorst, *Reaching for the Olive Branch*, 59–61, 71–80.

51. Avalon Project, "Camp David Accords; September 17, 1978," Yale Law School Library, last modified 2008, http://avalon.law.yale.edu/20th_century/campdav.asp; United Nations Development Programme, Programme of Assistance to the Palestinian People, "About UNDP/PAPP," accessed April 25, 2015, http://www.undp.ps/en/aboutundp/aboutpapp.html; Murphy, *United Nations Development Programme*, 11, 181–82, 187.

52. United Nations Development Programme, Programme of Assistance to the Palestinian People, "Unique Features of PAPP," accessed April 25, 2015, http://www.undp.ps/en/aboutundp/aboutpapp.html. See also Murphy, *United Nations Development Programme*, 11–12, 182; UNDP PAPP, *Twenty Years of Partnership in the West Bank and the Gaza Strip* (Jerusalem: UNDP/PAPP, 1999); John Olver, *Roadblocks and Mindblocks: Partnering with the PLO and Israel* (Rye, NY: self-published, 2002).

53. Talhami, *Palestinian Refugees*, 134–35.

54. For a short account of the Iran-Iraq War, see Hahn, *Crisis and Crossfire*, 82–85; the best current history of the conflict as a whole (based on academic reviews) is Dilip Hiro, *The Longest War: The Iran–Iraq Military Conflict* (London: Paladin, 1990), 7–212. There were quite a few contemporary studies of the Iran-Iraq War, but the aspiring researcher should

be aware, as one reviewer of this literature has said, that "in the race to beat competitors and to capitalize on a favorable publishing market, numerous books were hurriedly published, each with a title more eye-catching than the other, and each promising to have the definitive answers concerning Saddam [Hussein]'s territorial and military exploits. Sacrificed in the process were balance and objectivity, scholarly depth, and, often, an accurate understanding of the many political, economic, and diplomatic forces at work both in Iraq and in the larger Middle East" (Mehran Kamrava, review of Miron Rezun, "Saddam Hussein's Gulf Wars: Ambivalent Stakes in the Middle East," in *International Journal of Middle East Studies* 26, no. 1 [February 1994]: 168).

See also Bosco, *Five to Rule Them All*, 141–42; Javed Ali, "Chemical Weapons and the Iran–Iraq War: A Case Study in Non-compliance," *Nonproliferation Review* (Spring 2001): 43–58, accessed May 7, 2015, http://cns.miis.edu/npr/pdfs/81ali.pdf; United Nations Security Council, "Report of the Specialists Appointed by the Secretary General to Investigate Allegations by the Islamic Republic of Iran Concerning the Use of Chemical Weapons," March 26, 1984, Document S/16433, http://repository.un.org/bitstream/handle/11176/63929/S_16433-EN.pdf?sequence=3&isAllowed=y; Bahram Mostaghimi and Masoud Taromsari, "Double Standard: The Security Council and the Two Wars," in *Iranian Perspectives on the Iran-Iraq War*, ed. Farhang Rajaee (Gainesville: University Press of Florida, 1997), 62–72.

55. Janice Gross Stein, "The Wrong Strategy in the Right Place: The United States in the Gulf," *International Security* 13, no. 3 (Winter 1988–89): 147–48, 151; Bosco, *Five to Rule Them All*, 148; Javier Pérez de Cuéllar, *Pilgrimage for Peace: A Secretary-General's Memoir* (New York: St. Martin's Press, 1997), 49.

56. U.N., "Iran-Iraq—UNIIMOG: Background," accessed 6 May 2015, http://www.un.org/en/peacekeeping/missions/past/uniimogbackgr.html; Bosco, *Five to Rule Them All*, 150–53; Cameron R. Hume, *The United Nations, Iran, and Iraq: How Peacemaking Changed* (Bloomington: Indiana University Press, 1994), 55–102; Stein, "Wrong Strategy in the Right Place," 142, 148–51, 153; Hiro, *Longest War*, 223–50; Djamchid Momtaz, "The Implementation of UN Resolution 598," in *Iranian Perspectives on the Iran-Iraq War*, 123–32; Smith, "United Nations Iran-Iraq Military Observer Group," in *Evolution of UN Peacekeeping*, 237–57.

57. Estimates of deaths and casualties vary. The UNRWA numbers come from Schiff, *Refugees unto the Third Generation*, 237–38, and the others from Shlaim, *Iron Wall*, 451. See also Shlaim, *Iron Wall*, 450–54; Hahn, *Crisis and Crossfire*, 88–89.

58. For the 1987–88 school year, all West Bank schools were closed from February until late May, losing 40 percent of class-time; sporadic closings in Gaza led to the loss of 35 percent of the year's class-time. The 1988–89 school year saw West Bank schools open only in December and January and the Israeli officials banning the distribution of home-schooling materials; while in the Gaza Strip schools 50 percent of class-time was lost, and Israeli officials forbade the extension of the school year into the summer. The 1989–90 school year witnessed much of the same, with Gaza students losing 40 percent of class-time and West Bank schools closed for three months (but the school year was extended through July to make up some of this time). Forty percent of class-time was also lost in 1990–91. See Schiff, *Refugees unto the Third Generation*, 10, 227, 234, 247, 259, 265; Hahn, *Crisis and Crossfire*, 89; Shlaim, *Iron Wall*, 454–67; Talhami, *Palestinian Refugees*, 136; Gerhard Pulfer and Ingrid Jaradat Gassner, *UNRWA: Between Refugee Aid and Power Politics* (Jerusalem: Alternative Information Center, 1997), 11.

59. As quoted in Hahn, *Crisis and Crossfire*, 90. See also ibid., 89–90; Shlaim, *Iron Wall*, 454–67; Quandt, *Peace Process*, 364–73, 385–92; Palestine National Council, "Declaration of Independence," November 15, 1988, http://www.nad-plo.org/userfiles/file/Document/

declaration%20of%20independence%20En.pdf; "Yasser Arafat, Speech at UN General Assembly," *Le Monde diplomatique*, English edition, December 13, 1998, http://mondediplo.com/focus/mideast/arafat88-en; George P. Shultz, *Turmoil and Triumph: Diplomacy, Power, and the Victory of the American Deal* (New York: Scribner, 2010), 1016–45; James A. Baker, *The Politics of Diplomacy: Revolution, War, and Peace, 1989–1992* (New York: Putnam, 1995), 115–32.

60. Poorvi Chitalkar and David M. Malone, "The UN Security Council and Iraq," United Nations University Working Paper series, no. 1 (November 2013), https://collections.unu.edu/eserv/UNU:5/wp01_theunscandiraq1.pdf; Jan Bury, "United Nations Iraq-Kuwait Observation Mission (UNIKOM)" in *The Oxford Handbook of United Nations Peacekeeping Operations*, ed. Joachim A. Koops, Norrie MacQueen, Thierry Tardy, and Paul D. Williams (Oxford: Oxford University Press, 2015), 314–24; Bosco, *Five to Rule Them All*, 155–63; U.N. Security Council Resolution 672 (October 12, 1990), http://palestineun.org/wp-content/uploads/2013/08/SC-672-1990.pdf; U.N. Security Council Resolution 673 (October 24, 1990), https://unispal.un.org/DPA/DPR/unispal.nsf/1ce874ab1832a53e852570bb006dfaf6/3b28c7d6384fe1ea852560dd00639476?OpenDocument; Margaret Thatcher, *The Downing Street Years* (New York: HarperCollins, 1993), 821, 828; Paul Conlon, *United Nations Sanctions Management: A Case Study of the Iraq Sanctions Committee, 1990–1994* (Ardsley, NY: Transnational, 2000); Elaine Sciolino and Eric Pace, "Putting Teeth in an Embargo: How U.S. Convinced the U.N.," *New York Times*, August 30, 1990, A1, http://www.nytimes.com/1990/08/30/world/un-s-watershed-special-report-confrontation-gulf-put ting-teeth-embargo-us.html; Baker, *Politics of Diplomacy*, 305, 321, 325–26; Ilyana Kuziemko and Eric Werker, "How Much Is a Seat on the Security Council Worth? Foreign Aid and Bribery at the United Nations," *Journal of Political Economy* 114, no. 5 (2006): 907.

61. Bosco, *Five to Rule Them All*, 163–64; Jean E. Krasno and James S. Sutterlin, *The United Nations and Iraq: Defanging the Viper* (Westport, CT: Praeger, 2003), 5, 19–22; Sarah Graham-Brown, *Sanctioning Saddam: The Politics of Intervention in Iraq* (New York: Tauris, 1999), 56–104.

62. Schiff, *Refugees unto the Third Generation*, xiv, 266–67.

63. Hahn, *Crisis and Crossfire*, 92–93; Dennis Ross, *The Missing Peace: The Inside Story of the Fight for Middle East Peace* (New York: Farrar, Straus, and Giroux, 2004), 101–104; Quandt, *Peace Process*, 404–12; Shlaim, *Iron Wall*, 502–12; Avalon Project, "Israel-Palestine Liberation Organization Agreement: 1993," http://avalon.law.yale.edu/20th_century/isrplo.asp; Baker, *Politics of Diplomacy*, 512; Warren Christopher, *Chances of a Lifetime* (New York: Scribner, 2001), 194–204; Bill Clinton, *My Life* (New York: Knopf, 2004), 541–45.

64. Schiff, *Refugees unto the Third Generation*, 10, 282–83; Talhami, *Palestinian Refugees*, 136–37, 141; Pulfer and Gassner, *UNRWA*, 11–12, 15; Dina Craissanti, "New NGOs and Democratic Governance in Palestine: A Pioneering Model for the Arab World?," in *NGOs and Governance in the Arab World*, ed. Sarah Ben Néfissa, Nabil Abd al-Fattah, Sari Hanafi, and Carlos Milani (Cairo: American University in Cairo Press, 2005), 181; Saad Eddin Ibrahim, "Civil Society and Prospects of Democratization in the Arab World," in *Civil Society in the Middle East*, vol. 1, ed. A. R. Norton (Leiden, Netherlands: E. J. Brill, 1995), 27–54.

65. Murphy, *United Nations Development Programme*, 184–86; Olver, *Roadblocks and Mindblocks*, 166–70; Timothy S. Rothermel, "Palestinian Elections: Chance for a Model Democracy," *Christian Science Monitor*, December 27, 2004, http://www.csmonitor.com/2004/1227/p09s01-coop.html; UNDP, *Partnership for Peace-Building: Palestine*, accessed May 13, 2015, http://www.undp.ps/en/newsroom/publications/pdf/other/japan.pdf; UNDP/PAPP, *TOKTEN: 10 Years of Brain Gain* (Jerusalem: UNDP/PAPP, 2004), http://www.undp.ps/en/newsroom/publications/pdf/other/Tokten05.pdf; Elisabeth Rehn and

Jean Claude Aime, *UNDP in the Occupied Palestinian Territory: Programme Review 2005* (New York: UNDP, 2005), 31, accessed May 13, 2015, http://www.undp.ps/en/newsroom/publications/pdf/other/progreview.pdf.

66. Hahn, *Crisis and Crossfire*, 93–94; Ross, *Missing Peace*, 122–36, 188–93, 195–208; Christopher, *Chances of a Lifetime*, 205–208, 211–16; "1995 Oslo Interim Agreement," ProCon.org, last modified April 24, 2008, http://israelipalestinian.procon.org/view.background-resource.php?resourceID=000921; Rothermel, "Palestinian Elections"; Clinton, *My Life*, 609–10, 625–26; Warren Christopher, *In the Stream of History: Shaping Foreign Policy for a New Era* (Stanford, CA: Stanford University Press, 1998), 195–202.

67. Hahn, *Crisis and Crossfire*, 93–95; U.N. General Assembly, "Tenth Emergency Special Session: Illegal Israeli Actions in Occupied East Jerusalem and the Rest of the Occupied Palestinian Territory," accessed July 24, 2015, http://www.un.org/en/ga/sessions/emergency10th.shtml; Madeleine Albright, *Madam Secretary: A Memoir* (New York: Miramax, 2003), 291–92; Clinton, *My Life*, 626, 747–48; Christopher, *In the Stream of History*, 497–504; Christopher, *Chances of a Lifetime*, 205–08, 216–24; Ross, *Missing Peace*, 122–36, 137–63, 188–208, 216–45; Bowker, *Palestinian Refugees*, 181–214; Talhami, *Palestinian Refugees*, 135–37, 141–43.

68. Hahn, *Crisis and Crossfire*, 95–96; Ross, *Missing Peace*, 415–59, 650–711; Clinton, *My Life*, 814–20, 832–33, 911–16; Albright, *Madam Secretary*, 288–318, 484–93; Talhami, *Palestinian Refugees*, 144; "Wye River Memorandum [Excerpts]," in *A History of the Arab-Israeli Conflict*, 6th ed., ed. Ian J. Bickerton and Carla L. Klausner (Boston: Prentice Hall, 2010), 327–30.

69. Hahn, *Crisis and Crossfire*, 96–99; "A Performance-Based Roadmap to a Permanent Two-State Solution to the Israeli-Palestinian Conflict," in Bickerton and Klausner, *A History*, 364–66; Bosco, *Five to Rule Them All*, 220; U.N. Security Council Resolution 1405, April 19, 2002, https://unispal.un.org/DPA/DPR/unispal.nsf/5ba47a5c6cef541b802563 e000493b8c/9d8245ad174f11d785256ba3004c8663?OpenDocument; Ross, *Missing Peace*, 536–90, 742–58; Talhami, *Palestinian Refugees*, 146–49; Ian Williams, "In Advance of Jenin Report, Lantos, AIPAC Wage Campaign against UNRWA," *Washington Report on Middle East Affairs* 21, no. 6 (August 2002): 43, 58, http://www.wrmea.org/2002-august/in-advance-of-jenin-report-lantos-aipac-wage-campaign-agai nst-unrwa.html; U.S. Department of State, "A Performance-Based Roadmap to a Permanent Two-State Solution to the Israeli-Palestinian Conflict," April 30, 2003, in *Israel in the Middle East: Documents and Readings on Society, Politics, and Foreign Relations, Pre-1948 to the Present*, 2nd ed., ed. Itamar Rabinovich and Jehuda Reinharz (Lebanon, NH: University Press of New England, 2007), 536–37; Clinton, *My Life*, 883–88, 903–04, 925–26, 929, 935–38, 943–45; Albright, *Madam Secretary*, 473–82, 495–98; Murphy, *United Nations Development Programme*, 182–83; U.N., *The Question of Palestine and the United Nations* (New York: United Nations, 2008), https://unispal.un.org/pdfs/DPI2499.pdf.

70. World Bank, "Palestinian Reform and Development Plan Trust Fund," last modified 2013, http://go.worldbank.org/BCF0DGPRR0; idem, "Trust Fund Details," last modified 2013, http://go.worldbank.org/JJUOZ8HYI0. Someone wanting to understand the current work of UNDP's PAPP could fruitfully start by looking at the online publications of the organization (including *UNDP Monthly* and the quarterly *Focus* by the PAPP Communications Office, with copies from 2000 to 2005) to get an overview: http://www.undp.ps/en/newsroom/publications.html.

71. U.N., "UNIFIL—United Nations Interim Force in Lebanon."

72. Ibid.; Novosseloff, "Expanded United Nations Interim Force in Lebanon (UNIFIL II)," 767–78.

Chapter 8

1. Kenneth Cmiel, "The Recent History of Human Rights," in *The Human Rights Revolution: An International History*, ed. Akira Iriye, Petra Goedde, and William I. Hitchcock (New York: Oxford University Press, 2012), 27–52, sees one major approach within the historiography of human rights being an exploration of the change over time in the language and meaning of human rights. See also Akira Iriye and Petra Goedde, "Introduction: Human Rights as History," in *Human Rights Revolution*, 4; Paul Gordon Lauren, *The Evolution of International Human Rights: Visions Seen* (Philadelphia: University of Pennsylvania Press, 1999), 73.
2. Roger Normand and Sarah Zaidi, *Human Rights at the UN: The Political History of Universal Justice* (Bloomington: Indiana University Press, 2008), 1; Stefan-Ludwig Hoffman, "Introduction: Genealogies of Human Rights," in *Human Rights in the Twentieth Century*, ed. Stefan-Ludwig Hoffmann (Cambridge: Cambridge University Press, 2011), 1–26; Jolly, Emmerij, and Weiss, *UN Ideas*, 51–58; Tom J. Farer, "The United Nations and Human Rights: More Than a Whimper," *Human Rights Quarterly* 9 (1987): 550–86.
3. Iriye and Goedde, "Introduction," 6.
4. Steven Jensen, *The Making of International Human Rights: The 1960s, Decolonization, and the Reconstruction of Global Values* (Cambridge: Cambridge University Press, 2016); Iriye and Goedde, "Introduction," 12–13; A. W. Brian Simpson, *Human Rights and the End of Empire: Britain and the Genesis of the European Convention* (New York: Oxford University Press, 2001); Javier Garcia Roca and Pablo Santolaya, eds., *Europe of Rights: A Compendium of the European Convention of Human Rights* (Leiden, Netherlands: Martinus Nijhoff Publishers, 2012); Michael D. Goldhaber, *A People's History of the European Court of Human Rights* (New Brunswick, NJ: Rutgers University Press, 2007); Anna P. Schreiber, *The Inter-American Commission on Human Rights* (Leyden, Netherlands: A. W. Sijthoff, 1970).
5. Mary Ann Glendon, *A World Made New: Eleanor Roosevelt and the Universal Declaration of Human Rights* (New York: Random House, 2002), 73–78; Benjamin Nathans, "Soviet Rights—Talk in the Post-Stalin Era," Andreas Eckert, "African Nationalists and Human Rights, 1940s–1970s," and Fabian Klose, "'Sources of Embarrassment': Human Rights, State of Emergency, and the Wars of Decolonization," all in *Human Rights in the Twentieth Century*, 168–69, 189–90, 285–86, 237–38.
6. United Nations Human Rights, Office of the High Commissioner for Human Rights, "International Convention on the Elimination of All Forms of Racial Discrimination," accessed June 2, 2015, http://www.ohchr.org/EN/ProfessionalInterest/Pages/CERD.aspx; Normand and Zaidi, *Human Rights at the UN*, 260; Barbara J. Keys, *Reclaiming American Virtue: The Human Rights Revolution of the 1970s* (Cambridge, MA: Harvard University Press, 2014), 48–74.
7. *Final Act of the International Conference on Human Rights: Teheran, 22 April to 13 May 1968* (New York: United Nations, 1968), A/CONF.32/41, http://legal.un.org/avl/pdf/ha/fatchr/Final_Act_of_TehranConf.pdf. See also Iriye and Goedde, "Introduction," 5–6, 9; Stephen Hopgood, *Keepers of the Flame: Understanding Amnesty International* (Ithaca, NY: Cornell University Press, 2006); Volker Schneider, "The Global Social Capital of Human Rights Movements: A Case Study on Amnesty International," in *Private Organizations in Global Politics*, ed. Karsten Ronit and Volker Schneider (London: Routledge, 2000), 146–64; Roland Burke, "From Individual Rights to National Development: The First UN International Conference on Human Rights, Tehran 1968," *Journal of World History* 19, no. 3 (September 2008): 275–96.

8. Iriye and Goedde, "Introduction," Paul Rubinson, "'For Our Soviet Colleagues': Scientific Internationalism, Human Rights, and the Cold War," and Sarah B. Snyder, "Principles Overwhelming Tanks: Human Rights and the End of the Cold War," all in *Human Rights Revolution*, 17–18, 245–64, 265–83; Schreiber, *Inter-American Commission on Human Rights*; Thomas E. McCarthy and Karel Vasak, *The Inter-American Commission on Human Rights: Cases and Materials* (Strasbourg, France: International Institute of Human Rights, 1978).
9. Iriye and Goedde, "Introduction," 11–12; Asian Cultural Forum on Development, *Our Voice: Bangkok NGO Declaration on Human Rights* (Bangkok: Asian Cultural Forum on Development); William Korey, *NGOs and the Universal Declaration of Human Rights: A Curious Grapevine* (New York: Palgrave Macmillan, 1998), 472–91; Frans Viljoen, *International Human Rights in Africa* (Oxford: Oxford University Press, 2007); Manisuli Ssenyonjo, ed., *The African Regional Human Rights System: Thirty Years after the African Charter on Human and Peoples' Rights* (Leiden, Netherlands: Martinus Nijhoff Publishers, 2012).
10. Iriye and Goedde, "Introduction," 5. A sample of works by scholars and practitioners of international law includes Simpson, *Human Rights and the End of Empire*; Arnold McNair, *The Development of International Justice: Two Lectures Delivered at the Law Center of New York University in December, 1953* (New York: New York University Press, 1954); Egon Schwelb, *Human Rights and the International Community: The Roots and Growth of the Universal Declaration of Human Rights, 1948–1963* (Chicago: Quadrangle Books, 1964). For works by political scientists, see, for example, William Korey, *The Key to Human Rights Implementation* (New York: Carnegie Endowment for International Peace, 1968); M. Glen Johnson, "Historical Perspectives on Human Rights and U.S. Foreign Policy," *Universal Human Rights* 2, no. 3 (July–September 1980): 1–18.
11. Jensen, *Making of International Human Rights*; Yogesh Tyagi, *The UN Human Rights Committee: Practice and Procedure* (Cambridge: Cambridge University Press, 2011), 4.
12. Cmiel, "Recent History of Human Rights," 40–42. See also ibid., 27–52; Normand and Zaidi, *Human Rights at the UN*, xxi.
13. Sarah B. Snyder, "Human Rights and U.S. Foreign Relations: A Historiographical Review," *Passport* 44 (April 2013): 19. See also Mark Philip Bradley, "Approaching the Universal Declaration of Human Rights," in *Human Rights Revolution*, 327–43.
14. Iriye and Goedde, "Introduction," 3. See also Nathan J. Citino, "The Global Frontier: Comparative History and the Frontier-Borderlands Approach," in *Explaining the History of American Foreign Relations*, ed. Michael J. Hogan and Thomas G. Paterson, 2nd ed. (Cambridge: Cambridge University Press, 2004), 195.
15. Iriye and Goedde, "Introduction," 4; Irvine, *Between Justice and Politics*; Lauren, *Evolution of Human Rights*, 73.
16. ILO, "Declaration Concerning the Aims and Purposes of the International Labour Organisation (Declaration of Philadelphia)," last modified 2012, http://www.ilo.org/dyn/normlex/en/f?p=1000:62:0::NO:62:P62_LIST_ENTRIE_ID:2453907:NO#declaration. See also Daniel Roger Maul, "The International Labour Organization and the Globalization of Human Rights," in *Human Rights in the Twentieth Century*, 301.
17. Iriye and Goedde, "Introduction," 4–5; Glendon, *World Made New*, 32, 35–51; Dag Hammarskjöld Library, "Research Guide: Drafting of the Universal Declaration of Human Rights," last updated January 27, 2016, http://research.un.org/en/undhr. The first Commission included delegates from Australia, Belgium, Byelorussia, Chile, China, Egypt, France, Great Britain, India, Iran, Lebanon, Panama, the Philippines, the Soviet Union, Ukraine, the United States, Uruguay, and Yugoslavia.

18. Glendon, *World Made New*, 36, 112; Iriye and Goedde, "Introduction," 6; Allida Black, "Are Women 'Human'? The UN and the Struggle to Recognize Women's Rights as Human Rights," in *Human Rights Revolution*, 135; Johannes Morsink, *The Universal Declaration of Human Rights: Origins, Drafting, and Intent* (Philadelphia: University of Pennsylvania Press, 1999); Glenda Sluga, "René Cassin: Les droits de l'homme and the Universality of Human Rights, 1945–1966," in *Human Rights in the Twentieth Century*, 108–10.

19. Normand and Zaidi, *Human Rights at the UN*, 197–99; Iriye and Goedde, "Introduction," 4–5; Jennifer Amos, "Embracing and Contesting: The Soviet Union and the Universal Declaration of Human Rights, 1948–1958," in *Human Rights in the Twentieth Century*, 147.

20. Citino, "Global Frontier," 197; U.N. Commission on Human Rights, "Summary Record of the 130th Meeting Held at Lake Success, New York, on Thursday, 16 June 1949," E/CN.4/SR 130, p. 10, http://hr-travaux.law.virginia.edu/content/summary-record-130th-meeting-held-lake-success-new-york-thursday-16-june-1949-commission. See also Gaiduk, *Divided Together*, 195; Anderson, *Eyes off the Prize*; Amos, "Embracing and Contesting," 147–65; Normand and Zaidi, *Human Rights at the UN*, 1, 197, 201–7, 210–11; Mary Dudziak, *Cold War Civil Rights: Race and the Image of American Democracy* (Princeton, NJ: Princeton University Press, 2000); United Nations, *The United Nations and Human Rights, 1945-1995* (New York: United Nations Department of Public Information, 1995).

21. Amos, "Embracing and Contesting," 147–65; Snyder, "Human Rights and U.S. Foreign Relations," 16; Iriye and Goedde, "Introduction," 7, 10, 16–17; Samuel Moyn, "Imperialism, Self- Determination, and the Rise of Human Rights," in *Human Rights Revolution*, 159–78; Roland Burke, "The Compelling Dialogue of Freedom: Human Rights in the 1955 Bandung Conference," *Human Rights Quarterly* 28, no. 4 (November 2006): 947–65; idem, *The Politics of Decolonization and the Evolution of the International Human Rights Project* (Philadelphia: University of Pennsylvania Press, 2010).

22. Normand and Zaidi, *Human Rights at the UN*, 200–201, 203, 209–10, 215–16.

23. Ibid., 197–98, 201–202, 212–32.

24. As quoted in Anderson, *Eyes off the Prize*, 239; Normand and Zaidi, *Human Rights at the UN*, 229. See also Anderson, *Eyes off the Prize*, 236–39; Normand and Zaidi, *Human Rights at the UN*, 198–99, 209, 229; Rowland Brucken, *A Most Uncertain Crusade: The United States, the United Nations, and Human Rights, 1941–1953* (DeKalb: Northern Illinois University Press, 2014); Black, "Are Women 'Human'?" 142; Tyagi, *UN Human Rights Committee.*

25. Tyagi, *UN Human Rights Committee*, 2n5, 3, 5. See also D. McGoldrick, *The Human Rights Committee: Its Role in the Development of the International Convention on Civil and Political Rights* (Oxford: Clarendon Press, 1991), 20–22; Alfred de Zayas, "The Potential for the United States Joining the Covenant Family," *Georgia Journal of International and Comparative Law* 20, no. 2 (1990): 309–10.

26. "1968: International Year for Human Rights, A/RES/2081 (XX)," accessed May 31, 2015, http://www.un.org/en/sections/observances/international-years/.

27. Normand and Zaidi, *Human Rights at the UN*, 47–48, 247–58; Sluga, "René Cassin," 107–24; G. Daniel Cohen, "The Holocaust and the 'Human Rights Revolution': A Reassessment," in *Human Rights Revolution*, 53–71; Charles D. Amoun, *Study of Discrimination in Education* (New York: U.N. Sub-Commission on Prevention of Discrimination and Protection of Minorities, 1957).

28. See, for example, Study of the Right of Everyone to Be Free from Arbitrary Arrest, *Detention and Exile* (New York: United Nations, 1964); Egranary Digital Library, "Global Disability

Rights Library," accessed March 11, 2016, http://www.widernet.org/egranary/gdrl; Luin Goldring and Sailaja Krishnamurti, eds., *Organizing the Transnational: Labour, Politics, and Social Change* (Vancouver, Canada: University of British Columbia Press, 2011); Douglas Sanders, "Getting Lesbian and Gay Issues on the International Human Rights Agenda," *Human Rights Quarterly* 18, no. 1 (February 1996): 67–106; Laura Belmonte, *The International LGBT Rights Movement*, New Approaches to International History series (London: Bloomsbury Publishing, forthcoming).

29. League of Nations, "Geneva Declaration of the Rights of the Child," September 26, 1924, http://www.un-documents.net/gdrc1924.htm. See also Geraldine Van Bueren, *The International Law on the Rights of the Child* (Dodrecht, Netherlands: Martinus Nijhoff, 1995), 3; Yves Beigbeder, "Children," in *Oxford Handbook on the U.N.*, 512.

30. As quoted in Normand and Zaidi, *Human Rights at the UN*, 283. See also ibid., 282–83; A. Ording, "The United Nations and the World's Children," *Annals of the American Academy of Political and Social Science* 252 (July 1947): 63–65; Black, *Children First*, chapter 1; Marta Balińska, *For the Good of Humanity: Ludwik Rajchman, Medical Stateman* (Budapest: Central European University Press, 1998), 201–34.

31. UNICEF, "Declaration of the Rights of the Child," accessed June 2, 2015, http://www.unicef.org/malaysia/1959-Declaration-of-the-Rights-of-the-Child.pdf. See also Normand and Zaidi, *Human Rights at the UN*, 282–83; Black, *Children First*, chapter 1; Joan Bel Geddes, "The Rights of Children in World Perspective," in *The Children's Rights Movement: Overcoming the Oppression of Young People*, ed. Beatrice Gross and Ronald Gross (Garden City, NY: Anchor Press, 1977), 214; Beigbeder, "Children," 512.

32. Normand and Zaidi, *Human Rights at the UN*, 283–85, 435n284; Cynthia P. Cohen, "The Role of Nongovernmental Organizations in the Drafting of the Convention on the Rights of the Child," *Human Rights Quarterly* 12, no. 1 (February 1990): 137–47; J. Le Blanc, *The Convention on the Rights of the Child* (Lincoln: University of Nebraska Press, 1995); Barbara Bennett Woodhouse, *Hidden in Plain Sight: The Tragedy of Children's Rights from Ben Franklin to Lionel Tate* (Princeton, NJ: Princeton University Press, 2008), 10–11, 29, 31.

33. Geddes, "Rights of Children in World Perspective," 215–16; Woodhouse, *Hidden in Plain Sight*, 2, 27, 30, 32–33; Beatrice Gross and Ronald Gross, "Introduction," in *Children's Rights Movement*, 1, 6–7; Normand and Zaidi, *Human Rights at the UN*, 283–86; UNICEF, "Convention on the Rights of the Child: Frequently Asked Questions," last modified November 30, 2005, http://www.unicef.org/crc/index_30229.html; Beigbeder, "Children," 513; UNICEF, "The African Charter on the Rights and Welfare of the Child," accessed June 2, 2015, http://www.unicef.org/esaro/children_youth_5930.html; Council of Europe, "European Convention on the Exercise of Children's Rights," accessed June 2, 2015, http://conventions.coe.int/treaty/en/Treaties/Html/160.htm.

34. UNICEF, "Information: Publications: A Promise to Children," June 2, 2015, http://www.unicef.org/wsc/; Beigbeder, "Children," 515–16; United Nations Special Session on Children, "World Leaders 'Say Yes' for Children," accessed June 2, 2015, http://www.unicef.org/specialsession/; Woodhouse, *Hidden in Plain Sight*, 304–05.

35. Subsequent meetings were held in Yokohama, Japan (2001) and in Brazil (2008), and significant international successes include the 2000 Protocol to Prevent, Suppress and Punish Trafficking in Persons, Especially Women and Children; the 2001 Convention on Cybercrime; and the coming into force on January 18, 2002, of the Convention on the Rights of the Child optional protocol on the sale of children, child prostitution, and child pornography. See "Declaration and Agenda for Action: 1st World Congress against Commercial Sexual Exploitation of Children, Stockholm, Sweden, 27–31 August," http://www.ecpat.net/sites/default/files/stockholm_declaration_1996.pdf; Beigbeder,

"Children," 515; Roger J. R. Levesque, *Sexual Abuse of Children: A Human Rights Perspective* (Bloomington: Indiana University Press, 1999).

36. Graça Machel, *The Impact of War on Children* (New York: Palgrave, 2001); Office of the Special Representative of the Secretary-General for Children and Armed Conflict, "The Machel Reports," accessed July 27, 2015, https://childrenandarmedconflict.un.org/mandate/the-machel-reports/.
37. Beigbeder, "Children," 516–17, 519–20; Kofi Annan, *We, the Children: End-Decade Review of the Follow-Up to the World Summit for Children: Report of the Secretary-General*, A/S-27/3, May 4, 2001, http://www.unicef.org/specialsession/documentation/documents/a-s-27-3e.pdf; Nelien Haspels and Michele Jankanish, eds., *Action against Child Labour* (Geneva: ILO, 2000).
38. As quoted in Karen Gamer, *Shaping a Global Women's Agenda: Women's NGOs and Global Governance, 1925–1985* (Manchester, UK: Manchester University Press, 2010), 141. See also Jain, *Women, Development, and the UN*, 4, 14; Kristine Midtgaard, "Bodil Begtrup and the Universal Declaration of Human Rights: Individual Agency, Transnationalism and Intergovernmentalism in Early UN Human Rights," *Scandinavian Journal of History* 36, no. 4 (2011): 479–99.
39. Black, "Are Women 'Human'?" 137–39; Arvonne S. Frazer, "Becoming Human: The Origins and Development of Women's Human Rights," *Human Rights Quarterly* 21, no. 4 (November 1999): 230; Morsink, *Universal Declaration of Human Rights*, 230.
40. Jain, *Women, Development, and the UN*, 22–24, 31–32, 62–65; *The United Nations and the Advancement of Women*, 164–66; U.N. Department of Public Information, "Four Global Women's Conferences, 1975–1995"; Black, "Are Women 'Human'?" 133, 139–40; Morsink, *Universal Declaration*, 199; UNESCO, "Legal Instruments: Convention against Discrimination in Education 1960, Paris, 14 December 1960," http://portal.unesco.org/en/ev.php-URL_ID=12949&URL_DO=DO_TOPIC&URL_SECTION=201.html.
41. Jain, *Women, Development, and the UN*, 23–24, 31–32; *The United Nations and the Advancement of Women*, 164–66; Black, "Are Women 'Human'?" 141–42.
42. Kelly J. Shannon, "The Right to Bodily Integrity: Women's Rights as Human Rights and the International Movement to End Female Genital Mutilation, 1970s–1990s," in *Human Rights Revolution*, 285–310; Nitza Berkovitch and Karen Bradley, "The Globalization of Women's Status: Consensus/Dissensus in the World Polity," *Sociological Perspectives* 42, no. 3 (Autumn 1999): 481–98; U.N. Human Rights Office of the High Commissioner for Human Rights, "Convention on Consent to Marriage, Minimum Age for Marriage and Registration of Marriages," accessed July 28, 2015, http://www.ohchr.org/EN/ProfessionalInterest/Pages/MinimumAgeForMarriage.aspx.
43. Jolly et al., *UN Contributions to Development Thinking and Practice*, 130; Jain, *Women, Development, and the UN*, 7. See also Jain, *Women, Development, and the UN*, 45–48.
44. Jain, *Women, Development, and the UN*, 48–51, 65–66; Galey, "Women Find a Place," 20; *The United Nations and the Advancement of Women*, 177–79.
45. Black, "Are Women 'Human'?" 144. See also ibid., 134, 143–45; Iriye and Goedde, "Introduction," 8; Jain, *Women, Development and the UN*, 7, 66–71; U.N. Department of Public Information, "Four Global Women's Conferences, 1975–1995."
46. Black, "Are Women 'Human'?" 144–45.
47. Ibid., 147; Margaret E. Galey, "The Nairobi Conference: The Powerless Majority," *PS* 19, no. 2 (Spring 1986): 255–65.

48. United Nations Human Rights, Office of the High Commissioner for Human Rights, "Vienna Declaration and Programme of Action: Adopted by the World Conference on Human Rights in Vienna on 25 June 1993," http://www.ohchr.org/EN/ProfessionalInterest/Pages/Vienna.aspx. See also Black, "Are Women 'Human'?" 148–49; Charlotte Bunch and Samantha Frost, "Women's Human Rights: An Introduction," Center for Women's Global Leadership, accessed July 28, 2015, http://www.cwgl.rutgers.edu/globalcenter/whr.html.

49. Black, "Are Women 'Human'?" 150. See also ibid., 149–51; Terra Viva, "U.S.-Women: Women's Conference Further Entangles China Policy," August 2, 1995, http://www.ips.org/TV/beijing15/u-s-women-womens-conference-further-entangles-china-policy/; U.N. Peacekeeping, "Women, Peace and Security," accessed July 28, 2015, http://www.un.org/en/peacekeeping/issues/women/wps.shtml (includes summaries of and links to the relevant Security Council resolutions); interview with Peter David Eicher (U.S. State Department Bureau of Democracy, Human Rights, and Labor) on Association for Diplomatic Studies and Training, "Moments in U.S. Diplomatic History: The Beijing Conference on Women," accessed July 28, 2015, http://adst.org/2014/08/the-beijing-conference-on-women/, for a personal account of attending and drafting the Beijing Declaration.

50. Black, "Are Women 'Human'?" 151.

51. Lauren, *Evolution of International Human Rights*, 105–38; Normand and Zaidi, *Human Rights at the UN*, 247–77, 427–28n194. The text of International Labour Conference's "Convention 107 Concerning Indigenous and Tribal Populations" is still posted as a pdf on the Organization of American States' website: Organization of American States, Secretariat for Legal Affairs (SLA), accessed May 28, 2013, http://www.oas.org/dil/1957_Convention_concerning_Indigenous_and_Tribal_Peoples_ILO_Convention_No_107).pdf. The current ILO website lists the differences between this convention and the new convention (No. 169) passed in June 1989 but no longer lists the original text of No. 107: International Labour Organization, "Convention No. 107," accessed May 28, 2013, http://www.ilo.org/indigenous/Conventions/no107/lang--en/index.htm.

52. Ibid., 273–77; Joseph Novitski, "For Indians of Brazil's Interior the Choice Is the Past or the Future," *New York Times*, July 28, 1970, 14; Victor Lusinchi, "Red Cross Says Aid Is Needed by Indians in Amazon Urgently," *New York Times*, February 24, 1971.

53. Normand and Zaidi, *Human Rights at the UN*, 273–77; Asbjørn Eide, "The Sub-Commission on Prevention of Discrimination and Protection of Minorities," in *The United Nations and Human Rights: A Critical Appraisal*, ed. Philip Alston (Oxford: Clarendon Press, 1992), 235–39; Russel Lawrence Barsch, "Indigenous Peoples: An Emerging Object of International Law," *American Journal of International Law* 80, no. 2 (April 1986): 369–85; idem, "Indigenous Peoples and the UN Commission on Human Rights: A Case of Immovable Object and the Irresistible Force," *Human Rights Quarterly* 18, no. 4 (November 1996): 782–813; Douglas Sanders, "The UN Working Group on Indigenous Populations," *Human Rights Quarterly* 11, no. 3 (August 1989): 406–33.

54. *Indigenous and Tribal Peoples' Rights in Practice: A Guide to ILO Convention No. 169* (Geneva: International Labour Organization, 2009), 5–7; Maul, "ILO and the Globalization of Human Rights," 301; William G. Martin, "Conclusion: World Movement Waves and World Transformations," in *Making Waves: Worldwide Social Movements, 1750–2005*, ed. William G. Martin, Fernand Braudel Center series (Boulder, CO: Pardigm Publishers, 2008), 152–53.

55. U.N. Permanent Forum on Indigenous Issues, "About Us/Members," accessed July 27, 2015, http://undesadspd.org/IndigenousPeoples/AboutUsMembers.aspx; U.N. Human Rights Office of the High Commissioner for Human Rights, "Special Rapporteur on the Rights

of Indigenous Peoples," accessed July 27, 2015, http://www.ohchr.org/EN/Issues/IPeoples/SRIndigenousPeoples/Pages/SRIPeoplesIndex.asp.

56. U.N. Permanent Forum on Indigenous Issues, "Declaration on the Rights of Indigenous Peoples: Frequently Asked Questions," accessed July 27, 2015, http://www.un.org/esa/socdev/unpfii/documents/faq_drips_en.pdf. See also U.N., "United Nations Declaration on the Rights of Indigenous Peoples," last modified March 2008, http://www.un.org/esa/socdev/unpfii/documents/DRIPS_en.pdf; U.N. Human Rights Office of the High Commissioner for Human Rights, "Expert Mechanism on the Rights of Indigenous Peoples," accessed July 27, 2015, http://www2.ohchr.org/english/issues/indigenous/ExpertMechanism/index.htm.

57. A very small sampling of the available work that can launch your research (see the online reference guide for more) includes Jacqueline A. Kalley, *South Africa under Apartheid: A Select and Annotated Bibliography* (Westport, CT: Meckler, 1989); Robert Davies, Don O'Meara, and Sipho Dlamini, *The Struggle for South Africa: A Reference Guide to Movements, Organizations, and Institutions* (London: Zed Books, 1984); U.N. Department of Public Information, *The United Nations and Apartheid, 1948–1994* (New York: U.N., 1994); Rob Skinner, *The Foundations of Anti-Apartheid: Liberal Humanitarians and Transnational Activists in Britain and the United States, c.1919–64* (Houndsmills, UK: Palgrave Macmillan, 2010); Håkan Thörn, *Anti-Apartheid and the Emergence of a Global Civil Society* (Houndsmills, UK: Palgrave Macmillan, 2006); Donald R. Culverson, "From Cold War to Global Interdependence: The Political Economy of African American Antiapartheid Activism, 1968–1988," in *Window on Freedom: Race, Civil Rights, and Foreign Affairs, 1945–1988*, ed. Brenda Gayle Plummer (Chapel Hill: University of North Carolina Press, 2003), 221–38; Nelson Mandela, *Long Walk to Freedom* (New York: Back Bay Books/Little, Brown, 1995); F. W. de Klerk, *The Last Trek—a New Beginning: The Autobiography* (New York: St. Martin's, 1999).

58. Pretoria is considered the de facto national capital, as it houses the executive/administrative functions of the national government. However, the legislative capital is Cape Town, and the judicial capital is Bloemfontein.

59. South African History Online (SAHO), "United Nations and Apartheid Timeline, 1946–1994," accessed June 7, 2015, http://www.sahistory.org.za/; "Paper on the Group Areas Act and Its Effects on the Indian People of Natal, May 1956," SAHO, accessed June 7, 2015, http://www.sahistory.org.za/archive/paper-group-areas-act-and-its-effects-indian-people-natal-may-1956.

60. SAHO, "U.N. and Apartheid Timeline"; Margaret P. Doxey, *Economic Sanctions and International Enforcement*, 2nd ed. (New York: Oxford University Press for the Royal Institute of International Affairs, 1980), 61; Robert Kinloch Massie, *Loosing the Bonds: The United States and South Africa in the Apartheid Years* (New York: Doubleday, 1997), 63–66; Mark David, "United States- South African Relations, 1962–67," in *Economic Coercion and U.S. Foreign Policy: Implications of Case Studies from the Johnson Administration*, ed. Sidney Weintraub (Boulder, CO: Westview Press, 1982), 217; Permanent Mission of India to the UN, "Historical Perspective: Decolonization and Apartheid," accessed July 28, 2015, https://www.pminewyork.org/pages.php?id=1981; Normand and Zaidi, *Human Rights at the UN*, 260–72; office of the United Nations High Commissioner for Human Rights, "Committee on the Elimination of Racial Discrimination: Monitoring Racial Equality and Non-Discrimination," accessed June 2, 2015, http://www2.ohchr.org/english/bodies/cerd/; Michael Banton, *International Action against Racial Discrimination* (Oxford: Clarendon Press, 1996), 51–60.

61. At the end of 1963, the Security Council expanded its resolution to encompass the equipment and materials that South Africa would need to manufacture its own military

supplies. Its Resolution 282 (1970) called on governments to strengthen the arms embargo against South Africa (12–0–3 with France, Great Britain, and the United States abstaining). Resolution 418 (1977), which was approved unanimously, imposed a mandatory arms embargo. In November 1986, the Security Council added spare parts and components to the list of embargoed items for both the South African military and police.

62. For U.N. action, see SAHO, "United Nations and Apartheid Timeline"; Peterson Institute for International Economics, "Case Studies in Sanctions and Terrorism: Case 85-1: US, Commonwealth v. South Africa (1985–91: Apartheid): Chronology of Key Events," accessed June 10, 2015, http://www.iie.com/research/topics/sanctions/southafrica.cfm#chronology; David, "United States-South African Relations, 1962–67," 218–19; Doxey, *Economic Sanctions*, 61–64; Merle Lipton, *Sanctions and South Africa: The Dynamics of Economic Isolation*, *Economist* Intelligence Unit Special Report no. 1119 (London: The Economist Publications, 1988), 15. For Rivonia trial, see, for example, Mandela, *Long Walk to Freedom*; African National Congress, "The Rivonia Trial," accessed June 7, 2015, http://www.anc.org.za/show.php?id=4839; Douglas Linder, "Famous Trials: The Nelson Mandela (Rivonia) Trial, 1963–64," 2010, Famous Trials, University of Missouri-Kansas City School of Law, accessed June 7, 2015, http://law2.umkc.edu/faculty/projects/ftrials/mandela/mandelahome.html.

63. SAHO, "United Nations and Apartheid Timeline." See, for example, the April 1973 International Conference of Experts for Support of Victims of Colonialism and Apartheid in Southern Africa, the June 1973 International Trade Union Conference against Apartheid organized by the ILO Workers' Group (a second conference followed in June 1977), the August 1977 World Conference for Action against Apartheid, the August 1984 Conference of Arab Solidarity with the Struggle for Liberation in Southern Africa, the May 1985 International Conference on Women and Children under Apartheid, the May 1985 International Conference on Sports Boycott against South Africa, and the August 1987 International Student Conference in Solidarity with the Struggle of the Students of Southern Africa.

64. SAHO, "United Nations and Apartheid Timeline."

65. Ibid.; Peterson Institute, "Case Studies."

66. General Assembly Resolution 3151 G (XXVIII), 33, December 14, 1973, https://documents-dds-y.un.org/doc/RESOLUTION/GEN/NR0/282/23/IMG/NR028223 .pdf?OpenElement; General Assembly Resolution 3207 (XXIX), December 30, 1974, https://documents-dds-ny.un.org/doc/RESOLUTION/GEN/NR0/738/09/IMG/NR073809 .pdf?Op enElement; General Assembly Resolution 3324 E (XXIX), 38, December 16, 1974, https://documents-dds-ny.un.org/doc/RESOLUTION/GEN/NR0/739/26/IMG/NR073926 .pdf?Op enElement. See also Bosco, *Five to Rule Them All*, 155; Edward C. Luck, *UN Security Council: Practice and Promise* (New York: Routledge, 2006), 58–67.

67. SAHO, "United Nations and Apartheid Timeline"; Noor Nieftagodien, *The Soweto Uprising* (Athens: Ohio University Press, 2014); James Sanders, *South Africa and the International Media, 1972–1979* (London: F. Cass, 2000); Elsabé Brink, *Soweto, 16 June 1976: Personal Accounts of the Uprising*, 2nd ed. (Cape Town, S. Afr.: Kwela Books, 2006).

68. SAHO, "United Nations and Apartheid Timeline."

69. Ibid.; Peterson Institute, "Case Studies"; John A. Marcum, "Africa: A Continent Adrift," *Foreign Affairs* 68 (1988–89): 161; Massie, *Loosing the Bonds*, 487–88.

70. SAHO, "United Nations and Apartheid Timeline"; SAHO, "United Democratic Front (UDF): Partial State of Emergency, July 1985," http://www.sahistory.org.za/partial-state-emergency-july-1985.

71. Peterson Institute, "Case Studies"; Massie, *Loosing the Bonds*, 584–85, 595, 604–18; Keith Ovenden and Tony Cole, *Apartheid and International Finance: A Program for Change* (Ringwood, Australia: Penguin, 1989), 82–83, 89, 128; Baker, *United States and South Africa*, 32–33, 42–45, appendix D; Lipton, *Sanctions and South Africa*, 16, 18, 29, appendix 6; Laurence Harris, "South Africa's External Debt Crisis," *Third World Quarterly* 8, no. 3 (July 1986): 793–817; SAHO, "United Nations and Apartheid Timeline"; Commonwealth Secretariat, *Independent Expert Study on the Evaluation of the Application and Impact of Sanctions: Final Report to the Commonwealth Committee of Foreign Ministers on Southern Africa* (London: Commonwealth Secretariat, April 1989), appendix 3, p. 3; J. P. Hayes, *Economic Effects of Sanctions on Southern Africa* (London: Trade Policy Research Centre, 1987), 1–2.

72. SAHO, "United Nations and Apartheid Timeline"; Peterson Institute, "Case Studies"; Piero Gleijeses, *Visions of Freedom: Havana, Washington, Pretoria, and the Struggle for Southern Africa, 1976–1991* (Chapel Hill: University of North Carolina Press, 2013); Christopher S. Wren, "Botha, Rebuffed by His Party, Quits South Africa Presidency," *New York Times*, August 15, 1989, http://www.nytimes.com/1989/08/15/world/botha-rebuffed-by-his-party-quits-south-africa-presidency.html.

73. On August 16, 1991, the High Commissioner and South African government initialed a memorandum of understanding granting voluntary repatriation and reintegration, a comprehensive amnesty for all political offenses, and freedom of movement to returnees that would be monitored by the presence of United Nations High Commissioner for Refugees representatives on the ground in South Africa. On December 1, 1992, UNICEF joined the effort, especially to assist in the reintegration of women and children returnees. The discovery of fraud and corruption in the National Coordinating Committee for the Repatriation of South African Exiles in mid-1993 led to UNHCR taking over primary responsibility for this task.

74. As quoted in SAHO, "United Nations and Apartheid Timeline." See also Peterson Institute, "Case Studies"; Muna Ndulo, "United Nations Observer Mission in South Africa (UNOMSA): Security Council Resolutions 772 (1992) and 894 (1994) and the South African Transition: Preventive Diplomacy and Peace-Keeping," in *African Yearbook of International Law*, ed. A. A. Yusuf (The Hague, Netherlands: Kluwer Law International, 1996), available through Cornell Law Library, Scholarship@Cornell Law: A Digital Repository, http://scholarship.law.cornell.edu/cgi/viewcontent.cgi?article=1060&context=facpub.

75. *Yearbook of the United Nations, 1991*, vol. 45 (Dordrecht, Netherlands: Martinus Nijhoff Publishers for U.N. Department of Public Information, 1993), 108, http://cdn.un.org/unyearbook/yun/pdf/1991/1991_119.pdf; SAHO, "The CODESA Negotiations: Convention for a Democratic South Africa (CODESA)," accessed March 12, 2016, http://www.sahistory.org.za/article/codesa-negotiations. See also SAHO, "United Nations and Apartheid Timeline."

76. On September 23, 1992, Jamaican Angela King, who headed UNOMSA (the acronym is a Zulu word that means "she who brings mercy"), and six of her observers arrived in Johannesburg to begin the mission, which eventually grew to 50 in October and then 500 in sixty locations. Its goal was to understand and report on the sources of the violence then occurring and to assist in a peaceful transition to democracy. Its staff swelled to 2,527 as it helped observe the national election in 1994, and members of that team were still gathering for an annual celebratory dinner on the anniversary of the elections in 2006.

77. "Address by Nelson Mandela at the United Nations, 24 September 1993," Nelson Rolihlahla Mandela memorial website, http://www.mandela.gov.za/mandela_speeches/1993/930924_un.htm. See also SAHO, "United Nations and Apartheid Timeline"; Angela E. V.

King, "Women, Peace and Posts—in United Nations Peace Operations," talk given on October 25, 2006, http://www.un.org/womenwatch/feature/angelaking/pdf/8-womenpeaceandposts251006.pdf.

78. SAHO, "United Nations and Apartheid Timeline."

79. G. Robertson, *Crimes against Humanity: The Struggle for Global Justice*, 4th ed. (New York: New Press, 1999), 447; David Scheffer, *All the Missing Souls: A Personal History of the War Crimes Tribunals* (Princeton, NJ: Princeton University Press, 2012), 2. See also Gerry J. Simpson, *Law, War and Crime: War Crimes, Trials and the Reinvention of International Law* (Cambridge: Polity Press, 2007); Scheffer, *All the Missing Souls*, 2–3, 5–7; Goldstone, "International Criminal Court," 465–66; Elizabeth Borgwardt, "'Constitutionalizing' Human Rights: The Rise and Rise of the Nuremberg Principles," in *Human Rights Revolution*, 73–92; Matthew Gillett, *Atrocity and Accountability: The Impact of International Criminal Tribunals on Peacemaking and Reconciliation*, Virginia and Derrick Sherman Emerging Scholar Lecture series (Wilmington: University of North Carolina Wilmington History Department, 2013), 6–7, 16. Online primary source collections for the aspiring ICTY researcher include the United Nations International Criminal Tribunal for the former Yugoslavia website—http://www.icty.org/—which includes background information, case information, a "legal library," an archive of press releases and statements, outreach resources, a section on crimes of sexual violence, a timeline for ICTY activities, ICTY court records, and several ICTY-produced documentary films that were part of its outreach efforts.

80. Scheffer, *All the Missing Souls*, 15–19; Roy Gutman, *A Witness to Genocide: The 1993 Pulitzer Prize-Winning Dispatches on the "Ethnic Cleansing" of Bosnia* (New York: Macmillan, 1993); Stewart Purvis and Jeff Hulbert, *When Reporters Cross the Line: The Heroes, the Villains, the Hackers and the Spies* (London: Biteback Publishing, 2013), chapter 1; Thierry Tardy, "United Nations Protection Force (UNPROFOR—Croatia)" and "United Nations Protection Force (UNPROFOR—Bosnia-Herzegovina)," both in *Oxford Handbook of United Nations Peacekeeping Operations*, 371–82, 383–94; Normand and Zaidi, *Human Rights at the UN*, 259; Samantha Power, *A Problem from Hell: America and the Age of Genocide* (New York: Basic Books, 2002); Gillett, *Atrocity and Accountability*, 8–9, 11–12.

81. "International Panel of Eminent Personalities (IPEP): Report on the 1994 Genocide in Rwanda and Surrounding Events (Selected Sections)," *International Legal Materials* 40, no. 1 (January 2001): 141–236; U.N. Mechanism for International Criminal Tribunals, "The Genocide," accessed June 6, 2015, http://unictr.unmict.org/en/genocide.

82. Linda Melvern homepage, "Conspiracy to Murder," accessed July 28, 2015, http://lindamelvern.com/index.php/19-books. Critical accounts include Normand and Zaidi, *Human Rights at the UN*, 258–59; Linda Melvern, *The Ultimate Crime: Who Betrayed the UN and Why* (London: Allison & Busby, 1995); idem, *The Rwandan Genocide and the International Community* (London: Verso, 2004); Michael Barnett, *Eyewitness to a Genocide: The United Nations and Rwanda* (Ithaca, NY: Cornell University Press, 2002); Philip Gourevitch, *We Wish to Inform You That Tomorrow We Will Be Killed with Our Families* (New York: Picador, 1998).

83. As quoted in press release, "Statement by Justice Louise Arbour, Prosecutor of the International Criminal Tribunal for Rwanda," September 4, 1998, CC/PIU/342-E, accessed June 5, 2015, http://www.icty.org/sid/7642. See also Gillett, *Atrocity and Accountability*, 13–14; Alexandra Stiglmayer, "Sexual Violence: Systematic Rape," Crimes of War Education Project, last modified 2011, http://www.crimesofwar.org/a-z-guide/sexual-violence-systematic-rape/; ICTY, "The ICTY in Brief," accessed June 6, 2015, http://www.unictr.org/en/tribunal. For earlier accounts of rape as a method of genocide that were not considered as such by the tribunal for the former Yugoslavia, see Beverly Allen, *Rape Warfare: The*

Hidden Genocide in Bosnia-Herzegovina and Croatia (Minneapolis: University of Minnesota Press, 1996); Gutman, *Witness to Genocide* (New York: Macmillan, 1993). The ICTR's original website is now (since December 31, 2015) maintained by the U.N. Mechanism for International Criminal Tribunals (UNMICT), accessed February 3, 2016, http://unictr.unmict.org.

84. Office of the Special Adviser on the Prevention of Genocide, "The Mandate and Role of the Office," http://www.un.org/en/preventgenocide/adviser/background.shtml, and "The Responsibility to Protect," both accessed June 5, 2015, http://www.un.org/en/preventgenocide/adviser/responsibility.shtml, with links to the relevant U.N. documents.
85. Normand and Zaidi, *Human Rights at the UN*, 259; Iriye and Goedde, "Introduction," 14; International Criminal Court, "About the Court," accessed June 6, 2015, http://www.icc-cpi.int/en_menus/icc/about%20the%20court/Pages/about%20the%20court.aspx; David Bosco, *Rough Justice: The International Criminal Court in a World of Power Politics* (Oxford: Oxford University Press, 2014); Benjamin Schiff, *Building the International Criminal Court* (Cambridge: Cambridge University Press, 2008); Bosco, *Five to Rule Them All*, 220–22, 245.
86. Gillett, *Atrocity and Accountability*, 8, 17–19; Global Policy Forum, "Special Court for Sierra Leone," accessed June 5, 2015, https://www.globalpolicy.org/international-justice/international-criminal-tribunals-and-special-courts/special-court-for-sierra-leone.html; Special Court for Sierra Leone/Residual Special Court for Sierra Leone, "Legacy Projects," accessed June 5, 2015, http://www.rscsl.org/legacy.html; Sierra Leone Peace Museum, accessed June 5, 2015, http://www.slpeacemuseum.org/; Special Court for Sierra Leone/Residual Special Court for Sierra Leone, "The Special Court for Sierra Leone: Its History and Jurisprudence," "The Special Court Trials," "Court Records: Special Court Jurisprudence," and "The Residual Special Court: Its Operations and Mandate," all accessed June 5, 2015, http://www.rscsl.org/.
87. TRack Impunity Always (TRIAL), "Criminal Court for Cambodia: Establishment of Extraordinary Chambers Responsible for the Prosecution of Crimes Committed by the Khmer Rouge in Cambodia," accessed June 5, 2015, http://www.trial-ch.org/en/resources/tribunals/hybrid-tribunals/criminal-court-for-cambodia.html; Seth Mydans, "Judge Quits Tribunal in Khmer Rouge Inquiry," *New York Times*, October 10, 2011, http://www.nytimes.com/2011/10/11/world/asia/judge-quits-cambodia-tribunal.html?_r=0; U.N. News Centre, "UN Voices Concern as Second Judge Resigns from Cambodia Genocide Court," March 19, 2012, http://www.un.org/apps/news/story.asp?NewsID=41578#.VXIcgVQo5ok; Charlie Campbell, "Cambodia's Khmer Rouge Trials Are a Shocking Failure," *Time* (February 13, 2014), http://time.com/6997/cambodias-khmer-rouge-trials-are-a-shocking-failure/; ECCC, "Nuon Chea and Khieu Samphan Sentenced to Life Imprisonment for Crimes against Humanity," posted August 7, 2014, http://www.eccc.gov.kh/en/articles/nuon-chea-and-khieu-samphan-sentenced-life-imprisonment-crimes-against-humanity; ECCC, "Key Events," last updated August 7, 2014, http://www.eccc.gov.kh/en/keyevents; Global Policy Forum, "Special Tribunal for Cambodia," accessed June 5, 2015, https://www.globalpolicy.org/international-justice/international-criminal-tribunals-and-special-courts/special-tribunal-for-cambodia.html. Additionally, Northwestern University School of Law's Center for International Human Rights and the Documentation Center of Cambodia maintain an archive of material before 2013 as well as history and court filing information as Cambodia Tribunal Monitor, http://www.cambodiatribunal.org/.
88. Mehlis's reports to the U.N. Security Council in the fall of 2005 identified fifteen other bombings that targeted Lebanese ministers, deputies, and journalists who opposed Syria and found "converging evidence pointing at both Lebanese and Syrian involvement in the assassination." The Security Council then extended the mandate of the commission

(now under the leadership of Belgian Serge Brammertz) to investigate these other attacks. Brammertz made three additional reports to the Security Council and, on September 25, 2006, urged it to create a tribunal to bring these perpetrators to justice, which contributed to its decision to move forward without formal ratification by the Lebanese parliament (TRIAL, "Special Court for Lebanon: Introduction," accessed June 5, 2015, http://www.trial-ch.org/en/resources/tribunals/hybrid-tribunals/special-court-for-lebanon.html).

89. The United States at the time sought to put international pressure on Syria, which it thought was responsible for the flow of arms to Hezbollah in southern Lebanon and the flow of arms and fighters into Iraq to counter American forces there. In fact, Syria did withdraw its troops from Lebanon in April 2005, ending a nearly thirty-year presence there. See United Nations, "Special Tribunal for Lebanon," accessed June 5, 2015, http://www.un.org/apps/news/infocus/lebanon/tribunal/; TRIAL, "Special Court for Lebanon: Introduction"; Global Policy Forum, "Special Tribunal for Lebanon," accessed June 5, 2015, https://www.globalpolicy.org/international-justice/international-criminal-tribunals-and-special-courts/special-tribunal-for-lebanon.html (this website also includes links to relevant UN documents from 2005 to 2008 and news about the court as it developed); United Nations, "Timeline: Special Tribunal for Lebanon," accessed June 5, 2015, http://www.un.org/apps/news/infocus/lebanon/tribunal/timeline.shtml#top.

90. United Nations, "Ayyash et al. (STL-11-01): Accused," accessed February 27, 2016, http://www.stl-tsl.org/en/the-cases/stl-11-01/accused; U.N., "Special Tribunal for Lebanon"; United Nations, "Factsheet: Special Tribunal for Lebanon," accessed June 5, 2015, http://www.un.org/apps/news/infocus/lebanon/tribunal/factsheet.shtml; United Nations, "Timeline: Special Tribunal for Lebanon"; TRIAL, "Special Court for Lebanon: Introduction"; Gillett, *Atrocity and Accountability*, 8–9; Special Tribunal for Lebanon, "About the STL," accessed June 5, 2015, http://www.stl-tsl.org/en/about-the-stl; Global Policy Forum, "Special Tribunal for Lebanon"; David Tolbert, "Introduction: A Very Special Tribunal," in *The Special Tribunal for Lebanon: Law and Practice*, ed. Amal Alamuddin, Nidal Nabil Jurdi, and David Tolbert (New York: Oxford University Press, 2014), 1–9. This volume's contributors include Judge Howard Morisson, former judge at the Special Tribunal for Lebanon, and Bahije Tabbarah, former minister of justice of Lebanon.

91. Aryeh Neier, *The International Human Rights Movement: A History* (Princeton, NJ: Princeton University Press, 2012), 2–3; Iriye and Goedde, "Introduction," 15; United Nations Human Rights Office of the High Commissioner, "United Nations Human Rights Council," accessed July 28, 2015, http://www.ohchr.org/en/hrbodies/hrc/pages/hrcindex.aspx.

INDEX